ORACLE® *Oracle Press*™

Oracle Collaboration Suite Handbook

About the Author

Ronald J. Zapar is the CEO of Re-Quest, Inc. He has over 18 years of experience with the Oracle technology and e-Business Suite products. He began his Oracle career when he joined their consulting organization in the North Central region in early 1988. Ron left Oracle in late 1991 to start his first integration firm centered on Oracle core technology and Oracle applications. In 2003, he made a significant investment in Oracle's emerging Collaboration Suite technology. As CEO, Ron has led Re-Quest's effort to gain regional as well as national recognition around their expertise in successfully implementing Oracle Collaboration Suite in all types of environments for all types of customers. In 2003, Re-Quest was named one of the premier North American systems integrators for Oracle Collaboration Suite. Ron is frequently interviewed by industry publications for his comments on current trends and events. He resides in Naperville, Illinois with his wife Cece and daughter Ashley.

Re-Quest, Inc. is a leading Systems Integrator and Managed Services provider focused on Oracle solutions based in the Chicago area. Re-Quest provides consulting and managed services for all of Oracle products, and was one of the early adopters of the Oracle Collaboration Suite. Re-Quest has implemented, and currently manages, Oracle Collaboration Suite environments for a variety of customers across the United States. The Re-Quest Collaboration Suite methodology provides a complete end-to-end strategy for successfully architecting, implementing, and managing an Oracle Collaboration Suite solution.

ORACLE®   *Oracle Press*™

Oracle Collaboration Suite Handbook

Ron Zapar

McGraw Hill

New York Chicago San Francisco
Lisbon London Madrid Mexico City
Milan New Delhi San Juan
Seoul Singapore Sydney Toronto

The McGraw·Hill Companies

Cataloging-in-Publication Data is on file with the Library of Congress

McGraw-Hill books are available at special quantity discounts to use as premiums and sales promotions, or for use in corporate training programs. For more information, please write to the Director of Special Sales, Professional Publishing, McGraw-Hill, Two Penn Plaza, New York, NY 10121-2298. Or contact your local bookstore.

Oracle Collaboration Suite Handbook

1234567890 FGR FGR 01987

ISBN-13: 978-0-07-226300-8
ISBN-10:0-07-226300-8

Sponsoring Editor	**Technical Editor**	**Composition**
Lisa McClain	Shruthi Ravindranath Esthuri	International Typesetting and Composition
Editorial Supervisor	**Copy Editor**	**Illustration**
Jody McKenzie	Bob Campbell	International Typesetting and Composition
Project Editor	**Proofreader**	
Carolyn Welch	Carolyn Welch	**Art Director, Cover**
Acquisitions Coordinators	**Indexer**	Jeff Weeks
Alexander McDonald	Claire Splan	**Cover Designer**
Mandy Canales	**Production Supervisor**	Pattie Lee
	George Anderson	

To Mom: From Bucktown to the bookshelf,
I dedicate this work to her.

Contents at a Glance

PART IV
Oracle Content Services

Contents

PART I
Getting Started

PART II
Installation and Configuration of OCS

PART III

Managing Your OCS Environment

PART IV
Oracle Content Services

Acknowledgments

The idea to write this book first crossed my mind after having several successful implementations of the Oracle Collaboration Suite under my belt. I realized that with such an early commitment to the product that I might just have the unique opportunity to write a book on an Oracle subject that nobody had ever written about before. Early on there were not many Oracle partners, integrators, or consulting firms investing time or resources into learning the ins and outs of this new product line from Oracle. Collaboration Suite was different — way different — from anything Oracle had ever attempted before, so the more traditional Oracle people were a little tentative as to whether the product was something that would take hold in the marketplace. Okay, maybe "ever attempted" is too strong a phrase, but certainly it had been longer than most people remembered since Oracle made a concerted effort to break into a market previously uncharted by the database giant, except those of us that had been around in the early days of Oracle Applications or Oracle Application Server. But to me, the product made perfect sense, and a book presenting the results of real life experiences dealing with a new product such as this was adding real value to the cause of getting it out in the marketplace.

As cliché as it sounds I have always thought about writing a book. Maybe it is the Liberal Arts component of my education kicking in (Hail to Purple, Hail to White), or maybe it's just the creative side of my brain taking over, but I have for a long time now wanted to take on the challenge of writing. What I didn't realize when having those creative yearnings is just how demanding a challenge it would be, especially when trying to build and run a successful business at the same time! But Mom always said, what doesn't kill you makes you stronger. So here it is, and here I am…alive and well, writing the acknowledgments.

But this was not a solo effort by any means, and there are many, many people I need to thank for helping make this project a success. First, I want to thank all the folks at McGraw-Hill, especially Lisa McClain and Alexander McDonald, a.k.a. the Triple Mac Attack. Lisa, thanks for taking the idea from our first phone conversation to an accepted project at Oracle Press, and all the support you provided every step of the way. Alex, thanks for helping me get things done properly when I had no concept of how the process worked. And thanks also for your always-present balance between the push to get the project completed on time and understanding my need to run my company and have a life in parallel with this effort. There is no way I would have ever gotten through this project without the intense commitment from both of you. And thanks to Mandy Canales, also from McGraw-Hill, for finishing what Alex started. Finally, thanks to Carolyn Welch for walking me through the final editorial process and getting the book from word processor documents to print.

Any good system integrator worth their salt will tell you that you cannot get "there" — there being the mastery of a particular product — without having relationships with key customers willing to take a risk on the product before it has proven itself in the marketplace. Early adopters provide the artist with the canvas for painting the masterpiece. For me, the early adopters were customers like Steve Small and Rick Fox at AMLI Residential, and Sue Koebel at Aux Sable. Thank you for your willingness to invest in the technology when there weren't many proof points, and for trusting me to get you there. Also, to Ted Fines at Macalester College, thanks for your commitment to our relationship around the Collaboration Suite platform, and making the journey an interesting one.

I would also like to thank Mike Boduch, for helping with content in key areas in the book. This would have been much harder without your commitment to seeing things through to completion.

Also, thanks to the Oracle Collaboration Suite partner support group, who supported not only me but the entire Re-Quest team as we took on new and ever more complex implementations of the Collaboration Suite. You always gave us the access to the necessary inside development, deployment, and support resources to help us set direction and do things the right way when implementing the product. Stephen L. Smith, Mike Popelka, Kevin de

Smidt, John Hutchison, Marc Ottenville, Tait McCarthy, and the rest of the Oracle Collaboration Suite Partner team, thanks.

And last but not least, I would like to thank my family for their unwavering support during the entire process. I especially want to thank my wife Cece for knowing that this was something I needed to do, giving me the freedom to do it, and the much-needed encouragement along the way. Thanks to my daughter Ashley, for understanding how very important this project was to me, and for knowing when I just needed to lock myself in the office and focus, or when I needed to leave things alone for a while and go have fun. I also want to thank her for taking the time to help me through some tough grammatical predicaments, run-on sentences, and poorly structured paragraphs. It's nice to see the investment in that education is paying off! And thanks to my Mom, who along with my late Father, gave me the work ethic and common sense to tackle new challenges such as this one, while not necessarily having either the slightest idea where things would end up, or how to get there, when I started.

Introduction

racle Collaboration Suite 10g is an integrated collection of software applications built upon the foundational technology components of the Oracle Database and Application Server, that provide business users with the ability to communicate, exchange critical information, and work together in real-time regardless of where they are physically relative to each other. Oracle Collaboration Suite provides end-users with tools to exchange emails, voice mails and faxes, coordinate calendar entries, share and store content of any type, and collaborate through an array of tools that facilitate online communications. All of this functionality is provided through a single web portal interface, through standard desktop tools such as Microsoft Outlook and Explorer, or via wireless devices ... anywhere, anytime. Oracle Collaboration Suite 10g, the product upon which this book focuses, is part of the overall Oracle Fusion Middleware platform, which includes other products such as the Application Server, Data Hubs, Integration Server, Business Intelligence and Business Process Integration solutions, as well as Identity Management and Portal.

The Oracle Collaboration Suite Email solution allows users to send and receive emails, as well as receive faxes and voice mails right into their Inbox to be played or viewed right on their workstation. Email can be sent and retrieved by all of the common messaging standards such as POP, IMAP, and SMTP. The Calendar function allows users to create appointment entries, check real-time availability for a meeting time across a list of users, and to book pre-defined resources (e.g., conference room or overhead projector) for those meetings in addition to sharing calendar information with each other. Content Services provides the end user with the ability to upload, store, manage and publish all types of content within a database repository with an application front-end that provides combined file server, workflow and document management system functionality. This content can then be shared with a self-defined group of colleagues, with the access type controlled down to the file level, and the entire process driven by automated workflow functionality. Workspaces allow users to define and manage project, department or work group sets of documents in one place, with versioning, locking and access rights functionality. All of the above solutions — Email, Calendar, Content Services, and Workspaces — can be accessed either through standard Windows PC desktop tools such as Windows Explorer and Outlook, or through a portal framework set of web deployed user interfaces, which provides the same level of robust functionality and performance as their desktop client counterparts. Real-Time Collaboration (RTC) — available only through the web interface and proprietary downloaded clients for obvious reasons — gives users the ability to establish online meetings to share documents, demonstrate applications, control other user's desktops, and present all types of real-time information securely across the Internet, as well as carry on real-time messaging and chat sessions.

The concept of collaboration really began to take hold in the market a few years ago, when headcount at companies was continually reduced by the downward forces of the economy, but delivery demands on remaining resources became more pressing than ever. The concept seemed to flourish as companies looked for ways in which they could continue to build teams of geographically disparate individuals to work together to deliver company projects, but keep the travel required for such projects to a minimum. With the ability to store project content centrally, yet make it accessible globally through a standard set of web-based tools in real-time, companies could now have resources in multiple geographical locations work together productively without ever stepping foot on an airplane. And, speaking of the economy, with the onset of compliance requirements such as Sarbanes-Oxley (not to mention HIPAA, the U.S. Patriot Act, and the European Data Privacy Act), the ability to search and manage unstructured data across the enterprise to guarantee accuracy and accountability for decisions drove even more interest in the collaborative product market.

Oracle Corporation was a late entry to the collaboration race, but as usual they made their presence felt almost immediately. Actually, the individual components of the Collaboration Suite product have been around for quite a while in Oracle's product arsenal, albeit as strong stand-alone offerings.

For example, Oracle Mail has been in existence since the early 90's. (I actually used a version of Oracle Mail during that time as an Oracle employee.) Oracle Files, which was also called iFS, has been a production product for more than six years now. In addition to the Oracle developed products, Oracle also acquired best-of-breed calendar solution from Steltor as well as established web conferencing technologies, both with strong existing client bases. All the individual application products were then bundled together, storing all critical information in the Oracle Database and providing an integrated portal interface and single sign-on security through Oracle Application Server OID and Portal functionality. Oracle gained an instant technical leg up on the competition by delivering their collaboration solution on top of their Database and Application Server platforms. With the reliability of running on top of a world-class database and app server platform — versus the file system based architecture of the competition — availability, manageability, and security concerns of centralized critical information were greatly reduced. The possibility of the consolidation of email and file servers into a single database added synergy to the Oracle Collaboration Suite story, as by doing so any given architecture would require fewer centralized servers to provide better messaging and content management. Fewer servers mean lower annual hardware maintenance costs and fewer administrators necessary for managing the same amount of information. The idea sat well with CIOs looking to remove cost from their shops without reducing the service level to the end-user. It was especially appealing to the CIOs who were already managing Oracle environments in their shops currently.

We first got involved with the Oracle Collaboration Suite product shortly after Release 1 was introduced. It was a process we were fairly familiar with ... learning to implement a new Oracle product. You see, we have had a lot of experience in implementing new Oracle technologies throughout our 18+ years of working with Oracle, from implementing various versions of the database, to working with the first release of Oracle Web Server in the mid 90's, to completing one of the first 10.7 to 11i Oracle Applications upgrades ever done. It was because of some of this previous experience that we decided to take what was perceived a considerable risk at the time and invest significant resource into learning what made this new solution tick. Where many Oracle professionals have only touched certain categories of Oracle's vast product offerings, my team and I have pretty much worked with them all. We have spent a fair amount of time blazing the Oracle trail with leading edge—and sometimes bleeding edge—technologies from the Redwood City giant, so this was just another opportunity to do so ... but with a slightly different payoff. When Release 2 of Oracle Collaboration Suite came out we invested heavily in learning the product and building a services practice around the entire life-cycle implementation of Oracle Collaboration Suite, and have since become a leader in the market for providing successful client implementations (*successful* being the key word in this sentence). We have spent countless hours with both the sales and technical resources from Oracle Corporation responsible for moving the product forward, and have done extensive work with this latest release of the product, Oracle Collaboration Suite 10*g*, the release upon which this book is based.

It is my intent with this book to provide a roadmap for a successful Oracle Collaboration Suite implementation, not through extreme methodologies or rigid standards, but rather by sharing with the reader our experiences with what works and what doesn't work in terms of planning, installing, implementing, and later managing this product. I will attempt to let the reader know when things have to be done a specific way, and where they have choices. I will make the effort to take the guesswork out of the vast amounts of documentation, Metalink notes, available web content, etc., and provide straightforward instructions and/or recommendations where possible.

Who Should Read This Book

This book is intended mainly for a technical audience, namely, those individuals who will be responsible for architecting the appropriate hardware environment on which to install and configure the base Collaboration Suite product. Also, the book has value for those responsible for migrating email, calendar entries and files from legacy solutions, and, of course, those responsible for the care and feeding of the product, its environment and its users on an on-going basis. It will also be of value to those individuals chartered with considering and comparing collaborative solutions for their companies. Technical implementers, Oracle engineers considering Oracle Collaboration Suite 10*g* for their companies, and folks chartered with moving their organizations from stand-alone point solutions to integrated suites will all hopefully gain immense value from the content contained herein.

What This Book Is

This book is about technical architecture, product implementation, and post-production management of the Oracle Collaboration Suite 10*g* platform. It covers the Oracle Collaboration Suite 10*g* foundational components of the Oracle Database and Application Server, as well as the individual applications that make up Oracle Collaboration Suite 10*g* and what is needed to successfully install and implement the entire product. I provide information germane to installing Oracle environments, such as operating system prerequisites, running the Oracle Installer, defining directory structures, App Server requirements, database requirements, and requirements specific to the individual Oracle Collaboration Suite 10*g* applications.

   This book is intended as practical reference material, based upon real-life experience at clients with the products. The book is peppered with facts from Oracle Collaboration Suite 10*g* resources, development and support, and presents the right way to implement this product without providing an overbearing quantity of methodology.

What This Book Is Not

This book is not a Functional User Guide to Oracle Collaboration Suite 10*g*. That subject needs a book of its own. This book is also not an Email Administrator's Guide. We cover the components of Oracle Email as they relate to implementing and managing the Oracle Collaboration Suite 10*g* environment to the extent that they do not overshadow the other important value-added components of Oracle Collaboration Suite 10*g*. Email Administration, while given much attention in this book, is left to the Oracle manual for details involving the many aspects of managing an Oracle Email environment. This book is not about "Extreme Methodology." It's all about practical decision-making based upon real-life experiences and situations as they relate to implementing Oracle Collaboration Suite 10*g*. It is not an installation manual full of general theory. Finally, this book is not stuffy, because I hate stuffy! I am a technician who writes, not a writer who attempts technology ... so please read it as such. WARNING: There may be a dangling participle or two in here (I would fix them if I knew exactly what they were ...☺)! Enjoy!

PART
I

Getting Started

CHAPTER
1

An Overview of Oracle Collaboration Suite 10g

It is the framework which changes with each new
technology and not just the picture within the frame.

—Marshall McLuhan

O racle Collaboration Suite 10*g* represents a huge paradigm shift not only in the software industry today, but also in the business world. Until recently, if a company wanted its employees to communicate, cooperate, and collaborate on documents, projects, and ideas, and do so on a real-time basis, they had only one choice: incur the travel expense to get all members of the team to a single location to work together on the required deliverables. Add to the mix the propensity of today's companies to work more closely with business partners—consultants, suppliers, architects, lawyers—on projects as they are defined ("projects" in this context can mean everything from a new product to a commercial high-rise building to a software application to a multibillion-dollar corporate merger), and the requirements to get all their schedules coordinated, location and length of meetings defined, travel expense and loss of productivity covered, and you exponentially increased the cost and complexity of getting projects off the ground. There were many great ideas that were never undertaken because the timing, complexity, and cost of collaboration between necessary parties made the project logistically prohibitive.

Many software companies saw an opportunity to create products to address this functional need for collaboration. However, just as in any evolving market in its early stages, many software vendors were only successful at targeting specific business functions such as conferencing over the web, communicating via chat, or sharing thoughts and documents via email. This left businesses with the daunting task of choosing, implementing, and then managing multiple point solutions from multiple vendors in an attempt to meet a portion of the growing requirements of collaboration from the business users. And unfortunately, this approach only attempted to address the functional side. It didn't take into account the administrative and technical complexities introduced by trying to protect and synchronize unstructured data in a disconnected group of applications, and make these environments available, scalable, and manageable. Oracle Corporation delivered Oracle Collaboration Suite to the market in the hopes of addressing all requirements—technical as well as functional—in an integrated set of applications, with a standard look and feel, all developed and deployed on the Oracle Database and Oracle Application Server platforms.

Oracle entered the market in 2002 with Release 1 of Oracle Collaboration Suite (Version 9.0.3), not only to address the functional concerns but also to provide a secure, integrated architecture and set of applications that worked together and provided a common access point and look and feel. Although not perfect, Release 1 of the Collaboration Suite defined the next level of product functionality and manageability. Release 2 (Version 9.0.4), which was announced production-ready in 2003, addressed many of the initial shortcomings experienced with any first release product, and convinced many companies to move along the technology adoption lifecycle curve. After almost two years in the market, Release 2 was able to get Oracle to the point where it had enough input and momentum to be able to deliver Oracle Collaboration Suite 10*g*, a completely redesigned, feature-rich set of applications deployed on Oracle's latest and greatest 10*g* technology stack. Oracle Collaboration Suite 10*g* not only surpasses any competitors in the integrated collaborative solution space, but application by application it can stand toe to toe with point solutions for best-of-breed functionality, ease of management, and scalability.

In this first chapter, I will provide an overview of the two main areas of Oracle Collaboration Suite 10*g* that are critical for anyone evaluating, implementing, or managing the product: technology components and functional components. This chapter should provide someone who is not intimately familiar with Oracle products a basic understanding of how the Oracle Database and Oracle Application Server platforms are used to deliver the integrated applications. It offers a solid overview of all the technical components and where they reside, and describes what end-user applications are available in Oracle Collaboration Suite 10*g* and how to navigate through the Collaboration Suite functional map to access their various features and functions. Figure 1-1 illustrates the high-level architecture of Oracle Collaboration Suite 10*g*, including the technical as well as the application layers.

Core Technology Components

The core technology products of Oracle Database 10*g* and Application Server 10*g* form the foundational base for the Oracle Collaboration Suite 10*g* architecture. This core infrastructure architecture is what provides the combination of scalability, availability, and manageability for the product,

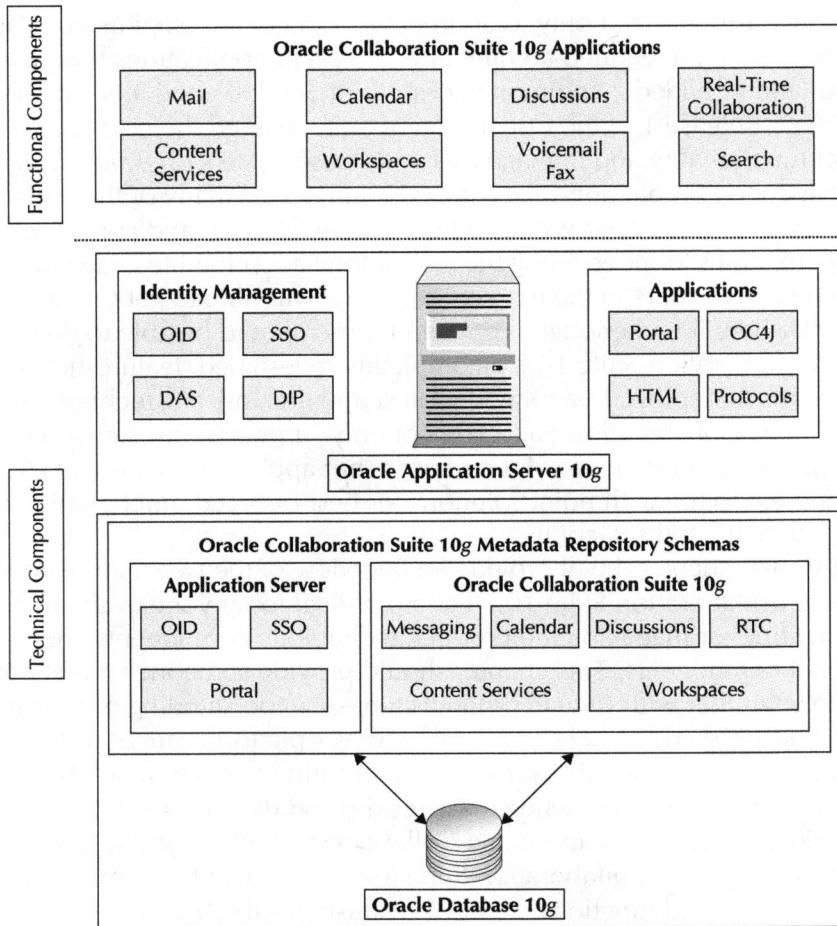

FIGURE 1-1. *Oracle Collaboration Suite high-level architecture*

as well as the security for end-user authentication and application data.
These core technology components are also what provide Oracle Collaboration
Suite 10*g* developers with the perfect platform to create functional web-based
user interfaces, integration services for desktop applications, and administrative
functions.

Oracle Database 10*g*

Oracle Database 10*g* provides the repository for Oracle Internet Directory and Oracle Application Server Metadata Repository, as well as for the schemas of the various component applications that make up the Oracle Collaboration Suite 10*g* Database.

The Enterprise Edition of Oracle Database 10*g* gives Oracle Collaboration Suite 10*g* a scalable data platform that will handle large amounts of unstructured data, ranging from emails to discussions to documents and other content. The Oracle Collaboration Suite 10*g* architecture also takes advantage of various database options such as partitioning and Real Application Clusters to increase the scalability and availability of the database platform within the architecture.

Oracle Internet Directory

Oracle Internet Directory (OID) is a general-purpose Lightweight Directory Access Protocol (LDAP) service, which provides a standard centralized structure for storing all user profile and application management information for Oracle Collaboration Suite 10*g*. It contains all user authentication information, profile information, and application access and responsibility detail. Because it is stored in Oracle Database 10*g*, it provides enterprise-scale support of user creation, as well as fast retrieval and centralized management of information about all users and all processes of Oracle Collaboration Suite 10*g*, regardless of location.

Oracle Collaboration Suite 10*g* Metadata Repository and Database

Oracle Application Server Metadata Repository is a standard and required component of any Oracle Application Server 10*g* installation. Oracle Application Server Metadata Repository is a set of schemas preseeded into an Oracle Database 10*g* instance that support the various components of the Oracle Application Server 10*g*. These stored schemas are used by Oracle Application Server 10*g* for organizing metadata in the Oracle Database about the Oracle Application Server 10*g* installation, configuration, and base function such as Single Sign-On and Portal, as well as details regarding any applications that are deployed on that Application Server platform's Middle Tier. Each component application of Oracle Collaboration Suite 10*g* has an associated schema or set of schemas stored in the Oracle Collaboration Suite 10*g* Database. These schemas contain structures created for managing the data for the individual component applications of Oracle Collaboration Suite 10*g*. Email, Content Services, Real-Time Collaboration, Discussions, and other features all have schemas that contain data, index, and logic structures to support their functionality. (Oracle Calendar still resides in its own proprietary database structure.) In most deployment scenarios, both the Application Server 10*g* Metadata Repository and Oracle Collaboration Suite 10*g* schemas are created in a single database instance, unless the size of the implementation warrants separation for management and performance reasons.

Oracle Application Server 10g

Oracle Application Server 10*g* provides the components of the architecture for Identity Management, Application Integration, and Application Deployment. The Identity Management components—Oracle Application Server Single Sign-On, Oracle Delegated Administration Services, and Oracle Directory Integration and Provisioning—provide Oracle Collaboration Suite 10*g* with the ability to manage users, their access, and their privileges in a central location, all stored in the Oracle Database 10*g* repository as described previously. The Single Sign-On component of Oracle Application Server 10*g* is utilized throughout Oracle Collaboration Suite 10*g* to provide secured access to all component applications, features, and accounts within Oracle Collaboration Suite 10*g*, at the properly defined level, while only requiring the end user to enter a username and password one time. Oracle Delegated Administration Services provides Oracle Collaboration Suite 10*g* Administrators with the ability to delegate responsibility for managing responsibilities to other administrators or end users. Oracle Directory Integration and Provisioning keeps all the information stored in the Oracle Internet Directory synchronized with other connected directories such as Microsoft Active Directory and the Oracle Collaboration Suite 10*g*'s individual applications security schemes. All applications within Oracle Collaboration Suite 10*g* (with the exception of Oracle Calendar) are deployed through the Oracle Containers for Java (OC4J) engine of the Oracle Application Server 10*g* and can either be accessed via the web through individual URLs or through a Portal that provides a single consistent interface for all functions an end user is allowed to access. Access to Oracle Collaboration Suite 10*g* functionality such as Content Services, Email, Calendar, and Messaging from client interfaces is also provided for in the infrastructure via standard open protocols such as WEBDAV (Content Services), POP3, IMAP4, and SMTP (Email).

Functional Components

Oracle Collaboration Suite 10*g* consists of several closely integrated applications, each providing a set of business functions that together give the end user a complete toolkit for collaborating with peers, management, and partners. For example, Email and Discussions allow communication between one or more members of a team. Calendar provides a shared real-time view of schedules and availability, Content Services allows the management of all types of content—structured as well as unstructured— and easy search through that content for finding necessary information quickly. Real-Time Collaboration provides a web-based meeting tool for multiple users to collaborate on documents, presentations, designs, etc., everyone viewing and changing the same information at the same time.

Oracle Collaboration Suite 10*g* applications have been developed to support end users' having multiple access methods to both functionality and data. All Oracle Collaboration Suite 10*g* applications can be accessed via a web browser through the Oracle Collaboration Suite 10*g* Portal, shown in Figure 1-2. Also, the Oracle Collaboration Suite 10*g* Welcome page allows access to the individual application pages (Mail, Calendar, Real-Time

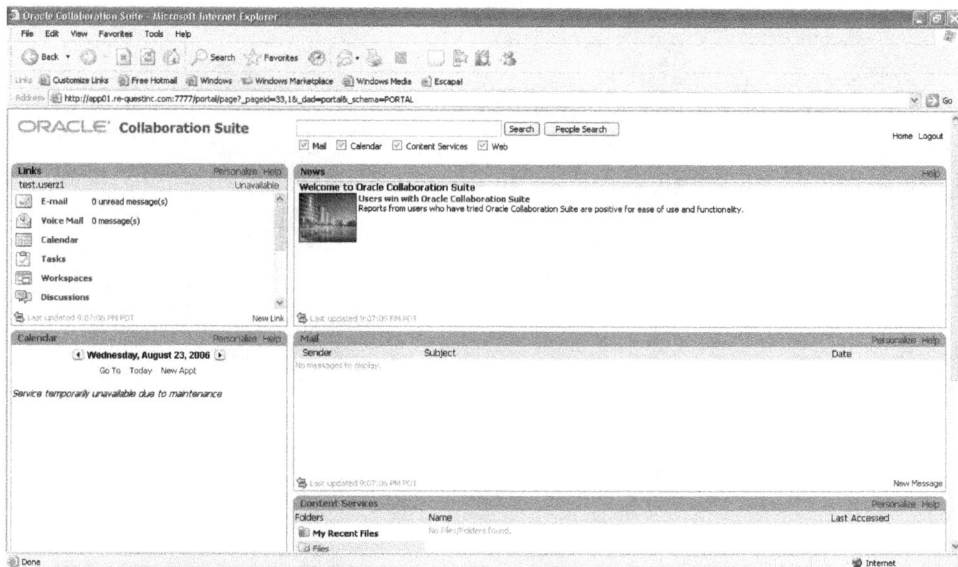

FIGURE 1-2. *Oracle Collaboration Suite 10g Portal*

Collaboration, etc.) as well as to the administrative applications such as Oracle Collaboration Suite Control (Enterprise Manager) and Downloads for Connectors, Oracle Drive, etc. Figure 1-3 shows the Welcome page for Oracle Collaboration Suite 10*g*.

Many applications—whenever it is useful—can be accessed through standard Windows desktop features or desktop application interfaces. For example, Oracle Collaboration Suite 10*g* Mail can be accessed via any desktop email client, using standard open messaging protocols such as IMAP4, SMTP, and POP3. Oracle Collaboration Suite 10*g* Calendar can be accessed via the Windows Outlook client, for example (see Figure 1-4), as well as through a desktop calendar client provided as a download from Oracle Collaboration Suite 10*g*. Oracle Collaboration Suite Content Services can be accessed through Windows Explorer via standard open communication protocols such as WEBDAV and SAMBA, as well as through Oracle Drive (another desktop tool downloadable from Oracle Collaboration Suite 10*g*

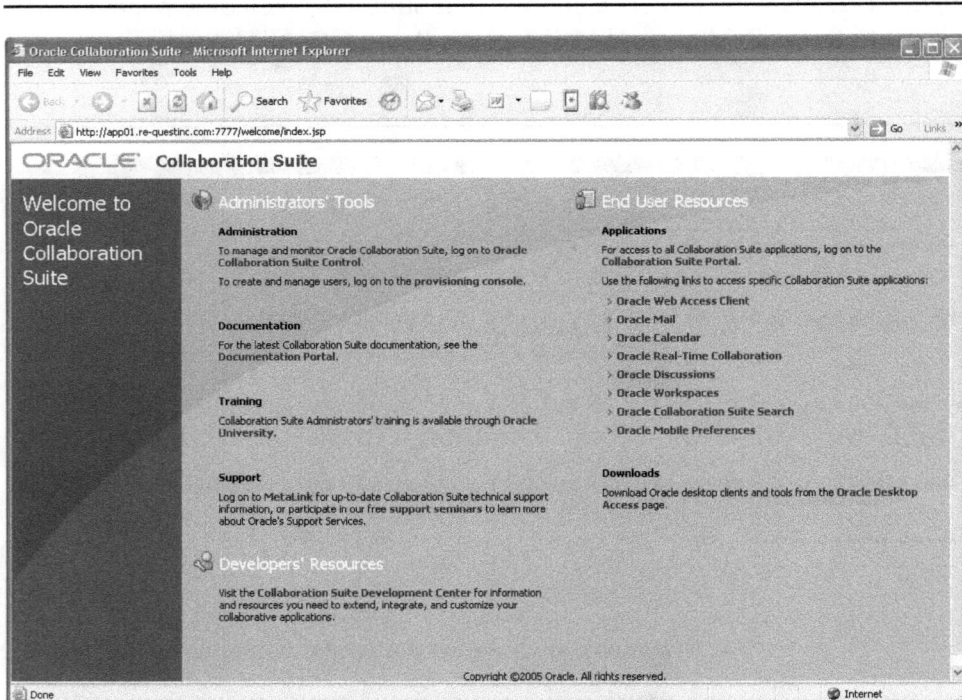

FIGURE 1-3. *Oracle Collaboration Suite 10*g *Welcome page*

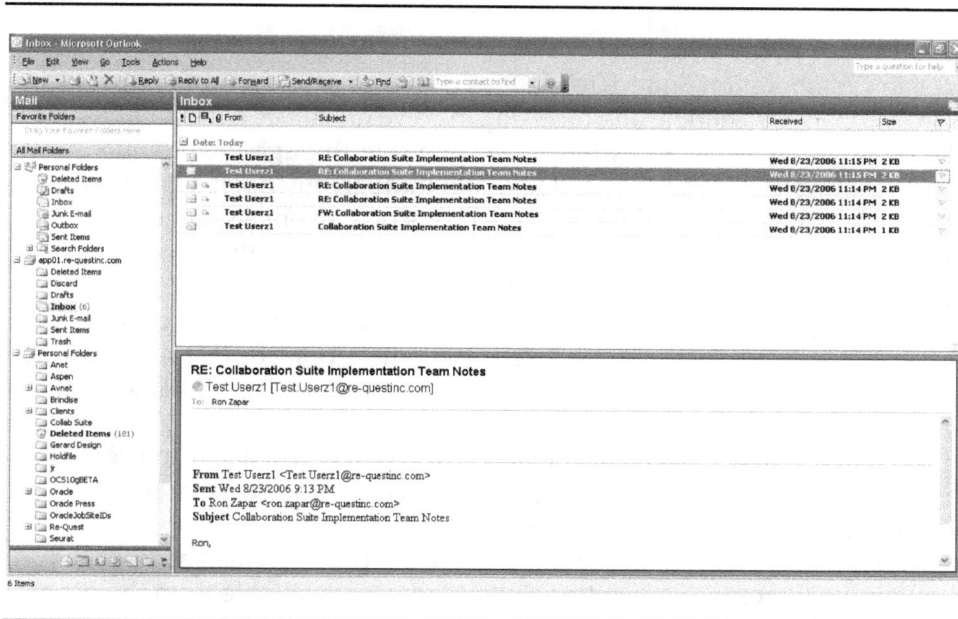

FIGURE 1-4. *Standard Windows Desktop Applications Access Oracle Collaboration Suite 10*g

that uses cookieless WEBDAV to communicate back to the Oracle Collaboration Suite 10*g* Content Services application).

The applications provided in Oracle Collaboration Suite 10*g* are

- Oracle Collaboration Suite 10*g* Mail

- Oracle Collaboration Suite 10*g* Calendar

- Oracle Collaboration Suite 10*g* Discussions

- Oracle Collaboration Suite 10*g* Voicemail and Fax

- Oracle Collaboration Suite 10*g* Workspaces

- Oracle Collaboration Suite 10*g* Content Services

- Oracle Collaboration Suite 10*g* Real-Time Collaboration

- Oracle Collaboration Suite 10*g* Mobile Collaboration

- Oracle Collaboration Suite 10*g* Federated Search

Mail

Oracle Collaboration Suite 10*g* Mail is an enterprise-class unified messaging system capable of sending and receiving massive quantities of email messages, voicemails, and faxes, accessible to the end user through the provided web interface, through Microsoft Outlook, and through any open standard email client compatible with IMAP4 or POP3 protocols. All emails, attachments, voicemails, and faxes are stored in tables housed within the Oracle Database 10*g* Database Email and Voicemail schemas. This provides for ease of management and higher scalability to support more users, and more messages per user, than standard email systems. Contacts, distribution lists, and other directory services are provided in Oracle Mail via Oracle Internet Directory.

Users have many choices when it comes to mail interfaces to use with Oracle Collaboration Suite 10*g* Mail. They can use the web-based Email application that comes with Oracle Collaboration Suite 10*g* and is accessible from the Collaboration Suite Portal. They can also access mail through the Oracle Collaboration Suite Mail page available from the list of the specific Oracle Collaboration Suite applications on the Oracle Collaboration Suite 10*g* Welcome page. This is a thin, simple Mail interface for sending and receiving unified messages to/from the Oracle Collaboration Suite 10*g* Mail application. End users may also use any of the IMAP4 or POP3 standards–based email clients available through various vendors and open-source providers in the market. As long as the email application supports one of the preceding protocols for receiving email and standard SMTP for sending email, it can be used with Oracle Collaboration Suite 10*g* Mail. Finally, anyone wanting to use Microsoft Outlook as their Mail (and Calendar) client with Oracle Collaboration Suite 10*g* can do so by downloading and installing the Outlook Connector for Oracle Collaboration Suite 10*g*.

Through the Oracle Collaboration Suite Email application accessed from the Portal a user gets a feature-rich "thick" client feel but through a web-based interface. The web client is very "Outlook-like" in its look and feel, giving end users access to Mail folders and Contacts from the two main functional sections of the page. In the Mail section the Inbox, Sent Items, Drafts, and Deleted Items are available as part of the Oracle Mail folder tree, and the Shared Folders area provides access to any user-defined shared folders, as well as to Categories and Forums for that user in the Oracle Collaboration Suite 10*g* Discussions application. Figure 1-5 shows the

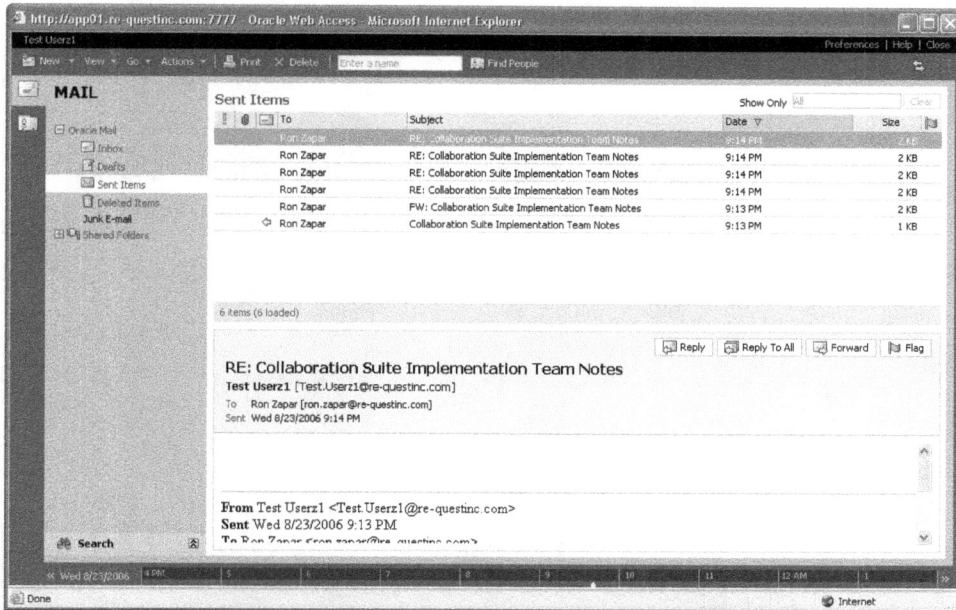

FIGURE 1-5. *Oracle Collaboration Suite 10g Mail client*

Oracle Application Server 10*g* Mail web client. When a subitem of Oracle Mail is highlighted, say Inbox, the list of messages held in that subitem is displayed in the top portion of the main window to the right of the folder tree. The bottom portion displays a preview window for the highlighted item in the preceding list. In the Contacts section My Address Book entries as well as Corporate Directory information are available. This section provides a search engine to find contacts through a keyword search. A Calendar bar is also displayed at the bottom of the client page so that Calendar can easily be accessed from the Email web client.

The Oracle Collaboration Suite Mail web interface, shown in Figure 1-6, is accessed through the link directly from the Welcome page for Oracle Collaboration Suite 10*g*. This client is designed to be more like a webmail interface, focusing on lightweight functionality targeted at composing, sending, and receiving mail messages. It is basically the old Mail interface from Oracle Collaboration Suite 9.0.4.

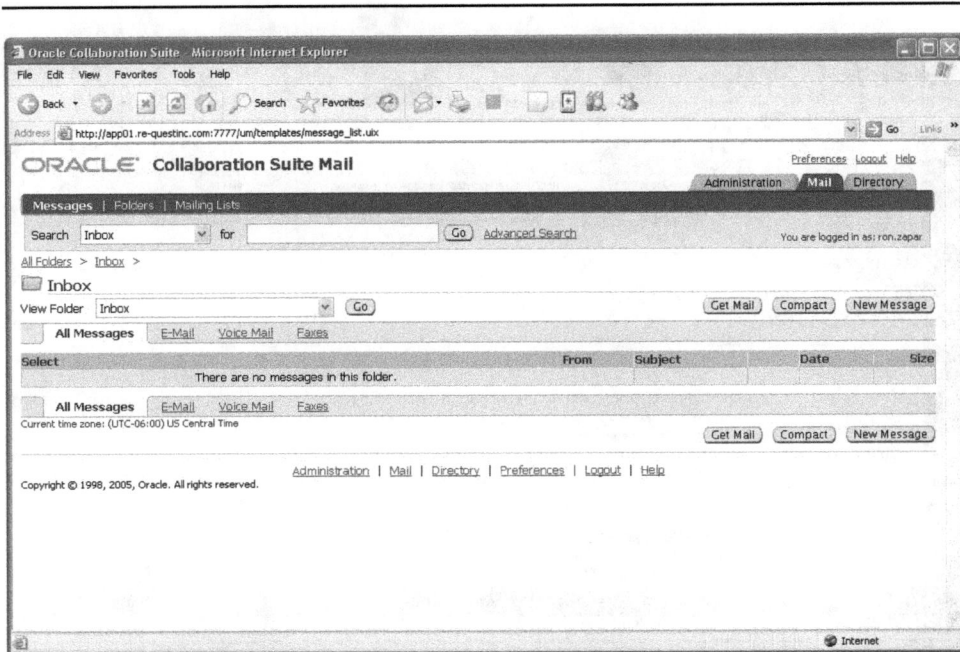

FIGURE 1-6. *Oracle Collaboration Suite 10g Mail web interface*

The open-standards email clients allow end users to use their favorite email client against Oracle Collaboration Suite 10g Mail. As long as they have a valid username and the appropriate server names for the Oracle Collaboration Suite 10g Mail IMAP4, POP3, and SMTP servers, users can connect their email client to Oracle Collaboration Suite 10g Mail as if it were any open-standards email server running those protocols.

The Outlook Connector allows the end user to use Outlook with all of its full-featured functionality against Oracle Collaboration Suite 10g. This connector allows the use of Outlook to be tightly integrated with Oracle Collaboration Suite 10g Mail and Calendar functionality and vice versa. Users can use shared folders, access other allowed Inboxes, manage contact lists, schedule real-time availability of other users and resources, and more through the Outlook interface into Oracle Collaboration Suite 10g. The Outlook Connector is available through the Oracle Desktop Access page in the Downloads section on the Oracle Collaboration Suite 10g Welcome page.

There is not very much a user can do today with Outlook connected to one of its more native messaging servers—guess which one I'm talking about . . . hmmm—that they cannot do connected to Oracle Collaboration Suite 10*g* using the Outlook Connector.

From an administrator's perspective, the Oracle Collaboration Suite 10*g* Mail client (this web interface) provides administrative capabilities to maintain Domain, User, List, Alias, News, and Policy settings right through the Administration tab. The details of Email Administration will be covered in Chapter 12.

Voicemail and Fax

Oracle Collaboration Suite 10*g* Voicemail and Fax provide the end user the ability to receive voicemails and faxes directly into his or her messaging Inbox. The voicemails and faxes are stored in the Oracle Collaboration Suite 10*g* Datastore along with other email messages, all in standard MIME format, so they are manageable as well as secure, and accessible through the webmail interface or any desktop email client using the standard email protocols IMAP4 or POP3. Faxes are received into a user's Inbox as an attachment to a mail message in standard MIME compliant .tif format. Voicemails are received in the same manner, except they are attachments in the standard .wav format. This allows users to review voicemails and fax attachments using any standard tool available that can "play" .wav files or view .tif files, respectively. Also, because these attachments come right into the user's Inbox, a user can synchronize their laptop email applications with the server, download voicemails and faxes along with other standard email messages, and review them offline from a network connection, say on an airplane or in their home office later that night. Voicemails can also be accessed through the traditional method of listening to them on a telephone.

It is important to note that in order to support the voicemail and/or fax options of Oracle Collaboration Suite 10*g*, additional hardware is required. Any company wishing to implement Collaboration Suite 10*g* Voicemail must install a voicemail and fax server, which gives Oracle Collaboration Suite 10*g* the ability to "connect" to the company's telecommunications equipment—specifically its PBX switch—in order for the voicemails to be transmitted to the Oracle Collaboration Suite 10*g* Voicemail function. A voicemail and fax server is another server in the environment that runs the voicemail and fax server software from the Oracle Collaboration Suite 10*g*. This software is integrated with Intel's NetMerge CCS 3.0 CT server, which provides a separation layer between Oracle Voicemail and Fax software and proprietary telecom architectures, eliminating the need for custom application code for each PBX switch Oracle wishes to integrate with the Oracle Collaboration Suite 10*g* voicemail and fax functions. More detailed information regarding architecture choices, hardware options, and compatibility with telecom equipment can be found in Chapter 12 of the *Oracle Collaboration Suite Deployment Guide 10g Release 1 (10.1.2)*.

Calendar

Oracle Collaboration Suite 10*g* Calendar is a feature-rich people and resource (conference rooms, equipment, etc.) scheduling solution. It maintains all user and resource schedule information in a central repository, so it can be checked by other users for accurate availability. It is a real-time solution, which means that schedule updates happen as they are made, with no delays for processing as in other message-based calendar solutions. As with Email, Calendar can be accessed with the Oracle Collaboration Suite 10*g* web client, through Microsoft Outlook via the Oracle Collaboration Suite 10*g* Outlook Connector, or through an included desktop client.

Unlike many web clients that provide limited functionality from their applications as compared to the desktop clients themselves, Oracle Collaboration Suite 10*g* provides the full functionality available from the Oracle Collaboration Suite 10*g* Calendar application through its web interface: the ability to add, update, and delete calendar entries, view other users' schedules (as they allow of course), change views of the calendar from day to week to month, and switch from Planner Mode to List Mode. Figure 1-7 shows the Calendar web interface.

Oracle Collaboration Suite 10*g* Calendar users can access their calendar data in two modes: Planner Mode and List Mode. Planner Mode provides an interface that looks much like that of a typical "day planner," with Daily, Weekly, and Monthly views. The Daily view of Planner Mode presents a screen with meetings on the left side and a daily notes and events as well as task lists on the right. The Weekly view of Planner Mode shows the days of a week (default Monday through Friday) in columnar form, with appointment times listed down the left-hand side (start day for the week and whether Saturdays and/or Sundays are displayed are preference options). The Monthly

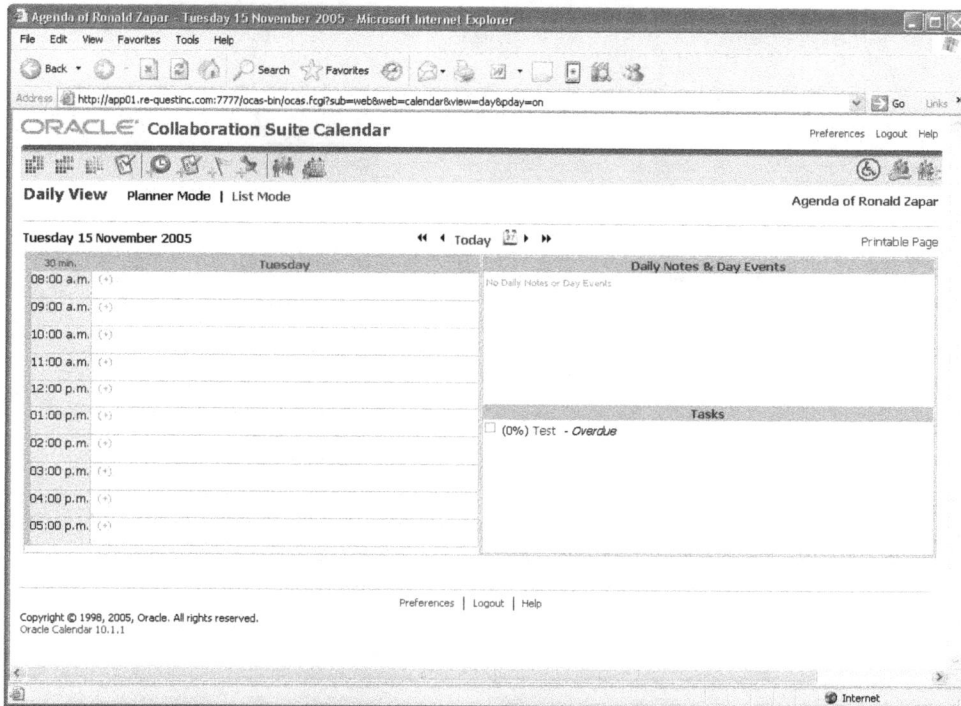

FIGURE 1-7. *The Oracle Collaboration Suite 10g Calendar web interface*

view of Planner Mode shows all days of the month in a view that resembles most wall or desktop blotter calendars (a grid of squares, one for each day of the month). List Mode looks and feels more like a task list program, with meetings listed out on the top portion of the web page and tasks listed on the bottom portion of the web page. Figure 1-8 shows the List Mode view of the Oracle Collaboration Suite 10*g* Calendar interface. The Daily view of List Mode shows lists of meetings and tasks for the day, the Weekly view of List Mode shows the days of the week across the top, with lists of schedule items going down under the days, and the Monthly view shows the grid again.

In addition to the Mode links and Daily, Weekly, and Monthly View change buttons, the toolbar on the web interface provides buttons for creating meetings, adding tasks to task lists, and creating day events and

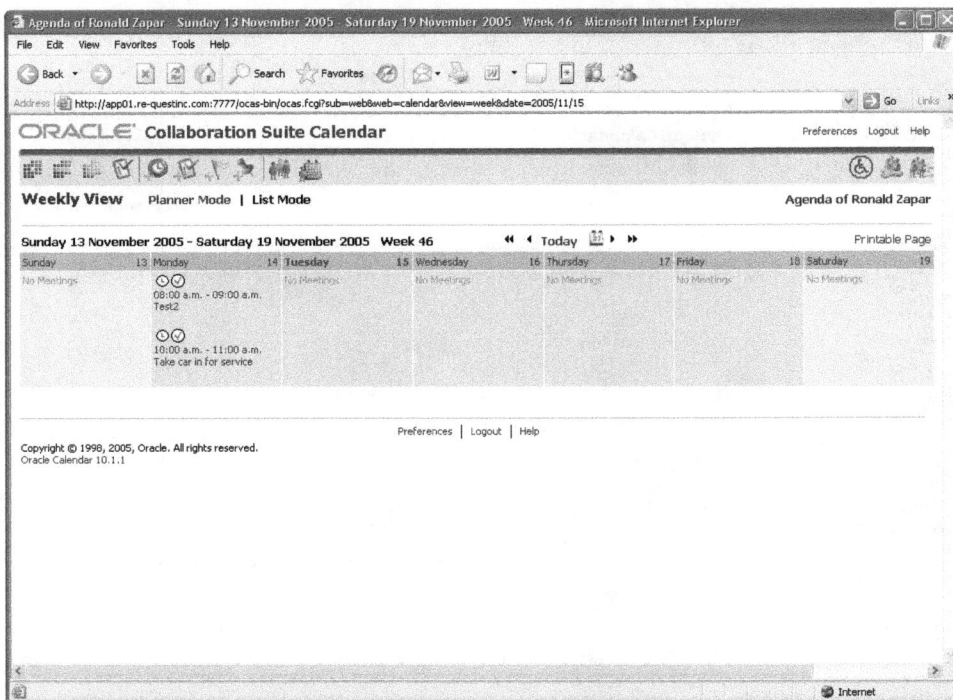

FIGURE 1-8. *Oracle Collaboration Suite 10g Calendar List Mode Weekly view*

daily notes. It also opens the group functions of Scheduler—in order to schedule a calendar entry for multiple users—and Agenda Viewer, which gives the user the ability to do an OID lookup of a user and see his or her calendar entries. There is also an icon for switching to Accessibility Mode, as well as two Administrative icons for managing user groups and access rights. Figure 1-9 shows the toolbar from the Oracle Collaboration Suite 10g Calendar web interface.

FIGURE 1-9. *Oracle Collaboration Suite 10g Calendar toolbar*

Discussions

Oracle Collaboration Suite 10*g* Discussions is a tool that provides Oracle Collaboration Suite 10*g* users with all of the standard functionality of message boards and discussion forums. Discussion information is organized by Category, and then either by Category within a Category, or by Forum within a Category. Users can post questions to a Forum, and other users can comment, answer, etc., on the same thread of conversation. Search capabilities are also available so that users can search by keywords across all forums or select groups. Figure 1-10 shows the Oracle Collaboration Suite Discussion web interface.

From the Edit Configuration tab administrators can determine whether attachments are allowed in the Forum messages, what the default prefix for

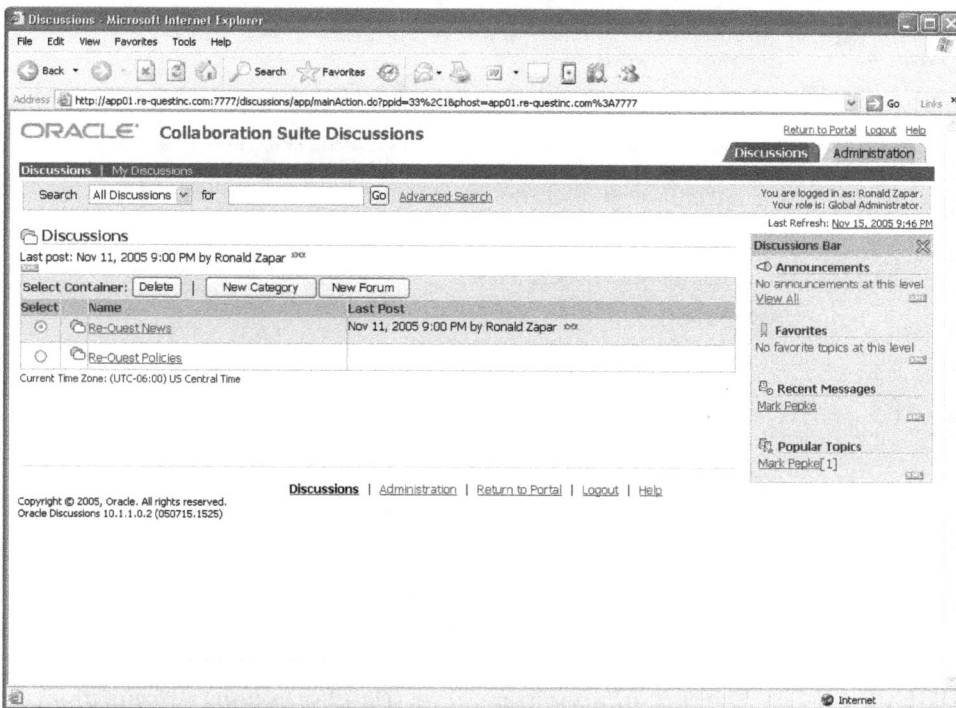

FIGURE 1-10. *Oracle Collaboration Suite 10g Discussions*

the message subject in replies should be, and whether or not the original message should be quoted in replies. They can also determine whether Forum Writers can edit and/or hide their messages in Forums, what the WebUI look and feel is for message threads and message editors, and the definition of the Public Policies on access to Forums (Forum Members only, Public Read-Only, or Public Read-Write). From the Edit Email Administration tab administrators can determine whether emails sent to the forum email address will be accepted into the Forum from Forum Writers, anyone, or not at all, and can determine the look and layout of subscription emails. Figure 1-11 shows the Administration page for Oracle Collaboration Suite 10*g* Discussions.

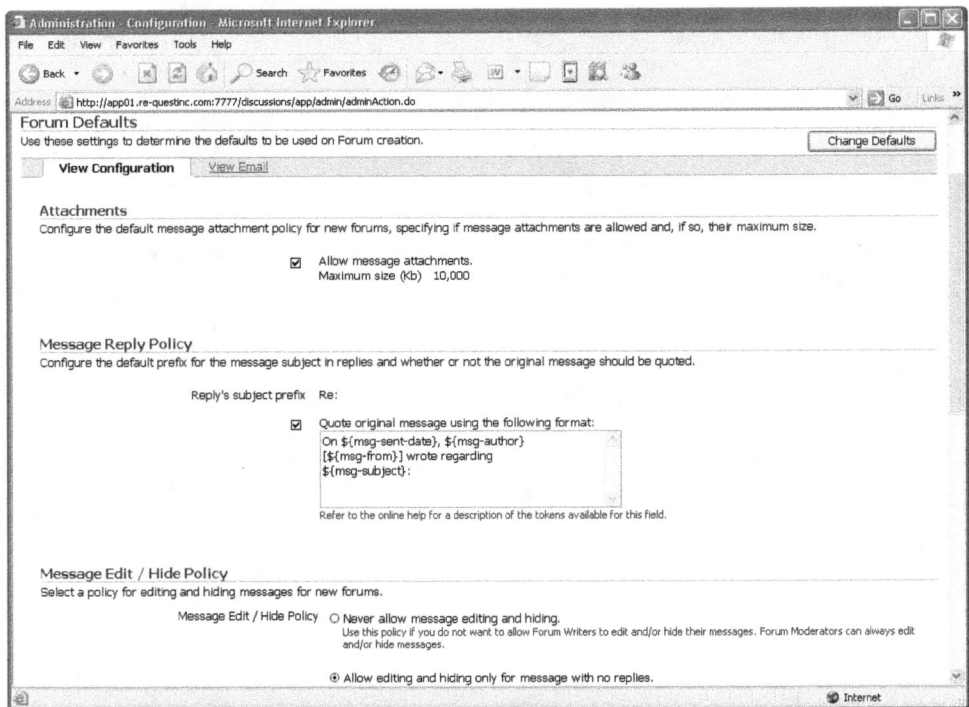

FIGURE 1-11. *Oracle Collaboration Suite 10*g *Discussions Administration*

Content Services

Oracle Collaboration Suite 10*g* Content Services is an application combining the file handling capabilities of file servers with the feature-rich functions and user interface of Content Management and Document Management solutions. All content is stored in Content Services schemas within the Oracle Collaboration Suite 10*g* Datastore. This allows the Content Services application to take advantage of the capabilities of the Oracle Database 10*g* database engine, so end users can store, index, and make available— through various standard protocols and interfaces—files, content, etc., that are stored in Oracle Collaboration Suite 10*g* Content Services. End users can use the web interface for Workspaces to access content specific to projects, or can use the SAMBA or WEBDAV protocol to map access points into their Oracle Collaboration Suite 10*g* Content Services repository from Windows Explorer, Internet Explorer, or any third-party application accessing file services through these open standards.

Content Services uses a delegated access method for security around files, folders, and workspaces. A user can be assigned as an Administrator for a specific workspace, and that user can then delegate the security for other users accessing that workspace. All folders and files under that workspace can be delegated by the Administrator for view-only or read/ write access.

Content Services has a broad scope for application of its functionality. For example, for companies/entities such as law firms where large amounts of documents need to be stored, secured, managed, and many times, searched, Content Services can provide all the necessary functionality of a document management system along with the security and scalability of storing the content in an Oracle database. Doctors, hospitals, and other entities chartered with managed medical records can use Content Services to meet their functional needs. Figure 1-12 shows the Content Services web interface.

Real-Time Collaboration

Oracle Collaboration Suite 10*g* Real-Time Collaboration consists of two main components: Web Conferencing and Instant Messaging. Web Conferencing provides users with a browser-based interface for holding online conferences. Users can schedule conferences, invite attendees, upload meeting materials for preconference access, and review archived web conferences from the web conferencing interface. Participants can be

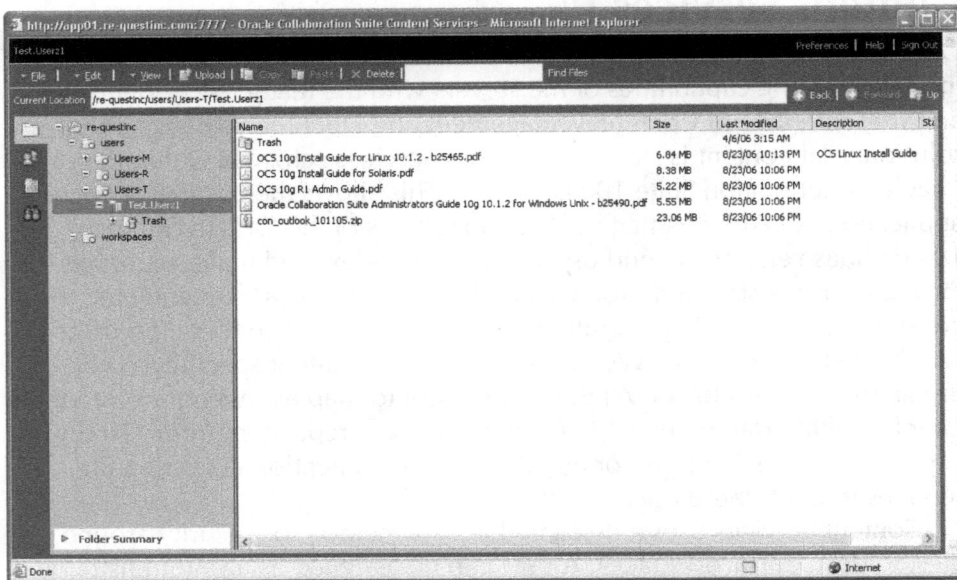

FIGURE 1-12. *Content Services web interface*

Oracle Collaboration Suite 10*g* users, or outside entities (as long as the application is made available to users outside the firewall). Figure 1-13 shows the Web Conferencing web interface for scheduling, starting, and joining a conference. The Instant Messaging client can be downloaded from the Oracle Collaboration Suite 10*g* Welcome Page or Portal (or the Real-Time Collaboration web page), and allows a user to open a fully functional chat session with any Oracle Collaboration Suite 10*g* user. Figure 1-14 shows the Oracle Messenger Console and Chat Interface.

The Web Conferencing console, shown in Figure 1-15, provides several tools for collaborating among a group of users on a web conference. A user in Presenter can show other attendees a document that has been previously uploaded to the Oracle Collaboration Suite 10*g* Web Conferencing application. A user can draw diagrams, illustrations, etc., using the Whiteboard functions. Web Conferencing also provides desktop sharing, with the ability for hosts to share their entire desktop, an area or portion of their desktop, or a single application running on their PC by choosing a

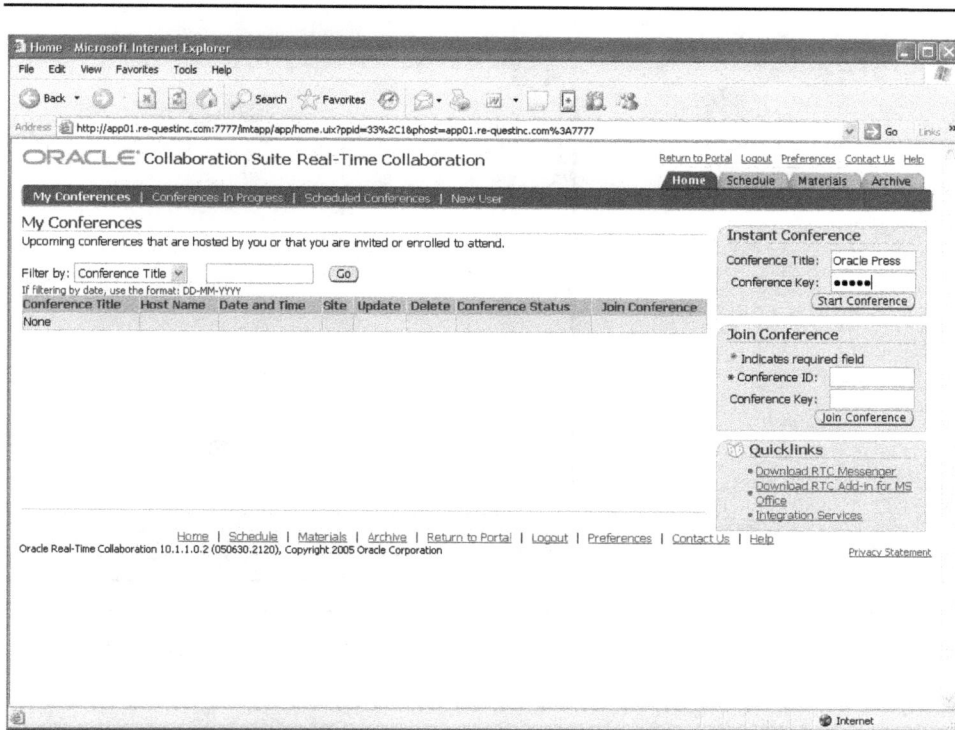

FIGURE 1-13.   *Oracle Collaboration Suite 10*g *Web Conferencing web interface*

share type from the pull-down Share menu once the Desktop Sharing Mode icon is selected. There is also the ability to co-browse a web site, where the Host or Presenter enters a web site and everyone on the web conference can view it. Users can decide how to view the Shared desktop window using the next two icons. Users can either view just the active portion of the Presenter's screen with the arrow icon or enable a scroll bar to control what portion of the Presenter's screen they view at any time with the Scroll Bar icon. A user can request Shared Control from a Presenter by clicking the mouse icon to the left of the conference's Attendee pull-down list. In the Attendee pull-down list, the Host can grant another attendee Presenter rights so they can share their desktop and make a presentation to the conference attendees. The Host can also request Shared Control of another user's desktop or grant Shared Control of his own desktop. This means he or she can manipulate

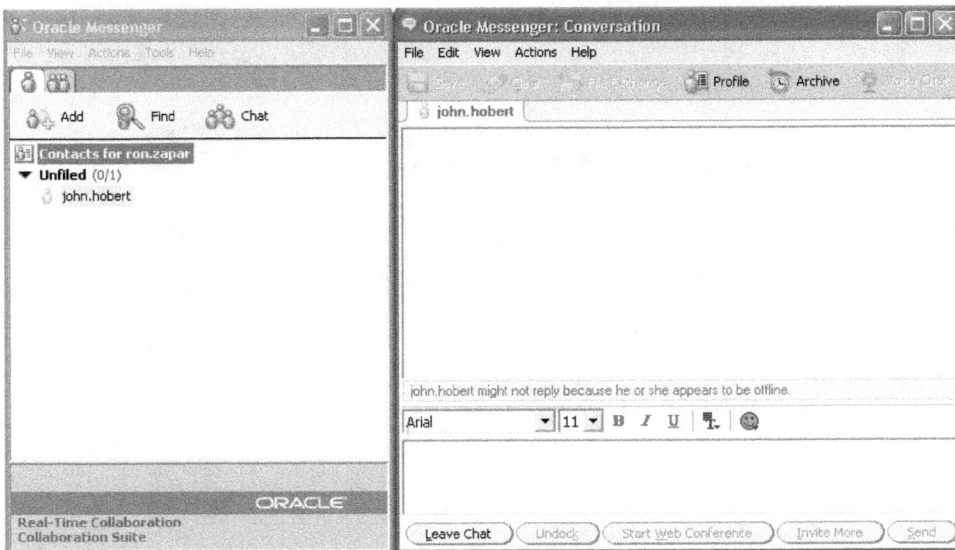

FIGURE 1-14. *Oracle Collaboration Suite 10g Instant Messenger client*

the mouse and keyboard of a remote attendee's PC in the web conference just as if sitting in front of the keyboard of that attendee's PC, or give another conference attendee the ability to manipulate his or her desktop. Finally, from within the Attendee pull-down list a Host can grant the Speaker role to a user so that user can use his or her microphone to speak to other attendees through voice streaming (bandwidth consumption considerations need to be taken into account here prior to allowing this functionality on a corporate network). The Chat icon allows a user to open the chat window and either

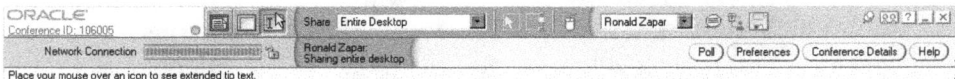

FIGURE 1-15. *Oracle Collaboration Suite 10g Web Conferencing Console*

hold a public chat—all attendees—or request a private chat with one attendee, or a group chat with multiple attendees. The Enable Voice Streaming icon allows a Host to use his or her PC microphone to speak to attendees, or dial into a conference call and stream the telephone audio over the web conference to other attendees. The Snapshot icon allows an attendee to take a snapshot of the screen of the web conference and save it to a file in .bmp format. The Recording icon allows a Host to record the presentation for playback later.

Workspaces

Oracle Collaboration Suite 10*g* Workspaces is a tool that provides a user interface that summarizes as well as organizes documents, content, schedules, resources, and people working together on common projects. All informational aspects of the entity—design, idea, project—that people are working on in a Workspace can be provided and managed within the Workspace. It is a concept rather than a function, where all information related to a common theme can be provided, accessed, and managed by the team of people working together on that theme.

A good analogy for an Oracle Collaboration Suite 10*g* Workspace is the carpenter's workshop. In his workshop the carpenter has everything he needs to create and review designs, build prototypes, work with others on refinements in the design or product, and ultimately deliver the production article. An Oracle Collaboration Suite 10*g* Workspace is a virtual carpenter's workshop for business people, where they can incubate ideas with coworkers and business partners, and have available to them the entire Oracle Collaboration Suite 10*g* set of functionality to do so. Figure 1-16 shows the Oracle Collaboration Suite 10*g* Workspaces web interface.

Mobile Collaboration

Oracle Collaboration Suite 10*g* Mobile Collaboration provides an out-of-the-box solution for the mobile user. With a full install of Oracle Collaboration Suite 10*g* the wireless functions are installed. Through the Mobile Preferences in the Oracle Collaboration Suite 10*g* Portal, or through the Oracle Mobile Preferences link on the Oracle Collaboration Suite 10*g* Welcome page, users can define certain preferences for how their mobile

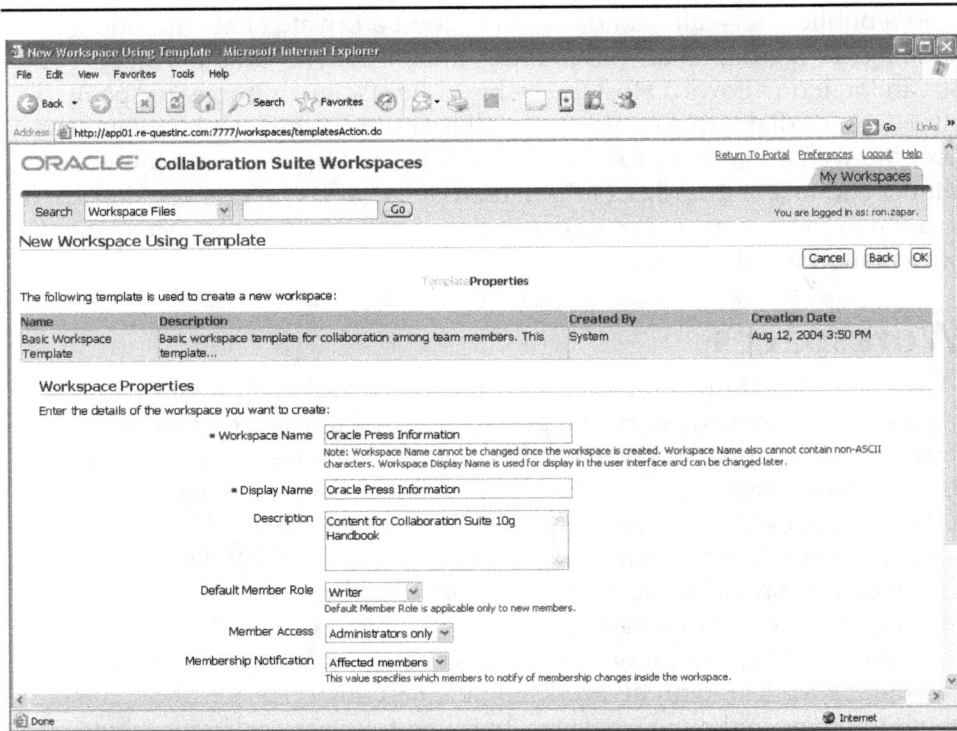

FIGURE 1-16. *Oracle Collaboration Suite 10g Workspaces web interface*

access to Oracle Collaboration Suite 10*g* will work. First, users must define their mobile sign-on information (Mobile Access Account ID—usually your mobile phone number—and Mobile Access PIN, which is different but related to your Oracle Collaboration Suite 10*g* SSO ID through the Oracle Internet Directory). A user can define notifications when Voicemails, Fax messages, or Urgent messages are received in Oracle Collaboration Suite 10*g*, or when emails are received from particular email addresses. Finally a user can define what the default view of the mobile Inbox is (today's messages, messages from the last 3 or 7 days, only faxes, etc.). In the Advanced options section of the mobile preferences, shown in Figure 1-17, a user can define Contact Rules according to where he or she is at any given point in time. For example, a user can define an "At My Desk" Contact Rule that says use corporate email, or an "On the Go" Contact Rule that says use

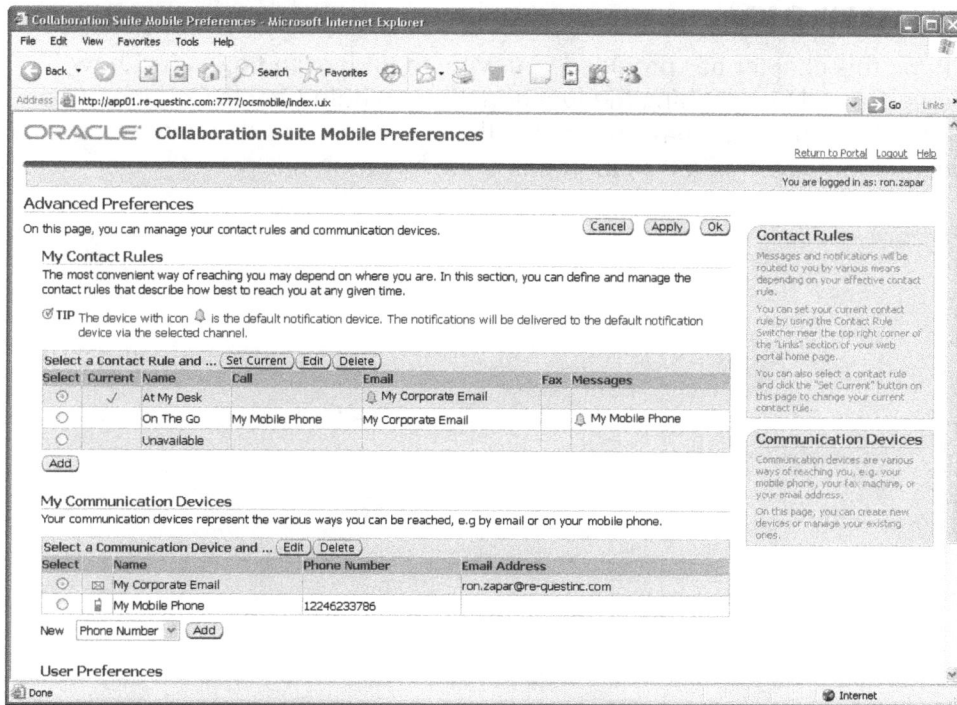

FIGURE 1-17.   *Oracle Collaboration Suite 10*g *Mobile Preferences Advanced Options*

the mobile phone. A user can also define different Communication Devices and how to contact them, depending upon the device type. Faxes, Pagers, PDAs, Email, and Mobile Phone are some of the Device Type choices.

If a user has a mobile device that is web-enabled, that user can access the Oracle Collaboration Suite 10*g* Mobile Portal by going to the Mobile Preferences page and entering his or her Mobile Access Account ID and Mobile Access PIN. From there, the user will be put into the Mobile Portal, where all Oracle Collaboration Suite 10*g* applications are accessible in their mobile form. A user can access Mail, Calendar, Address Book, Oracle Internet Directory (OID), Short Messaging, Files, and Fax via the URL OCSMid-Tier:port/ptg/rm.

Summary

I hope this chapter has provided you with an understanding of just how powerful and far-reaching the functionality is within Oracle Collaboration Suite 10*g*. Now that I have presented the overview, let's dive into some detail about creating a Collaboration Suite environment.

CHAPTER
2

Creating the Right Architecture for Your OCS Environment

*If we continue to develop our technology without wisdom
or prudence, our servant may prove to be our executioner.*
—Omar Bradley

One of the biggest value propositions the Oracle Collaboration Suite 10*g* product brings to the table is the fact that it is extremely flexible in how it can be installed and configured. Given the fact that the Oracle Collaboration Suite 10*g* infrastructure and applications are deployed on top of the Oracle Database 10*g* and Application Server 10*g* core technology stack, an Oracle Collaboration Suite solutions architect has an extreme amount of latitude in making implementation decisions. This flexibility also allows companies of every size and budget to be able to "right-size" an architecture for their needs . . . and pocketbook. Small companies, depending upon their messaging and content storage requirements, can implement Oracle Collaboration Suite 10*g* on a single server, while larger organizations can spread infrastructure and application components across several servers, taking advantage of the high availability and scalability options of Oracle Collaboration Suite 10*g*. This gives these larger companies the ability to distribute processes and take advantage of redundant architecture components not only to support more users but to do so with a higher uptime threshold. The main deployment metrics we will look at that drive architecture decisions are

- *Total user capacity*, or the number of users we can support with a given architecture, which is a function of concurrency, storage, interface deployment, and load

- *Access methods*, which means how will users get to Oracle Collaboration Suite 10*g* functionality; through the provided web interfaces or open standards protocols

- *High availability requirements/considerations*, and how the architecture of the Oracle Collaboration Suite 10*g* product can be deployed to best meet those needs

- *Company-specific requirements*, such as what servers/operating systems can/will IT support, what existing infrastructure components already in place can Oracle Collaboration Suite 10*g* take advantage of (for example, backup solutions, DMZ routers, System Administrator capacity)

But as we all know, with flexibility sometimes comes complexity, or at least multiple possible choices, which in some people's minds equals difficulty in deciding the correct path to take. This chapter is going to provide the reader with an understanding of the options for architecting an Oracle Collaboration Suite 10g environment, and what guidelines and decision points will assist someone in properly choosing among those options to best fit their specific company's needs.

Rather than attempting to dive right into the hardcore technical scope of defining an Oracle Collaboration Suite 10g architecture, I am going to start with the more intangible—or in other words nontechnical—factors that drive architecture decisions. User types, as in role within the company, technical savvy, etc., along with users' locations (which will determine bandwidth availability and security requirements), whether they are internal or external to the corporate network firewall, as well as their mobile access requirements, all factor into the architecture decisions, playing a huge part in how the solution is architected and deployed. Once we have discussed these high-level architecture drivers, we will get into the more traditional architecture considerations such as concurrency, storage requirements, scalability, and availability.

OCS User Community

The demographics of the user base that will be supported with a particular Oracle Collaboration Suite 10g implementation plays a key part in solution architecture decisions, in addition to affecting implementation, training, and rollout plans. Who, where, how, and why users will be using the various components of Oracle Collaboration Suite 10g will all drive architecture considerations, network and security requirements, and deployment methods for an implementation.

User Type

One of the main considerations within user demographics is user type, which is usually defined by a combination of job description—or role within the organization—and tech savvy-ness of the individual. For example, the CEO of a company will have a different set of requirements in terms of function, access, interface, availability, etc., than the plant manager, lead product engineer, product sales trainer or IT systems administrator. Users of each type will have a particular approach to how they utilize the tools within Oracle Collaboration Suite 10g to do their jobs as well as what components from Oracle Collaboration Suite 10g they rely on more often than others, all of which determine the most effective access method to enhancing their productivity.

I generally categorize users into four or five collective groupings: executives, administrators, sales, training, and IT professionals. Each job description defines a set of requirements for a successful Oracle Collaboration Suite 10g implementation. Executives are generally less technology-savvy (easy now, I said generally), so their user experience should be simple and nonthreatening. Implementing Oracle Collaboration Suite 10g Mail within their favorite mail client, for example, will get much closer to a successful executive user experience than, say, forcing them to log in to the Oracle Collaboration Suite 10g Portal or Welcome page Email link every time. Sales professionals are always moving around, so they may be best served by the Oracle Collaboration Suite 10g Portal interface, combined with mobile wireless access. Trainers generally don't care how they get to mail or files, but they definitely will rely heavily on scheduling, using archiving and replaying of web conferences. Administrators will require functionality such as delegated authority, 24 x 7 around-the-clock access to Mail, Calendar, and Files, as well as the ability to work on the run. IT professionals are generally the most adaptive and flexible user type but can also be the biggest critics of new technology rolled out in an organization. From a functional requirements perspective, they will also be the most creative—and driving—user group in terms of finding interesting new ways to stretch and deploy the functionality presented to them.

In general, user types will drive architecture decisions, as they mostly relate to the user interface and access method components of the architecture. Does the functionality of Oracle Collaboration Suite 10g need to meld seamlessly into their current user experience, or can it deploy its own set of user interface functions? User type will determine whether it is possible to roll out the Oracle Collaboration Suite 10g Portal web interface as the standard interface to everyone in the organization, or whether desktop connectivity and tools such as the Outlook Connector and/or Oracle Drive need to be deployed as well.

Location, Location, Location

Remember the old-time restaurateur's mantra, "location, location, location . . . it's everything to success!" In sticking with that theme, user logistics, or more precisely user location, is another important factor to consider in determining Oracle Collaboration Suite 10g architecture. If a company maintains a large user population that is distributed nationally or even globally across multiple physical locations, it must deal with certain requirements as they relate to architecting an environment that is secure and performs well. For example, if a high-tech electronics company has an office in Chicago and one in Singapore and plans on relying heavily on Oracle Collaboration Suite 10g Content Services for managing CAD drawings, close attention should be paid to the bandwidth requirements of moving large files across long distances between the offices. Otherwise, performance will be compromised. This is not an architecture requirement related to Oracle Collaboration Suite 10g functionality, but rather one that is required for any centralized store of large files where users are distributed across a wide area network (WAN). The performance of any application or process across a WAN will only be as good as the slowest segment in the network that any user must execute through in order to run the application. So I encourage anyone who is contemplating an Oracle Collaboration Suite 10g implementation in a distributed WAN environment that will include centralizing the storage of large files into Content Services to spend some time with their network architects/administrators to understand the bandwidth availability as compared to the requirements of moving large files across the WAN. With the proper attention to bandwidth requirements ahead of time, performance issues can be avoided. As an example, Oracle Corporation itself uses Oracle Collaboration Suite 10g, installed/maintained in a central location in the U.S., to service all offices' Content Services needs across the globe.

Internal vs. External Users

If a user requires significant access outside the four walls of the organization (with the availability of VPN connections for remote users today this literally means outside the corporate network), or an interface that can be used everywhere regardless of security or desktop configuration, or the ability to work closely with partners (read: contractors, suppliers, non-employees), architecture decisions need to be made to accommodate these requirements. If connectivity speed, security, and/or support levels are factors, then architecture considerations are affected as well. If outside contractors require the same or close to the same access to Oracle Collaboration Suite 10*g* as employees, then consideration of that fact also needs to come into play when making architecture decisions.

Mobile Requirements

If a company's user base travels, but what is more important, spends a lot of time on the road, away from internal network or secure Internet connectivity, then special considerations need to be given when architecting an Oracle Collaboration Suite 10*g* environment for these users. External accessibility of the Oracle Collaboration Suite 10*g* web client, along with possibly making available the Wireless option (which will install out of the box if it is not deselected), should be considered.

User Base Summary

So why is all the preceding information important in determining architecture? Well, it comes down to determining how to split up the components of Oracle Collaboration Suite 10*g* onto multiple servers, whether to install components outside the intranet firewall in the DMZ, and what types of security need to be implemented to protect corporate information being accessed outside the firewall.

In an environment where a measurable amount of access will take place by entities (employees, partners, contractors, etc.) that do not have secure access to the corporate network, then one might consider installing certain components of the infrastructure functions and Middle Tier applications in the DMZ. The other option is to install everything behind the intranet firewall and provide access to the Oracle Collaboration Suite 10*g* functions through specific IP/port combinations on the intranet firewall.

Previous User Experience

Another important consideration when architecting an Oracle Collaboration Suite 10*g* environment is what collaboration products end users have previously used or are currently using.

If a user base is heavily engaged in the Microsoft Exchange product with the Microsoft Outlook desktop tool, for example, a company will definitely need to either implement the Oracle Collaboration Suite 10*g* Outlook Connector or face a huge paradigm shift in the end users' acceptance of an Oracle Collaboration Suite 10*g* implementation. Exchange/Outlook users are going to be very biased in how they use their email and calendar tools, especially when it comes to some of the responsibility delegation and folder sharing that can be done in Exchange. A web-only interface will simply not fly for this user base. In addition, a company will most likely wind up implementing Content Services access through open protocols in Windows Explorer, or through Oracle Drive, rather than the web access through Oracle Collaboration Suite 10*g* Portal.

If a user base is accustomed to a less functional collaboration tool such as a standard POP email interface, then the issue becomes more of training the users to take advantage of more functionality. Examples are teaching users to share content through emailed links back to Workspaces rather than attaching the file directly to the email message, and using the scheduling tools in Calendar rather than sending an email message to coordinate a meeting. Heck, even getting everyone to *use* Calendar diligently to capture and manage schedule information will be a huge step forward with a group that is used to operating in a stand-alone manner.

The bottom line is, regardless of what environments end users are coming from, old habits die hard, so keep testing, knowledge transfer, and training high on the list of required tasks in your Oracle Collaboration Suite 10*g* implementation plan.

Architecture Components

Before beginning the task of describing the various solution architectures possible for implementing Oracle Collaboration Suite 10*g,* I should discuss the individual components of the architecture and how to decide which to use to build an Oracle Collaboration Suite 10*g* environment. Specifically, the components to review and make a decision on prior to architecting an Oracle Collaboration Suite 10*g* are

- Operating systems
- Server architectures

- Storage configurations
- Additional Oracle Collaboration Suite 10g architecture components (Fax, Voice, Document Conversion)

Operating Systems

The first decision point for the Oracle Collaboration Suite 10g architecture components is upon what operating system to deploy the application. There are many factors that can be considered when determining the operating system to run on: primary or Tier 1 development and deployment platform of the vendor (in this case Oracle Corporation); ease of installation/configuration/deployment of the product; internal experience with operating system platforms; market trends; cost; and of course the architectural pillars of availability, scalability, and manageability. In many cases we see a distinct line drawn in any IT shop. In terms of deploying solutions to the enterprise, they are either big Microsoft Windows shops or rely heavily on some type of Unix platform for larger implementations. Although Linux is becoming more prevalent as it becomes more mainstream in the marketplace, it is still less often as of this writing that you see many enterprise-class applications implemented on Linux unless a company's IT leader is an early adopter type. However, given that much of the success story of Oracle Collaboration Suite 10g is based upon lower total cost of ownership, I always recommend Linux, specifically Red Hat Linux with Oracle Unbreakable Linux support, as the operating system in our Oracle Collaboration Suite 10g implementations, unless a company's IT staff have a different operating system preference. I have had more success with Linux than any other operating system in our Oracle Collaboration Suite 10g installations, Oracle Support will support Red Hat directly without having to go to Red Hat for technical questions, and Oracle works with Red Hat to define the operating system to run Oracle better and faster than other operating systems. I have used other flavors of Unix, for example Solaris and HP-UX, but I deploy more Oracle on Red Hat Linux than on all the other operating system platforms combined.

Server Architectures

Given the wide range of choices available for purchasing server hardware in the market today, and the commodity-like pricing available from most hardware vendors, it is recommended that a company purchase as much in the way of server resources for an Oracle Collaboration Suite 10*g* implementation as the budget can support, without sacrificing quality of components, of course. This is sometimes a difficult concept to get across to customers, but there is a certain minimum set of resource requirements just to get the product installed and have its components start up successfully in the environment. I cannot count how many times I have had customers try to talk us into installing Oracle Collaboration Suite 10*g* on a single Intel server running 512MB of RAM and 10GB of available disk space for a proof-of-concept pilot. I tell them the only thing you're going to prove is that it cannot be done! I know the Oracle Collaboration Suite 10*g* Installation Guide says 1GB of RAM for each of the three tiers (Applications, Database, and Infrastructure), or 2GB for a single-box install, but trust me on this one folks, all anyone will be able to do is install it and have one or two users bring up the Oracle Collaboration Suite 10*g* Portal.

It is always recommended that a company procure a brand name server platform rather than a "white-box" generic server platform, although successful Oracle Collaboration Suite 10*g* implementations have been completed on the latter as well, especially using Linux as the operating system. I have implemented Oracle Collaboration Suite 10*g* successfully on many server platforms, so I cannot say that one will be better than another, but I can suggest various configuration footprints that work.

Hardware configuration and sizing are going to be a factor in the number of servers one plans to implement in the architecture along with the workload each tier of the Oracle Collaboration Suite 10*g* will put on the particular server it runs on. In general, when possible, I like to configure the servers in the architecture to be as close to identical as possible to each other, within reason. This means if one tier of the architecture requires a bit more or a bit less horsepower, I will throttle the lower requirements up to match those of the tier requiring the higher resource. For example, if I have a two-server architecture, one running the Applications Tier and one running the Infrastructure Tier, and the Infrastructure Tier requires 8GB of memory to support the database and SSO components, then I would increment the memory of the Applications Tier server from, say, 6GB to 8GB so that they match. The reasoning for incrementing memory on the Applications Tier server is it a) gives you additional room to grow on that tier, b) maintains a standard configuration across the multiple servers in the architecture, and c) provides flexibility in the future deployment of the servers into different configurations (RAC, clustered midtiers, etc.). There are times, of course, when a particular tier will require measurably more of a particular resource, for example memory, than the other servers at the time of implementation and it is just not feasible to bring all servers in the architecture up to that equivalent level of resources.

When planning an environment, given no predisposed preference from the customer, I try to start out with a standard server configuration of a dual processor machine. I usually ask the customer to purchase the fastest processors available at the time, since the hardware costs are generally not differentiable between the latest and greatest chips and the next step down . . . you know, last week's model! We then scale the processor requirements on each Applications Tier according to the following general formula:

Total# of CPUs = round((Max # of concurrent connected users / 250) * 1.25)

where max# of concurrent connected users is the number of users logged in and executing a process at the peak hour of the day, and the 1.25 multiplier is to add a 25 percent overhead amount to the total. If you are unsure of a way to estimate the Max# of concurrent connected users, you can use 0.25 to 0.33 of the total users.

In terms of memory, I like to start out with 6GB of RAM. If you are on a tight budget, I would consider 4GB of RAM a minimum, unless you are implementing a single-box install of Oracle Collaboration Suite 10*g* in Production, in which case I would definitely not go lower than 6GB of RAM, regardless of the number of users. To calculate the necessary RAM for the Applications Tier, I use the following general formula:

Total Amount of RAM in GB = round((Number of users / 250) * 1.25) + 4

In this scenario Number of users is the total number of users to be serviced, the overhead factor is the same as in the preceding example, and we always start with a minimum of 4GB of RAM. In the case of a single-box install I would increase my multiplier to 1.5 or 2.

Some factors that will affect server architecture decisions are such things as a large number of Oracle Collaboration Suite 10*g* web client users, massive quantities of large files being loaded into the Content Services repository, or a large number of concurrent web conferences. In general, the more activity related to Application Server processes such as the Oracle Collaboration Suite 10*g* Portal and its associated applications, the more memory is required to adequately service the requests. If large quantities of

Server Designation	# of Processors	Amount of Memory
Single-box install	2	6GB–12GB

TABLE 2-1.   *1–500 Oracle Collaboration Suite 10g Users*

I/O are being executed, that will require additional processor resources on the Datastore Tier. All these things need to be taken into account when defining server architectures for an Oracle Collaboration Suite 10*g* implementation. Tables 2-1, 2-2, and 2-3 show several examples of server architectures for sample implementation scenarios.

Storage Configuration

In my opinion the most important architecture component to get right for an Oracle Collaboration Suite 10*g* environment is storage, specifically as it relates to the Datastore Tier (where Oracle Collaboration Suite 10*g* Content, Email, Files, etc., are stored). You can always add processors and/or memory to a server, or change server backplanes to scale, but the total amount of available disk storage is limited by the size of the individual disk drives in the architecture and the "container" they live in, whether that be internal to a server, directly attached to a server or cluster of servers, or in a SAN/NAS device attached through some type of switch technology. (I won't go into detail on SAN/NAS architectures in this book, but if I were recommending a solutions architecture that involved mass storage, I would recommend fiber-attached SAN technology over Ethernet-based NAS technology.) And if a company misses on this one, it is difficult to respond quickly, since changing storage strategies usually involves moving large quantities of database files around . . . which isn't easy.

Server Designation	# of Processors	Amount of Memory
Applications Tier	2–4	6GB–8GB
Infrastructure/Datastore Tier	2–4	8GB

TABLE 2-2.   *500–1000 Oracle Collaboration Suite 10g Users*

Server Designation	# of Processors	Amount of Memory
Infrastructure Tier	2	8GB
Datastore Tier	2	8GB
Applications Tier	4–8	8GB–16GB

TABLE 2-3. *1000–2500 Oracle Collaboration Suite 10g Users*

Again, the type of storage chosen for a Oracle Collaboration Suite 10g Database environment is in direct proportion to the number of users it will support (read: the amount of storage needed, as the two should be proportionate)—both now and over time—as well as budget constraints. It is generally acceptable for the Infrastructure Tier and the Applications Tier to run on internal disks of the application server(s) they reside on (the Infrastructure database can be installed as a stand-alone database instance separate from the Oracle Collaboration Suite 10g applications database, and if so, that needs to be taken into account in the internal storage scheme for the Infrastructure Tier server). However, using external or SAN storage will allow for easier switch-over of servers in the event of a hardware failure (basically, you just detach the failed server from the storage, configure a new server with same etc/hosts, services, oratab, and other files from an online backup from the original server, and then reattach the external storage). The Datastore Tier, however, may not be able to run on internal storage, depending upon total space requirements of the various Oracle Collaboration Suite 10g components, which I will discuss next.

Estimating Storage

You can see that estimating storage requirements is an extremely important exercise as it relates to architecting an Oracle Collaboration Suite 10g environment. Basically, in a nutshell, you need to look at each component of the Oracle Collaboration Suite 10g product to be implemented and estimate its storage requirements, and then summarize the results to find a total storage requirement for all of the Oracle Collaboration Suite 10g applications. Email, Calendar (Calendar is *not* stored in the Oracle database as of this release of the product), Content Services, RTC recordings, and

Messenger message dialogues all need to be taken into account to get a complete and total storage requirement, but the largest consumers of storage by far are the Email and Content Services components of Oracle Collaboration Suite 10g. Then you must calculate the amount of storage you desire to have available for administrative functions such as exports and online RMAN backups as well. This amount could multiply storage requirements by two or more, depending upon the chosen backup strategy.

One note of caution is to make sure the company doesn't architect itself into a storage corner. Leave enough space for space requirement growth for eighteen months if possible so that there are no storage requirement issues during the burn-in phase and the new Oracle Collaboration Suite 10g environment doesn't have any lengthy downtime issues in the first year of operation.

Estimating Email Storage　　When estimating Email storage, it is important to take several areas of storage requirements into account: current Inbox and Folder space consumption for all users that will be migrated to Oracle Collaboration Suite 10g, average Inbox size for each user, and overhead for Oracle Collaboration Suite 10g. The migration numbers should be one to one, with the exception of the additional overhead required by Oracle Collaboration Suite 10g to store and manage the email messages. The average Inbox should require between 20–30 percent less space over time after initial conversion (the initial conversion is a one-to-one size calculation plus 20 percent for overhead), at least at the overall user community level, because of the efficient way in which Oracle Collaboration Suite 10g stores messages (for internal users it will only store one copy of the message in the Database and create pointers for everyone on the Recipient list). Overhead is generally calculated at approximately 20 percent of the total storage requirement because of data dictionary information, normalized email schema structures, etc. So, the general formula for calculating email storage requirements is

Total email storage required = (total email size planned for migration * 1.20)

which takes into account space for all email messages a company plans on migrating plus 20 percent overhead amount to take care of internal Oracle Collaboration Suite 10g requirements.

Many Email Administrators take the migration from their legacy email system to Oracle Collaboration Suite 10*g* as an opportunity to clean up old email during the migration process (only migrating email messages that are, say, newer than two years old) and/or impose space utilization parameters on the end-user community. If it is desired to manage email space utilization, Email Administrators can implement quotas (general as well as per user), but care should be taken regarding the perception that the move to a new system is less robust than the old system because users are now "limited" in comparison to the old system.

Estimating Content Services Storage   There are three main areas to consider when estimating the space necessary for the Content Services portion of Oracle Collaboration Suite 10*g*: initial Content Services required storage, the total amount of space required to store all the files themselves, and overhead associated with storing files in Content Services. The general formula for calculating storage requirements for Oracle Collaboration Suite 10*g* Content Services is

Total CS Storage required = 4.5GB + (total file size * 1.20)

Oracle Collaboration Suite 10*g* Content Services requires 4.5GB of initial storage, and 20 percent is the general overhead number for indexes, metadata, etc., for storing and retrieving the files.

Storage Architecture Alternatives

Once the required storage sizing has been calculated for an Oracle Collaboration Suite 10*g* implementation, that information can be used to determine which storage architecture alternative best fits a company's needs and budget.

Internal Storage   Internal storage is the least expensive method for providing storage to a solution today. Individual disks installed into the available disk bays on a server have basically become a commodity in today's world of inexpensive hardware. However, internal storage has a severe limitation as it relates to scalability requirements. Basically, when a system runs out of internal disk space, choices are limited to a) adding disk drives, unless/until all drive bays are full, and then b) investing in an alternative external storage solution. Again, as I mentioned earlier in the chapter, internal storage is perfectly acceptable for the Infrastructure and

Applications Tiers of the architecture, as they generally will not have storage requirements that expand beyond the capabilities and capacity of internal disks; albeit it may limit options in implementing failover scenarios down the road.

The other architecture-related point to consider around an internal storage choice is how to configure the internal disk. You can build redundancy such as RAID and/or mirroring into the architecture, which require some overhead (the redundancy solution itself consumes disk space), or you can use every available block of disk space to store Oracle Collaboration Suite 10g database files, binaries, etc., and run the risk that the loss of a single disk drive will take down the entire Oracle Collaboration Suite 10g environment.

Direct-Attached Storage   The next level of storage choice above internal disk is the direct-attached storage option. This involves an external disk cabinet, often referred to as a disk array, that holds a number of disk drives. An external array has several appealing features; for instance, it can have multiple connections per server (with the appropriate product choice), it can be shared across servers, it has the ability to grow (again with the right choice of array), and it can provide another level of high availability in the architecture.

Options for direct-attached storage include using a single cabinet to attach to the Datastore Tier server (whether it runs just the Datastore Tier or not is irrelevant), or attaching all servers in the architecture to the array (the ability to do so will be determined by the type of storage array purchased and what options for multiple connections are available with that particular array). Generally speaking, however, the limited scalability of a direct-attached storage array really only benefits the Datastore Tier in the Oracle Collaboration Suite 10g environment.

SAN/NAS Solution   The most scalable and robust storage option is a storage area network (SAN) or network-attached storage (NAS). Both provide scalability for your storage, with the main difference being how the storage device is connected to, and communicates with, the servers. In a SAN environment servers are attached to the storage via fiber cable or SCSI cable that runs from the server into a switch and from the switch to the SAN cabinet. With NAS, the storage is connected to the servers through Ethernet connections, which usually run through an initiator (either hardware or software) that deciphers the network packets between the servers and the NAS cabinet making the storage requests.

SAN/NAS devices can scale to very large amounts of space and are usually found in enterprise architectures where terabytes or even petabytes of storage are needed across the company by different servers running different operating systems. SAN/NAS devices can provide storage to all kinds of servers simultaneously, and they can provide flexible storage allocations as an Oracle Collaboration Suite 10*g* datastore grows. Many SAN devices also have a set of tools to allow things like snapshot backups of file systems that give some assistance to high availability configurations.

Storage Summary   In summary, I would say that for most environments that do not already have a SAN/NAS environment to take advantage of, companies should look at direct-attached storage for the Datastore Tier and internal storage for the Infrastructure and Applications Tiers. Purchasing a SAN device for a single solutions architecture is a costly endeavor. However, if it is anticipated that the Datastore Tier of an Oracle Collaboration Suite 10*g* instance will grow to several terabytes, then a SAN/NAS device may be worth looking into. If asked for a recommendation, I always say that fiber-attached SAN technology is the best way to go, then SCSI-attached SAN, and then finally some flavor of NAS. Basically, for performance and availability reasons SAN devices have always out-performed NAS devices in database environments, although as NAS technology matures and network bandwidth becomes broader, NAS devices have become much more viable.

Additional Oracle Collaboration Suite 10*g* Architecture Components

In addition to the various architecture components already described, Oracle Collaboration Suite 10*g* has several optional architecture components that provide functionality specific to the Oracle Collaboration Suite 10*g* product.

Voicemail/Fax Server

If a company wishes to implement unified messaging, including voicemails and faxes coming directly into the users' Inboxes, then a voicemail/fax server needs to be added to the architecture. The voicemail server consists of a Windows CT Server with Dialogix cards installed that attach Oracle

Collaboration Suite 10*g* to the company's PBX switch, convert the analog voice to digital, and allow the voicemail messages to be delivered and stored as .wav attachments to an email (sent from the calling phone number extracted from the phone packet header). In addition, if faxes are to be delivered in the same manner to the Inbox, fax server software must be installed on the same or another server to receive inbound faxes and send them to Oracle Collaboration Suite 10*g* (faxes come in as .tif file attachments to an email message, again sent from the fax number where the fax originates).

Document and Voice Conversion Server
Oracle Collaboration Suite 10*g* may be installed on an operating system other than Microsoft Windows, and users may wish to have the functionality of uploading Microsoft Office documents to the Web Conferencing tool for download by conference attendees, or for display in Documentation Presentation mode (documents to be displayed in this manner must have been previously uploaded to Oracle Collaboration Suite 10*g* Web Conferencing). In this case, a Document Conversion Server must be implemented into the architecture. Basically, there is an Oracle Collaboration Suite 10*g* component that needs to be installed on a server running the Microsoft Windows operating system and has Microsoft Office installed. In addition, if voice conversion—having Oracle Collaboration Suite 10*g* read emails to an end user when that user dials in over the phone—is desired, this server also requires a Dialogix card in order to provide this functionality.

Architecture Categories
I generally like to put the various customer implementation requirements into categories so that I can then apply some architecture best practices to them and create a solution. The following are the categories:

- Single-box architectures
- Multiserver architectures
- High-availability architectures

Each of these (excluding the single-box architecture) can then be further qualified by whether they need to have components installed outside the intranet firewall.

Required Ports for Oracle Collaboration Suite 10g

All of the components, subcomponents, protocols, etc., for Oracle Collaboration Suite 10g communicate on specific ports on the server(s) on which they are installed. For functions to be accessible, their associated ports must be accessible as well. The installation process, which I cover in Chapters 3–6, can determine the ports on its own (default port values), and requires that certain preinstallation changes be made to /etc/services to ensure certain ports are available (or unavailable if assigned in the /etc/services file) for Oracle Collaboration Suite 10g (for example, 389 is the default non-SSL LDAP port). Otherwise, if an installer wishes to determine the ports to be used by certain components of Oracle Collaboration Suite 10g, then the installer should modify the staticports.ini file in the install/response directory of the Oracle Collaboration Suite 10g installation software image. Assuming the /etc/services files have been modified to allow usage of the standard LDAP and LDAPS ports (389 and 636, respectively), Tables 2-4 and 2-5 show the ports that will be assigned to the Infrastructure Tier and Applications Tier of Oracle Collaboration Suite 10g in a default single-box install.

Single-Box Architecture

Oracle Collaboration Suite 10g is really the first version of the Oracle Collaboration Suite product with which a single-server architecture is possible for production implementations. Prior to Oracle Collaboration Suite 10g the Oracle Collaboration Suite installation was designed to install individual components on a minimum of three separate servers and made installation on a single server nearly impossible, not to mention trying to maintain the environment for production users. Now in Oracle Collaboration Suite 10g the installation process actually has a "Default Option" to install everything on a single server (again, I cover the installation processes in detail in Chapters 3–6), allowing the Oracle Universal Installer to determine everything necessary to have the install work properly, including asking for

Port Usage	Port#
Oracle HTTP Server port	7777
Oracle HTTP Server Listen port	7777
Oracle HTTP Server SSL port	4443
Oracle HTTP Server Listen (SSL) port	4443
ASG port	7890
Application Server Control RMI port	1850
Java Object Cache port	7000
Oracle HTTP Server Diagnostic port	7200
Oracle Notification Server Request port	6003
Oracle Notification Server Local port	6101
Oracle Notification Server Remote port	6200
Log Loader port	44000
DCM Discovery port	7100
Oracle Management Agent Port	1157
Application Server Control port	1156
Oracle Internet Directory port	389
Oracle Internet Directory (SSL) port	636
Enterprise Manager Console HTTP port (ocsdb)	5500
Enterprise Manager Agent port (ocsdb)	1830

TABLE 2-4.   *Oracle Collaboration Suite 10g Default Infrastructure Tier Ports*

a single password for all "Administrative" users in the configuration (for example, sys, system, orcladmin).

Since this installation is limited to one server, the single-box architecture can really only be implemented two ways: 1) with the server inside the intranet firewall (optionally with a DMZ router configured to do reverse proxy for the HTTP and HTTPS requests for Oracle Collaboration Suite 10*g*), or 2) with the server outside the intranet firewall but inside the DMZ firewall.

Port Usage	Port#
Oracle HTTP Server port	7778
Oracle HTTP Server Listen port	7779
Oracle HTTP Server SSL port	8250
Oracle HTTP Server Listen (SSL) port	4444
Oracle Notification Server Request port	6004
Oracle Notification Server Local port	6102
Oracle Notification Server Remote port	6201
ASG port	7891
Oracle Mail IMAP4 port	143
Oracle Mail IMAP4 Secure port	993
Oracle Mail POP3 port	110
Oracle Mail POP3 Secure port	995
Oracle Mail SMTP port	25
Oracle Mail NNTP port	119
Oracle Mail NNTP Secure port	563
Application Server Control RMI port	1851
Oracle Management Agent port	1831
Oracle HTTP Server Diagnostic port	7201
Java Object Cache port	7001
Log Loader port	44001
DCM Discovery port	7101
Application Server Control port	1810
Web Cache HTTP Listen port	7778
Web Cache HTTP Listen (SSL) port	8250

TABLE 2-5. *Oracle Collaboration Suite 10g Default Applications Tier Ports*

Port Usage	Port#
Web Cache Administration port	9400
Web Cache Invalidation port	9401
Web Cache Statistics port	9402
Oracle Net Listener	1521
Oracle Calendar server	5730
Oracle Calendar server manager (CSM)	5734
Wireless PIM Notification Dispatcher port	9000
Push Mail UDP Listener port	9300
Push Mail TCP Listener port	9301
Push Mail TCP IPC port	9302
RTC redirector Server port	1026
RTC redirector MX port	1025
RTC redirector XMPP port	5222
RTC redirector Secure XMPP port	5223
RTC process monitor port	1027
RTC messenger directory server first port	7340
RTC messenger directory server second port	7341
RTC messenger multiuser chat port	7350
RTC messenger connection manager port	7351
RTC messenger statistics collection port	7370
RTC messenger server-to-server connection port	5269
RTC messenger group service port	7360
RTC messenger voice proxy listener port	3478

TABLE 2-5. *Oracle Collaboration Suite 10g Default Applications Tier Ports* (Continued)

With the first option, no access from entities outside the intranet firewall can occur unless either the firewall rules are modified to allow certain ports to be accessed on the server with inbound requests and certain ports are allowed to communicate outbound, or the users outside the intranet firewall are given a secure connection (Citrix server connection/portal, VPN connection, etc.) into the intranet network. With the DMZ installation, some configuration must take place on the DMZ firewall to allow access. It is possible it could be left wide open, which is not recommended, since the single-box install puts the Oracle Internet Directory on the server in the DMZ and potentially exposes user profile and password information to hacking (which can be encrypted for user sign-on using SSL, which we will discuss later in this chapter). In either case, if outside access is desired (especially for Real-Time Collaboration in web conferencing, since it does not support reverse proxy), certain ports must be opened to allow access outside the respective firewall(s) if the implementation is to work properly. Figure 2-1 shows a single-box install in the DMZ area of the network. If a company does not have a DMZ (many small companies may not), then the required ports must be opened in the Internet firewall to the

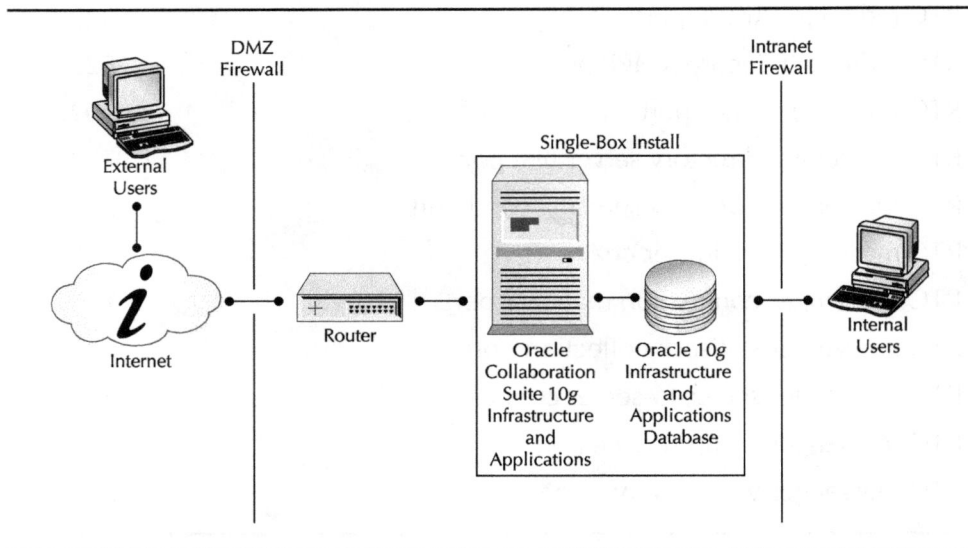

FIGURE 2-1. *Single-box Oracle Collaboration Suite 10g installation in the DMZ*

specific IP address of the Oracle Collaboration Suite 10*g* server for functionality to be allowed outside the intranet network. Another option is to use a reverse proxy configuration on the DMZ router to support HTTP and HTTPS requests to Oracle Collaboration Suite 10*g*, but note that Real-Time Collaboration console does not use HTTP or HTTPS, so this configuration will not allow web conferencing or instant messaging to be used outside the intranet network.

A lot of companies want to implement Oracle Collaboration Suite 10*g* on a single server. In many cases people are looking to implement a proof-of-concept setup to validate Oracle Collaboration Suite 10*g* functionality prior to purchasing the product, or they want a test environment to verify functionality, patches, parameter changes, etc. But in many cases companies can successfully roll out Oracle Collaboration Suite 10*g* into production on a single server as long as certain requirements are taken into account. Resource availability is, of course, the biggest question mark of the single-box install. The single-box install can only scale so far in terms of memory and processors, which means there is only so much "concurrency" that a single-box install can support. So, what does that mean to any given situation? Well, there is a multidimensional matrix of variables that drive to the threshold of how many users can be supported in a particular environment by a single server with a given set of resources. I know this seems a bit like dancing around the question, but in reality a particular server configuration may support 500 users at one company extremely well while failing to support 100 users at another, given heavy usage of functions that consume large amounts of resources in the 100-user case. In my opinion, the standard rule for the minimum server configuration that should be deployed for any tier in Oracle Collaboration Suite 10*g* is a dual processor (assume Intel as a reference point) with 4–6GB of RAM. However, if someone is deploying a single server to support upward of 250 users, I would suggest investing in a four-processor server and bumping the memory up to 8GB on the low end and 16GB on the high (read: comfortable) end. This configuration, assuming normal usage and a 50-50 split between web users and desktop native protocol users (Ex: WEBDAV, IMAP, SMB), should support up to 250+ total users with decent performance and an average amount of administration.

Multiserver Architectures

Once the Oracle Collaboration Suite 10*g* user base grows beyond about 500 users, a single-box implementation is no longer feasible, in my opinion. In this case the architect needs to look at splitting technical—and functional—

components of Oracle Collaboration Suite 10*g* onto separate servers in the architecture. Then administrators can tune specific components differently than if everything were contending for the same set of resources on a single server. It also allows the administrator to scale certain components as needed depending upon utilization requirements. The options for Multitier deployments are pretty broad, with everything from a two-server implementation separating Infrastructure and Applications components, to a large server farm with a server or set of servers dedicated to serving up each component application of Oracle Collaboration Suite 10*g*.

The simplest multitier Oracle Collaboration Suite 10*g* architecture is the two-server architecture. In this architecture the Oracle Collaboration Suite 10*g* Applications are installed on their own server while the Infrastructure components—including the Single Sign-On function as well as Oracle Internet Directory and Metadata Repository database—are installed on another server. This allows the administrators to tune the former for memory consumption while they tune the latter for I/O consumption. Figure 2-2 details the architecture for Oracle Collaboration Suite 10*g* using two servers.

The most common multitier architecture I implement for customers is a three-server configuration. In this architecture the Oracle Collaboration Suite 10*g* Applications, Infrastructure (Single Sign-On), and Datastore Tiers

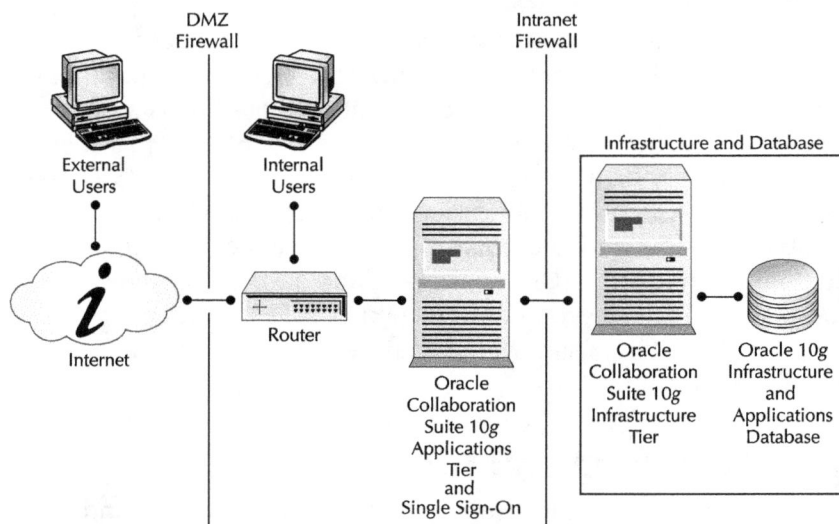

FIGURE 2-2. *Oracle Collaboration Suite 10*g *two-server architecture*

are all separated onto individual servers. This is the best architecture to ensure that performance and/or stability issues can be isolated to specific components in the software architecture. This architecture also allows the flexibility of determining what components get put in the DMZ and/or exposed to the Internet for outside the intranet network access. The three-server implementation also allows better flexibility in the Oracle Collaboration Suite 10g backup strategy, since only one server is focused on holding application data. Figure 2-3 illustrates a sample three-server configuration of Oracle Collaboration Suite 10g.

Once an implementation gets beyond supporting a couple of thousand users, more complex architectures are necessary to provide performance and availability of Oracle Collaboration Suite 10g. This includes implementing multiple midtier servers, each supporting a specific Oracle Collaboration Suite 10g application or set of applications. Figure 2-4 shows an example of implementing multiple Applications Tier servers to support a large implementation of several thousand users.

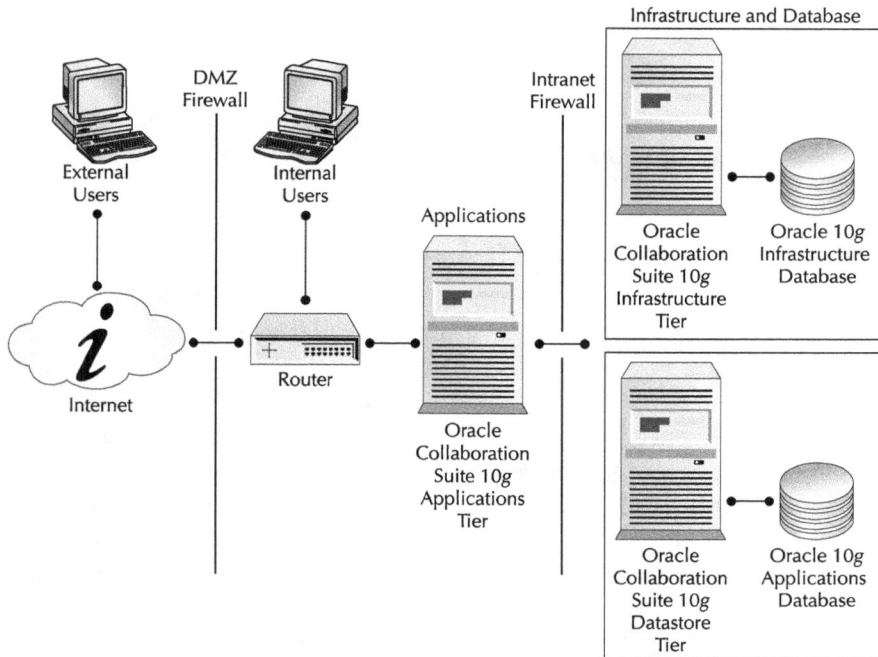

FIGURE 2-3. *Oracle Collaboration Suite 10g three-server architecture*

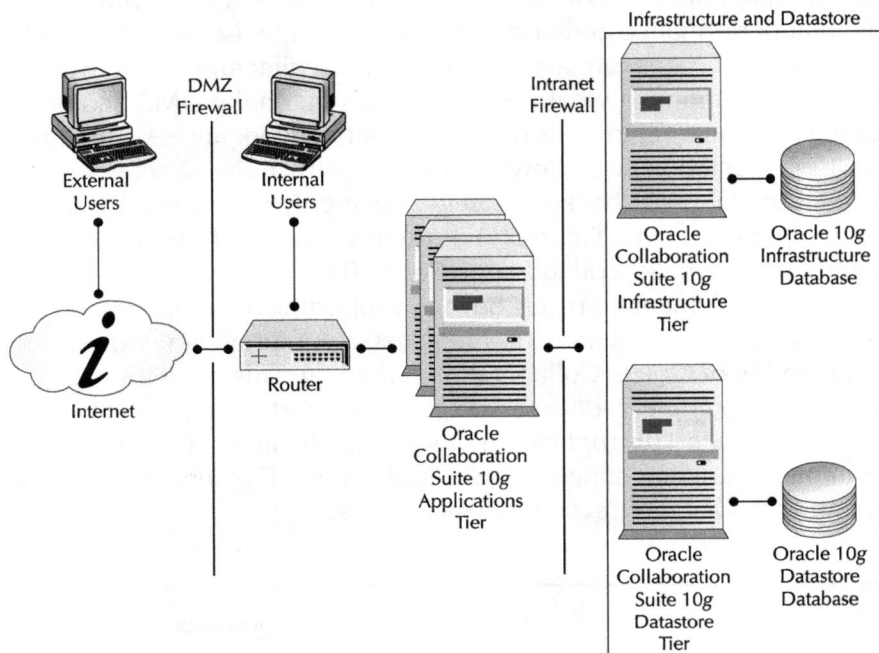

FIGURE 2-4. *Multiple Midtier server Oracle Collaboration Suite 10*g *architecture*

High Availability and OCS

In addition to architecting an environment for performance and resource requirements, it is possible to create a highly available architecture in Oracle Collaboration Suite 10*g*. With this latest release of the product using Oracle Application Server 10*g* Identity Management, the possibility exists to cluster not only the Applications database but also the Infrastructure database as well (they can even reside together now in a single database instance in Oracle Collaboration Suite 10*g*). So it is in fact possible to create an environment that is highly available at all tiers of the architecture. Figure 2-5 shows an example Oracle Collaboration Suite 10*g* High Availability ("HA") environment.

In the preceding example, the Applications Tier is made redundant through the ability to install multiple Applications Tier servers with connections managed by an up-front load-balancer. If one of the Applications Tier servers goes down, the other(s) in the architecture can continue to accept

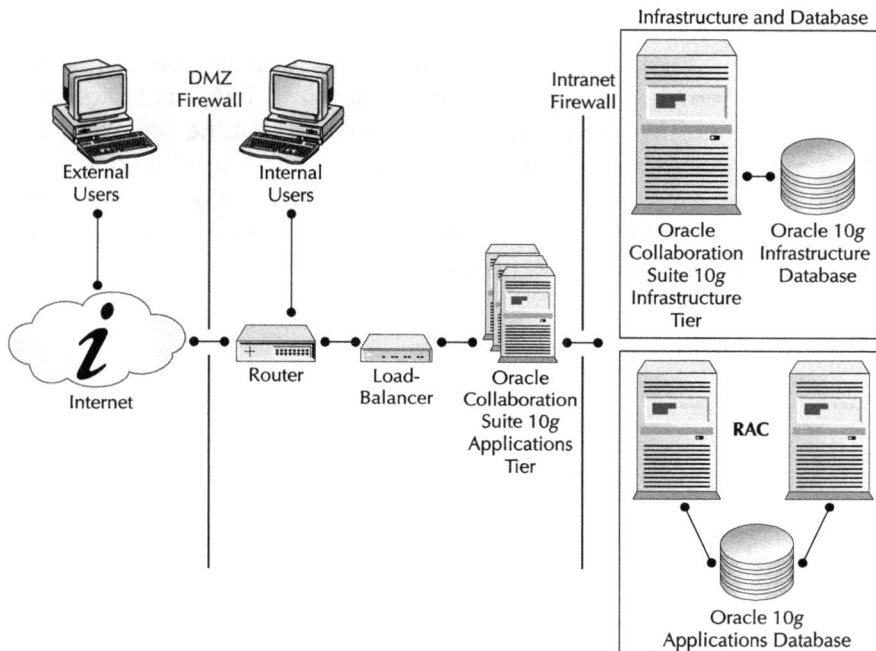

FIGURE 2-5. *Example Oracle Collaboration Suite 10*g *HA architecture*

connections and nobody is the wiser. (I will caution here that special attention needs to be paid to the Oracle Collaboration Suite 10*g* Calendar Server high availability requirements, because its database is still in the file system on the Applications Tier and *not* in the Oracle Database 10*g* Datastore like the rest of the Oracle Collaboration Suite 10*g* components' data). The Infrastructure Tier can also run on the Applications Tier servers, or as in Figure 2-5, multiple Infrastructure servers can be configured. Then a RAC cluster can be implemented at the Datastore Tier so that the Identity Management and Metadata Repository Oracle Database 10*g* instance can be made highly available as well. These High Availability architecture considerations can also have a bonus effect on the Oracle Collaboration Suite 10*g* environment as well. Having multiple servers at each tier in an active-active configuration provides increased resources for performance purposes as well.

Summary

I think it is safe to say that anyone architecting an Oracle Collaboration Suite 10g environment has many options in doing so, but great caution should be taken around planning and execution so that the options don't create unmanageable complexities in the process. I caution anyone attempting to deploy this product to invest in the correct hardware sizing and configuration for their requirements. Not doing so will cause both the product and the environment to run poorly.

PART

II

Installation and Configuration of OCS

CHAPTER
3

Before You Begin

I don't want to be left behind. In fact,
I want to be here before the action starts.

—Kerry Packer (on Technology)

As has been emphasized in the previous two chapters, the more architecture planning and analysis someone does up front before installing the first component of the Oracle Collaboration Suite 10*g* product, the smoother the installation, configuration, and implementation will go, *and* the less problematic the ongoing management and operations will be. The same theory can be applied to the implementation phase of the product. The more time spent up front planning important implementation decisions such as username and password conventions, port usage, user and email migration strategy and cut-over approach, the smoother the implementation will go; the less troublesome the install process, implementation steps, and production cut-over will be; and the higher the acceptance rating for the new product will be from the user community. Many Oracle Collaboration Suite 10*g* installations have failed because the preinstallation steps were not followed through to completion, or steps were skipped along the way, causing Oracle Collaboration Suite 10*g* components to not install properly, or not function properly once installed. In addition, many Oracle Collaboration Suite 10*g* implementations have failed because not enough up-front thought was put into steps such as the migration and production rollout, username naming conventions, etc., and answers to questions were provided in haste during these steps, making the users less than happy with the results after it was too late.

Please note that if the implementation plan does not include Oracle Collaboration Suite 10*g* Email, there are still many decisions that need to be made up front regarding implementation and rollout of the other components of Oracle Collaboration Suite 10*g*—and possibly migration if a company is moving from, say, a different calendar system to Oracle Collaboration Suite 10*g* Calendar—so this chapter will still contain some important information.

Username and Password Conventions

There is no better opportunity for an Administrator to clean up nonstandard naming conventions for usernames, passwords, email addresses, etc., than during a migration to a new system. Given the opportunity, proper planning for user naming conventions—and email address naming conventions if implementing Oracle Collaboration Suite 10g Email—as well as password policies should be part of the Oracle Collaboration Suite 10g implementation.

Oracle Collaboration Suite 10g gives the Administrator great flexibility as to how he/she wants to define usernames. Because the username information for Oracle Collaboration Suite 10g is stored in the Oracle Internet Directory/ Identity Management component of Oracle Application Server 10g, and therefore in the Oracle 10g Database, limitations such as username size, special characters, etc., get removed from the requirements. The Oracle Internet Directory/Identity Management component of the Oracle Application Server 10g username naming convention is based directly upon the LDAPv3 standard, so an Administrator can refer to that standard for specifics on what is and is not allowed when creating usernames for their Oracle Collaboration Suite 10g environment.

Many companies that have made the conversion to Oracle Collaboration Suite 10g have taken the opportunity to make a conversion from one username standard to another, say from the older tradition of first initial lastname to firstname.lastname (for example, John Smith was JSmith and is converted to John.Smith). This would default down to their email address as well unless another standard was used for email. There are several ways to migrate users themselves, either through the ExMigrate email migration tool provided and supported by Oracle, or through manual bulk load processes using ldif files extracted from the legacy system (or created from scratch for a migration not based on an LDAP legacy system source for user definitions).

In addition, password policies can be defined to meet a company's needs. Oracle Collaboration Suite 10g provides a default password policy out of the box for the realm created during the install. This policy states that a password must be a minimum of five characters, with a minimum of one of those characters being a number. To see all the information related to the default password policy created during the Oracle Collaboration Suite 10g install, an Administrator can go to the Infrastructure Tier server and run the Oracle Directory Manager tool. To run the Oracle Directory Manager, you must source the environment for the Infrastructure Tier—which should set the proper ORACLE_HOME—and run oidadmin at the command prompt. Figure 3-1 shows the sign-on screen for the Oracle Directory Manager tool. Notice on the background screen that the infra.env file is sourced (the infra.env file sets the appropriate environmental variables for the Infrastructure Tier),

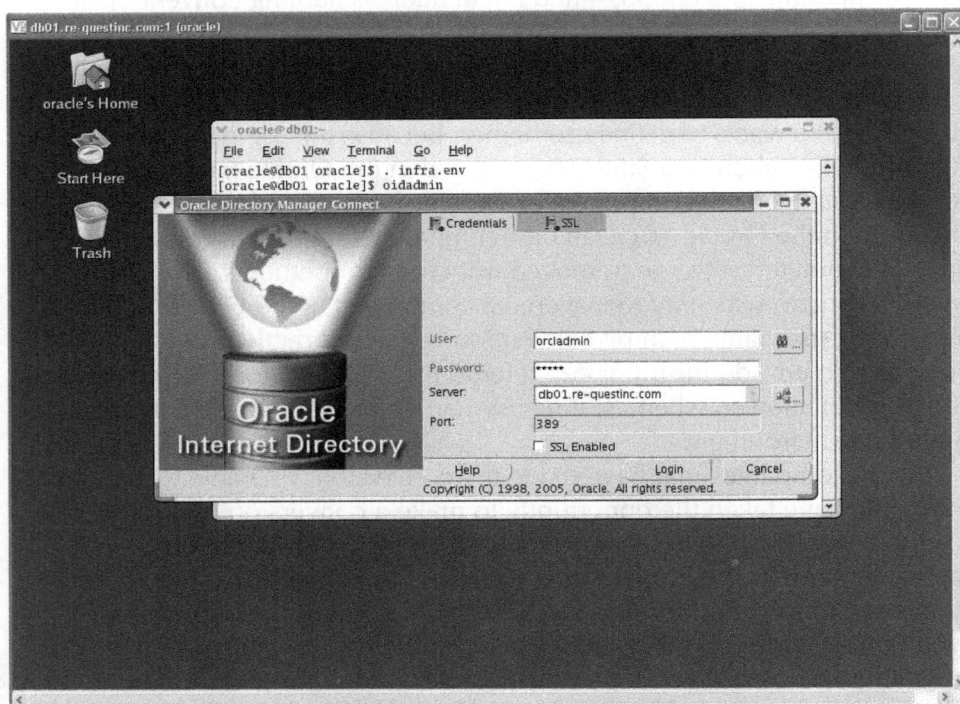

FIGURE 3-1. *Starting Oracle Directory Manager from the command line*

and then oidadmin is run, which brings up the Oracle Directory Manager Connect window. The Administrator must log in as the Oracle Identity Management user who manages the instance of the Oracle Internet Directory for the Oracle Collaboration Suite 10*g* Infrastructure (by default in an Oracle Collaboration Suite 10*g* installation this is the cn=orcladmin user).

Once logged in, the Administrator will get the navigator window for the Oracle Directory Manager as shown in Figure 3-2. To review/modify the default password policy for the Oracle Collaboration Suite 10*g* environment the Administrator must click the <+> to the left of the Password Policy Management system object to expand the section and display the password policy names. Choose the name "Password Policy for Realm dc=" that is defined there to view the default values Oracle sets for Oracle Collaboration

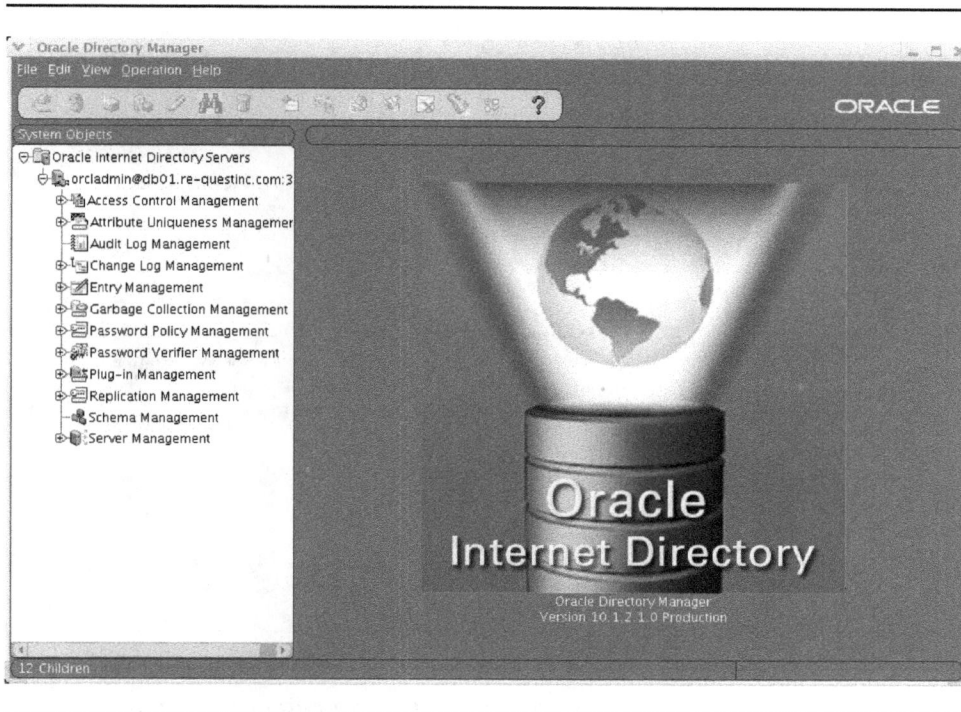

FIGURE 3-2. *Oracle Directory Manager Navigator window*

Suite 10*g* during the install. Figure 3-3 shows the expanded section and General tab of default options for the Password Policy for Oracle Collaboration Suite 10*g* that gets created during the install. Here, such things as whether the old password is required for a user to change their password, whether the OID Password Policy is enabled, what the password expiration time—in seconds—is set to, and whether to force users to reset their password the first time they log in can all be defined.

The most important tab to review is the Password Syntax tab, as seen in Figure 3-4. This defines the length, or number of total characters in the password, how many of the total characters must be numeric characters, the number of old passwords to hold in history (and therefore not allow to be reused when a password change is required), and any values an Administrator does not want people to use as passwords (Ex: oracle).

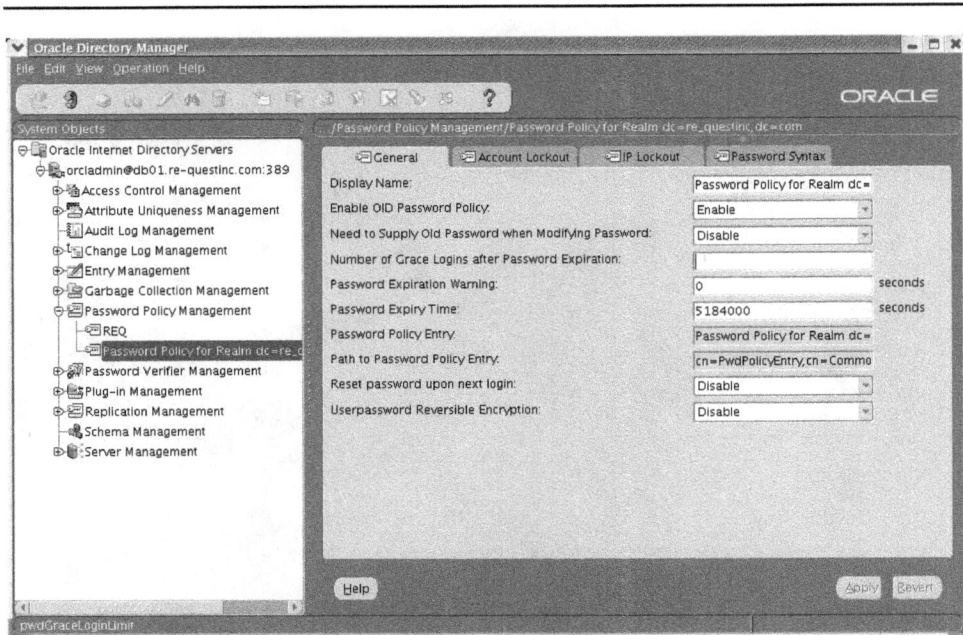

FIGURE 3-3. *Password policy viewing in Oracle Directory Manager*

Read the Installation Guide

Everyone in IT has heard it before. Actually, it's been said for every software product anyone has ever installed…"Read the documentation." But in the case of Oracle Collaboration Suite 10*g*, there is honestly a benefit to doing so. The Oracle Collaboration Suite 10*g* product deployment can be made so much easier by taking the time up front not only to plan for the implementation, but to actually read the Installation Guide for the intended platform. In the planning stages, Chapters 1 and 2 of the Installation Guide are very insightful, especially if the installer does not have an Oracle product background. Chapter 1 of the Installation Guide does a good job of explaining the high-level concepts anyone should know before installing the product, including important concepts such as product architecture. Chapter 2 covers the information, prerequisites, setups, etc., that need to occur before the Oracle Collaboration Suite 10*g* software install is started. This information is possibly the most important technical information to having a smooth

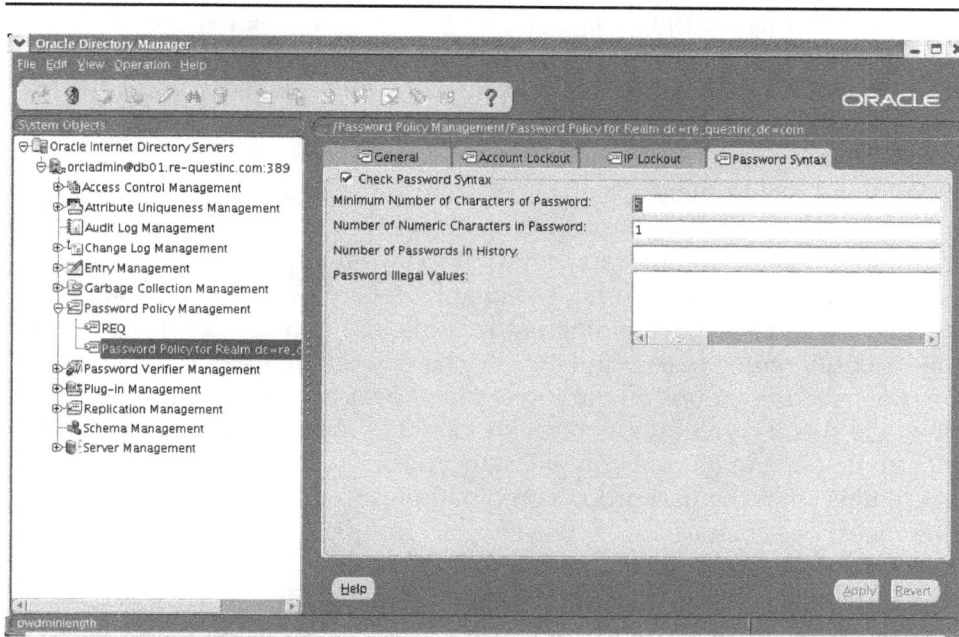

FIGURE 3-4.   *Password Syntax tab in password policy definition*

installation process. More Oracle Collaboration Suite 10*g* implementations have failed—or been less successful and entailed higher maintenance going forward than necessary—because the folks responsible for the installation process did not follow the preinstall checklist. The following sections cover some of the more important technical prerequisites to review in the implementation planning stage for Oracle Collaboration Suite 10*g*, in addition to the architecture and server hardware considerations that were covered in Chapter 2 of this book.

Creating the Oracle Operating System User and Group

In general I am comfortable with giving you some latitude in terms of the available choices when it comes to fulfilling the prerequisites for the installation discussed in the preceding paragraph. However, I am going to suggest that you do something specific—not demand, suggest—when it comes to creating the operating system userid that will be the owner of the Oracle software stack on each Oracle Collaboration Suite 10*g* server in your environment. While you can technically name the user and group anything you want, I am going to make the recommendation that the user be named oracle (all lowercase), and the group be named oinstall (again, all lowercase). In addition I would suggest being consistent with the actual user uid and group gid number values as well. Whenever I create these components—or advise the System Administrator on what to do—I use 500 for the oracle user uid and 501 for the oinstall group gid. I recommend these values because the uid and gid are different yet are close enough together that they can be easily remembered, and they are far enough up in the count for both the users and the groups on the server that they are generally available. Now, the specific values are not as important as the consistency, but I can tell you that at a minimum you will save yourself a ton of grief if you use oracle:oinstall as the user:group combination, since most documentation references these names (dba is used for the group as well, but I save that for pure database installs), and Oracle Support and other Oracle resources will be able to acclimate to your environment more quickly if you use something familiar and standard.

Software and Operating System Requirements

Most Oracle Collaboration Suite 10*g* installation issues arise from implementers' not taking the time to meet the correct ancillary software requirements such as supported browser versions, operating system kernel versions, necessary operating system software packages, and appropriate settings for kernel parameters. Even though the Oracle Universal Installer validates the kernel parameter values prior to installation of the Oracle Collaboration Suite 10*g* software, it is always better to review the required values for the target operating system platform and make the changes prior to attempting the install for the first time.

IP Addresses

It is imperative to get IP addresses nailed down for all servers in the Oracle Collaboration Suite 10*g* environment before beginning the installation. The best way to define IP addresses for an implementation is by using static

IP addresses for all servers in the Oracle Collaboration Suite 10*g* architecture. It is extremely difficult to change the IP address of any server running the Infrastructure Tier or Middle Tier of Oracle Collaboration Suite 10*g*, so it is best to get this right up front (it is not impossible to do so, especially with Oracle Collaboration Suite 10*g*, but it is very difficult). These IP addresses must be defined in the /etc/hosts file for each server in the architecture, as the Oracle Collaboration Suite 10*g* install process reads the IP address information from the /etc/hosts file on the server where the Oracle Universal Installer is running (not from DNS). It is extremely important to get the /etc/hosts file syntax and definition correct; otherwise, it is guaranteed the Oracle Collaboration Suite 10*g* software will have to be reinstalled. The localhost reference line should be left in as the first line of the /etc/hosts file, the server name—or server short name—should *not be entered* in the localhost line of the /etc/hosts file, and a separate entry line for each server should be made. The /etc/hosts file should look as follows when complete:

```
127.0.0.1        localhost.localdomain      localhost
111.111.111.1    ocs-1.testdomain.com       ocs-1
```

Ports

Verifying available ports and port ranges is another important preinstall task. There are some ports where using the default values is more or less a standard for the type of protocol running on that port (for example, 25 for SMTP and 389 for LDAP), while for others it doesn't really matter what specific port the process services requests from (for example, Application Server 10*g* WebCache component).

There are a couple of simple things that can be done prior to an installation on a server that will ensure using the correct ports for a given installation. First, if a company is going to install Oracle Collaboration Suite 10*g* Email on a Middle Tier, it should be verified that sendmail is not running on the server before beginning the install (some operating systems, Red Hat for example, install and start sendmail by default). The Oracle Collaboration Suite 10*g* installer actually checks whether sendmail is running, but it is best to stop it before beginning the install. There are a couple of ways to stop sendmail from running. The first is the brute force method. Simply log in as root and execute the following: "ps –ef | grep send". When this command returns, it should provide a listing of one or two processes running for sendmail. Simply execute a "kill –9 <processid>" command as root on those process IDs. The second method involves removing sendmail from the startup scripts for the operating system. To complete this, first, as the root user, shut down sendmail with the following command: "/etc/init.d/sendmail stop" (actually the preceding kill command will work as well, but this is a more graceful alternative and involves using the init.d). Next, execute the following command—again as root—so that sendmail does not start again when the server is rebooted: "chkconfig sendmail off" (a good alternative to shutting it down manually every time the server is rebooted, since the Oracle Collaboration Suite 10*g* Email components will not start up after a reboot if sendmail is running). Second, review the /etc/services file as root and *remove*—not comment out—any references to ldap or ldaps (there should be four entries altogether in a standard services file). Removing these references from the /etc/services file will allow the Oracle Collaboration Suite 10*g* Infrastructure Tier to deploy the Identity Management LDAP processes on standard LDAP ports 389 (nonsecure) and 636 (SSL). If the entries are not removed completely (but are only commented out), the Oracle Identity Management processes will run on high-numbered ports, which won't necessarily hurt anything, but they are a bit more difficult to identify when they are on nonstandard LDAP ports.

One other way to specify the ports to use is to update the staticports.ini file (found in the response subdirectory of the image of the Oracle Collaboration Suite 10*g* install software) with the port values for the individual services listed (one, several, or all of the port values can be updated and the installer will use default port values for those not specified in the file). Figure 3-5 shows a default staticports.ini file before being modified, with instructions at the top for how to set port values.

Migration

Another portion of an Oracle Collaboration Suite 10*g* implementation that should be thought through before starting the implementation project is the migration strategy. Specifically, a migration strategy or plan defines how a company plans to roll out the new Oracle Collaboration Suite 10*g* platform into production and therefore to the user community. When a company has a small number of employees, the migration plan is pretty straightforward. Simply send everyone out the door on a Friday night—after they sign off

```
oracle@db01:/u01/stage/OCS10g1012/response                          _ □ ✕

 File   Edit   View   Terminal   Go   Help
# staticports.ini Template File
#
# This file is a template for specifying port numbers at installation time.
# To specify a port number, uncomment the appropriate line (remove ) and
# replace "port_num" with the desired port number.
# You can then launch Oracle Universal Installer with special options to
# use this file.
# Please refer to Oracle Collaboration Suite 10.1.1.0.2 Installation Guide
# for instructions.

# Ports common to Infrastructure and Applications install

#Oracle HTTP Server port = port_num
#Oracle HTTP Server Listen port = port_num
#Oracle HTTP Server SSL port = port_num
#Oracle HTTP Server Listen (SSL) port = port_num
#Oracle HTTP Server Diagnostic port = port_num
#ASG port = port_num
#Application Server Control port = port_num
#Application Server Control RMI port = port_num
#Java Object Cache port = port_num
#Log Loader port = port_num
#DCM Discovery port = port_num
#Oracle Notification Server Request port = port_num
#Oracle Notification Server Local port = port_num
#Oracle Notification Server Remote port = port_num
#Oracle Management Agent Port = port_num

# Ports specific to Infrastructure install

#Oracle Internet Directory port = port_num
#Oracle Internet Directory (SSL) port = port_num
#Enterprise Manager Console HTTP Port = port_num
#Enterprise Manager Agent Port = port_num

# Ports specific to Applications install

#Web Cache HTTP Listen port = port_num
```

FIGURE 3-5.   *Sample staticports.ini file*

their email, file system etc.—and when they return on Monday morning
everything is running on Oracle Collaboration Suite 10*g* (okay, so maybe it's
not quite that simple, but we will cover migration in detail in Chapter 7).
We call this the Big Bang approach to migration. But keep in mind, as the
number of users to migrate increases, so does the complexity of the
migration plan. A migration plan might also simply run out of hours of
available downtime to migrate everyone at once, especially when migrating
a large amount of email message data is required. In addition to time, disk

space requirements on the migration machine need to be taken into consideration for each migration group, since the migration process first pulls migrated email data onto the migration machine and then loads it into Oracle Collaboration Suite 10*g* Email. So then the chess game begins—who gets migrated first, how are the users grouped for migration, and most important, how to get the email coming into the old environment and relayed to the new system for users who are migrated. This approach to migration is defined as a Phased Migration plan.

I follow a high-level migration plan that looks like this: First, migrate a small group of savvy users who can a) adapt quickly to new interfaces and functionality (in other words, users who don't have to hit the exact buttons in the exact order to feel two systems provide the same functionality) and b) provide quality testing and validation of the new Oracle Collaboration Suite 10*g* system in a constructive manner. Next, review the user base and determine groupings of users that can be migrated together, for example a) they work together closely, so they will benefit from migrating together (say a department or project group), and b) they provide a migration footprint that can be accomplished in a planned migration window (in other words, group users so as to always migrate a manageable and equitable amount of information per group, so group migration times stay consistent). If a migration plan can be defined that groups users to meet both criteria, great. But if not, managing migration time and complexity is more important than Mary and Jane from AP migrating together and helping each other through the learning curve. Keep in mind that if the approach is to execute a phased migration of email users, routing between the source and target email systems needs to be configured so that both systems—and more important, both sets of users—can continue to receive emails, since the source system is the one currently published on the Internet (via the MX record) to receive emails.

Another key component of a migration strategy is how much data to migrate (or in the case of email, how far back in time to go). A migration is a great way to get users to delete all those old emails and unused files. A migration can either limit users in terms of a quota (a maximum number of email messages and files that will migrate for any user) or limit the migration to a certain date, meaning no email messages received before a certain date or files that have not been touched since a certain date will be migrated (a little less straightforward, since some files that are used every day are *not* modified every day). Some customers have used one year, some two years, depending upon how much storage they budgeted for Oracle Collaboration Suite 10*g* Email in the architecture.

Another important decision to make when creating a migration strategy centers around functionality, i.e., what functionality of Oracle Collaboration Suite 10*g* is made available to the user community when. So, for example, if the plan is to deploy both the Oracle Collaboration Suite 10*g* Email and Content Services components, should the approach be to migrate and deploy the Email functionality first, and then go back and do Content Services, or vice versa, or else to deploy both simultaneously? The answer is, of course, it depends. If the plan is to make Oracle Collaboration Suite 10*g* Email and Content Services available only through the interfaces provided to the end user today (for example, Microsoft Outlook and Explorer), then a full-blown deployment of all functionality at once is much easier in terms of supporting the end user from a functional perspective. However, if the plan is to eliminate all desktop tools access and deploy only the Oracle Collaboration Suite 10*g* web interface, then a phased rollout of functionality is probably a safer approach, since giving the end user a new interface for both important functions simultaneously could generate a larger number of support inquiries and bury the implementation team.

Regardless of what migration strategy is chosen, Big Bang or Phased (limited or complete data, limited or complete functionality), the important point is to plan for the migration up front rather than waiting until the migration process is in the middle of the trees to try to plan the way out of the forest.

Implementation Planning and Documentation

A great way to ensure completion of all steps of an Oracle Collaboration Suite 10*g* implementation is to create an Implementation Planning document prior to embarking on any technical tasks. This document, if created properly, serves two very valuable purposes. First, it provides the task plan or roadmap for all the steps, in the proper order, for completing a successful installation, implementation, and rollout of Oracle Collaboration Suite 10*g*. Second, it provides a comprehensive technical document regarding the Oracle Collaboration Suite 10*g* environment, including product version specifics, values defined for technical prerequisites such as kernel parameters, answers provided to Oracle Universal Installer questions such as where to put the Oracle Home directory, and valuable things such as passwords for important operating system and Oracle userids. For customers that have used this document, it has proved invaluable when opening Oracle Support Requests, as all the answers to the up-front questions related to the environment that are asked when creating a Support Request are at their fingertips. Figure 3-6 shows the workbook tabs for a sample Implementation Planning technical document. Notice the Install Summary tab as well as the Pre-Install tab along with all the tabs for the individual Oracle Collaboration Suite 10g modules.

The Install Summary worksheet pictured in Figure 3-7 holds the most critical high-level technical information related to an Oracle Collaboration Suite 10g install. Notice the timing section at the top of the worksheet that shows the duration of each section of the implementation process as defined in the other worksheets of the document, and a summary of time for the entire implementation process. This may not be important for every Oracle Collaboration Suite 10g install, but it is useful for understanding where the time-consuming areas of an implementation are for future reference (as consultants we are constantly refining estimates and finding areas of implementations where we can save time, so having this reference for each implementation we have participated in provides a guideline for such activities).

The next section shows all servers in the environment, along with server/host names, IP addresses and location (inside or outside the firewall). This section of the sample Install Summary worksheet may not have enough information for every implementer's tastes, but at a minimum it helps implementers remember which Oracle Collaboration Suite 10g components are installed on which server(s). This section should be accompanied by an

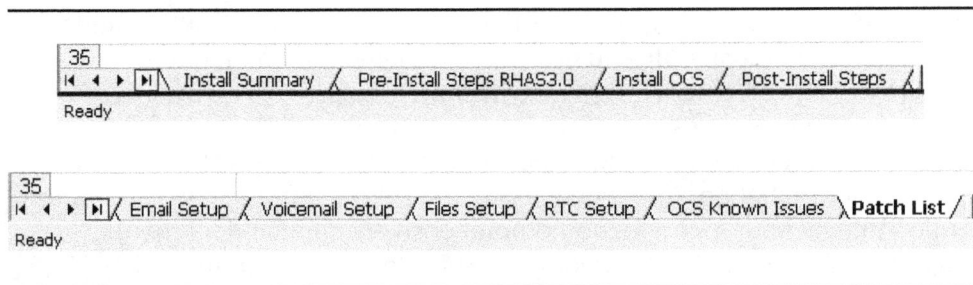

FIGURE 3-6. *Implementation Planning document sample tabs*

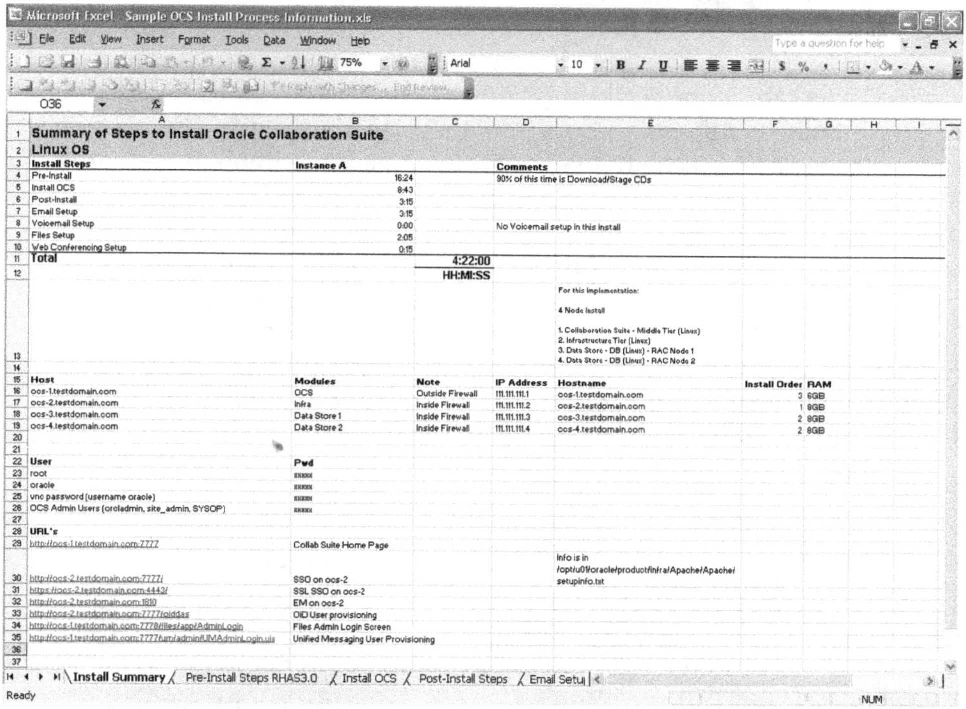

FIGURE 3-7.   *Implementation Planning document Install Summary worksheet*

architecture diagram showing a visualization of the environment, with servers and network components illustrated.

Notice there is an area in this sample Implementation Planning Install Summary worksheet for passwords for critical OS and Oracle usernames. Again, this may not be something every implementer wants to put in a document, but it at least provides a quick index of critical passwords during the implementation process. They can always be deleted afterward, or the document can be password-protected once the implementation is complete (or put in a secure reference document elsewhere, say on the server).

The final section of the Install Summary worksheet shows the various URLs for all the components of an Oracle Collaboration Suite 10*g* environment. This section is less important with Oracle Collaboration Suite 10*g* than it was with previous versions of the product, since Oracle Collaboration Suite 10*g* provides the Welcome page that provides links to all important URLs for the environment. However, it can still be useful to know how to access individual components of the Oracle Collaboration Suite 10*g* environment without having to go to the Welcome page.

The other tabs of the worksheet contain steps, tasks, important information, etc. for completing the various steps of the implementation. The information in these tabs can be as high-level or as detailed as the implementer prefers, but the sample in Figure 3-8 shows best practices of documenting the individual step(s) in the section and then documenting the values used in fulfilling the step's requirements in the specific environment. Again, this serves two purposes. First, it provides a record of what was done during the implementation, in case someone needs to go back and review it for any reason. Second, all the steps for the implementation are captured in one summary document, with the individual portions of the implementation sectioned off to allow for easy definition and later review.

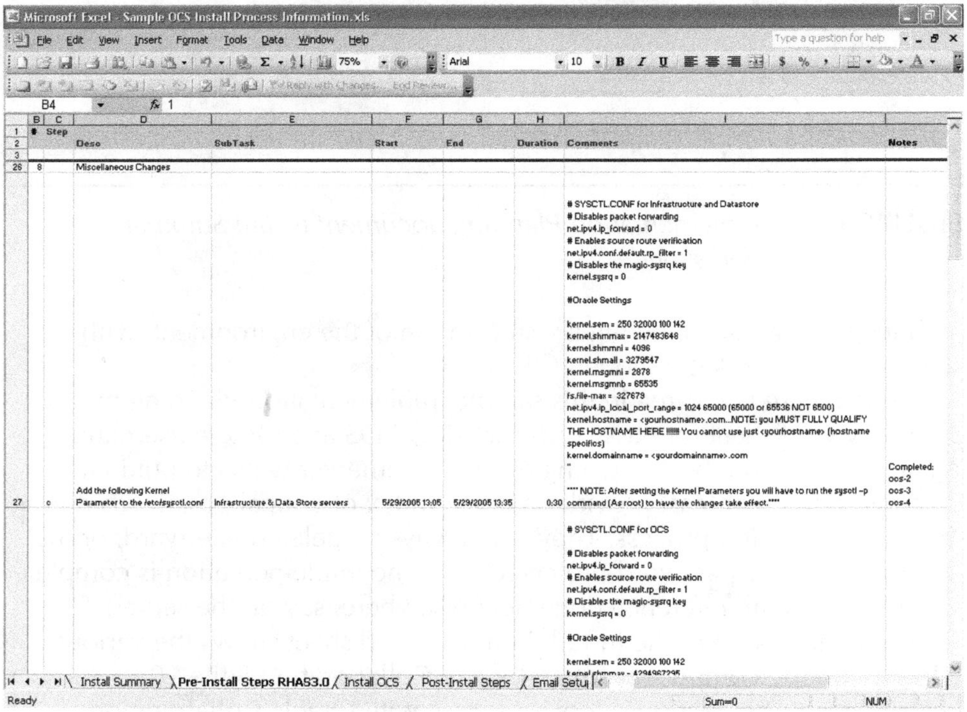

FIGURE 3-8. *Sample Implementation Planning document worksheet*

This implementation planning document shows the technical aspects of the Oracle Collaboration Suite 10*g* implementation plan. In addition, it is highly recommended that the implementation team create a project plan showing high-level tasks, responsible resources, duration, and timing. If a full-blown project management tool such as Microsoft Project is not available, a spreadsheet approach will work just fine as well. Figure 3-9 shows a sample task plan created in a spreadsheet tool. Remember, the end result here is to document and plan all the steps for the implementation, not to prove the ability to use a complex project management tool, so use whatever means available to document the steps—just get them documented prior to starting the implementation.

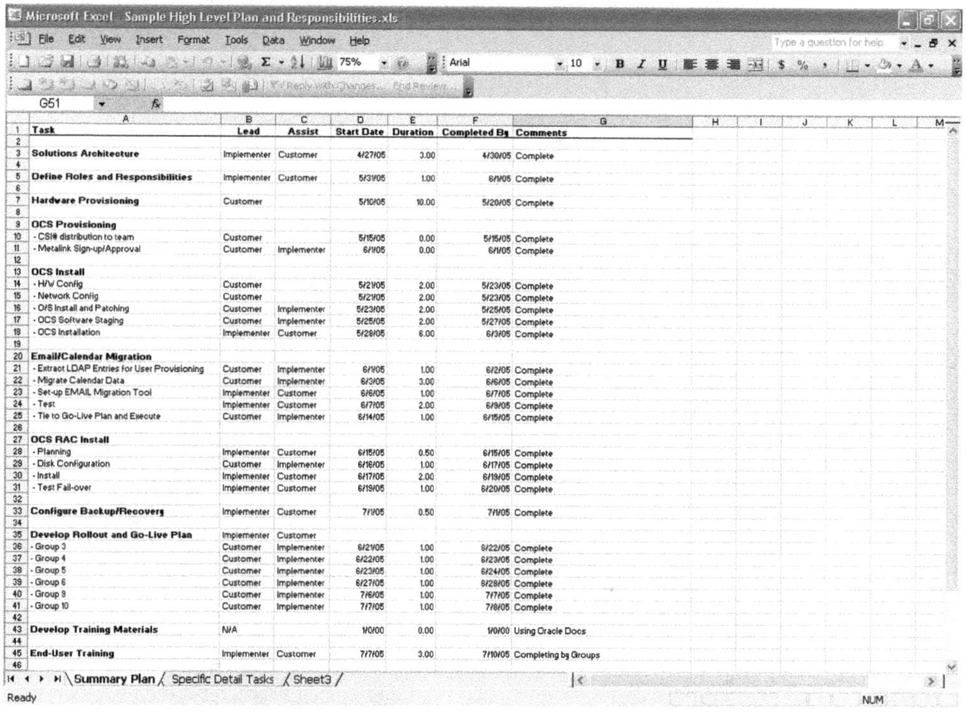

FIGURE 3-9. *Sample high-level Oracle Collaboration suite 10g task plan*

Summary

This chapter was intended to get the prospective implementation team members thinking ahead about the important preimplementation tasks for Oracle Collaboration Suite 10*g*. The most important concept to take away from this chapter is that up-front planning, with as much thought put into it as possible, is the key to the success of an Oracle Collaboration Suite 10*g* implementation. Planning forces an implementer to ask—and most times answer—difficult questions regarding an implementation before beginning, giving everyone time to think and react rather than stop and redo individual steps ... or potentially the entire implementation.

CHAPTER
4

Installing the Collaboration Suite Datastore Tier

America is the most inventive country in the
world because everybody has access to information.

　　　　　　　　　　　　　　　　　　　　　　　—Tom Clancy

T he next several chapters will take you through the details of an actual installation process for the Oracle Collaboration Suite 10*g* product. This is very valuable in planning the installation, as you can review the types of questions you will be asked during the actual installation process to better prepare for installing the product for the first time. During the narrative of the install process best practices, tips, explanations, etc., will be provided based upon previous experiences in deploying the Oracle Collaboration Suite 10*g* product.

As discussed in Chapter 2, there are many options for how to distribute the tiers of Oracle Collaboration Suite 10*g* across multiple servers in an architecture. This book will detail how to install the three main tiers— Infrastructure, Collaboration Suite Datastore, and Middle Tier—from a general perspective, without necessarily discussing the install in terms of any particular physical server architecture. It is assumed that the preinstallation tasks discussed in the preceding chapter have all been completed on every server you plan to use in the deployment, so the environment will not fail any of the preinstall checks in the Universal Installer installation process for any of the tiers, and that you are installing in a Linux/Unix environment (the Microsoft Windows installation process varies slightly from the Linux/Unix installation process).

Getting Started

In an Advanced install (versus a Basic or single-server install), the Collaboration Suite Datastore installation must be completed before either of the other two tiers can be installed, since they use the database instance created in this install to store their schemas and database objects. Note that you can install the Infrastructure Tier components and the Collaboration Suite Datastore during the same pass through the installation process, and this is completely acceptable if your approach is to have both Oracle Identity Management processes and the Collaboration Suite database processes running on the same server. The Collaboration Suite Datastore installation creates the repository that will hold the Infrastructure schemas and Collaboration Suite database schemas and objects. The general recommendation from an Oracle Collaboration Suite 10*g* perspective (unless there is a compelling reason otherwise, such as an incredibly large installation or an already-existing Infrastructure Tier in the environment) is to install both the Infrastructure database objects and Collaboration Suite database objects in the same Collaboration Suite database instance, rather than deploying them into separate database instances. The older releases of Oracle Collaboration Suite required separate database instances, which increased resource consumption as well as adding complexity to the management of the environment.

One recommendation prior to actually starting the installation process is to pre-create all the directory structures as the OS user that will own the Oracle software stack, for all the Oracle Homes on all servers in the architecture. This requires you to actually verify locations, disk space, directory permissions, etc., so that you won't have any issues running the Oracle Universal Installer to successful completion.

The Installation Process

First, the Oracle Collaboration Suite 10*g* installation image must be downloaded from the Oracle Technology Network web site (or edelivery.oracle.com), or the first installation CD must be mounted on the server. For the purposes of this dialogue the assumption will be that the software image was downloaded onto the server into a /u01/stage/OCS10g1012 directory. This is the recommended approach, since you can always get the latest release of the software and have it all staged at once. In order to run the Oracle Universal Installer, you must have an xterm environment such as VNC Server, and a monitor with a minimum of 256 color support. To begin the installation, simply change directories into the /u01/stage/OCS10g1012 directory and type in the ./runInstaller command at the command prompt. This will launch the Oracle Universal Installer tool for the Oracle Collaboration Suite 10*g* product. The initial screen for Oracle Collaboration Suite 10*g*, pictured in Figure 4-1, gives the option of executing a Basic Installation or Advanced Installation process. The Basic Installation process will ask only for a single password value and an Oracle Home directory to install the software into, and it will either provide default values for or read values from the environment and make assumptions before installing the entire Oracle Collaboration Suite 10*g* product on the single server from which you are

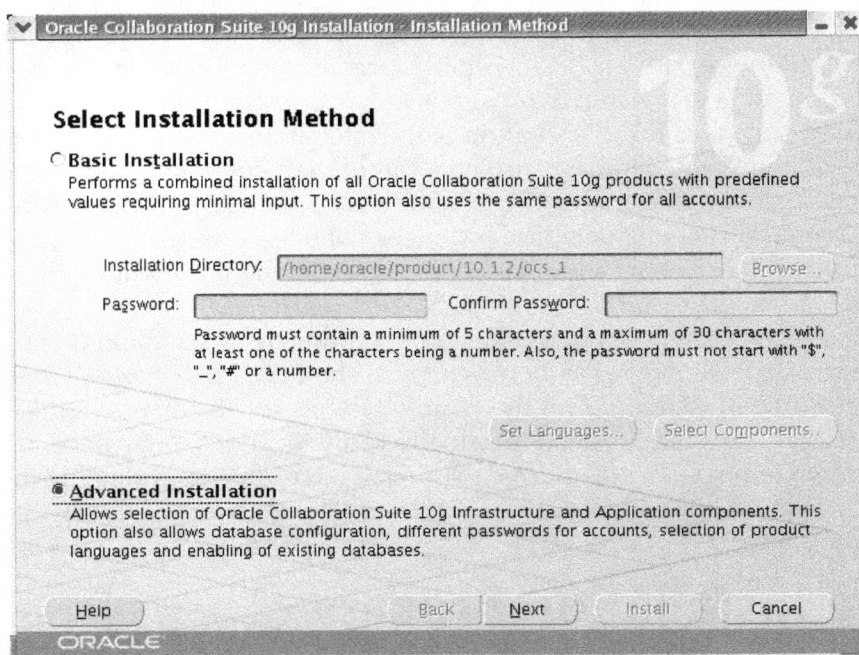

FIGURE 4-1. *Initial Oracle Collaboration Suite 10g Installer screen*

running the installation process. Since I am discussing the installation of each tier separately in this book, I will choose the Advanced Installation process, which allows the installation of each tier separately, and the ability to input specific values for installation parameters (such as database instance name and email domain name) instead of their being defaulted by the environment and/or the installer.

Executing an Advanced Installation

After choosing Advanced Installation, click the Next button to begin the Advanced Installation process. If this is the first time an Oracle installation has been executed on this server, a Specify Inventory Directory And Credentials screen will appear as in Figure 4-2, prompting for a directory path to create the oraInventory directory in as well as for the operating

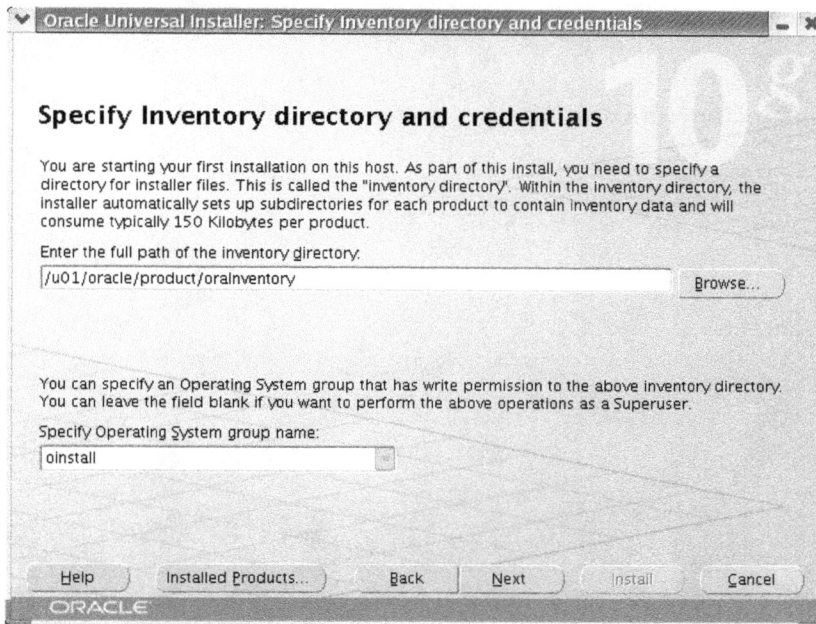

FIGURE 4-2. *Oracle Inventory Directory and Install Group screen*

system group name for the installation (the oraInventory directory tracks all names, versions, and install locations for Oracle products installed on the server). If Oracle installations have been executed on the server before, the Inventory and Credentials screen will not appear for this install. The first decision point in the Collaboration Suite Datastore Advanced Installation process is reached on the next screen of the Universal Installer, pictured in Figure 4-3. Here it asks for the path to the products.xml file holding the detail of the products you wish to install, and the Destination Oracle Home name and directory location. The path to the products.xml file should be defaulted correctly if the software image was properly downloaded and exploded. Enter the destination Oracle Home name and value for the Oracle Collaboration Suite 10g tier you are installing, in this case the Collaboration Suite Datastore Tier. The recommendation here is to specify both the Oracle Home Name and the directory name so that it is easy to recognize what is

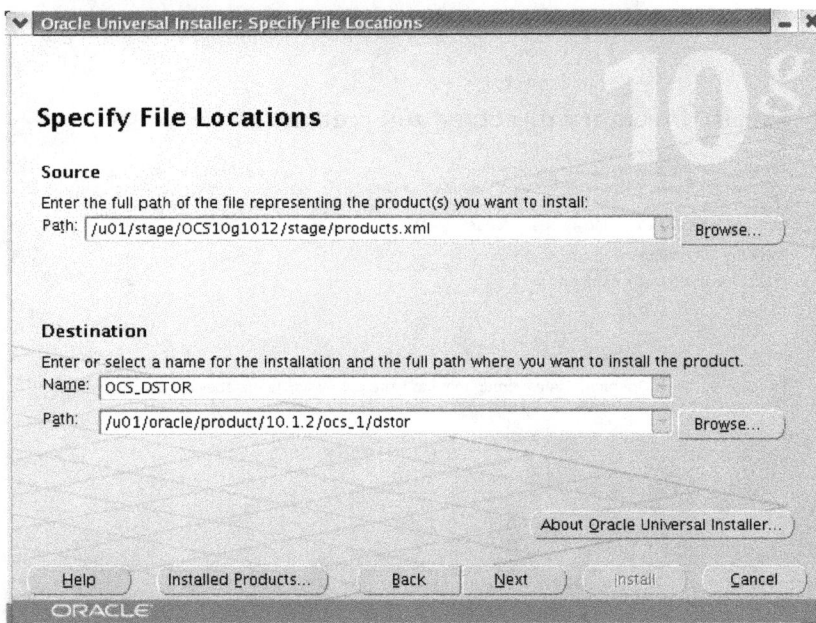

FIGURE 4-3. *Defining Source Path and Collaboration Suite Datastore Oracle Home*

installed there. In the example, the directory is named /u01/oracle/product/ 10.1.2/ocs_1/dstor. The first part of the directory name, /u01, is obviously the mount point name. The /oracle/product/<version#> segment follows the standard naming convention for an Oracle product directory. The theory here is you can install multiple product versions down the same path but still keep them separated by version. Another approach is to put the product name first, i.e., /u01/oracle/product/ocs, then the version numbers under that, such as /u01/oracle/product/ocs/10.1.2, so that you can keep several Oracle products with several versions of each under the same generic Oracle Home path (/u01/oracle/product). The dstor acronym is a holdover from the default name for the Datastore Tier in previous releases of the Oracle Collaboration Suite product, but it works for the purposes defined here because it meets the criteria of describing what component is installed there.

Choosing Components to Install

Once the Oracle Home Name and Path values have been defined, click Next to move to the next screen of the Installer, where you choose what Product—or more precisely, what Oracle Collaboration Suite 10g Product component(s)—to install. You have the option of installing everything at once (Infrastructure and Applications) or just the Infrastructure or Applications separately. You would choose the first option to install everything at the same time (similar to the Basic Installation option from the first screen, except it does not default any of the option values), which would put all components of the product on the same server. If you are installing each component separately, the Collaboration Suite database is part of the Infrastructure install, so the Oracle Collaboration Suite Infrastructure option is the correct choice on the Products screen as shown in Figure 4-4.

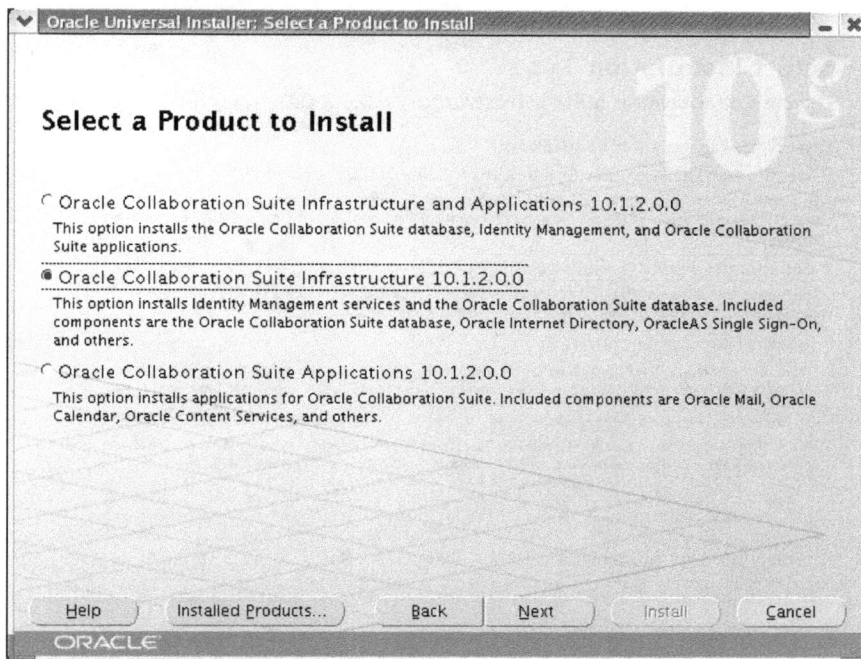

FIGURE 4-4.   *Oracle Collaboration Suite 10g Install Products screen*

Choosing an Installation Type

Clicking Next from the Products screen takes you to the Select Installation Type screen, which displays all the types of install combinations available for the product chosen on the previous screen. In this case we would choose the Collaboration Suite Database installation type as shown in Figure 4-5. Clicking Next from here takes you to the System Verification process, where all the prerequisites discussed in the preceding chapter and in the Installation and Configuration Guide are checked on the server.

It is critical that all automatic checks come back as Succeeded as shown in Figure 4-6. If they do not, you should not continue the install process. Not successfully completing the prerequisite setups to satisfy these checks is the single highest cause of failure of an Oracle Collaboration Suite 10*g* installation.

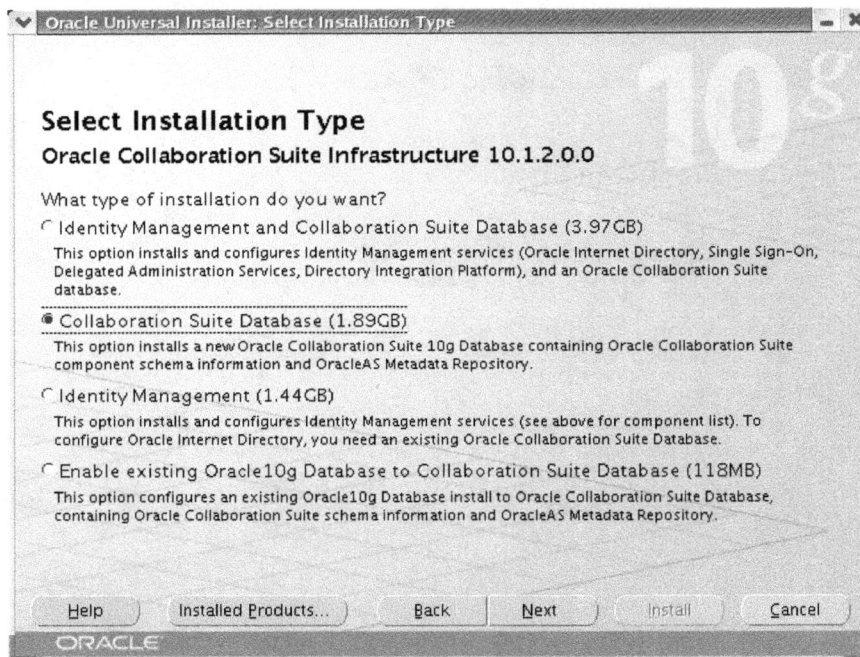

FIGURE 4-5. *Oracle Collaboration Suite 10*g *Installation Types screen*

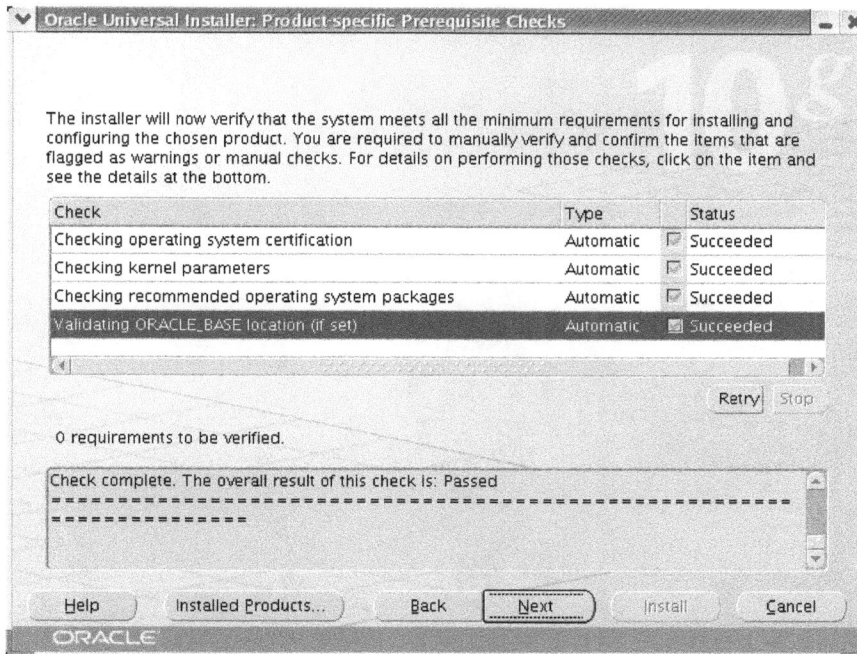

FIGURE 4-6. *System Verification Process screen*

The product may actually install fine even after failing one or more of these checks, but it will not run successfully in many cases (and the exact results of what these failed checks affect are unpredictable at best). It is possible in some cases to address the issue uncovered by the verification process in another VNC window or another connection into the server and then, back in the Installer, check the box for the failed check and click Retry.

Choosing a Language

Once the verifications have completed successfully, click Next to arrive at the Language Selection screen, pictured in Figure 4-7. English is preselected, but to select other languages, you must highlight them on the left and click the >> button to move to the selected pane. If you incorrectly select a language, you can always highlight it in the pane on the right and click the << button to remove it from the selected list.

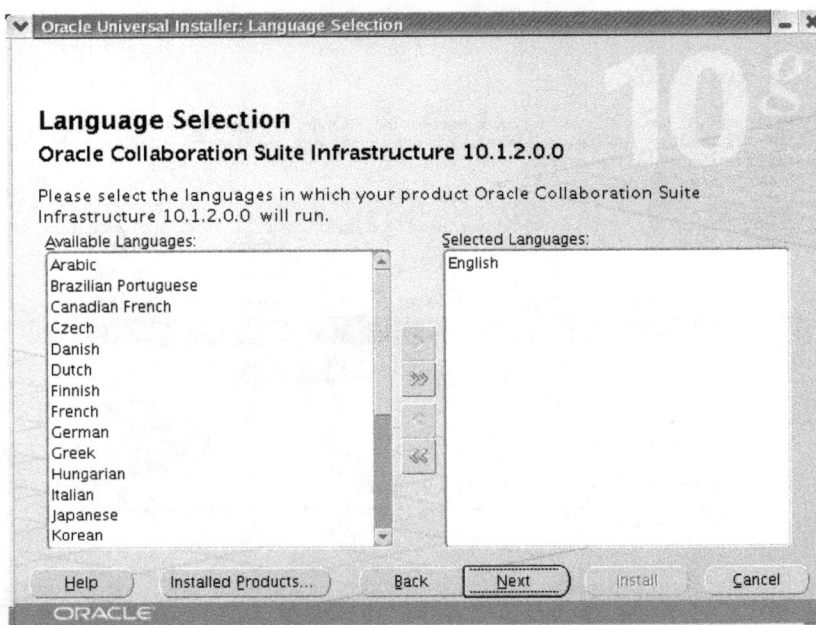

FIGURE 4-7. *Language Selection screen*

Creating the Database

Once you have selected all the languages you wish to install, click Next again and the Installer will bring up the Database Creation screen. Here you have a choice to have the Installer create the database instance for you, or to have the Installer simply install the binaries so that you can create the database manually by yourself. Best practices say you should have a database instance specifically for Oracle Collaboration Suite 10g, so you should answer Yes here as shown in Figure 4-8 and allow the Installer to create a database instance for the initial install of the Collaboration Suite Datastore. It is much simpler to let the Installer create the database instance—you can always go back later and reconfigure the database file layout, control files, redo log files, etc., to meet your environment's best practices and standards. This way, there is no concern for missing something for the database creation that the Oracle Collaboration Suite 10g install

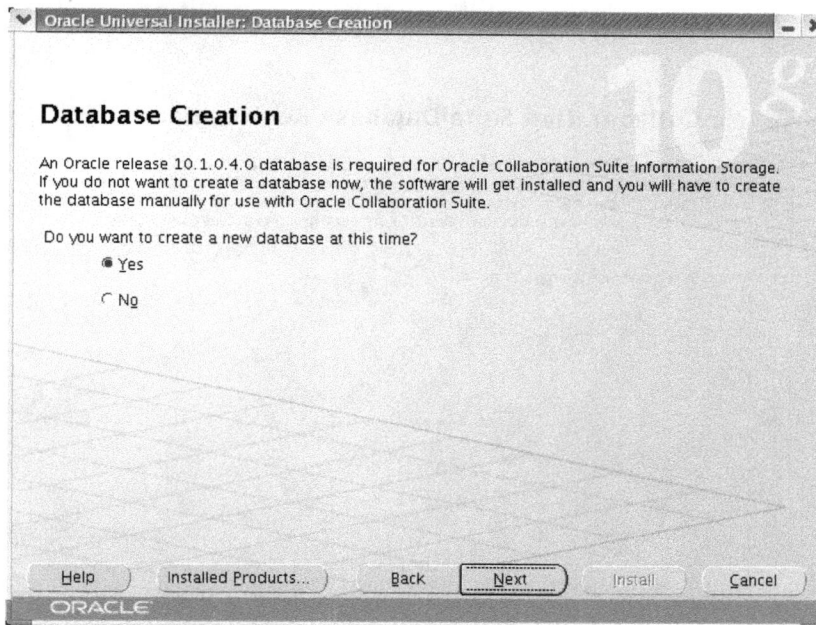

FIGURE 4-8. *Database Creation screen*

expects. Now, you could always answer No to this question if you wanted to create the Collaboration Suite Datastore inside another existing database instance in your environment, or execute the entire process—creating the initial database instance and then installing the Collaboration Suite Datastore inside—manually. Remember, however, version compatibility is extremely important with regard to the Oracle core technology stack underneath Oracle Collaboration Suite 10*g*, so if you decide to use another database instance, you must make sure the version of the target database instance is compatible with the Oracle Collaboration Suite 10*g* version you are installing.

Clicking Next on the Database Creation screen will take you to the Database Registration Screen pictured in Figure 4-9. Since we do not yet have the Infrastructure Tier installed (which would install the Oracle Internet Directory), you should select No here and then click Next to take you to the screen to Specify Database Identification.

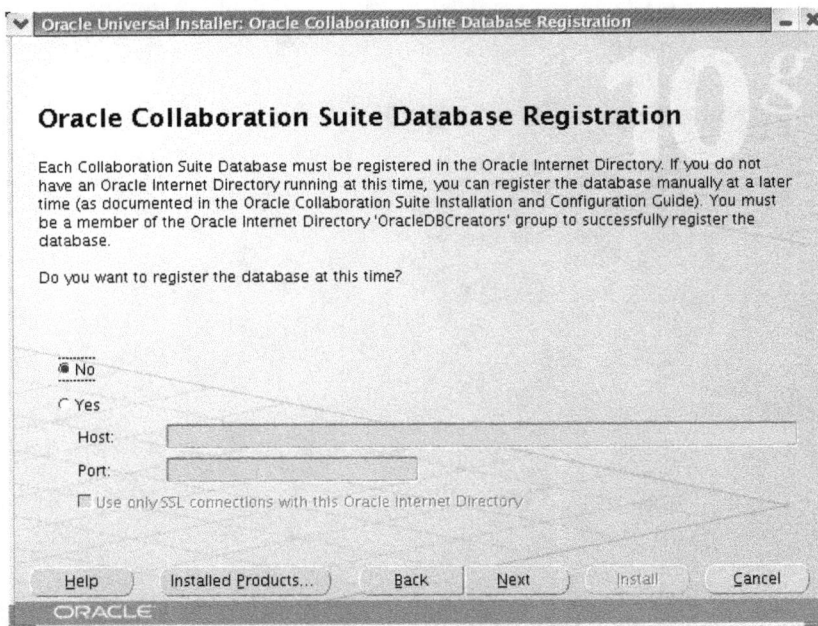

FIGURE 4-9. *Database Registration screen*

Naming Your Database Instance

In choosing the name for your database instance to hold the Collaboration Suite Datastore objects, it is recommended that you use a naming convention that again will easily identify this database instance as being tied to the Oracle Collaboration Suite 10g install in your environment. In the example pictured in Figure 4-10, the database instance is created as ocsdb. (I actually edited the Global Database Name, which in turn automatically changes the SID to match the first part of the GDN.) Now, if you wish to run more than one database instance associated with an Oracle Collaboration Suite 10g install, then you may want to get more descriptive with the SID, such as ocststdb vs. ocsprddb, or ocs10gdb vs. ocs92db. If you are not familiar with an Oracle database name, note that it is used in SQL*Net and JDBC connection strings for when applications need to communicate to the database.

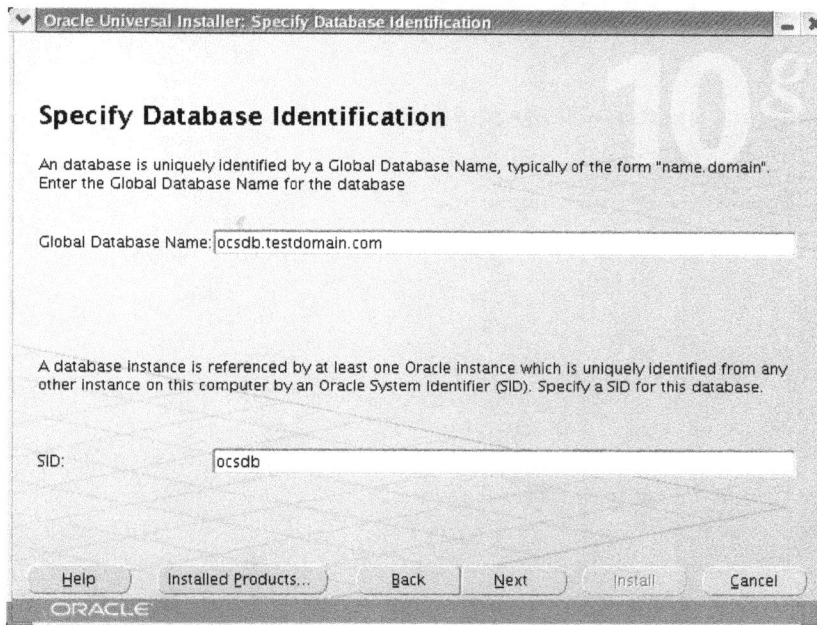

FIGURE 4-10. *Specify Database Identification screen*

Setting Management Options

Once you are satisfied with your database SID, click Next to go to the
Database Management Option screen, pictured in Figure 4-11.

If you are running Oracle Database 10*g* Grid Control in your environment,
then it is recommended that you use Grid Control to manage the 10*g*
database instance under Oracle Collaboration Suite 10*g*. If this is the only
Oracle database instance in your environment (possible for a company
implementing Oracle Collaboration Suite 10*g* as its first Oracle application),
or if you do not yet have Grid Control set up to centrally manage your
Oracle database environments, then choose the second option to manage
your database locally on this server with Oracle Enterprise Manager 10*g*
Database Control. Either way, it is strongly recommended to set up an email

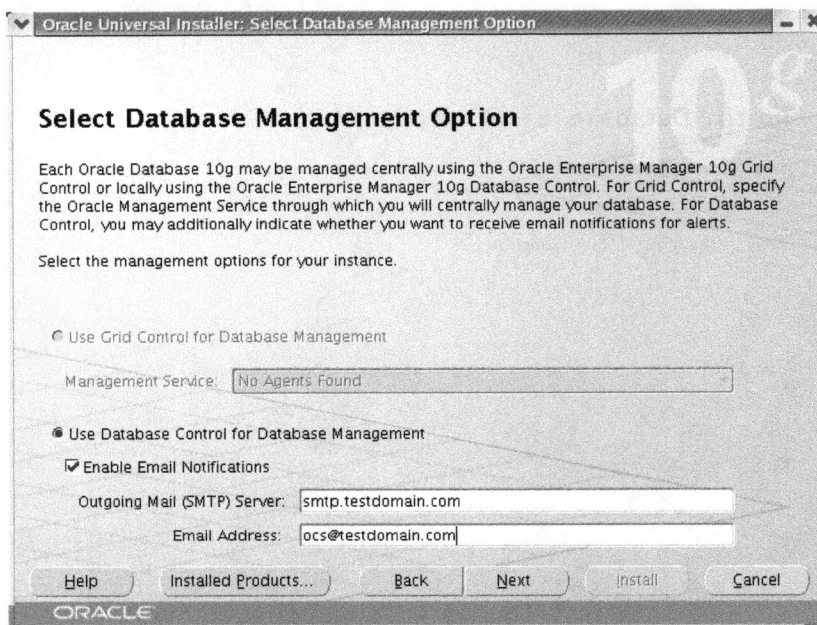

FIGURE 4-11. *Select Database Management Option screen*

address for Oracle management tools email notifications and provide it along with your environment's SMTP server to enable Email Notification for this database instance. This will help tremendously with proactively managing the database environment for this Oracle Collaboration Suite 10*g* environment by notifying the Administration email address provided when certain threshold values such as disk space utilization or tablespace free space are exceeded in the database. It is not intended to go into technical depth on every tier of the Oracle Collaboration Suite 10*g* architecture in this book, so for further detail on Enterprise Manager, 10*g* Grid Control, Oracle 10*g* database constructs, etc., please refer to the Oracle 10*g* R1 Database Installation and Administration Guides available directly from Oracle Corporation or on the Oracle Technology Network web site, or other publications available from Oracle Press.

Specifying the File Storage Mechanism

Once you have completed the selections on the Database Management Option screen of the installation process, click Next and proceed to the Specify Database File Storage Option screen. Here, as pictured in Figure 4-12, you must select the type of storage you want to use for the data files associated with this new database instance. The most common storage method for Oracle database files is File System, which is what we will choose here, but Automatic Storage Management (ASM) or Raw Devices are also possible storage methods. It is strongly recommended that unless you are familiar with deploying Oracle databases on either of the latter options (ASM or raw), you should use File System.

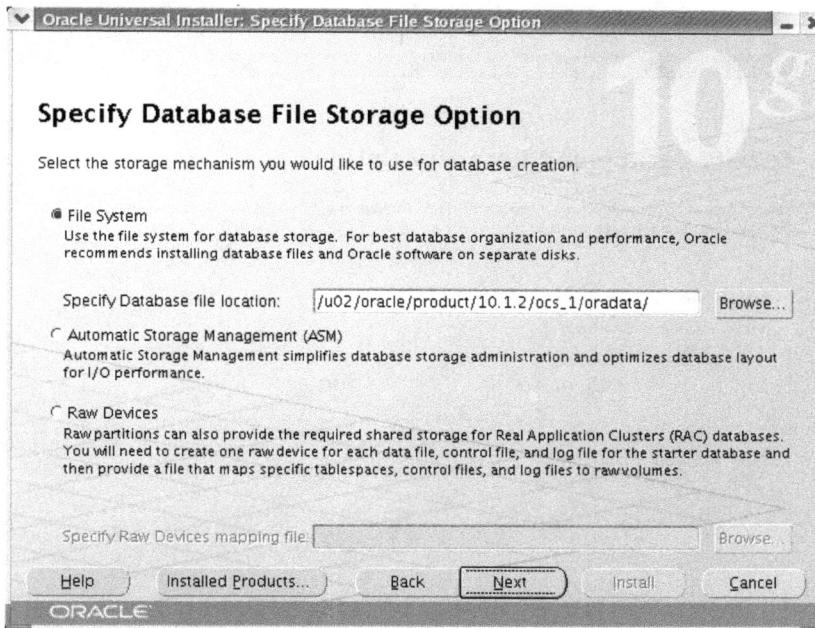

FIGURE 4-12.   *Specify Database File Storage Option screen*

Specifying Backup and Recovery Options

Once you have specified your file storage option, click Next to navigate to the Specify Backup And Recovery Options screen. It is recommended that you choose not to enable automated backups at this time during installation, but rather go back and manually configure your backup and recovery process after the entire product is installed. There are too many moving parts in an Oracle database backup and recovery process, and too many things that have to be done outside of the install process to try to have the Universal Installer coordinate and complete it successfully. It is just one of those things that you leave for the postinstall steps to get it right (we will discuss backup and recovery in a later chapter). The Specify Backup And Recovery Options screen is shown in Figure 4-13.

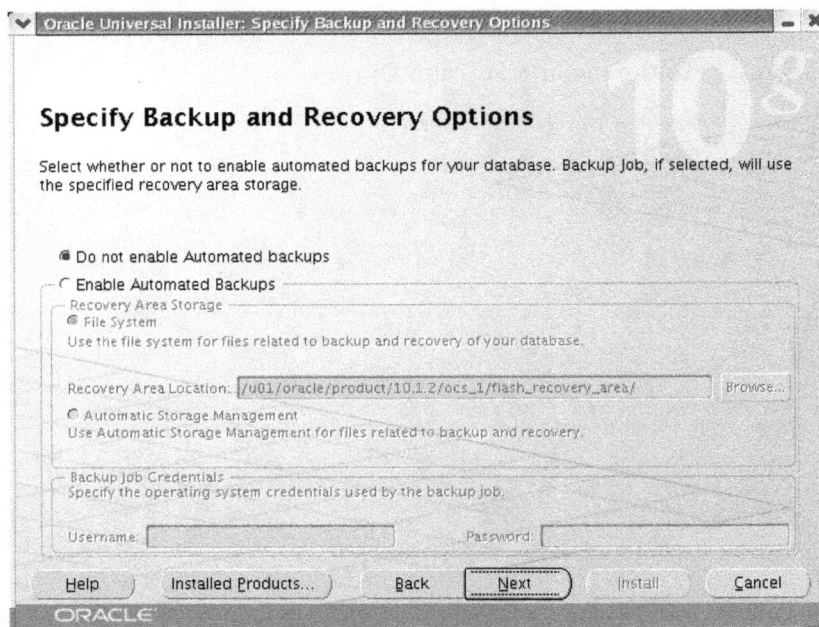

FIGURE 4-13. *Specify Backup And Recovery Options screen*

Specifying Database Schema Passwords

After clicking Next from the Backup and Recovery Options screen, you will arrive at the Specify Database Schema Passwords screen. As shown in Figure 4-14, it is recommended that you choose the option to use the same password for all the accounts. Now, this may seem against standard Oracle Database Administration best practices (or at least Oracle Database Security best practices), but it is not only recommended that you set all database account passwords the same, it is recommended that you set every password in the Oracle Collaboration Suite 10g environment the same, at least until you are completely comfortable with what username is required for what administrative function or application or process. There are several places during the install of the other tiers where you will be prompted for a password for a particular administrative account, but you are not necessarily told which account/username it is related to. So, if you set every password to something different, it is highly unlikely you will be able to relate the Oracle Collaboration Suite 10g function to the correct username and therefore the

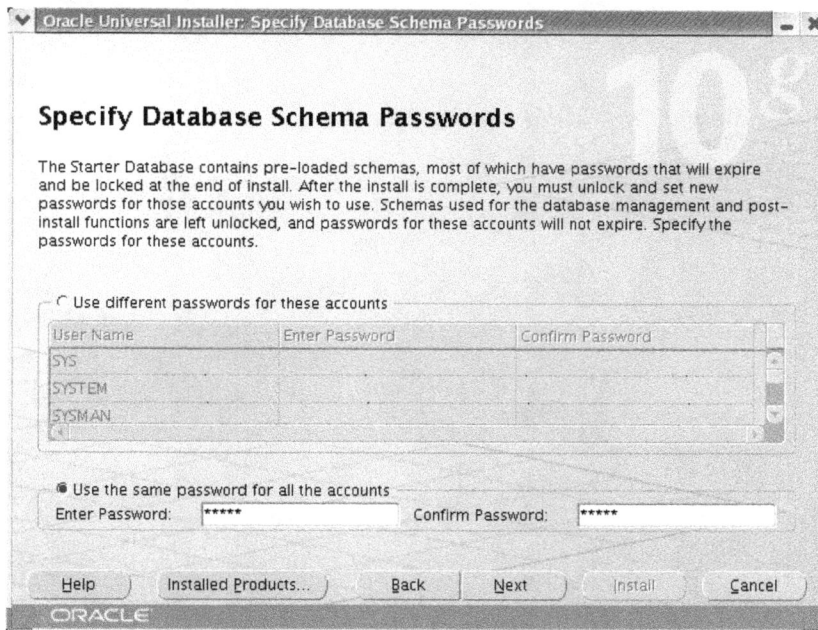

FIGURE 4-14. *Specify database schema passwords*

correct password until you spend some significant time managing the Oracle Collaboration Suite 10g environment. All passwords are modifiable, either through database functions or application functions or Oracle Internet Directory Manager. Another recommendation is to use a five-character password beginning with a letter and having at least one number. The Oracle Internet Directory requires a minimum of a five-character password with one character being a number, but Oracle Calendar has a requirement of a maximum of five characters for the administrative password, so setting your password the same, at five characters with one of them a number, meets every component's requirement for administrative password policy.

Defining Privileged Operating System Groups

After selecting Next, you will be placed on the screen for defining the Privileged Operating System Groups shown in Figure 4-15. It is recommended that you use the group you defined for your oracle account for both the OSDBA and OSOPER group assignments; the oinstall group

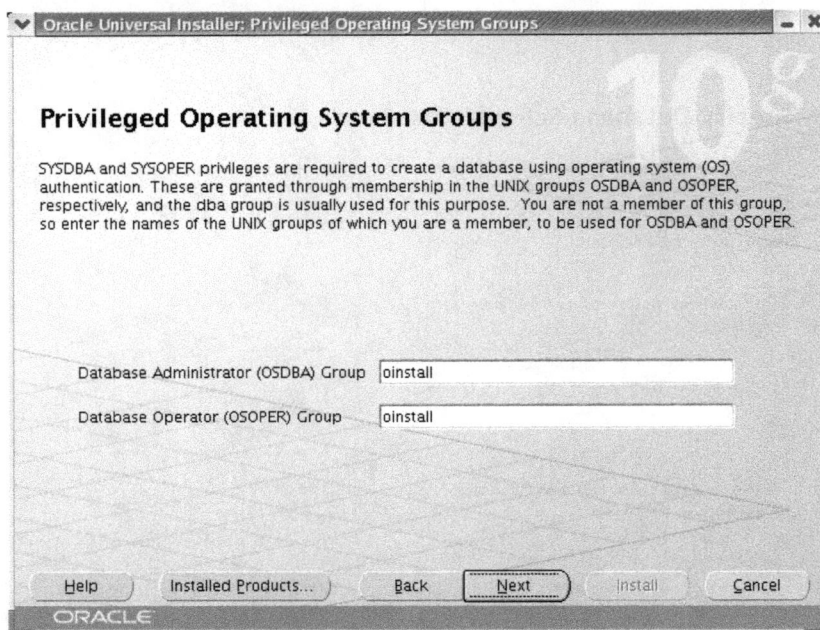

FIGURE 4-15. *Privileged operating system groups*

name is a holdover standard from previous releases of the Oracle Collaboration Suite product when only having a group named oinstall would work for all tiers. So if you have a different scheme in your organization, feel free to use it, but oinstall is a standard derived from previous usage that works and is even still used for stand-alone Oracle core technology installs outside of the Oracle Collaboration Suite 10g product. It is also my recommended standard.

Completing the Installation

Once you have defined your OSDBA and OSOPER groups, you can click Next to move to the Install Summary screen. As you can see from the image shown in Figure 4-16, this screen simply recaps the products you are going to install in this pass through the Universal Installer. Selecting the Install button here will begin the actual install of the Collaboration Suite Datastore component of the Infrastructure Tier.

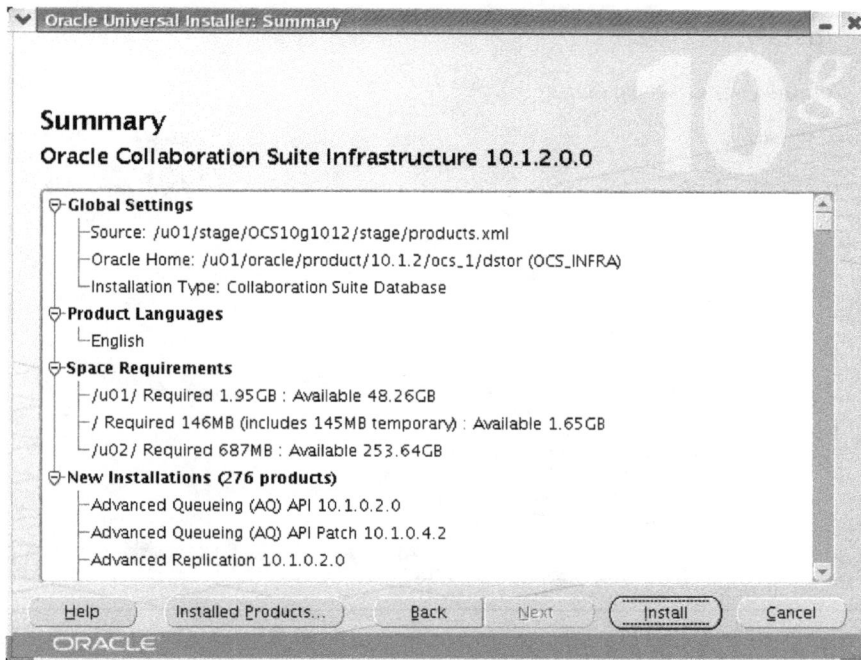

FIGURE 4-16. *Oracle Collaboration Suite Datastore Install Summary screen*

The install process will begin as shown in Figure 4-17 and will run through copy, link, and setup phases. If there are no issues during these phases, a Setup Privileges window will pop up as shown in Figure 4-18 and ask you to run a script located in the Oracle Home you defined earlier, which will set some root privileges for the Oracle environment.

You will need to go to another session in the server, logged in as root, and change directories to the directory referenced in the pop-up window to run the root.sh shell script to set the environment properly in order for the install to continue properly. Figure 4-19 shows the results of the execution of the root.sh script in another root window.

Clicking OK on the Setup Privileges window will display the Configuration Assistants window and begin the final configuration of the Collaboration Suite Datastore. You will see the Installer configure several

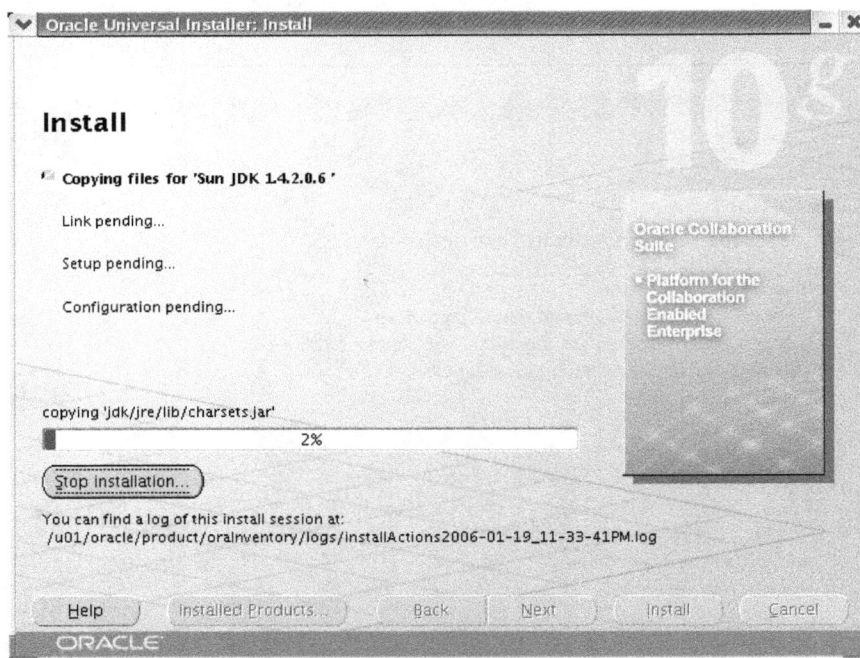

FIGURE 4-17. *Oracle Universal Installer Install screen*

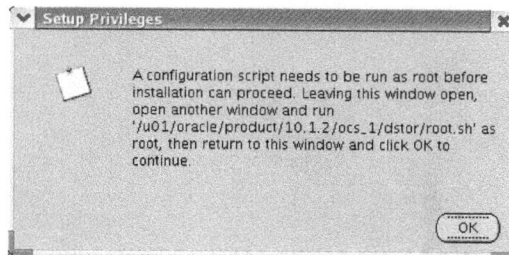

FIGURE 4-18. *Install Setup Privileges pop-up window*

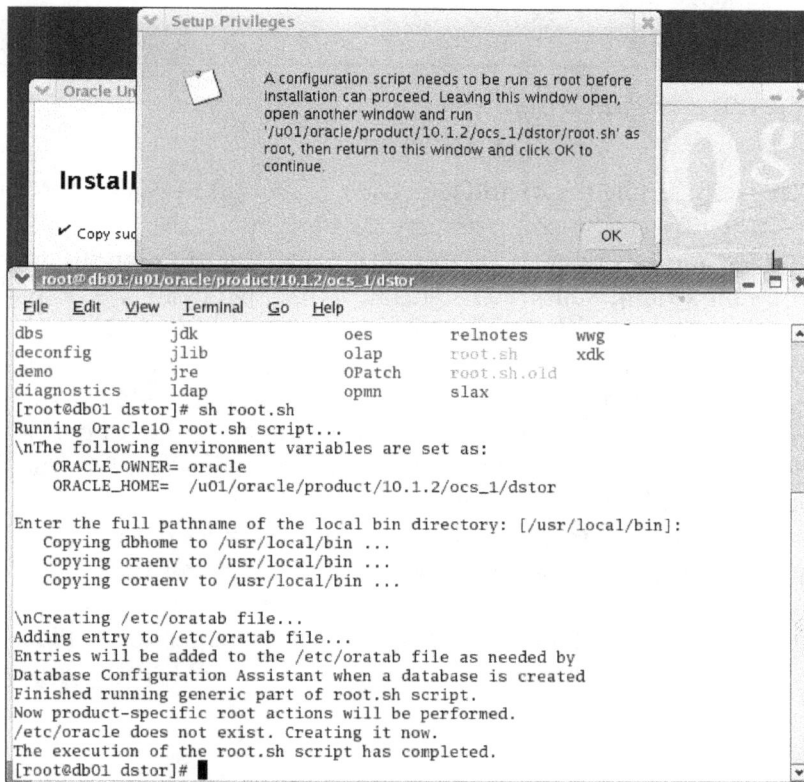

FIGURE 4-19. *Execution of the Root.sh script*

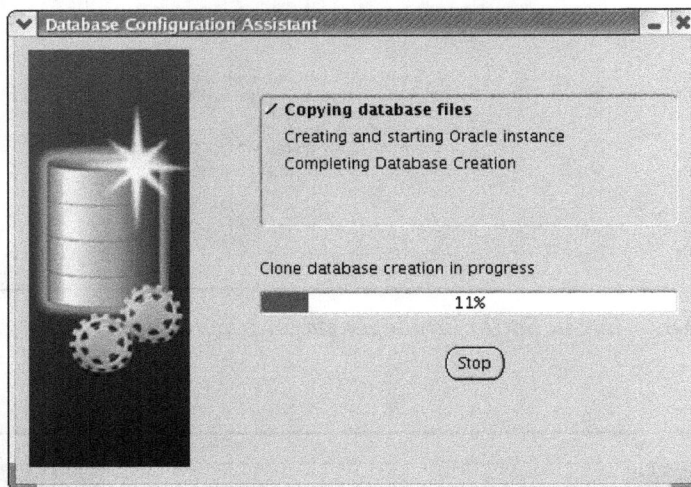

FIGURE 4-20. *Database Configuration Assistant execution*

components, including the main Database Configuration Assistant pictured in Figure 4-20. This is the configuration assistant that copies the default database files and sets up the Collaboration Suite Datastore on the server.

After all the Configuration Assistants have run successfully, you will see the summary pop-up window shown in Figure 4-21, which gives you all the important information about the newly created database instance, such as the SID, the Global Database Name, where the parameter file is located, and where to check the install log files. You have the option of performing Password Management on the other database accounts inside the Collaboration Suite Datastore and unlocking them and setting their passwords. It is recommended that unless asked to do so by some future requirement, for security purposes you should just leave all other database users locked. Clicking OK here will show the End Of Installation screen, which contains information about important URLs for Enterprise Manager, iSQL*Plus, etc.

The End of Installation screen is shown in Figure 4-22. This completes the installation of the Collaboration Suite Datastore.

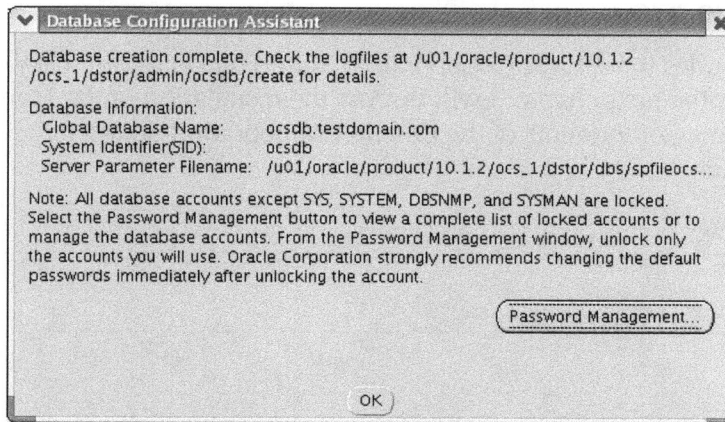

FIGURE 4-21.   *Database Configuration Assistant Completion Summary pop-up*

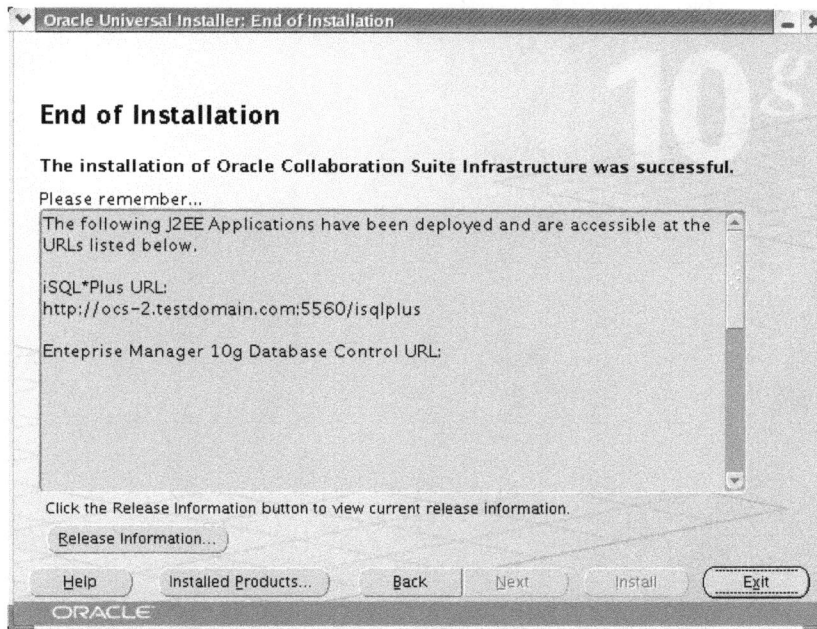

FIGURE 4-22.   *End of Installation screen*

Summary

This concludes the Oracle Collaboration Suite 10*g* Datastore installation chapter. In the next chapter I will discuss the installation of the Identity Management components of the Oracle Collaboration Suite 10*g* environment.

CHAPTER
5

Installing the Identity
Management Component
of the Infrastructure Tier

The value of identity of course is that
so often with it comes purpose.

—Richard R. Grant

N ow that you have successfully created a new Oracle 10*g*
database instance and installed the Collaboration Suite
Datastore component of the Oracle Collaboration Suite 10*g*
Infrastructure Tier into that instance (see Chapter 4), you can
now install the Identity Management component of the
Oracle Collaboration Suite 10*g* Infrastructure Tier. This component of the
Oracle Collaboration Suite 10*g* product architecture provides the user
management, directory, and security functionality for the Oracle
Collaboration Suite 10*g* environment. When users are provisioned in Oracle
Collaboration Suite 10*g*, the information about username, password,
applications they are granted access to and the associated level of access,
etc., are all stored in the Infrastructure Tier in Oracle Identity Management
10*g*. In addition to user information, information related to the status of
Oracle Collaboration Suite 10*g* applications and the processes that run on
the various tiers of Oracle Collaboration Suite 10*g* to support those
applications are also stored in the Infrastructure Tier in Oracle Identity
Management 10*g*. Oracle Internet Directory, Single Sign-On, Delegated
Administrative Services, Oracle Application Server 10*g* Certificate Authority,
and Directory Integration and Provisioning functionality are also part of the
Oracle Collaboration Suite 10*g* Infrastructure Tier Identity Management
installation.

Getting Started

The assumption here is that the preinstall steps outlined in the previous
chapters of this book and detailed in the Oracle Collaboration Suite 10*g*
Installation Guide have already been completed. It is also assumed that the
Oracle Collaboration Suite 10*g* install image has been downloaded and
unzipped, and the Collaboration Suite Datastore installation detailed in
Chapter 4 has also already been completed. If the plan is to install the
Oracle Collaboration Suite 10*g* Infrastructure Tier on a separate server from
the database install completed in Chapter 4, then the Oracle Inventory And
Install Credentials screen will be shown again during this chapter's install if
Oracle has never been installed on this server before.

The Installation Process

The installation process for the Identity Management component of the Oracle Collaboration Suite 10*g* Infrastructure Tier begins just as the database installation process did, with the execution of the ./runInstaller command at the command prompt from the /u01/stage/OCS10g1012 directory where the install image was unzipped. This will bring up the initial screen in the Oracle Collaboration Suite 10*g* install process shown in Figure 5-1, where the Installer prompts for the installation type. Since you are completing the Advanced Installation you started in Chapter 4, you should choose the Advanced Installation option as illustrated to continue the component install process.

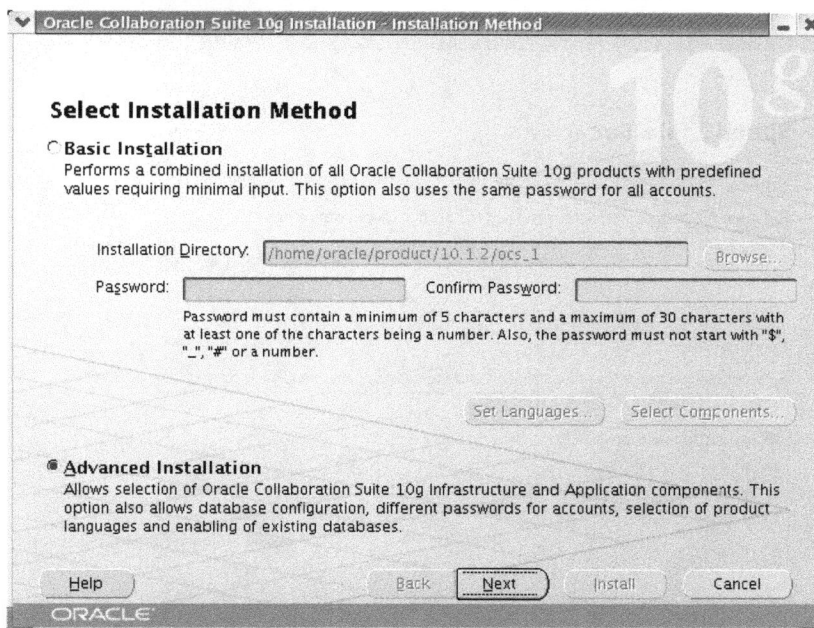

FIGURE 5-1. *Oracle Collaboration Suite 10g Select Installation Method screen*

Specifying File Locations

Clicking Next here will bring up the Specify File Locations screen, where you give the Universal Installer the location of the products.xml file, which lists the products for possible install (this value should default correctly if you are in the correct install image directory) and the name and location of the Oracle Home in which to install this component of the Oracle Collaboration Suite 10g product. In this case OCS_INFRA is chosen for the Oracle Home name, since you are installing the Infrastructure Tier, and the directory is placed down the same path as the Collaboration Suite Database installation, but in its own /infra subdirectory, as shown in Figure 5-2. Again, it is suggested that the directory structures be precreated prior to running the

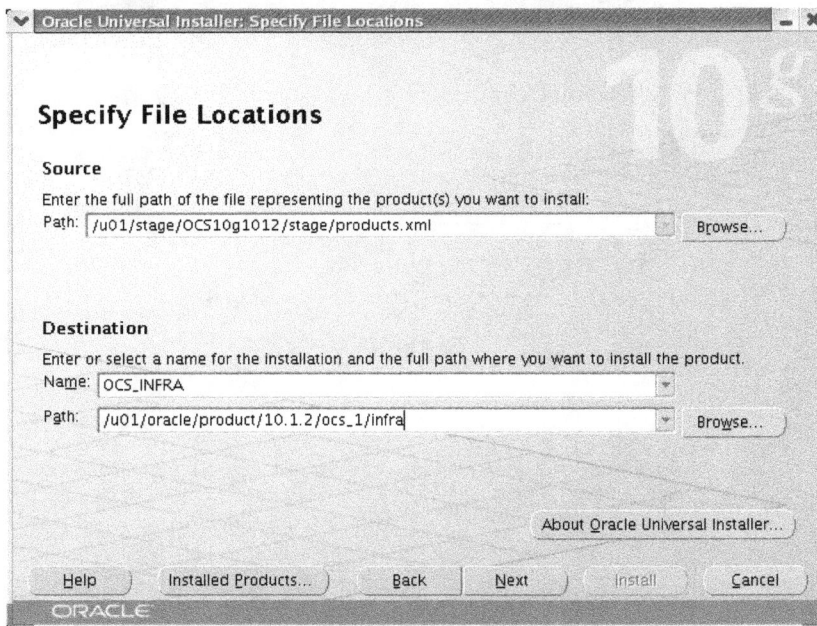

FIGURE 5-2. *Specify Files Location screen for the Infrastructure Tier install*

Oracle Universal Installer so that there are no rights/permissions issues
during the install process.

Selecting a Product to Install

Once the Oracle Home name and location are defined, click Next to
display the Select A Product To Install screen illustrated in Figure 5-3. Again,
just as in the Collaboration Suite Database install from Chapter 4, select the
Oracle Collaboration Suite Infrastructure as the product to install.

Selecting an Installation Type

Once selected, click Next to move to the Select Installation Type screen,
where you can select the Identity Management option as shown in Figure 5-4.
This option assumes you have an existing Collaboration Suite Database
installed like the one we completed in Chapter 4.

FIGURE 5-3. *Select A Product To Install screen*

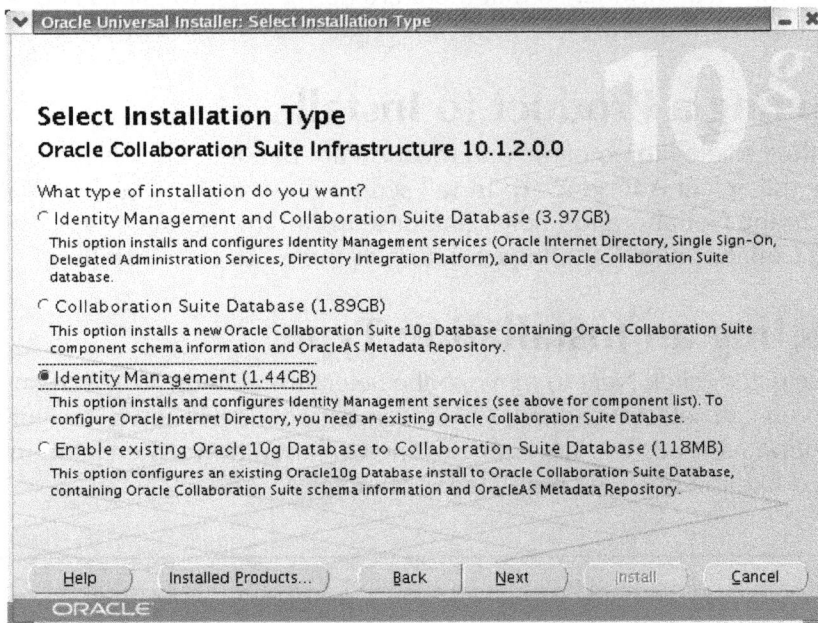

FIGURE 5-4. *Select Installation Type screen*

Clicking Next here takes you to the place in the install process where the environment is checked for the minimum requirements for the install. In every pass through the Oracle Collaboration Suite 10*g* install process, the environment you are attempting to install on will be verified for operating system version, installed packages, and kernel parameter settings. Again, just as in the Collaboration Suite Database install, all requirements should be met before continuing the installation process; otherwise, unpredictable results can occur. Once the process completes, all boxes should be checked and each line marked as Succeeded as shown in Figure 5-5. If one or more of these validation checks fails or gives a warning, review the log information provided in the window in the bottom half of the screen (or go to the directory defined for the oraInventory location at the beginning of the installation process and look in the /logs subdirectory for the log for your install and review there) and resolve the OS setting, the package version number—whatever the error might be—before continuing. It may be

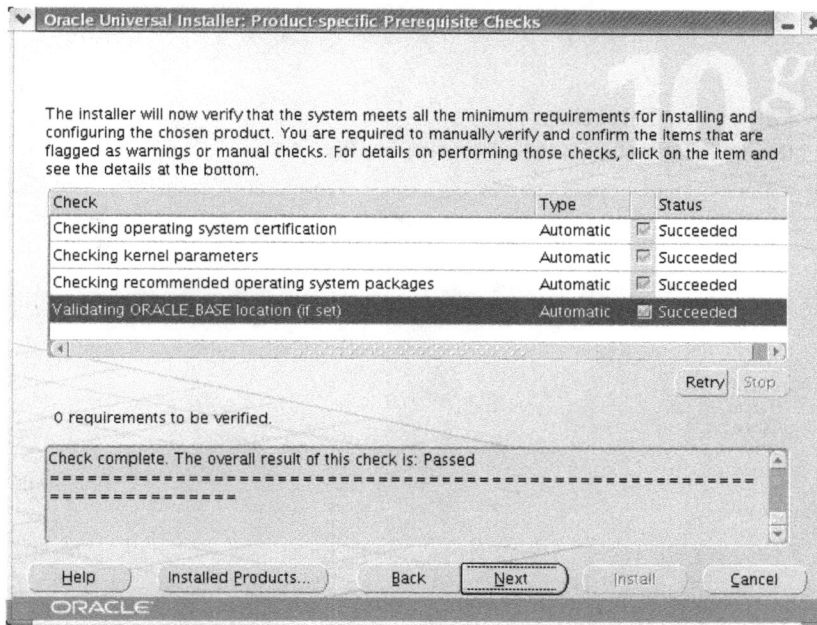

FIGURE 5-5. *Validating the Environment for Minimum Installation Requirements*

necessary, as in the case of certain kernel parameter values, to reboot the system to force changes to take effect. In that case cancel the install process by clicking the Cancel button in the lower right-hand corner of the installer window, answering Yes to the pop-up question on whether you want to cancel, and then rebooting the system. Once the system is rebooted, you can begin the install again, following the steps indicated at the beginning of this chapter.

Selecting a Language

After the validations are complete and successful, click Next to navigate to the Language Selection screen shown in Figure 5-6. I recommend being consistent by selecting the same languages in every pass through the Universal Installer that you selected in the first pass through the installation process for the first component.

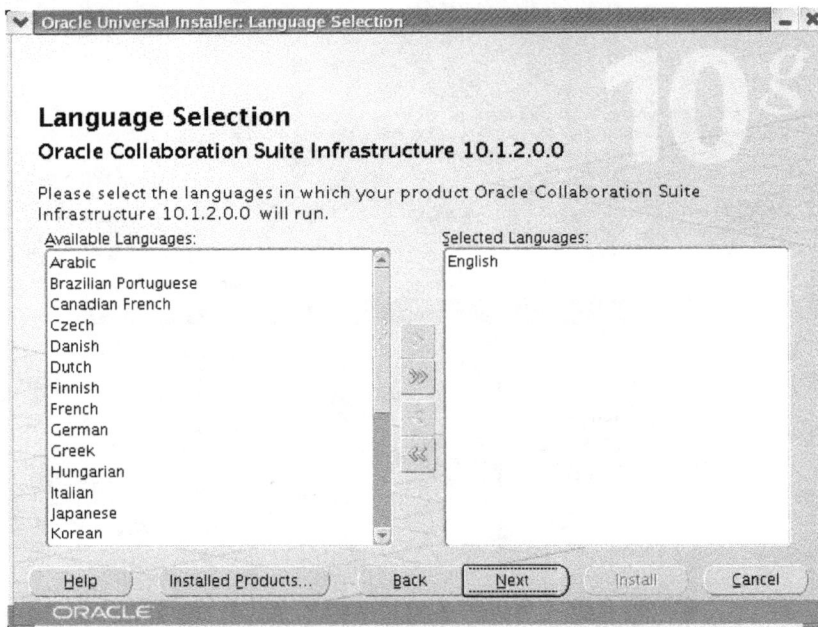

FIGURE 5-6. *Language Selection for Identity Management Install*

Selecting Configuration Options

Once the languages have been selected in the Language Selection Screen, click Next to move from this screen to the Select Configuration Options screen. Note that by default the first optional Available Component (one that can be selected or deselected, by contrast with the grayed-out boxes at the top, which cannot be deselected), Oracle Internet Directory, is not checked. This is because although an Oracle Internet Directory instance is necessary to successfully install Identity Management, you do not need to install that particular Oracle Internet Directory instance during this pass through the installer to successfully install the Oracle Collaboration Suite Identity Management component. It may be that an Oracle Internet Directory instance is already installed and running in the environment. For example, many Oracle Application Server users have installed Oracle Collaboration

Suite 10*g* into the existing Oracle Internet Directory instance for their Oracle Application Server environment. Since you are doing a component-by-component install, meaning you are not installing the entire Infrastructure Tier at once (Identity Management and Collaboration Suite database, which would take care of an Oracle Internet Directory install), you need to check that box so that the Oracle Internet Directory gets installed with the rest of the Identity Management items in this pass through the Installer. If you don't select the Oracle Internet Directory component here, you will be required to provide the Oracle Internet Directory to register the remaining Application Server components into during the install, or be directed to return to this screen and select the Oracle Internet Directory component. Take a look at Figure 5-7 to see all the recommended Available Components to select for an initial Identity Management install.

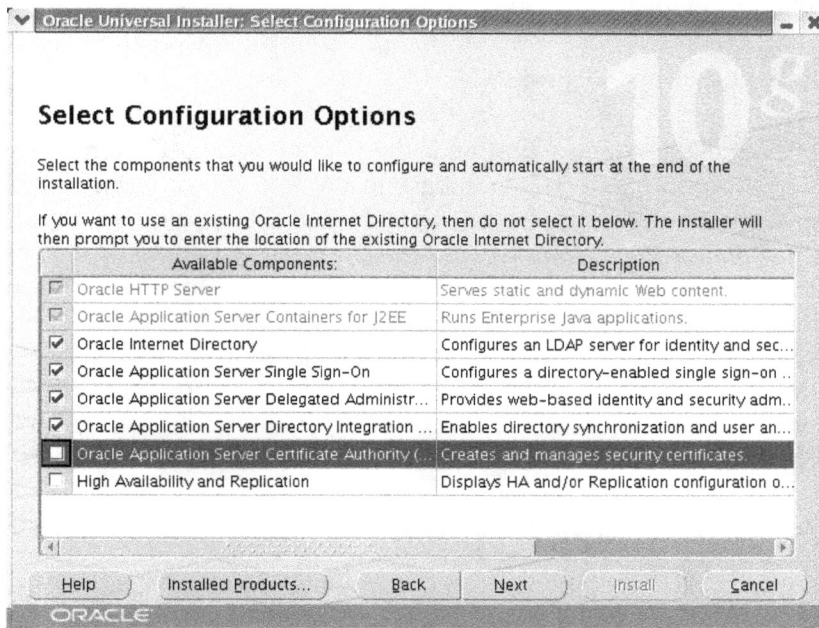

FIGURE 5-7.   *Select Configuration Options window of Identity Management installation*

Specifying a Repository

Once you have selected all the Available Components that you want to install, click Next to move to the Specify Repository screen. Here is where you tell the Universal Installer which Metadata Repository instance to install the Identity Management instance into. In this case, this is the Collaboration Suite database instance you created in the Chapter 4 installation process. A DBA login must be provided, since this is a new instance for the purposes of this installation process. The SYS account—and its associated password—is recommended here, since you can verify the install will work when it is provided. The hostname:port combination is the DNS registered server name along with the SQL*Net listener port that the listener for the Collaboration Suite database is running on. If nothing is changed in the Collaboration Suite installation process, this value will be 1521 (the default port for any Oracle SQL*Net listener). In the case of installing Oracle Collaboration Suite 10*g* into a RAC'd database environment, the hostname and port are provided as follows:

Virtual_hostname_on_node1:1521^Virtual_hostname_on_node2:1521

The Service Name at the bottom is the Global Database Name provided in the Collaboration Suite 10*g* Database install (see Figure 4-9 in Chapter 4). Figure 5-8 shows an example of the Specify Repository window populated for this installation.

Clicking Next at this point will cause the Universal Installer to verify all the values entered in the Specify Repository screen. If the Universal Installer cannot connect using the connect string formulated from the values populated on this screen, an error will display and you will not be allowed to continue until you get the values corrected such that the Universal Installer can verify them.

Specifying a Namespace

Once the Universal Installer verifies it can connect to the Metadata Repository specified, it will move to the next screen in the Identity Management installation process, the Specify Namespace screen, shown in Figure 5-9. Here, you are asked to define the default namespace for the Oracle Collaboration Suite 10*g* users to be defined in the Oracle Internet Directory for the Identity Management instance being installed. Remember

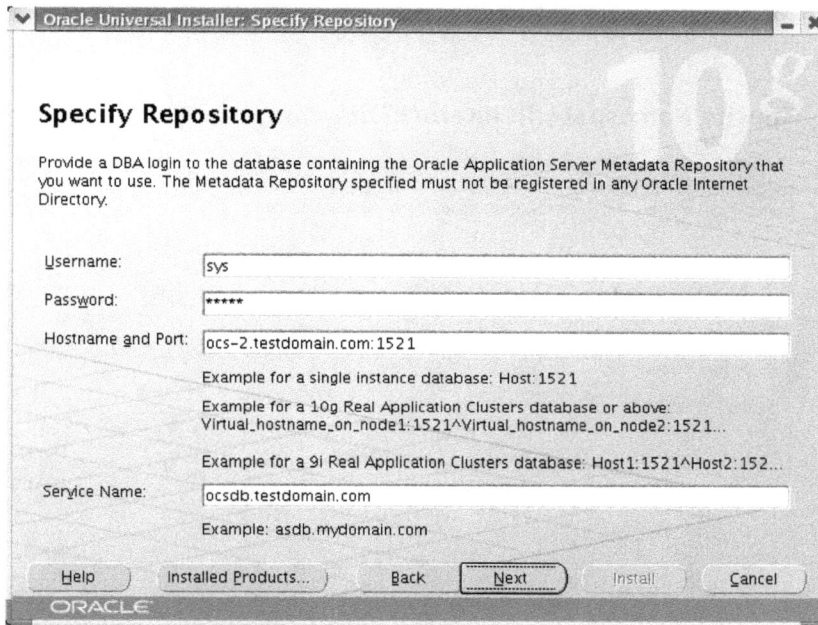

FIGURE 5-8.   *Specify Repository window of the Identity Management
installation*

the architecture components; the Oracle Internet Directory is the LDAP
repository that all Oracle Application Server 10*g* implementations—
including the one supporting this Oracle Collaboration Suite 10*g*
environment—use to hold their Identity Management, component status,
and user/group detail information.

Generally, the Suggested Namespace is correct, but sometimes it is
necessary to override the suggested namespace with a Custom Namespace
for a given Oracle Collaboration Suite 10*g* implementation. This will
especially be the case if you are installing the Oracle Collaboration Suite
10*g* components into an Oracle Internet Directory that already exists in an
environment that is being used for some other applications. In this case,
I do not want Oracle Collaboration Suite 10*g* security information and
component status information to mix with existing application LDAP
content, so I would create a custom namespace.

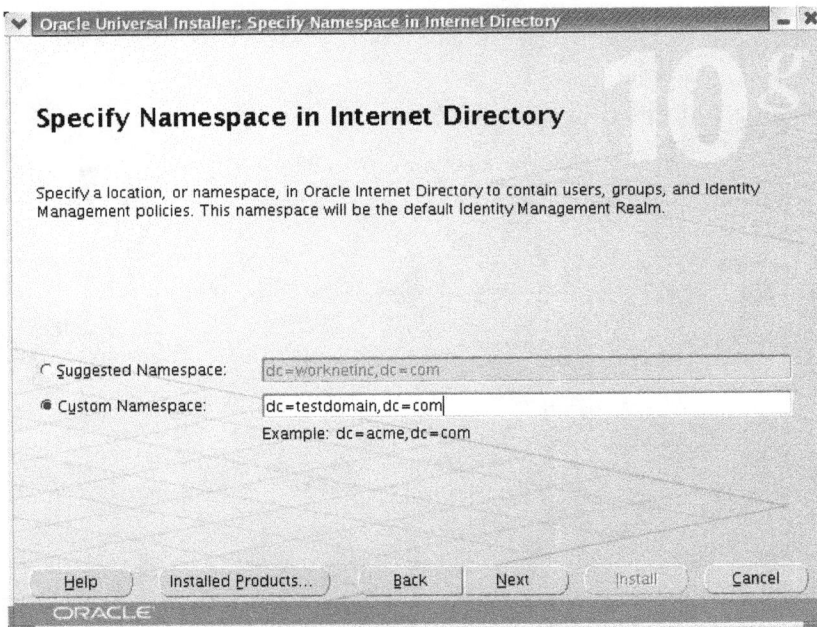

FIGURE 5-9. *Specify Namespace screen for the Identity Management installation*

Specifying Port Configuration Options

Once the namespace value has been defined, click Next to move to the Specify Port Configuration Options screen. This is where the Universal Installer is given the ports to be assigned to the various components of the Oracle Internet Directory and Identity Management components during this install. If the Automatic Port Selection option is chosen, the Universal Installer will first attempt to use the default port values normally assigned to the various components—for example, port 389 will be the first port attempted for the Oracle Internet Directory, since it is the universal default port for LDAP connectivity, 636 being its SSL counterpart—and if they are in use by some other process running on the server, the Oracle Universal Installer will attempt to increment up until an open port value can be found. If manual port selection is preferred, scroll through the component list in the

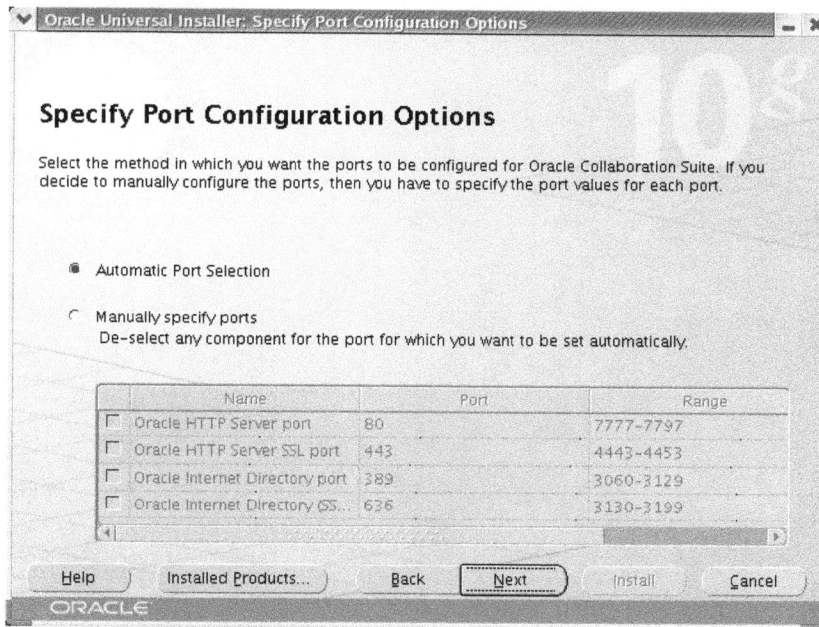

FIGURE 5-10.   *The Specify Port Configuration screen*

bottom box and enter a port for the component or deselect its check box to
have the default value instantiate, or populate the staticports.ini file with all
desired port values and reference it during the install. Figure 5-10 shows the
Specify Port Configuration screen and its options. The recommended choice
on this screen, unless a company has specific ports it uses that are not the
default values for the given component, is to first validate that the default
ports are not in use (see Chapter 4 on preinstall steps) and then choose the
Automatic Port Selection option to allow the Universal Installer to select the
default ports to use for the individual components.

Choosing a Guest Account Password

Once port settings are complete, click Next to navigate to the Guest
Account Password screen, pictured here in Figure 5-11. The Oracle
Collaboration Suite 10g Infrastructure Tier installation creates a user account

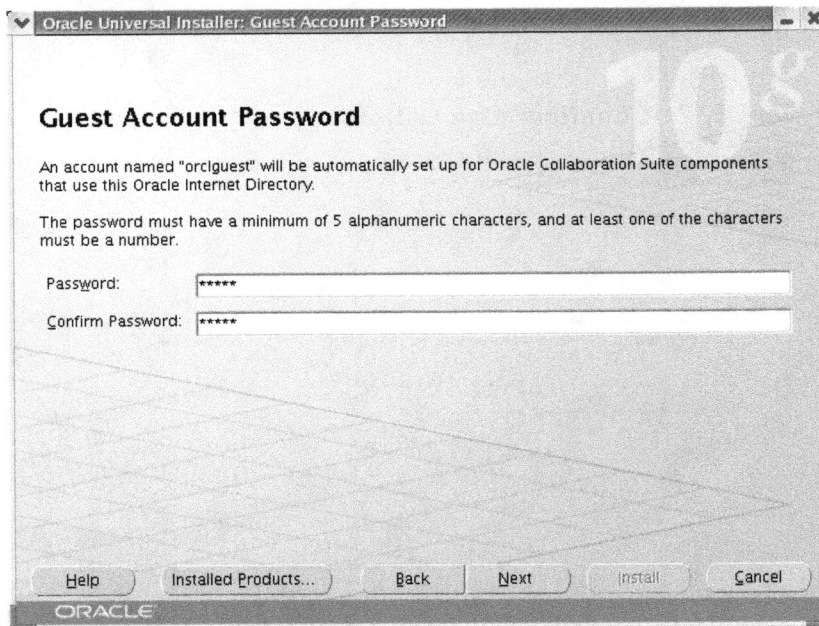

FIGURE 5-11. *Guest Account Password screen*

named ORCLGUEST, which is used to test user functionality, connectivity, etc., without requiring any users to be created by the Administrator (sort of the SCOTT/TIGER of the Oracle Collaboration Suite 10*g* environment, so to speak). This user can be used to log in to the Oracle Collaboration Suite 10*g* Portal once the Middle Tier installation is completed, for testing certain security or applications settings, pretty much anything one needs to do to "test" an Oracle Collaboration Suite 10*g* environment. The general recommendation on passwords stands here as well: set everything to the same password across the entire Oracle Collaboration Suite 10*g* install (exactly what the Basic or Single-Server installation process does) and change them once you get comfortable with what each user does in the environment. So, pick the password for the ORCLGUEST, recalling the rules that it needs to be a minimum of five characters long and at least one of those characters needs to be a number, and enter it on this screen, typing it in twice to confirm.

Specifying an Instance Name and ias_admin Password

Clicking Next from here takes you to the Specify Instance Name and ias_admin Password screen. This is where the name and administrator password for the Oracle Application Server 10*g* Infrastructure instance being installed here are defined (the username ias_admin is the Administrator user for Oracle Application Server 10*g*). Recommended best practices say to use ocs as the first part of the name so that you know that this particular infrastructure instance is part of your Oracle Collaboration Suite 10*g* installation, and infra1 to know this is the infrastructure instance of Oracle Application Server 10*g* that you are installing, and the 1 to identify it as the first infrastructure instance for this Oracle Collaboration Suite 10*g* environment. This way, if you decide later for high availability or performance reasons to install another infrastructure instance, you won't have issues with being able to identify it properly (for instance, ocs_infra2). See Figure 5-12 for an illustrated example.

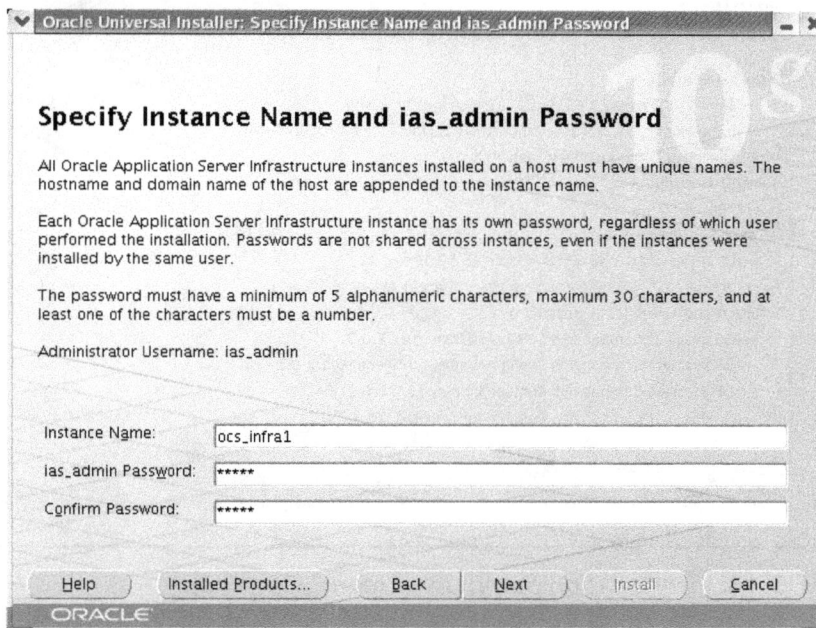

FIGURE 5-12. *Specify Instance Name and ias_admin Password screen*

Completing the Installation

Clicking Next here will navigate to the Installation Summary screen shown in Figure 5-13, indicating the Universal Installer is ready to commence installing the chosen components according to the parameter values entered throughout the Universal Installer dialogue just reviewed. Clicking Install here will start the installation process for the Oracle Internet directory and Identity Management components of this Oracle Collaboration Suite 10g environment.

Once the installation process begins, Configuration Assistants will begin running one by one, as indicated by the entries in the list in the top window of the Configuration Assistants screen shown in Figure 5-14.

If they haven't run yet, they will be marked as Pending, as shown in Figure 5-15.

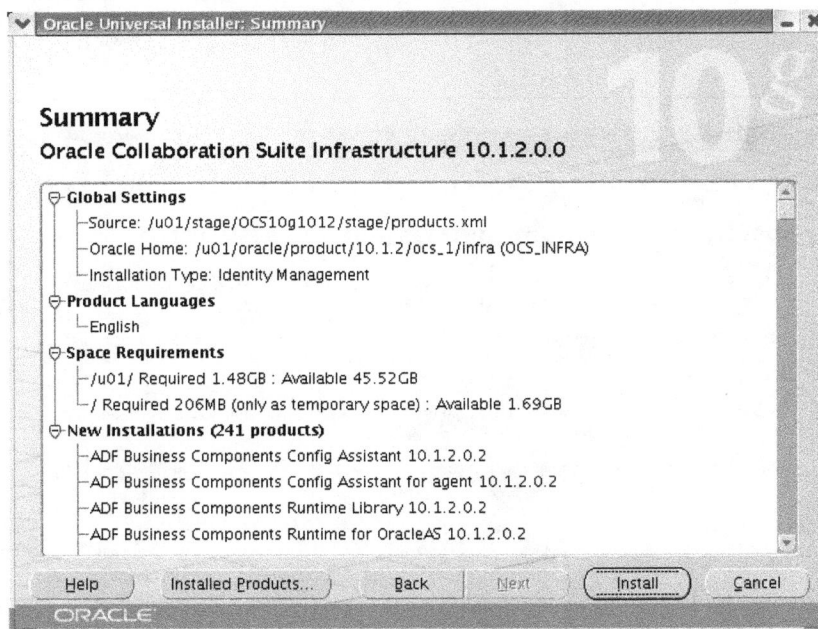

FIGURE 5-13. *Installation Summary screen*

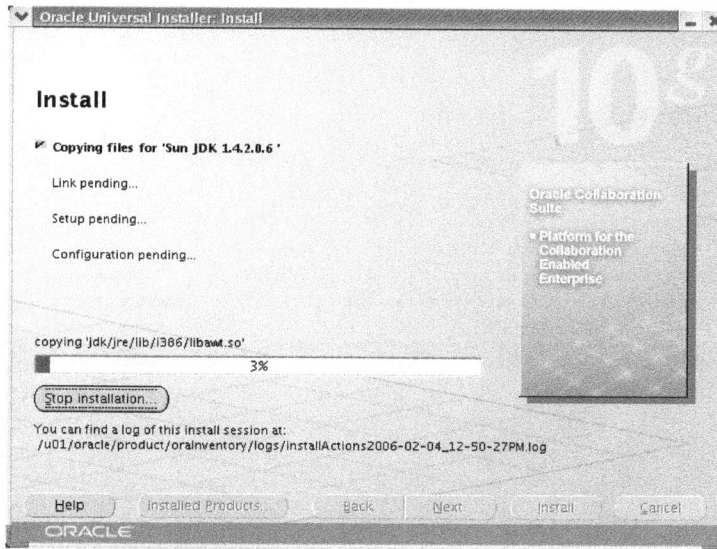

FIGURE 5-14. *Configuration Assistants screen*

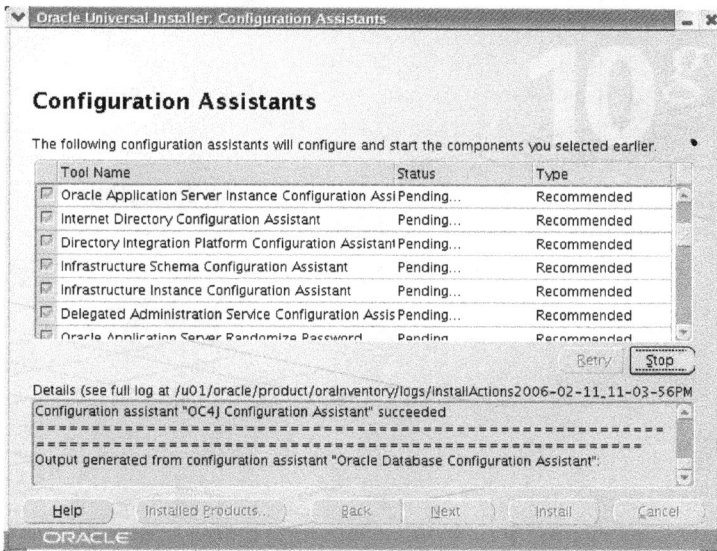

FIGURE 5-15. *Configuration Assistants Pending*

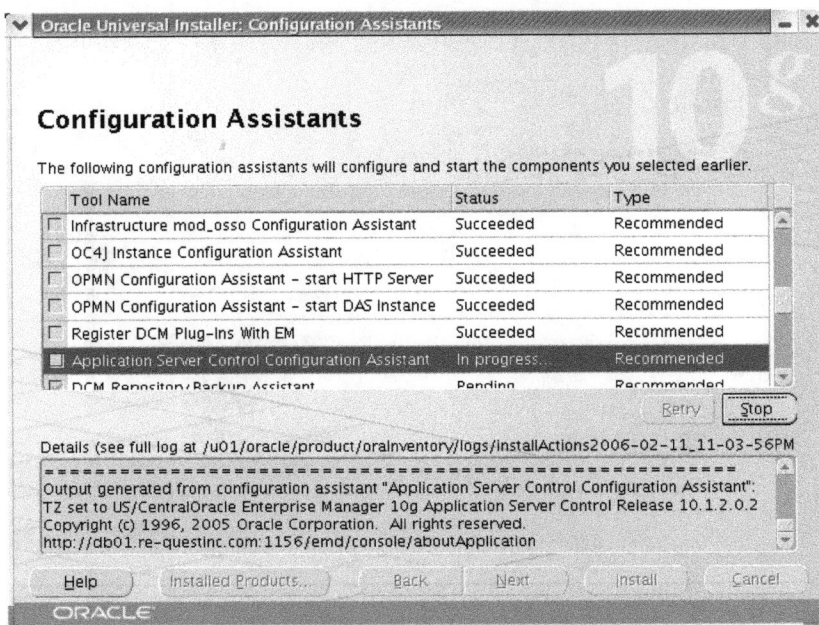

FIGURE 5-16. *Configuration Assistants Succeeded*

Once completed, the individual configuration assistants will show a status of Succeeded as seen in an already-running Configuration Assistant process illustrated in Figure 5-16. If for some reason they fail, a red Failed will show up in the status column.

Once the installation has completed, an End Of Installation screen will display, as shown in Figure 5-17, indicating whether the installation was successful and what the component URLs are for the installed environment.

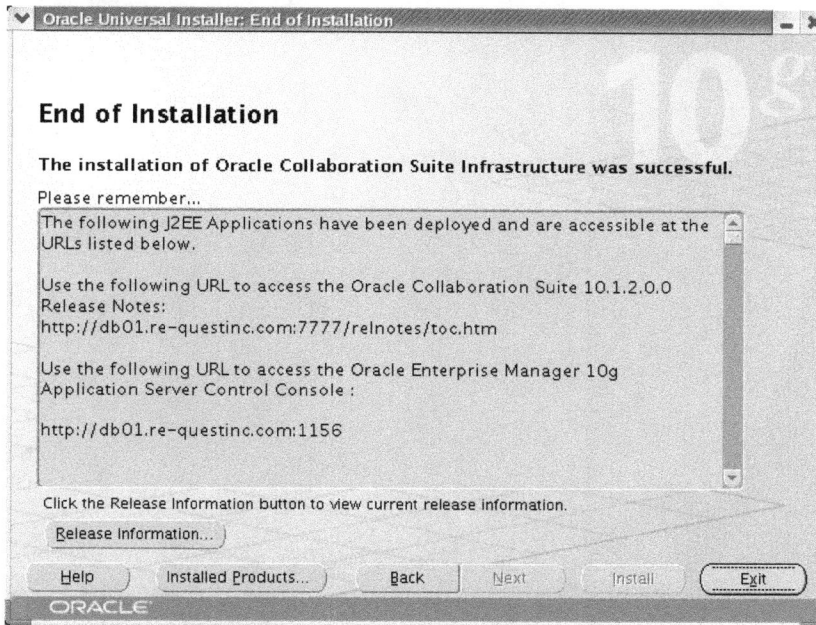

FIGURE 5-17. *End of Installation screen*

Summary

This completes the chapter on installing the Identity Management and Infrastructure components of the Oracle Collaboration Suite 10*g*. Next, we will explore installing the Oracle Collaboration Suite Applications Tier of the environment.

CHAPTER
6

Installing the
Applications Tier

You can have information and ease of use
and have artistic integrity at the same time.

—Mike Davidson

N ow that you have successfully installed the complete Oracle
Collaboration Suite 10*g* Infrastructure Tier, you can move on
to install the Oracle Collaboration Suite 10*g* Applications
Tier, also referred to as the Collaboration Suite 10*g* Middle
Tier and Applications. This chapter assumes that the installation
process has been followed as defined in the previous chapters and that a
Collaboration Suite Datastore and an Identity Management instance have
been successfully created and made available. Both are necessary in order
to successfully complete the installation of the Oracle Collaboration Suite
10*g* Applications Tier.

Getting Started

As with all other components of the Oracle Collaboration Suite 10*g* product,
I suggest precreating the Oracle Home directory structure. Then go to the
directory where the Oracle Collaboration Suite 10*g* install software has been
staged on the server/disk and type in the **./runInstaller** command. This will
bring up the same Installation Method screen as seen with the other Universal
Installer passes in the preceding two chapters. Again select the Advanced
Installation option as illustrated in Figure 6-1, since like the other installs
thus far, this will not be a Basic Install.

The Installation Process

Once the Advanced Installation option is selected, clicking Next will
navigate to the Specify Inventory directory and credentials screen shown in
Figure 6-2. (Note that if the Applications Tier is being installed on a server
that already has Oracle installed on it, this screen will not display.)

The Operating System group value should default to the group that was
assigned to the oracle operating system user when it was created prior to
staging the software (if not, exit the installer and verify that the operating

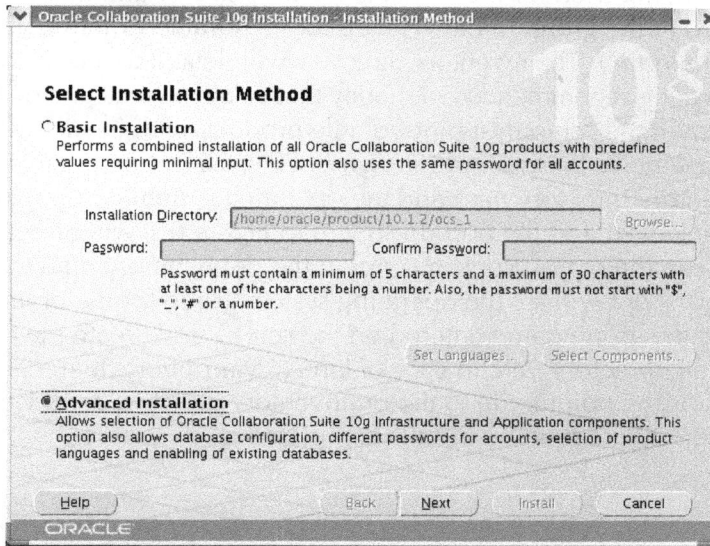

FIGURE 6-1. *Select Installation Method—Advanced Installation selected*

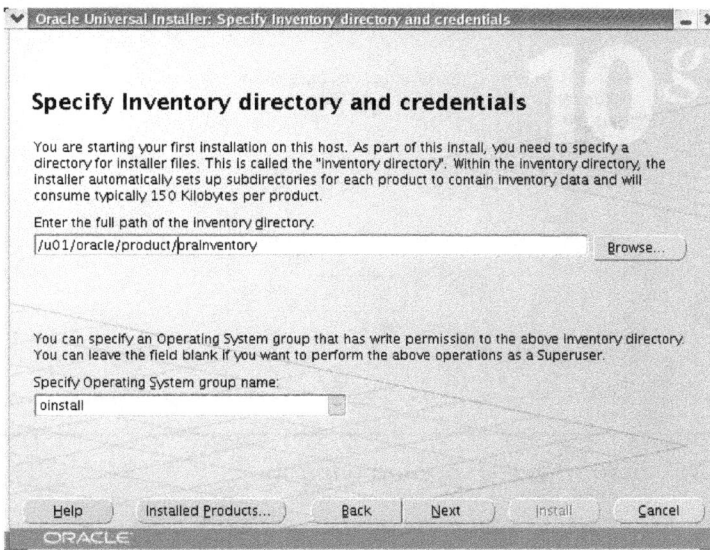

FIGURE 6-2. *Specify Inventory Directory And Credentials screen*

system user being used for the install is the proper user and that this user is still assigned to the group initially set up for the Oracle Collaboration Suite 10g software install). The inventory directory will default to /home/<os-user>/ oraInventory. It is recommended to modify that value to create the oraInventory directory down the /<mount-point>/oracle/product/ path in such a way that the value resembles the example shown in Figure 6-2. Once satisfied with the oraInventory directory path and the operating system group name entered, click Next and the pop-up shown in Figure 6-3 will direct the installer to run the orainstRoot.sh script in the oraInventory directory as root. Running this script will set the operating system group for the oraInventory directory to the group name entered on the screen and create the oraInst.loc file in the /etc directory (/etc in case of Linux, /var/opt/oracle in case of Solaris) that is the pointer file to the oraInventory directory for this install and all other Oracle product installs completed on this server.

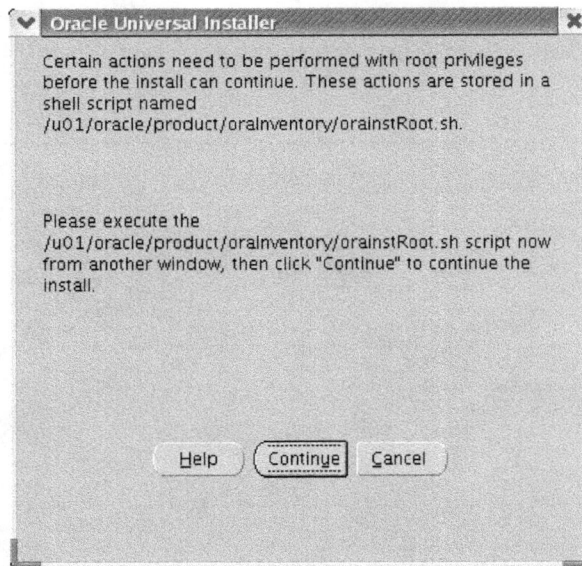

FIGURE 6-3. *orainstRoot.sh pop-up window*

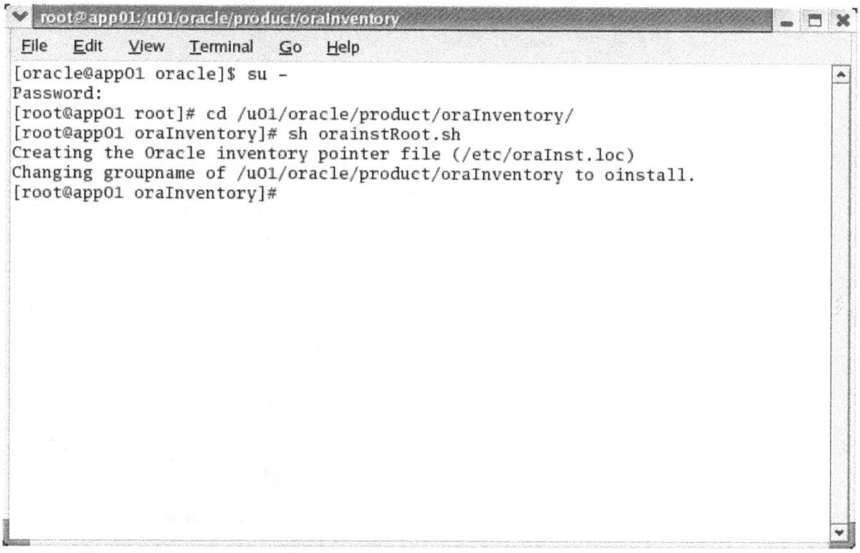

```
[oracle@app01 oracle]$ su -
Password:
[root@app01 root]# cd /u01/oracle/product/oraInventory/
[root@app01 oraInventory]# sh orainstRoot.sh
Creating the Oracle inventory pointer file (/etc/oraInst.loc)
Changing groupname of /u01/oracle/product/oraInventory to oinstall.
[root@app01 oraInventory]#
```

FIGURE 6-4. *Completed orainstRoot.sh shell script*

To run orainstRoot.sh, establish another operating system connection/
session as root, change directory to the oraInventory directory, and enter
either **./orainstRoot.sh** or **sh orainstRoot.sh** at the operating system prompt.
Once the script is completed, as shown in Figure 6-4, return to the pop-up
window and click Continue to remove the pop-up and move into the
Specify File Locations window shown in Figure 6-5.

Specifying File Locations

As with the other installations you went through in the previous chapters, if
the software is staged properly the Source directory should be correct. The
Oracle Home name should be modified as shown in Figure 6-5 to reflect
that this is the Apps or Middle Tier (using the 1 at the end is optional, but it
provides clarity in managing the environments later on if multiple Middle/
Applications Tiers are added to the architecture.) Then enter the complete
path of where to install the Oracle Collaboration Suite 10*g* Applications Tier
home directory on the server/disk.

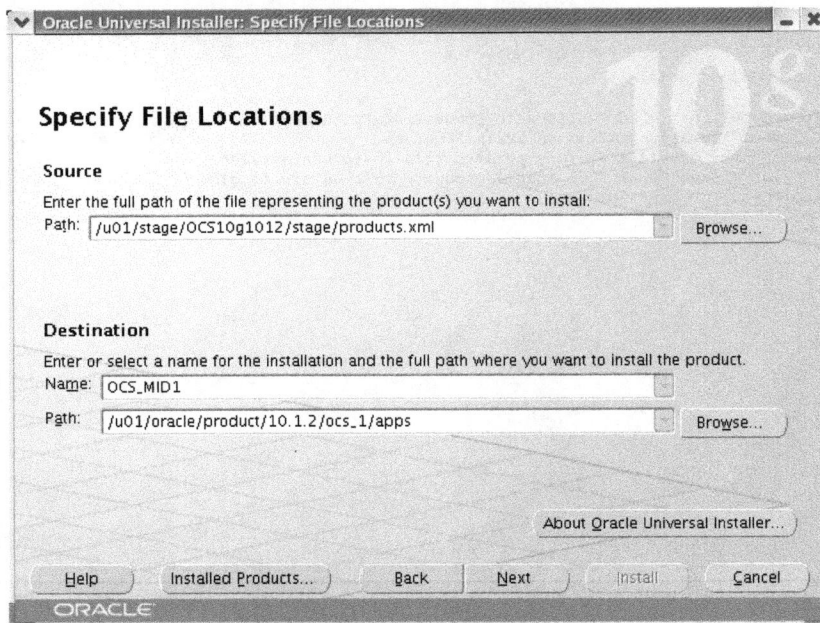

FIGURE 6-5. *Specify File Locations window for the Applications Tier install*

Selecting a Product

Once satisfied with the name and directory path for the Applications Tier Oracle Home, click Next to move to the next step in the Universal Installer process, the Product Selection screen, pictured in Figure 6-6.

Since it is assumed that all other necessary components of the Oracle Collaboration Suite 10*g* environment have already been installed, select the Oracle Collaboration Suite Applications 10.1.2.0.0 option as shown in Figure 6-6. Clicking Next here navigates the Universal Installer to where the Prerequisite Checks are performed on the operating system version, parameters, and installed packages. Again, just as in the previous installs, all checks should complete with a Succeeded status. If this is not the case, any issues

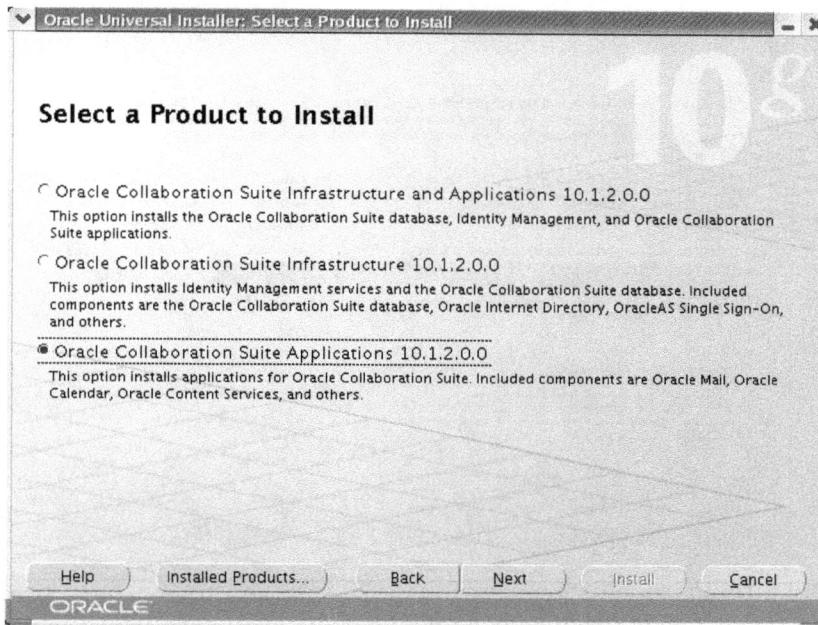

FIGURE 6-6. *The Product Selection screen*

should be rectified before continuing the install; otherwise, unpredictable (read *bad*) results may occur. An example of a prerequisite check completed successfully for all checks during an Applications Tier install is shown in Figure 6-7.

Selecting a Language

Once the prerequisite checks have been completed successfully, navigate on to the Language Selection screen shown in Figure 6-8 by clicking Next. Again, make sure to choose the same languages as chosen in the previous passes through the Universal Installer for the other tiers of this Oracle Collaboration Suite 10*g* install. Not matching the language choices up for all tiers in the same installation will present issues in terms of end users being able to use the languages later on.

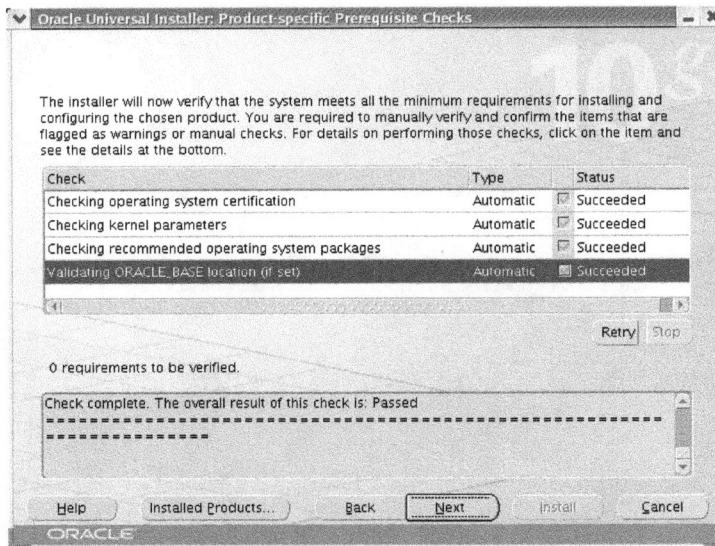

FIGURE 6-7. *Prerequisite Checks screen*

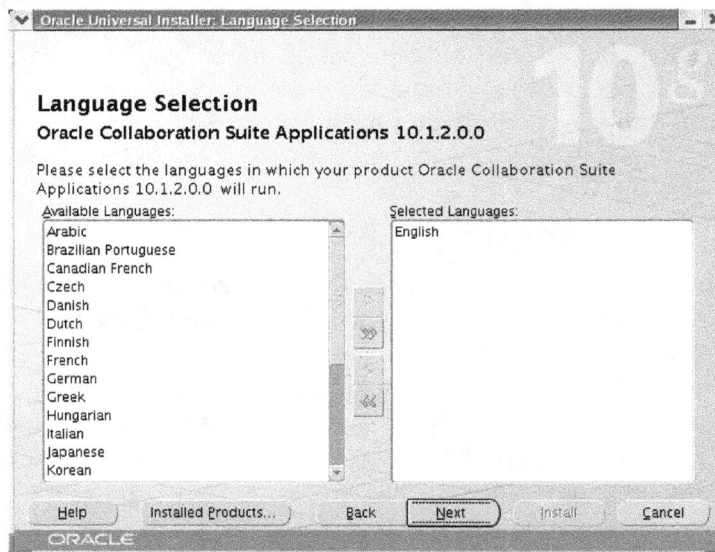

FIGURE 6-8. *Language Selection screen*

Selecting Components

Once all the languages to be installed have been selected, click Next to navigate to the Component Selection screen shown in Figure 6-9. This is where the installer needs to decide which components of the Oracle Collaboration Suite 10g Applications Tier are to be installed and configured during this Mid-Tier installation. By default all components are selected.

Now, here is some advice in terms of the component selection that has proved valuable for me in previous implementations. Even if there is not a plan to run all the components immediately in the environment, it is strongly recommended to install and configure all application components now and disable them later, rather than just picking the components planned for rollout today and assuming others can be added later. There are two reasons

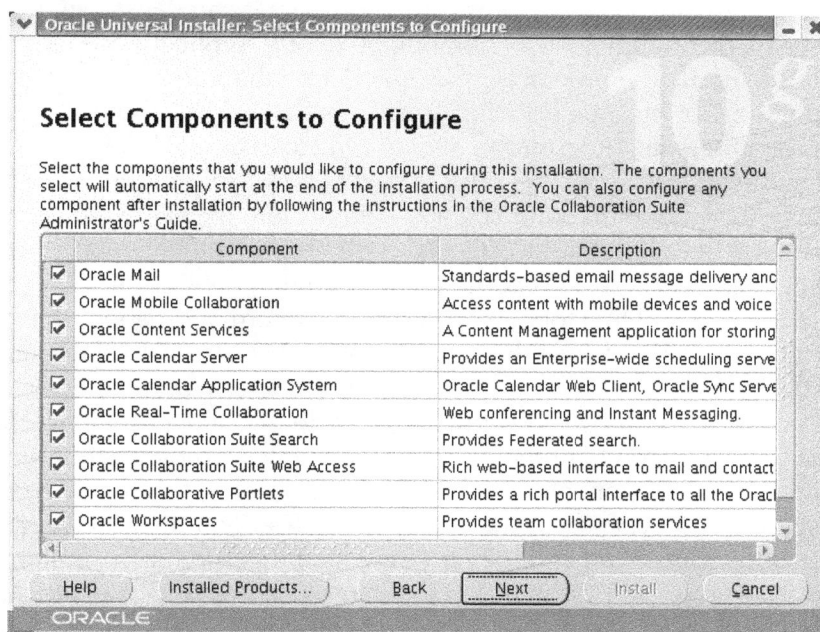

FIGURE 6-9. *Component Selection screen*

for this. First, there is a fair amount of dependency—necessary or not—between the objects of the various application components. In the past when either I or a client attempted an install that did not include the entire Applications Tier set of components, unpredictable results were observed. Second, it is extremely difficult, if not impossible, to add components at a later time, so if there is even a remote chance of rolling out a component in the future, just install and configure it from the beginning. There is always the option of either not provisioning that application to any user, or removing it from the welcome page, portal page, etc., so nobody can access it until the company is ready to make it available, if ever.

Registering the Instance

Once all the components to install/configure have been chosen, click Next to move to the Oracle Internet Directory registration screen. This is basically when the Universal Installer needs the server name and port where the Oracle Internet directory service is running so that it can register all the components of the Oracle Collaboration Suite 10*g* Applications Tier that are about to be installed. Remember, the Oracle Collaboration Suite 10*g* Infrastructure Tier must be installed, which includes a Collaboration Suite Datastore, a Metadata Repository, and an Oracle Internet Directory, prior to installing this Applications Tier. This is so the Universal Installer can register the Oracle Collaboration Suite 10*g* applications into the same Infrastructure Tier that Oracle Collaboration Suite 10*g* will use for authenticating users, providing application-level security, and presenting applications to users. The Oracle Internet Directory also holds status information about the background processes for all the components of the Oracle Collaboration Suite 10*g* Applications Tier, whether they are up or down, how they are administered, where they reside, etc. So, Oracle Collaboration Suite 10*g* uses the Oracle Internet Directory to hold not only user information but also application and component information. As shown in Figure 6-10, enter the hostname of the server where the Infrastructure Tier Identity Management component was installed and the port on which that service is running on that server. (Again, 389 is the non-SSL default, 636 is the SSL default, and both should be available if you followed the instructions under "Ports" in Chapter 3 and deleted references to their usage from the /etc/services file prior to executing the Identity Management portion of the Infrastructure Tier install.)

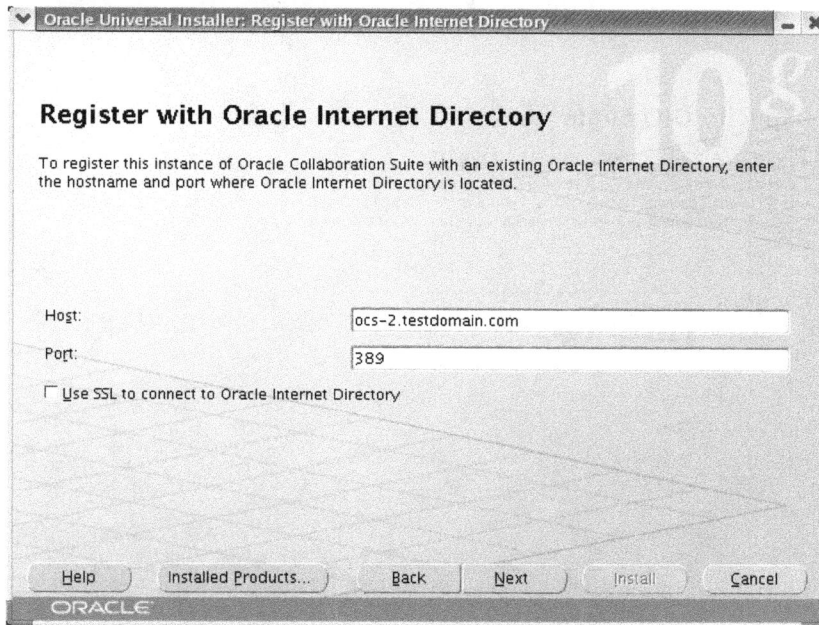

FIGURE 6-10. *Oracle Internet Directory Registration screen*

Specifying an OID Login

Clicking Next here will execute two steps. First, it will validate that the Universal Installer can connect to the Oracle Internet Directory through the provided server and port combination. If either the server or the port number is incorrect, the Universal Installer will display an error message, stating that it cannot find an Oracle Internet directory instance at the server/port specified. If they are both correct, the Universal Installer will move to the Specify OID Login screen as the second step. This screen, pictured in Figure 6-11, prompts for an Administrator Username and Password to connect to the Oracle Internet Directory location specified on the OID Registration screen. The default username for this and all purposes of managing Oracle Internet Directory information is cn=orcladmin, and the password is whatever you specified during the installation of the Oracle Identity Management component

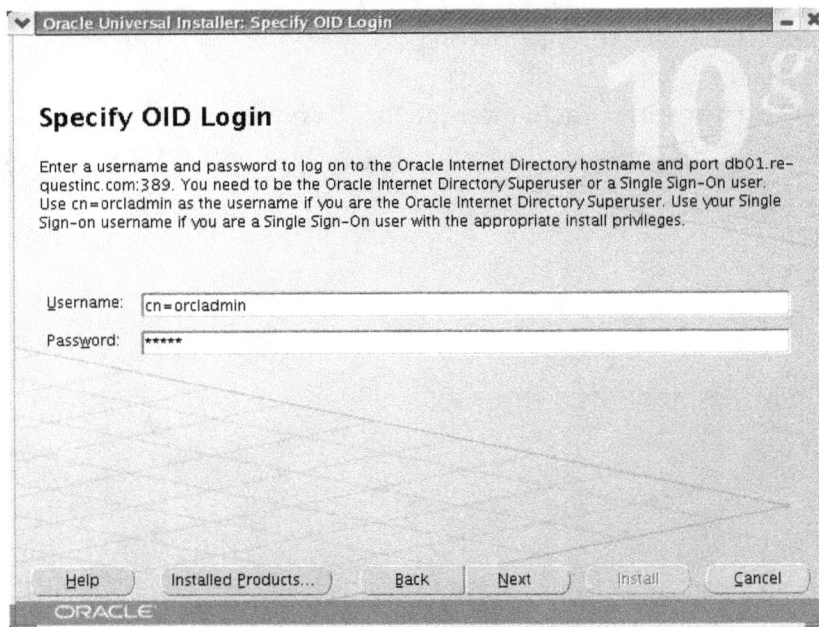

FIGURE 6-11. *Specify OID Login screen*

of the Infrastructure Tier from the preceding chapter. (Now you are beginning to see why it is recommended that *all* Administrative passwords in Oracle Collaboration Suite 10*g* be set to the same value initially!)

When the Username and Password values are populated, click Next, and the Universal Installer will once again validate everything by attempting to connect to the Oracle Internet Directory instance on the server and port provided in the previous screen with the Username and Password provided on this screen before it will allow the installation to continue. If either value—Username or Password—is incorrect, the install will not be allowed to progress further. Without available Oracle Internet Directory access the installation process will not be successful.

Selecting a Metadata Repository

If the validation of the Username, Password, Server Name, and Port value combination succeeds, the Universal Installer will move to the OracleAS Metadata Repository selection screen pictured in Figure 6-12. This information

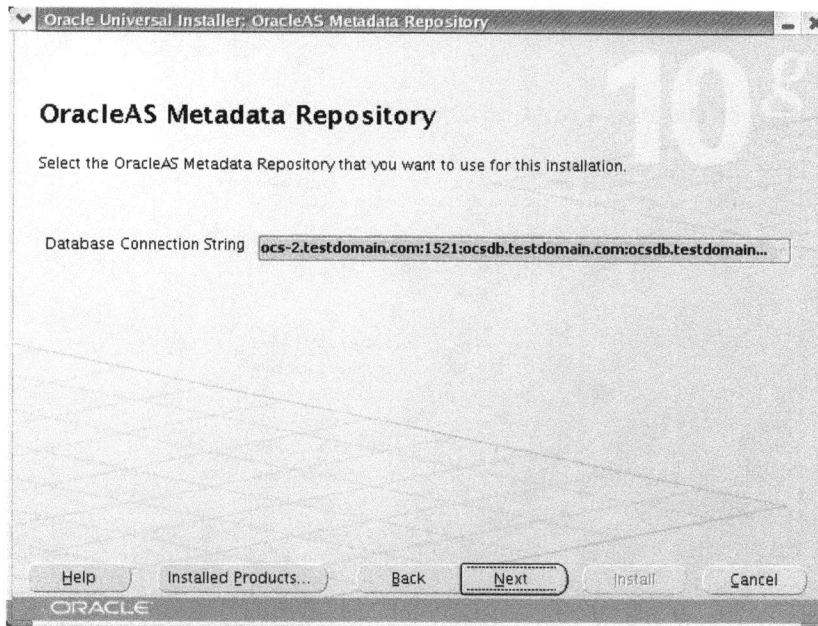

FIGURE 6-12.   *OracleAS Metadata Repository Selection screen*

was retrieved from the Oracle Internet Directory connected in the previous Installer step, where Metadata Repository information is stored for all Oracle Application Server instances. In the case of a stand-alone Oracle Collaboration Suite 10*g* installation, there will be only one Metadata Repository listed here, but if the Oracle Collaboration Suite 10*g* install is being run in an environment where an Oracle Application Server 10*g* Infrastructure Tier already exists, there may be more than one Metadata Repository to choose from in this list.

Selecting a Database for Components

For purposes of this book, I am going to assume there is only one choice here, so clicking Next will select the Metadata Repository listed as the only choice and navigate to the Select Database For Components screen shown in Figure 6-13. This screen is where the Installer needs the service name for

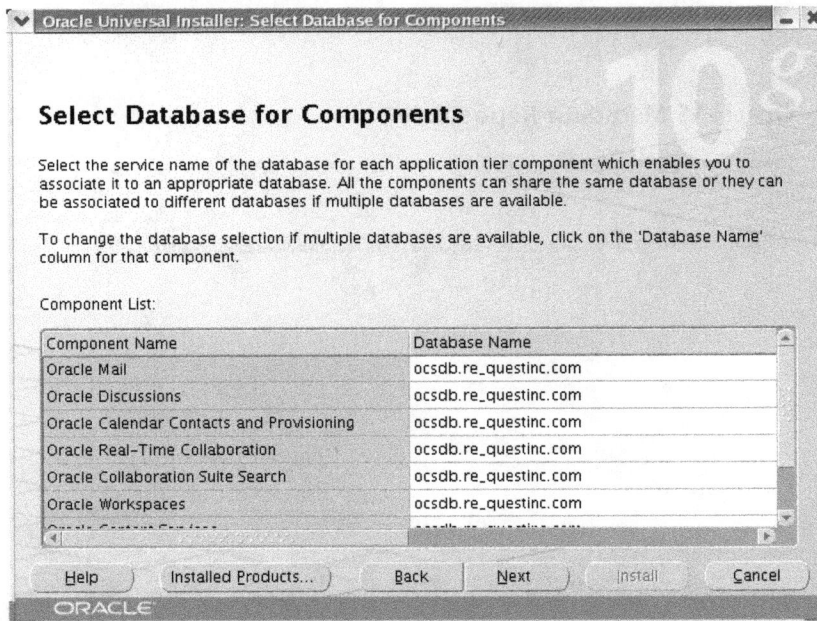

FIGURE 6-13. *Select Database For Components screen*

the database instance in which to install the schemas, database objects, seed
data, etc., associated with each Applications Tier component chosen on the
Component Selection screen earlier in this install pass. This value will
default to the service name for the database where the Collaboration Suite
10*g* database was installed as the first step in the overall install. The Installer
requires a Collaboration Suite database here, so unless there is another one
installed someplace else, leave the defaults and move on!

Specifying Port Configuration Options

Clicking Next from this screen navigates to the Specify Port Configuration
Options screen shown in Figure 6-14. This is exactly the same screen as
seen in the other passes through the Universal Installer you completed in the
previous chapters. You can either point the Universal Installer at a
staticports.ini file listing custom port preferences for the Applications Tier

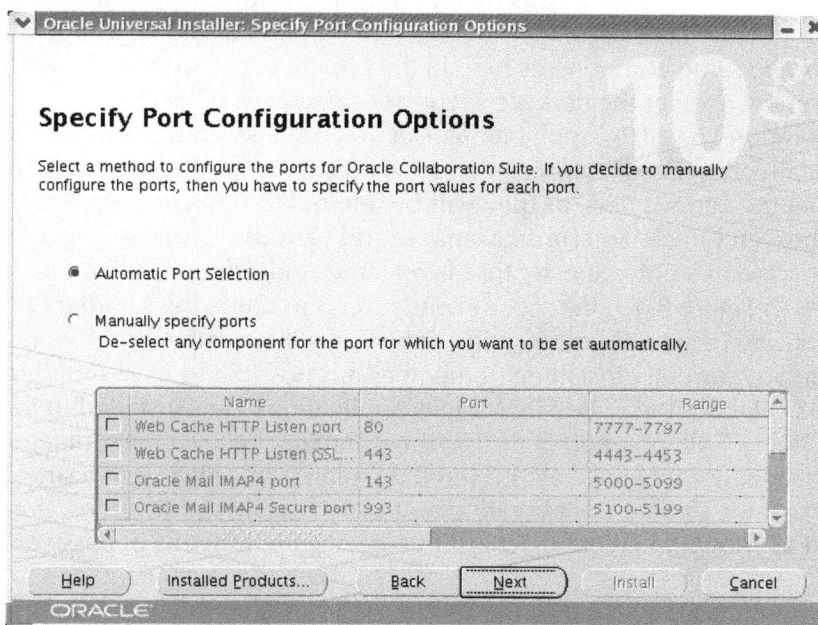

FIGURE 6-14.   *Specify Port Configuration Options screen*

components or accept the default port values determined by the Automatic Port Selection process. Again, it is recommended that rather than trying to provide a custom port list via the staticports.ini file on this screen, you actually make sure the standard default ports are available (for instance, port 389 for LDAP) so that the Universal Installer configures the components to use those default ports automatically.

Specifying an Instance Name and Administrative Password

Clicking Next here will navigate to the screen where the Installer wants an Instance Name and an Administrative Password specified. Without going too deep into the Oracle Application Server 10*g* architecture, it is important for anyone installing Oracle Collaboration Suite 10*g* to understand that it is the install process that actually installs a full-blown Oracle Application Server 10*g* environment, as well as a set of Collaboration applications on top of that

Oracle Application Server 10g environment. The Oracle Application Server 10g architecture consists of an Infrastructure Tier and a Middle Tier (hence the need for the same components here in the Oracle Collaboration Suite 10g environment, except the tiers are set up specifically to support the Collaboration Suite 10g Applications Tier you are installing in this chapter). The Installer requires the application server instances to be named when installing the various tiers, as they will be referred to by name when managing them through Oracle Enterprise Manager and various command-line tools. As shown in the example, Specify Instance Name And Administrative Password pictured in Figure 6-15, the recommendation is to name the Middle/Applications Tier instance ocs_mid$n$, where n is the number of the Middle Tier you are currently installing (remember it is possible to have multiple Oracle Collaboration Suite 10g Middle/Applications Tiers installed in the same Oracle Collaboration Suite 10g environment, each running different applications, components, etc.). Even if the plan is to only install a single instance of the Oracle Collaboration Suite 10g Middle/Applications Tier, name it as shown in Figure 6-15 just in case. Again, in terms of password

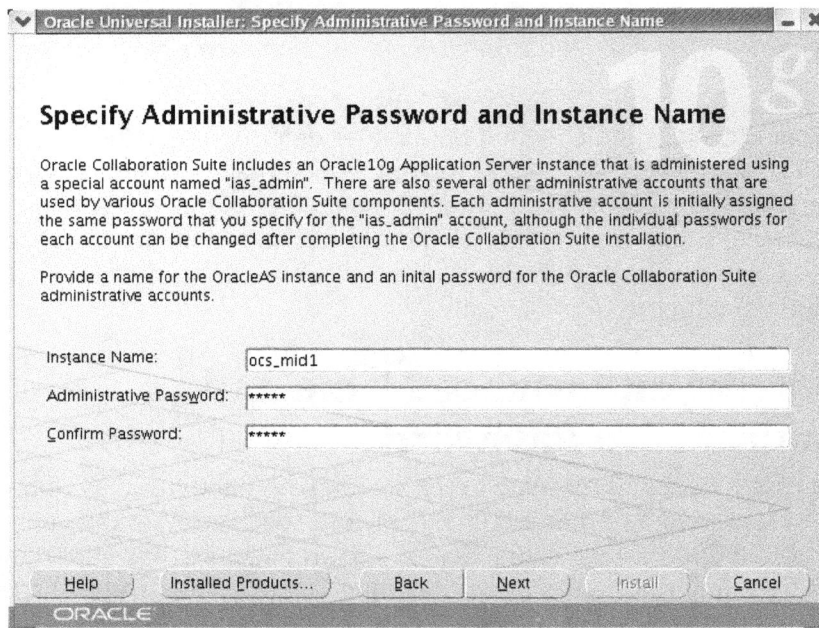

FIGURE 6-15. *Specify Instance Name And Administrative Password screen*

values, repeat after me . . . "Use the same password for *all* Administrative users within the Oracle Collaboration Suite 10*g* environment." So use the same password here for the ias_admin user (Middle/Applications Tier Administrator) that was used for the ias_admin user on the Infrastructure Tier, and for the sys and system database users, and the orcladmin user, etc.

Specifying a Calendar Server Host

Once you are satisfied with the Middle/Applications Tier instance name and ias_admin password, click Next to a) validate the Administrative Password field against the Confirm Password field to make sure the same value was entered twice in a row, and b) to navigate to the Oracle Calendar Host Alias screen shown in Figure 6-16. This value is defaulted to the hostname of your Middle/Applications Tier server but could be modified to be an Alias or Virtual hostname to accommodate the ability to move the Calendar Server instance to another physical machine at some point without having to attempt to deinstall and reinstall the Oracle Calendar Server. To use an alias,

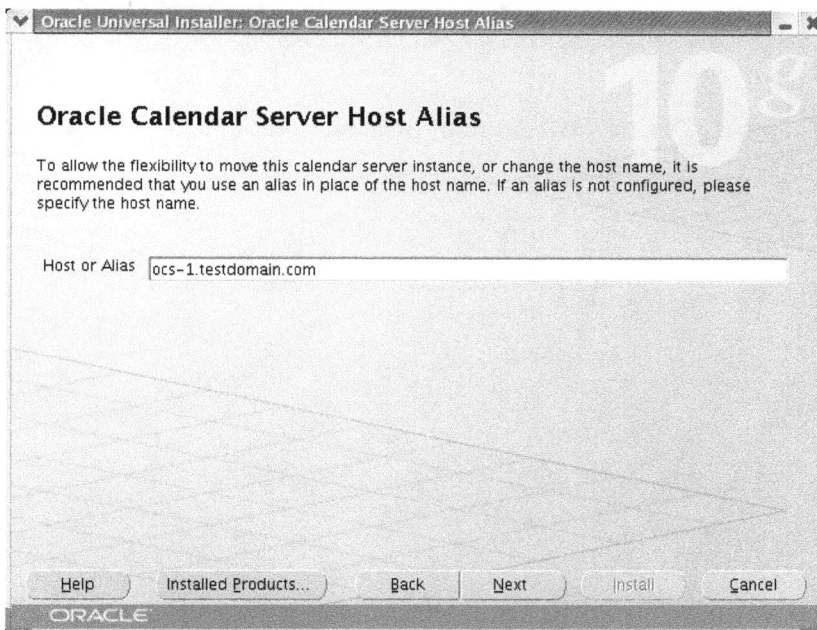

FIGURE 6-16.   *Oracle Calendar Host Alias screen*

you simply change the IP address to which the alias points (to the new physical server's IP address), migrate the Calendar Server instance to the new physical server, and start it up! The chances of having to do this exercise—moving the Calendar Server instance to another physical server—will be a product of how well that hardware was initially sized against the data and resource requirements of the user base. If the server was initially sized to hold 12 months of data for 50 users and it winds up having to support 500 users and allowing them to each retain five years of Oracle Calendar entries, then as was echoed from the communication of the then-in-trouble Apollo 13 spacecraft, "Houston, we have a problem." If, however, it is not anticipated to ever have to move Oracle Calendar, just use the server name for the Middle/Applications install and be done with it.

Specifying the Oracle Mail Domain

Once the Host or Alias value has been chosen, click Next to navigate to the Specify Oracle Mail Domain Information screen shown in Figure 6-17. This is extremely important to get correct if a company is planning on

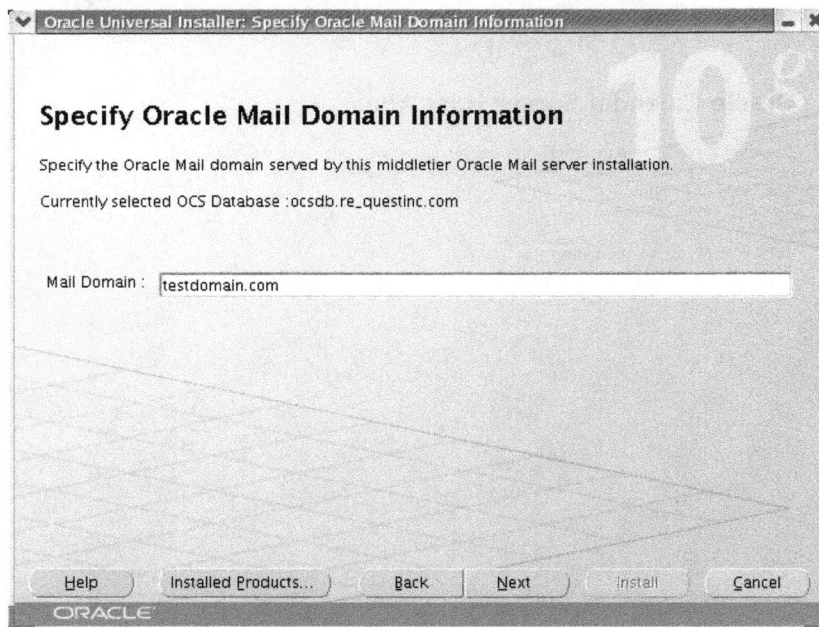

FIGURE 6-17. *Specify Oracle Mail Domain Information screen*

implementing Oracle Collaboration Suite 10*g* Email, as this defines the domain for email addresses, the email configuration, etc., during the installation/configuration process to follow shortly.

It is always possible, of course, to go in and manually configure an email domain at any time through the Administrative tools, but getting it right here makes life so much easier down the road.

Completing the Installation

Once the email domain name value has been determined and entered in the available field on the Specify Oracle Mail Domain Information screen, click Next to navigate to the Installation Summary screen shown in Figure 6-18. Just as in the other Universal Installer runs described in the previous chapters, this screen details what values were entered/determined during the pass through the Universal Installer screens, what applications are going to be installed, how much space they are going to take up, etc.; pretty much everything about the pending install process that was entered and would

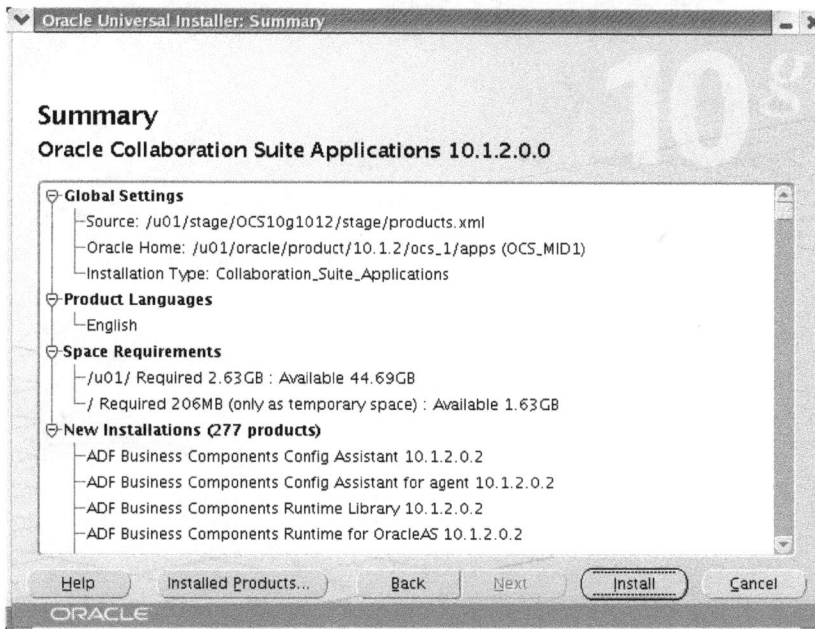

FIGURE 6-18. *Installation Summary*

need to be verified. Review the information carefully, and if something is incorrect or you are not satisfied with something, now is the time to use the Back button to navigate back through the Universal Installer screens and modify the answers and/or choices to make sure things are right *before* starting the installation process.

Once all the values have been verified, click the Install button to begin the Oracle Collaboration Suite 10*g* Applications installation process. An Install screen will appear just like the one pictured in Figure 6-19, showing the progress throughout the Copy, Link, Setup, and Configuration steps of the install process.

Once the Universal Installer has gone through the first three steps of copying the files for the install to the Oracle Home, linking all Oracle executables necessary in this operating system environment, and setting up for the configuration and when it is about to run the configuration assistants, it will again prompt, as shown in Figure 6-20, to run a script in the newly

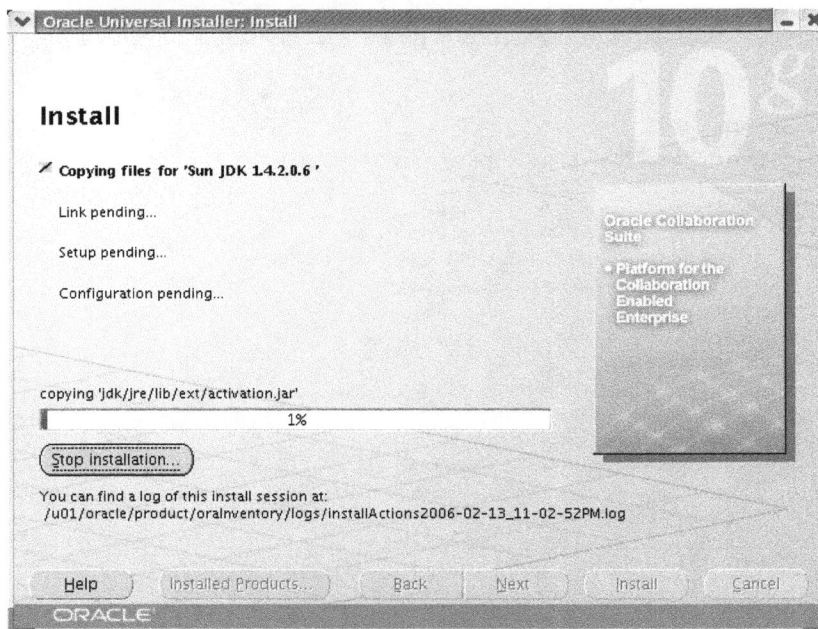

FIGURE 6-19. *Install Process screen*

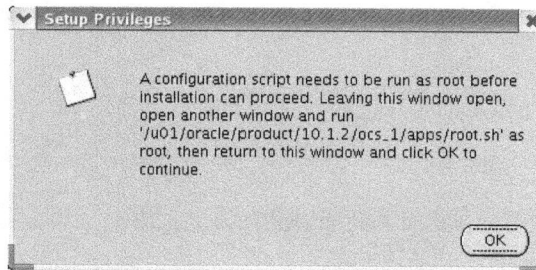

FIGURE 6-20.   *Run Script as Root User prompt*

defined Oracle Home for the Oracle Collaboration Suite 10*g* Applications Tier as the root user on the server.

Opening another connection to the server (or VNC window in the case of this install process), log in as root, change the directory to the specified directory, and execute the root.sh script. Accept the default value for the local bin directory (unless of course it is incorrect) and hit ENTER. The output of the script is shown in Figure 6-21.

FIGURE 6-21.   *Output of executing the root.sh script*

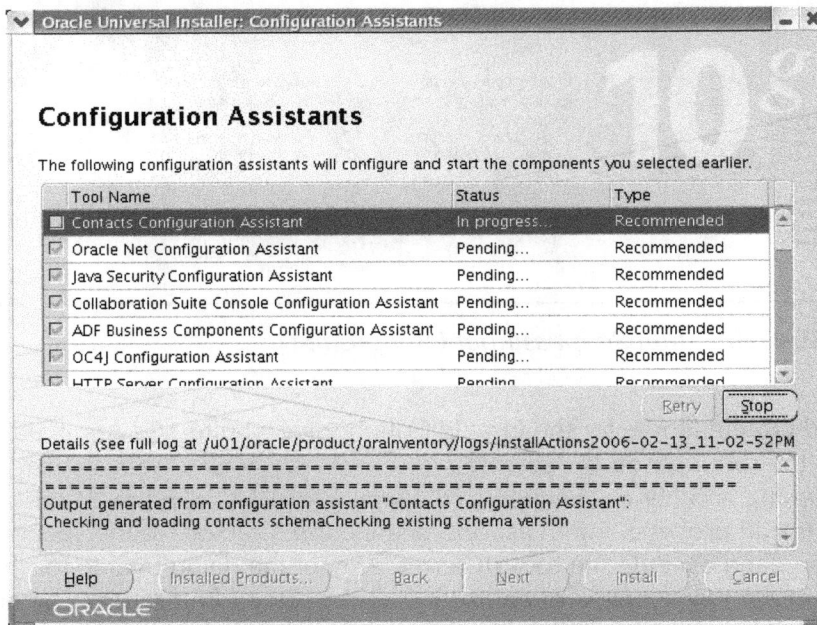

FIGURE 6-22. *Configuration Assistants screen*

After executing the root.sh script in another connection as root, click OK on the prompt window shown in Figure 6-20; the Configuration Assistants screen shown in Figure 6-22 will pop up and execute each configuration assistant as was defined by this pass through the Universal Installer. If there is an issue with a configuration assistant, an error message will display and the process will halt so that the issue can be reviewed and resolved; otherwise, an Installation Complete screen with values for URLs, ports, etc., will be displayed as in the other install processes.

Summary

Successfully completing the Applications Tier install concludes the installation process for the Oracle Collaboration Suite 10*g* product. Now that we have a successful installation, let's start the implementation!

CHAPTER
7

Migrating to the New
Oracle Collaboration
Suite 10g Environment

It is not the strongest of the species that survive,
nor the most intelligent, but the one most responsive to change.
                                                   —Charles Darwin

S o now that the soon-to-be production Oracle Collaboration Suite
10*g* environment has been successfully installed, you may be
thinking—to quote the singer Pink—"let's get this party started."
But, alas, now comes the "fun" part . . . the often ignored, and
always dreaded—or often ignored *because* it is dreaded—
migration process. Ignored because all us technical folks ever think about
when defining a successful implementation are lit-up servers, installs with
no errors in the log files, and shiny new applications showing up in someone's
browser. So, when we complete that install, man, life is good. But from an
end user's perspective, the most important—read *s-c-a-r-y*—part of a new
system implementation is always, "What is going to happen to my <insert
important data here>?" So, before you crack open the Dommie-P and
celebrate the success at the controls of the USS Oracle Universal Installer,
you need to take a step back and figure out how you get user definitions,
data, functionality mappings, etc., from the old system to the new system
(unless, of course, you are one of those lucky folks that isn't migrating from
anything or anywhere, to whom I say this is the time to go get a cold one
and watch the fellow Collaboration Suiters toil . . . we'll meet you at
Chapter 8, thank you very much!).

Seriously however, the concept—and effort—of a migration can be very
different for any implementation of Oracle Collaboration Suite 10*g*, big or
small. Each environment has its own definition and associated critical
components for a migration, which means each has its own unique set of
requirements, execution plan, test plan, and criteria for success. For some
it's getting every last email housed in their current Microsoft Exchange
environment into the same user's account on the new Oracle Collaboration
Suite 10*g* Email platform. For others it's using the migration to Oracle
Collaboration Suite 10*g* as an opportunity to force users to purge documents,
emails, attachments, whatever, such that their "stuff" (I loved that George
Carlin monologue on "stuff") fits into a certain size container, or is less than
two years old, or has been used within the last six months. Still others see
automating the creation of all usernames, passwords, and provisioning
of applications—anything so they don't have to type them in by hand—in
the new Oracle Collaboration suite 10*g* environment as their criteria for

a successful migration. Whatever the definition for migration and the criteria for its success, this chapter will hopefully expose the reader to things everyone should think about and plan for before beginning the migration and production rollout exercise.

As an informational note here in this chapter, the reference to the term *data* will be used generically to interchangeably exemplify email, calendar entries, files, user definitions, and profiles, depending upon the context in which it is used. The main concept to rationalize in this chapter is that the process of migrating from an existing legacy system to Oracle Collaboration Suite 10*g* has many possible constructs, mostly driven by factors of what data/functionality you are starting with or can extract from the current system(s) and what Oracle Collaboration Suite 10*g* components and functions you will be enabling and implementing.

Migration Planning Considerations

Just as it was important to architect, plan, and execute properly during the installation process for Oracle Collaboration Suite 10*g*, it is also extremely important to plan the migration process that will move both users and data from the legacy system(s) into the Oracle Collaboration Suite 10*g* system. There are many things to consider when planning for this type of migration, including who, what, when, and how to move users and data. In addition, you need to plan for technical requirements for the migration machine as well as the target environment (sometimes the horsepower required to migrate everything far exceeds what is required to support the user base in normal Oracle Collaboration Suite 10*g* operation once the migration is complete).

Migration Resources

Whenever you plan a migration, it is important to be realistic about how much you can get done in a given time period, or migration window. Properly setting the values for all the variables you have control over that are part of the migration is a critical component to the planning and execution of the migration process. You need to review each variable, determine its impact on the migration process in terms of time and effort, define acceptable but realistic values for those variables, and plug them into the migration equation. Okay, so you are probably wondering what the heck I'm talking about, right? Well, what I meant to say in plain English is that there are many variables that affect the overall size (read: timeline and complexity) of the migration, some of which have concrete values/limitations you have no control over, as well as others that you can control. Therefore, you must look at everything in the migration matrix and realistically base the choices for the variables you can control on the limitations you face for the variables you cannot control.

For example, there are environmental limitations such as the amount of memory and disk space that exist on the machine (PC or server) where you plan on running the migration tool/process. Because the migration is executed as a two-step process—premigration and then migration—the data extracted from the legacy system is held on an interim basis on the designated storage device of the migration machine. This means you can only migrate as much email such that all user data in a migration batch does not exceed the available storage on the migration machine (we will go into more detail around migration batches later, in the section "Migration Tools"). The memory required during the migration process is determined by several factors as well, such as size of messages and overall volume of data to be migrated, concurrency of the migration process with other migration processes running simultaneously, and the profile of the Datastore (whether the Datastore server is a slow processing machine with local disk and minimal memory or a monster server with fiber-attached SAN storage and gobs of memory will make a drastic difference in how quickly the Datastore instance accepts the migrated data). A good general guideline for the minimum amount of memory in the migration machine is 1GB of RAM, but if you are running a large migration process and wish to execute it on a single migration machine, it would be recommended to temporarily allocate a Windows server that has 4GB of RAM or more.

Bandwidth is another key limitation to the overall time the migration process will run. The bandwidth available between the legacy system and the migration machine is critical to migration processing speed. The higher the bandwidth between the legacy system and the migration machine, the faster the data will move between the two environments and therefore the faster the migration process will run. The smaller the "pipe" between the two systems, the slower the migration process will run. This means the migration window is effectively smaller, i.e., you can move less data in any given amount of time with a smaller "pipe" than you can with a bigger "pipe." The same holds true for the bandwidth available between the migration machine and the Oracle Collaboration Suite 10*g* system . . . the bigger the "pipe," the faster the process runs. Think of it as drinking though a straw. Regardless of how hard you draw on the straw, the amount of liquid you can take in will most likely be constrained by the size of the straw and not the ability to drink it. I recommend to many clients that they try to maximize available bandwidth during migrations, even if it means some type of short-term investment in network architecture during the migration process. For example, I recommend customers increase bandwidth by installing the fastest possible network cards into every machine in the environment (hopefully you did this already for the Oracle Collaboration Suite server[s] since they were just built), and even upgrading the router they are plugged into in the data center backbone to increase bandwidth. Today 100MB cards are extremely affordable, and it is also not uncommon to see Gig-E (short for Gigabit Ethernet) throughput in network cards in servers as well as throughout entire backbones—Gig-E routers, switches, etc.—in data center network architectures. It is even better if you invest in higher-bandwidth components and simultaneously create some type of "dedicated" network for the migration environment if possible. This includes adding high-bandwidth network cards to all legacy servers, all Oracle Collaboration Suite 10*g* servers, and any migration machines in the environment and plugging them all directly into a high-speed switch so that they can communicate directly over the fastest "pipe" possible. Using a dedicated network guarantees that all bandwidth in the network is available to communication between the legacy system and the migration machine and the migration machine and the Oracle Collaboration Suite 10*g* server(s). This also eliminates the concern with other things such as backups consuming network bandwidth during the migration process.

In addition, there are limitations on just how much processing power is available on the legacy system, the migration machine itself, and the Oracle Collaboration Suite 10*g* environment. It has been my experience that legacy systems have a couple of characteristics in common, especially if someone is replacing them and moving to a new environment. They are generally older machines and more often than not overworked. This means the migration process will be limited on the legacy system side by the horsepower available to execute the extraction tasks of the migration process. One way to increase processing power is by making the legacy system unavailable for normal user access during migration runs. This way, all processing power is dedicated to the migration process and not consumed by user requests. Also, the speed of the processor(s) in the migration machine will determine overall migration process performance as well. The faster the processor(s) in the migration machine, the faster the migration process will run, and vice versa. In addition, since you can group the users you are going to migrate, you can actually use multiple migration machines, so each machine can migrate its own set of users in parallel. This can give you some additional scale, but of course this approach is also limited by the available processing power of the source and target environments, as well as available bandwidth to/from the legacy environment.

The total number of users and the total amount of data (email, calendar and/or content services) that must be migrated are both driven more by business requirements than anything else; therefore, they could be considered concrete limitations to the overall migration process as well. However, the variables where some choice is available in this area include the number of users you migrate at one time compared to the amount of data each user has that needs to be migrated. This basically means it all comes down to planning the groups of users for migration such that they fit within the migration window defined by the limitations of the migration environment.

Clean-Up and Space Management During Migration

A migration to a new email and/or file system is a perfect opportunity to get everyone to clean up their old emails and files. Moving everything—every email, shared folder entry, saved file, etc.—that a user has currently saved is not very productive and will increase the overall amount of time and effort the migration will take. Also, the older the data, the higher the chance it will cause some type of issue during the migration process (for instance, older Microsoft Exchange emails were more susceptible to malformed headers that won't be accepted into the Oracle Collaboration Suite 10*g* Mail repository). I strongly suggest either enforcing a size limitation, i.e., telling the users "you will only be allowed to move a total of 10GB of email," or putting a date stamp limitation on them, such as only migrating emails that are one year old or newer, and only moving files that have been updated in the last six months (be careful with this one so that valuable information saved in files that doesn't need to be updated anymore, such as Board of Director meeting minutes and company policies, isn't inadvertently lost). If users still want to save things that fall outside the migration criteria, they can always archive information into .pst files for example (if they are using Outlook), but put a stake in the ground and only commit to moving the data that is necessary.

Another space management concept to consider when migrating to a new email and/or files solution like Oracle Collaboration Suite 10g is the implementation of quotas. Moving to a new environment when the user definitions are mass-created is a perfect opportunity to implement standard quotas across the board. I would take a look at my user base and calculate the average amount of space consumed across the entire group for email (do the same for files if you are implementing Content Services). If that amount is manageable, then make that the quota (how many people are in the user base, versus the number of very large space consumers, versus total space allocated to Oracle Collaboration Suite 10g may require adjustment to that number), or pick a manageable quota for each component based upon available space in the new environment and enforce that across the board, at least to start. Remember to account for at least 12 months worth of overall growth in this scenario. The last thing anyone wants immediately after going through the pain of moving to a new system that is supposed to manage information better and more efficiently than legacy systems is to have to requisition more hardware than was originally calculated for the first year.

However, take special note of a warning here. Regardless of how hard anyone tries to enforce the migration limitations and/or the standard quotas, someone of some importance—or someone suffering from squeaky wheel syndrome will complain to someone of said importance—that this is too limiting and they need their information, because it is important to the company, blah, blah, blah. Anyway, don't say I didn't warn you; be prepared to make exceptions.

Desktop Configuration

If the user base is using a desktop tool today, I think it is imperative for them to be allowed to continue to do so after the migration to Oracle Collaboration Suite 10g. Even though Oracle Collaboration Suite 10g Email Web Client is extremely robust and desktop-like in its functionality, unless there is some company edict about moving to web-based interfaces only, users asked to move out of their comfort zone will require a large amount of premigration testing, training, and familiarization in the form of more detailed user documentation and a longer proof-of-concept phase. Remember, as I have discussed numerous times in this book, user happiness equals project success, so spend the time with the integration to their desktop tool instead of convincing them that the Web Client will work.

If users are using Microsoft Outlook, the download and installation of the Outlook Connector is pretty straightforward and really works close to 100 percent of the time. However, I would suggest going out to the Oracle Technology Network site, downloading the latest version of the Outlook Connector, and replacing the one that comes with the Oracle Collaboration Suite 10*g* install with the most recent version downloaded from OTN. The file comes loaded into the $ORACLE_HOME/Apache/Apache/htdocs/ clientsdl/Calendar/OutlookConnector/ directory on the Applications Tier, so rename the con_outlook_ <version>.exe file that exists there and replace it with the one you downloaded from OTN. This way, all the users can make the download themselves if you wish.

For other desktop tools such as Outlook Express, Mozilla Thunderbird, and Netscape Mail, the setup is identical to how access was set up to the existing email system for these tools. Simply populate the POP or IMAP and SMTP server name fields with the Oracle Collaboration Suite 10*g* Application tier server name and fill out the rest of the user-specific information.

Admin and User Training

Administrator and User training is a critical component in the migration plan. I would say that for the most part the Oracle Collaboration Suite 10*g* Web Access Client is pretty intuitive for people used to using a web interface, so user training might be overkill in certain situations. In most cases a document created from screen prints with detailed text and good examples would suffice for user training. However, moving users to a new environment without properly training the folks that are to be the Administrators is a disaster waiting to happen. I highly recommend involving the targeted Administrator(s) in the Oracle Collaboration Suite 10*g* implementation and migration process as a start, but knowledge transfer on Administrative tools and considerations is also very important. I will cover the administrative concepts in a later chapter, but make sure the chosen implementation firm is contracted for administrative knowledge transfer, or go directly to Oracle University for official Oracle Collaboration Suite 10*g* training classes.

Phasing the Migration

I highly recommend to every organization I work with to phase their migration over several weeks and several sets of users. This approach is critical to success, in my opinion. Unless there is only have a handful of users (under 50) and they are all using desktop interfaces for email and calendar functionality (and plan to keep it that way), break the users up into logical groups to minimize any disruptions in communication between members of the same organizational unit and migrate the groups over a period of time. Make sure everyone involved in the migration feels comfortable about providing support for the migrated users while at the same time still staying on track with the migration schedule for the remaining users. Logical user groups could be anything, but typically doing a department or team at a time makes sense, or lining up users so the migration is always moving about the same amount of data each time is another effective migration grouping strategy. Moving too many users at once opens the migration team up to being overwhelmed with end-user questions or issues, and also provides for the opportunity for more—or bigger—things to go wrong during each migration group.

Types of Migrations

As mentioned in the preceding introduction, there are many requirements, processes, and definitions that fit into the broad category of performing a migration when moving an enterprise into a widely functional solution such as Oracle Collaboration Suite 10*g*. In addition, there are also many factors that determine the type and/or depth of a migration:

- The type of system users are being migrated from

- The type of data the enterprise can/wants to migrate

- The amount of data there is in relation to the space available for migration to Collaboration Suite 10*g*

- The different types of functionality the user base is starting with versus what functionality to implement in the new environment

It is truly a paradigm of choices and factors that determine the proper approach for moving from the current legacy system to going live on Oracle Collaboration Suite 10*g*.

Migrating User Definitions

Whenever and wherever possible I recommend automating the process of creating users in the Oracle Collaboration Suite 10*g* system during the migration process. There are several possible ways to accomplish this, but each depends upon two critical requirements: 1) does the source system have users defined in a manner that they can be extracted into a usable format that can be migrated to Oracle Collaboration Suite 10g, and 2) is there an approach and/or a tool available to complete the extraction on the legacy system side of the equation, and a counterpart to accept the extracted information and successfully load it into Oracle Collaboration Suite 10g Identity Management?

The most common—and easiest—approach to user migration into Oracle Collaboration Suite 10g is to use the Oracle Collaboration Suite Email Migration tool to extract user definitions from the legacy system and provision them into Oracle Collaboration Suite 10g Identity Management. Even if email data is not being migrated from a legacy system, the Email Migration tool provides an easy-to-use Java-based interface to assist the management of the user provisioning process. Another approach—if user definitions are stored in LDAP and someone in the organization has LDAP experience—is to use standard LDAP commands like *ldapsearch* against the legacy system user directory to extract user profiles into an ldif file. That ldif file can then be converted into an entry format compatible with the Oracle Collaboration Suite 10g Identity Management by running the LDAP command *ldifmigrator* provided in the $ORACLE_HOME/bin directory of the Infrastructure Tier. Once converted, the users can finally be loaded into the Oracle Collaboration Suite 10g Identity Management using LDAP command *ldapadd,* also provided in the $ORACLE_HOME/bin directory of the Infrastructure Tier Oracle Home ($ORACLE_HOME/bin where $ORACLE_HOME=/<mount-point>/<infrastructure tier oracle directory>/).

If the legacy system is not LDAP enabled, one of these two options can still used to provision the users, but source user profile definitions need to be created in an ldif file manually, and then one of these tools will need to be used to get the user definitions into Oracle Collaboration Suite 10g Identity Management. Each option has its own expected format for the input ldif file. The Email Migration tool expects the user profile information to be defined in a file named user_profiles.ldif, which must be placed in the C:\ocs\oes\migration\files directory on the migration machine prior to running the Email Migration tool (I cover this in detail in the later section "Migration Tools"). The LDAP command option is of course less formal, since the user specifically tells it what the filename is and where it is located during execution of the specific LDAP command at the command line.

One other option for user provisioning is to execute a bulk user load through the Oracle Identity Management Self-Service console. Basically this works the same as using the LDAP commands from the command line, but instead of placing an exactly named file in a specific directory, the user browses for the file location for the ldif file into the Self-Service page and tells it to bulk-create the users. The process works like this: As a migration team member with OID Administrator access, log in to the Oracle Identity Management Self-Service Provisioning Console as orcladmin (or another LDAP Administrator). Initially you will be placed on the main page for the Provisioning console as shown in Figure 7-1.

Click the Bulk button in the Users section of the page to go to the Bulk load page shown in Figure 7-2 and then click Browse and navigate to the location on their PC where the ldif file is located for the users to be

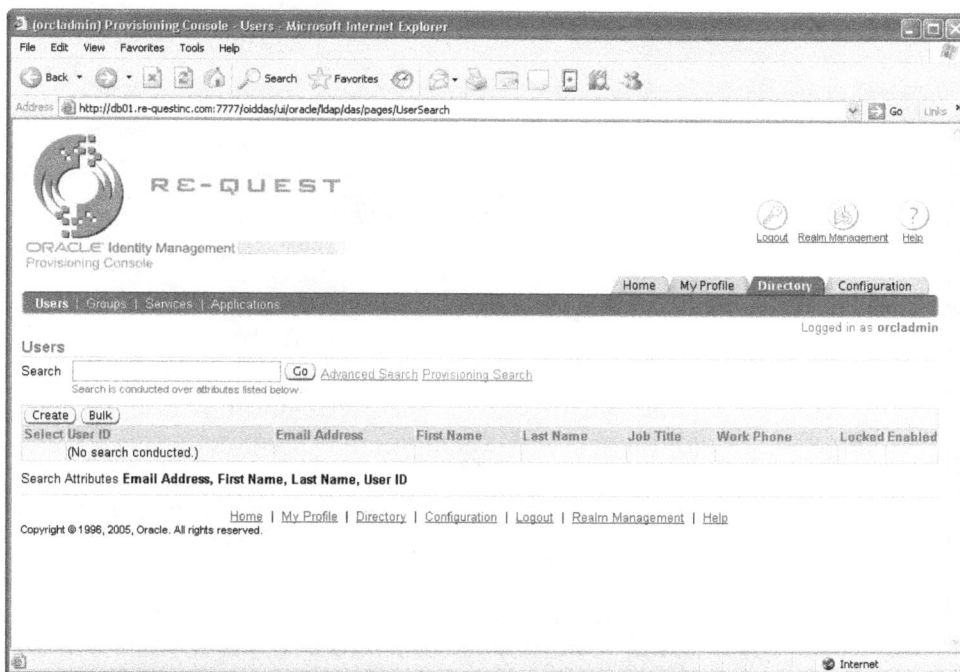

FIGURE 7-1. *Oracle Identity Management Self-Service Provisioning Console Main page*

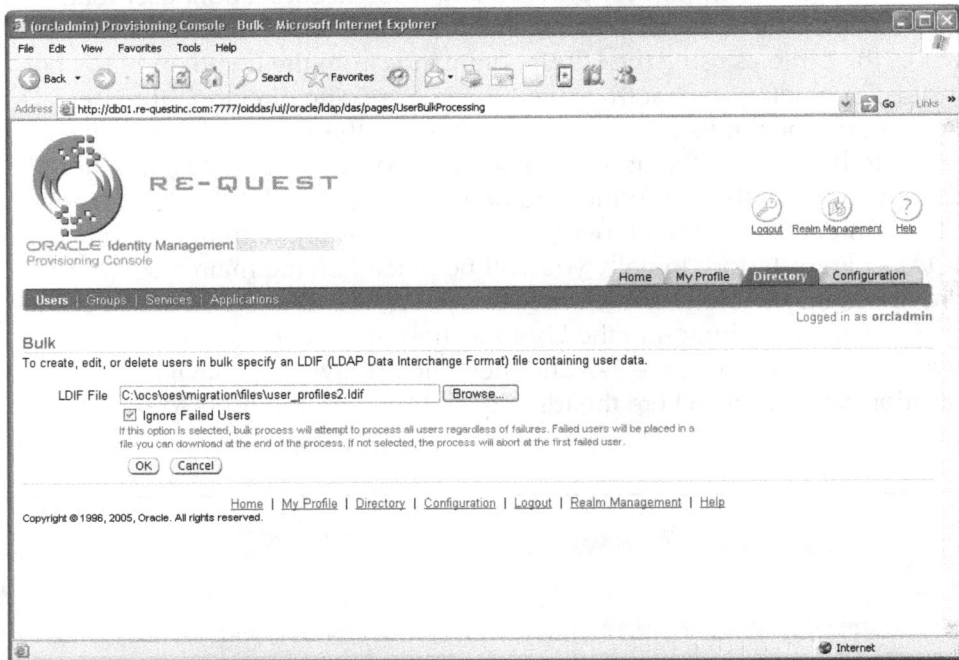

FIGURE 7-2. *Oracle Identity Management Bulk User Load page*

provisioned (or this can be accessed right from the migration machine, keeping all user profile definitions in one place). Highlight the file and click OK to come back to the Bulk Load page. I suggest leaving the Ignore Failed Users box checked so that at least some of the users—those whose data is without errors—get provisioned. It will put the users it cannot provision in another file called <ldif-file-name>.ldif.failed.

Once the process completes, you will get a page with information on the bulk load process as shown in Figure 7-3. You can click the individual filenames to view them there in the browser.

When users are provisioned into the Oracle Collaboration Suite 10*g* Identity Management in the default container (cn=Users, dn=<domainname>, dn=<.com, .org, .edu>), background DIP (Directory Integration Processes) processes run and provision the individual user for each Oracle Collaboration Suite 10*g* Component enabled for default provisioning (for example, Email, RTC, Files).

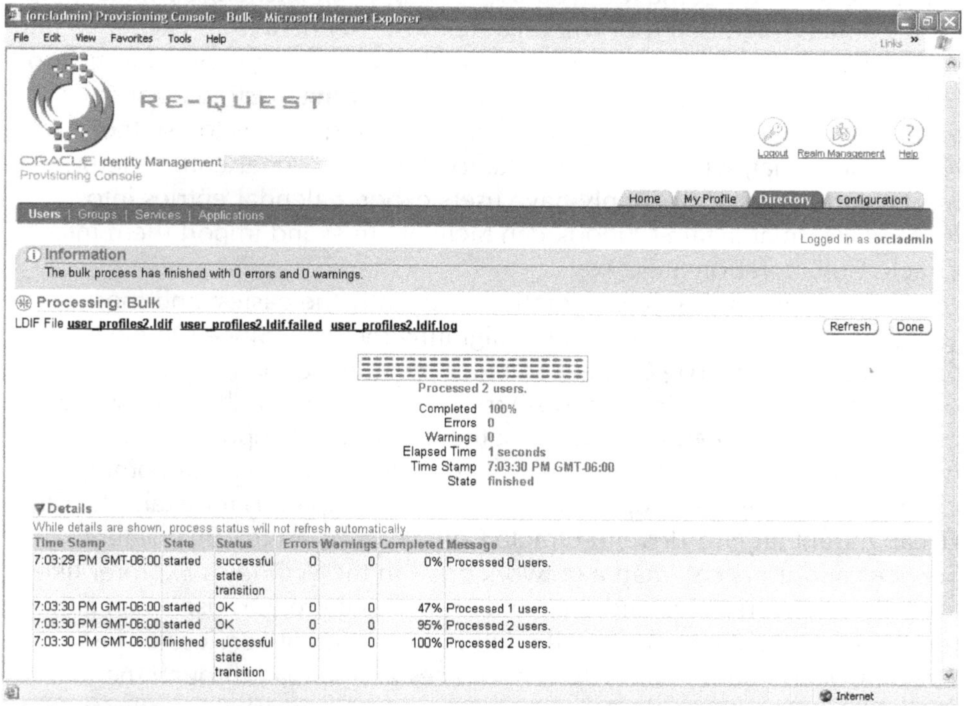

FIGURE 7-3.   *Bulk User Load Processing Summary page*

Data Migration

Once the approach for user definition migration is finalized, it is imperative to focus on what data is going to be migrated. Email is critical information to a company today, so in most cases, if implementing Oracle Collaboration Suite 10*g* Mail is part of the plan, there is an email migration in the plan as well. How much and when? See the previous section "Migration Planning Considerations" for some ideas.

Calendar entries are another story. There are tools/techniques available if the current company-wide calendar system is Exchange or Steltor (Steltor is the Calendar product Oracle purchased and integrated into Oracle Collaboration Suite). The Calendar data can be easily migrated from

Exchange using the same tool you use for migrating Exchange emails. (The Oracle Email Migration tool will migrate most user data from Exchange into Oracle Collaboration Suite including emails, calendar entries, address book entries, and server-side rules.) Otherwise, converting existing calendar entries is very time-consuming and difficult. One option is to use the iCalendar format, which is a universal format for calendar entries across most calendar systems. Simply have users export calendar entries into iCalendar format (again Outlook can facilitate this) and import them into Oracle Collaboration Suite 10*g*.

Files or Content Services migration is actually the easiest and most straightforward in terms of actually migrating the data. Since Oracle Collaboration Suite 10*g* Content Services provides so many options in terms of how the files stored in the repository can be accessed, that means it also provides as many options for loading the files into the repository. Users can map a drive using Oracle Drive (I will cover this setup in an upcoming chapter) and drag and drop files as in Windows Explorer, for example. Or, IT can mount an NFS drive to Oracle Collaboration Suite 10*g* Content Services and users can map a network drive in the Windows Explorer like any other network drive and drag and drop files there. Or, users can either use the web interface to access the full-blown Content Services or just Oracle Collaboration Suite 10*g* Workspaces and upload through the available tools in the web client. Nothing special is needed in order to move files into Oracle Collaboration Suite 10*g* Content Services other than the proper connection or tool setup and security to put them where they should be stored. My recommendation is to get people using Oracle Drive right away, since it is the least intrusive into the environment (uses cookieless WebDav protocol) and most user-friendly, because it doesn't require anyone to learn any new user interfaces.

Legacy Source System (Exchange, Lotus, GroupWise, Mbox)

The legacy source system a company is migrating from will in many cases determine many of the choices during the migration, as well as what can be migrated. Remember, the Email Migration tool uses plug-ins for the various legacy environments it supports, so the types of objects that are migrated are determined by the plug-ins. Therefore, the objects that can be migrated depend on the source system availability as well as the ability of the associated plug-in to migrate that object. For example, public aliases cannot be migrated from Microsoft Exchange (any version from 5.0 through 2003) but can be migrated from Novell GroupWise and Samsung Contact, while server-side rules can be migrated from all versions of Microsoft Exchange but not from Novell GroupWise or Samsung Contact.

To offer a complete picture of what types of migration are available from each legacy platform, Oracle has published a matrix in their Migration and Coexistence Guide available for download from the Oracle Technology Network Oracle Collaboration Suite 10*g* documentation section.

Migration Tools

One of the first things to understand when approaching a migration such as this is what tools are available to help complete the task at hand. In terms of Oracle Collaboration Suite 10*g* there are really only two choices: the Oracle Collaboration Suite 10*g* Email Migration tool and custom home-grown tools such as ldif scripting. Each has its value depending upon the variables you are presented with in a given migration scenario.

Email Migration Tool (ExMigrate)

By far the best choice for a tool to assist in the migration to Oracle Collaboration Suite 10*g*, provided you are migrating from one of the supported source systems, is the Email Migration tool—also known as ExMigrate—that comes with the Oracle Collaboration Suite 10*g* product. Not only does it provide the base extraction and load functionality for Email and Calendar data (certain platforms only—see the section "Calendar Migration Tools" later in this chapter), but it also will extract user profile definitions and allow you to manage the entire migration process by using its framework for two-pass migration, grouping, and batch processing. The current supported source platforms that you can migrate from using the Email Migration tool are Microsoft Exchange Server (5.0, 5.5, 2000, and 2003), Lotus Domino Server (release 5), Novell GroupWise (6.0), HP OpenMail (now known as Samsung Contact 7.1.0), and any IMAP4 rev1–compliant email server.

ExMigrate can only be installed on a Windows 2000 or XP machine (Server or Workstation), and the Outlook client is also required. It also cannot be installed on any server running Microsoft Exchange, including the server you plan on migrating from in an Exchange migration.

My advice is to do a Metalink search for the ExMigrate tool, or simply open an SR (Support Request) on Metalink and ask what the patch number is for the latest version of the Email Migration tool. I would provide a patch number here, but chances are that by the time this book gets into your hands, the tool will be updated, and therefore so will the patch number. Anyway, once the patch number for the latest version of the tool is provided by Support, click the Patches and Updates tab on the top of the Metalink page, choose the Simple Search link, and enter the patch number in the search field. Once it displays the patch info, click Download and save it to disk somewhere that it can be retrieved in a few minutes during setup.

Some helpful tips for installing the Oracle Collaboration Suite 10*g* Email Migration tool:

- If the company is migrating from Exchange, it is critical to have the machine where you install the Email Migration tool in the same domain as the Exchange Server data is being migrated from, but it cannot run on same server where Exchange Server is running.

- Download and install the Outlook Connector on the migration machine. The ExMigrate tool uses Microsoft Outlook and the Outlook Connector to move data between the Exchange and Oracle Collaboration Suite 10*g* environments.

- Create a directory directly off the root of C:\ (call it ocs or oracle . . . I *always* use ocs) to be used as the Oracle Home directory, and pre-create the \oes\migration directory structure under it. This tool setup is not dynamic, and the migrate.cmd file assumes this directory structure is in place and the ORACLE_HOME environmental variable is set. Also, make sure the directory path names don't have any spaces in them.

- Copy the Zip file downloaded from the Metalink patch into the C:\ocs\oes\migration directory, and extract it there. It will create several subdirectories to the migration directory, such as /bin, /files, /log etc.

- A Java runtime environment needs to be installed (1.4.2 or higher) for the migration tool to function. The Email Migration tool requires the JREHOME environmental variable be set prior to the tool being started, or it won't start up.

- Set the ORACLE_HOME variable to the initial directory created in an earlier step (Ex: C:\ > set ORACLE_HOME=C:\ocs) in a command window on the migration machine.

- Set the JREHOME environmental variable to the location where the JRE was installed (for example, set JREHOME=C:\Program Files\ Java\jre1.5.0_06).

Once the install and environment setup has been completed as described in the preceding steps, the ExMigrate tool is ready for use. Depending upon the source system and what is being migrated (users, email, calendar entries, or a combination), the following detailed information regarding the Email Migration tool may vary slightly from what is actually seen. I refer you to the Oracle Collaboration Suite 10*g* Migration and Coexistence Guide for further details on all possible configurations of the Email Migration tool.

To begin, open a command window on the migration machine, change directories to the %ORACLE_HOME%/oes/migration/bin directory, and type **migrate.cmd** as shown in Figure 7-4.

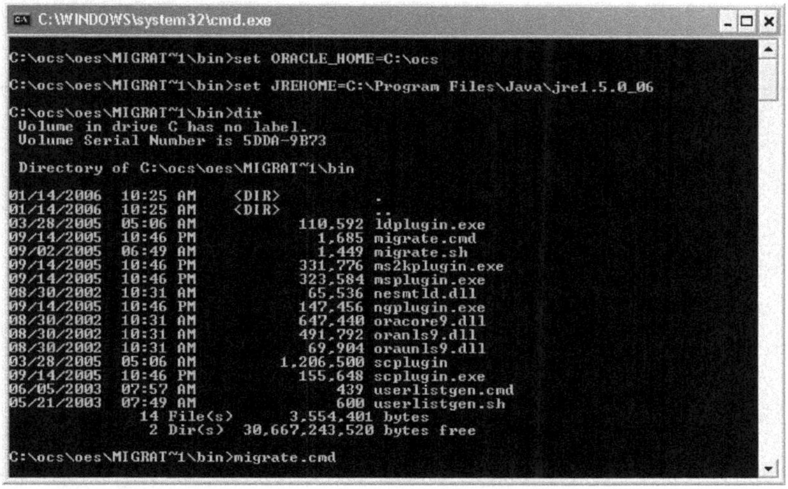

FIGURE 7-4. *Setting the environment and starting the Email Migration tool*

If the environmental variables have been set correctly and the installation of the patch file completed properly, the initial Java screen for the Email Migration tool should display along with a pop-up window prompting you for connection information to the Oracle Collaboration Suite 10*g* installation's Oracle Internet Directory Server as pictured in Figure 7-5.

The Email Migration tool uses the Oracle Internet Directory to store information about the migration process, including user lists, batches, statuses, etc., as well as of course to provision users if they are provided either through an extraction from the legacy system or through ldif files as discussed earlier in this chapter. You should have this information if you were following the recommendation of documenting this detail during the installation process. Once you have populated the information for the OID server name, the port OID is running on (default is 389), and the password for the orcladmin account (prompted for this during install), click OK. The tool will attempt to log in to the OID server. You will see a pop-up on the screen similar to the one shown in Figure 7-6 while the tool attempts to establish the connection.

Once you have successfully logged the Email Migration tool in to the Oracle Internet Directory for the installation for the first time, you will be prompted to create a migration instance, since one does not exist yet, and you can begin the setup of the migration process as shown in Figure 7-7. Click OK to begin the process of defining the parameters for the first migration attempt.

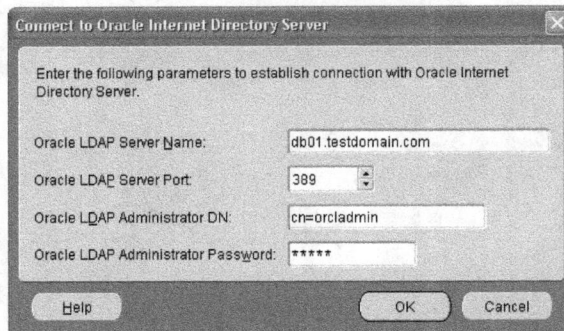

FIGURE 7-5. *Initial Email Migration tool screen and OID Connection pop-up*

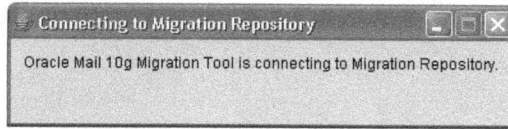

FIGURE 7-6.   *Email Migration tool connects to the Oracle Internet Directory*

Once you click OK, the Welcome screen for the Migration Wizard will display, explaining the information you will be asked to provide during the setup in the wizard. Figure 7-8 shows this list.

Review the information requested and either click Next now or come back to this screen after you have gathered the information requested. I would suggest reading through the remainder of this walk through the

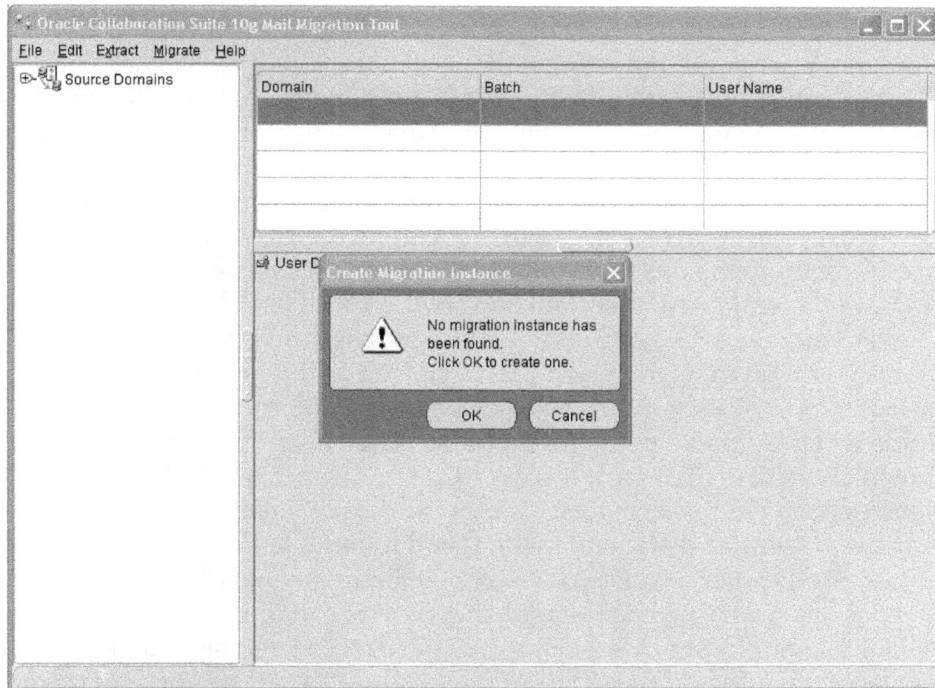

FIGURE 7-7.   *Creating a migration instance in Oracle Internet Directory*

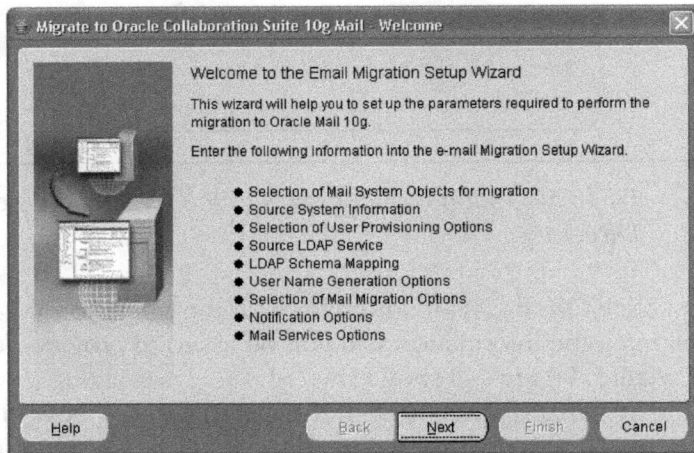

FIGURE 7-8. *Email Migration Wizard Welcome screen*

wizard as it will provide you with a good idea of not only the category of information you need, but the specifics.

Once you are ready to move on, click Next and move to the Mail System Objects window, where you will tell the Email Migration tool what source system you are migrating from and what objects you want to migrate from that system. The check boxes on the left side of the objects will either be available for selection or grayed out, depending upon which source system you choose from the pull-down menu. Figure 7-9 shows an example of the window if you choose Other Mail Servers.

After you choose the email system you are migrating from and what objects you wish to migrate, you will click Next and navigate to the User Provisioning Options window shown in Figure 7-10. You will need to decide whether you want to Provision Base Users, and if so whether you want to connect to the legacy system's LDAP Server or use a User Profiles File to define the users. You can also set the default email quota value for all users here (I suggest doing that in the User Profiles File if you use one). As we discussed earlier, even if you don't plan on migrating any email or calendar data with the Email Migration tool, you can in fact use it to mass-define the user profiles by selecting the User Profile File option and populating the user_profiles.ldif file in the $ORACLE_HOME/oes/migration/ files directory with the user definitions you wish to provision.

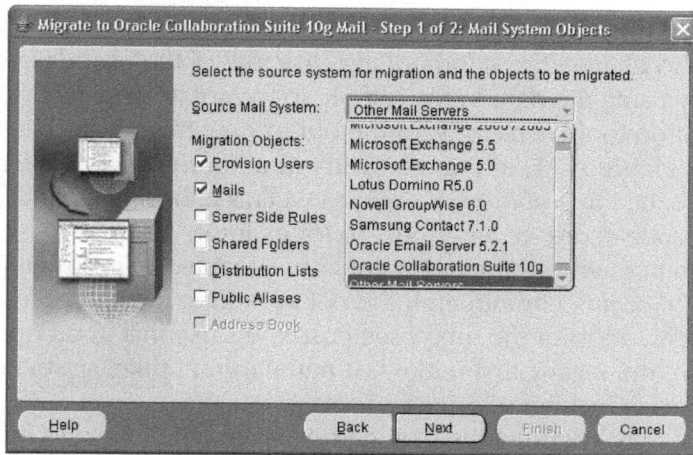

FIGURE 7-9.   *Email Migration tool Mail System Objects window*

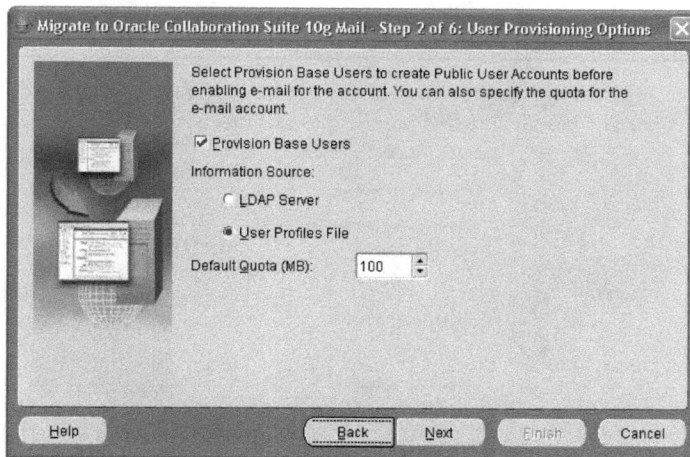

FIGURE 7-10.   *Email Migration tool User Provisioning window*

Clicking Next from here will take you to the User Name Generation screen. When migrating to Oracle Collaboration Suite 10*g*, you have the opportunity to change the standard and structure of the userids and email addresses by using the data in the ldif file to formulate new values while the Email Migration tool keeps track of the old-to-new migration. The options, as shown in Figure 7-11, are to retain any or all of the users' first, middle, or last names, or some portion of each, as well as choosing a name separator (a dash, an underscore, or a period). So for example, the username jsmith belongs to John Matthew Smith. He could be migrated to jmsmith, john.smith, john.m.smith, or any combination thereof by setting the values accordingly in this window. Most of the time I see customers use this as an opportunity to move from the legacy first initial last name format (like jsmith here), to today's common firstname.lastname format.

Once you have defined the user name format, click Next to move to the Notification window as shown in Figure 7-12. Here you can choose to notify the user and additionally the administrator of the user creation details and the migration report for that user when successfully created and migrated by the Email Migration tool.

An example of the email sent after user creation is shown here in Figure 7-13.

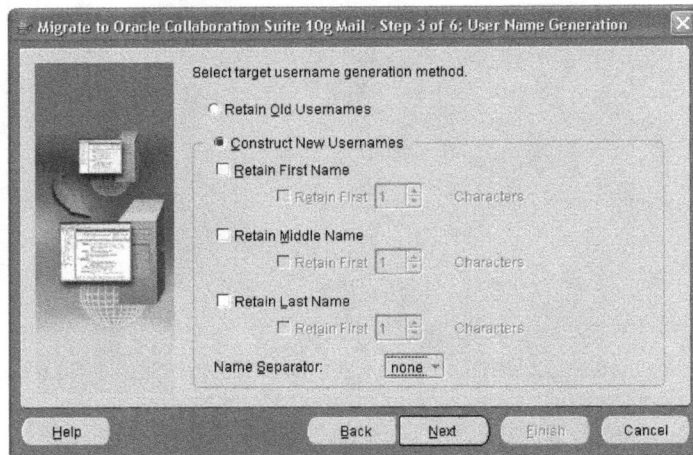

FIGURE 7-11. *Email Migration tool User Name Generation window*

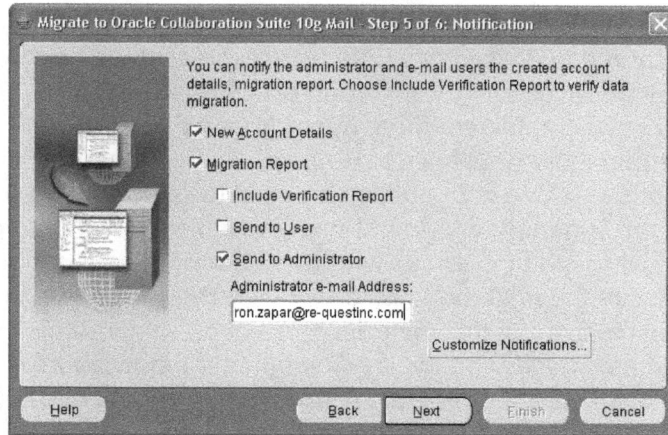

FIGURE 7-12. *Email Migration tool User/Administrator Notification Options*

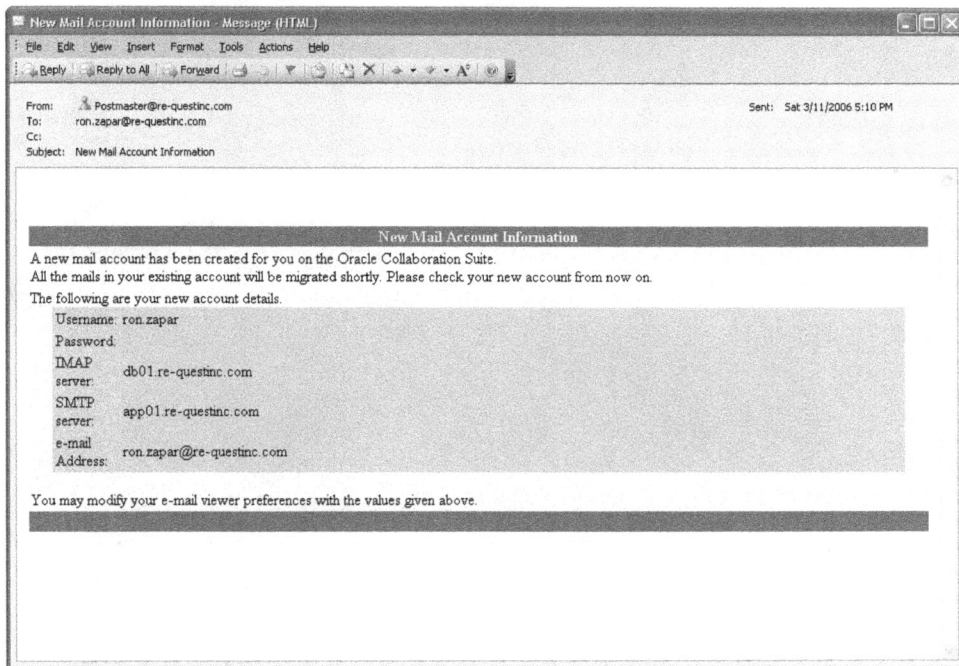

FIGURE 7-13. *Sample notification email to Administrator*

Clicking Next from here will take you to the window where you define the source and target email services. You will need to type in the source domain and source IMAP server values; the rest, as shown by the example in Figure 7-14, are available through pull-down lists.

Once you have completed filling in or choosing values for all the fields in the Services window (you have to populate everything; otherwise, the tool will not allow you to continue), click Next to complete the setup steps and move to the Summary window shown in Figure 7-15. Here you can either go back through the various windows and modify values or choose Finish to populate the migration repository with the values you just entered in the various windows of the wizard.

Clicking Finish moves you back to the initial window and sets you up to start the actual migration process. If you were to exit now, the information would still be saved in the migration repository so that you could return at a later time and continue the migration. Notice that now the domain is listed under the Source Domains branch of the migration tree, as shown in Figure 7-16. Additionally, if you decided for some reason this was not the

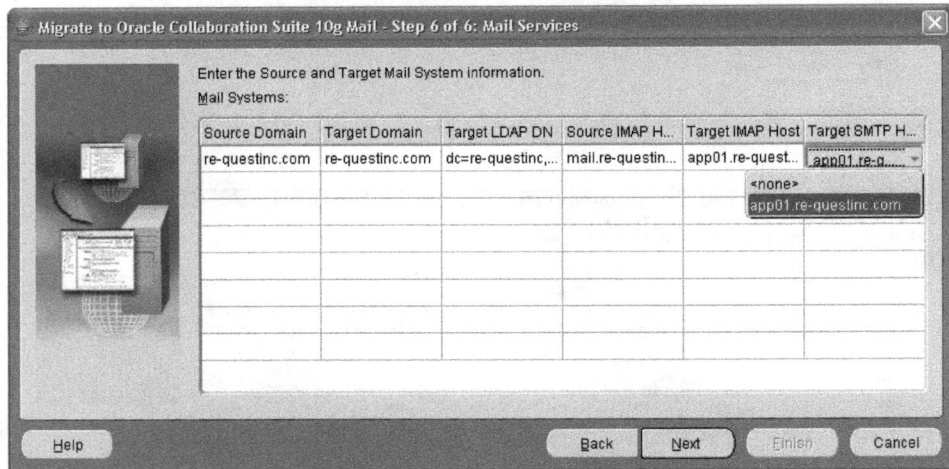

FIGURE 7-14. *Email Migration tool Source and Target Services window*

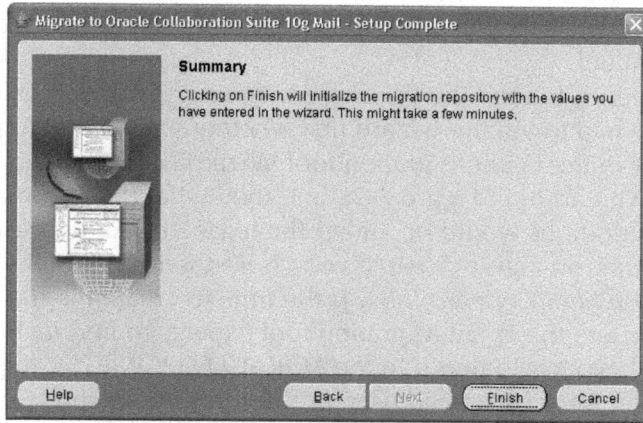

FIGURE 7-15.   *Email Migration tool Setup Wizard Summary window*

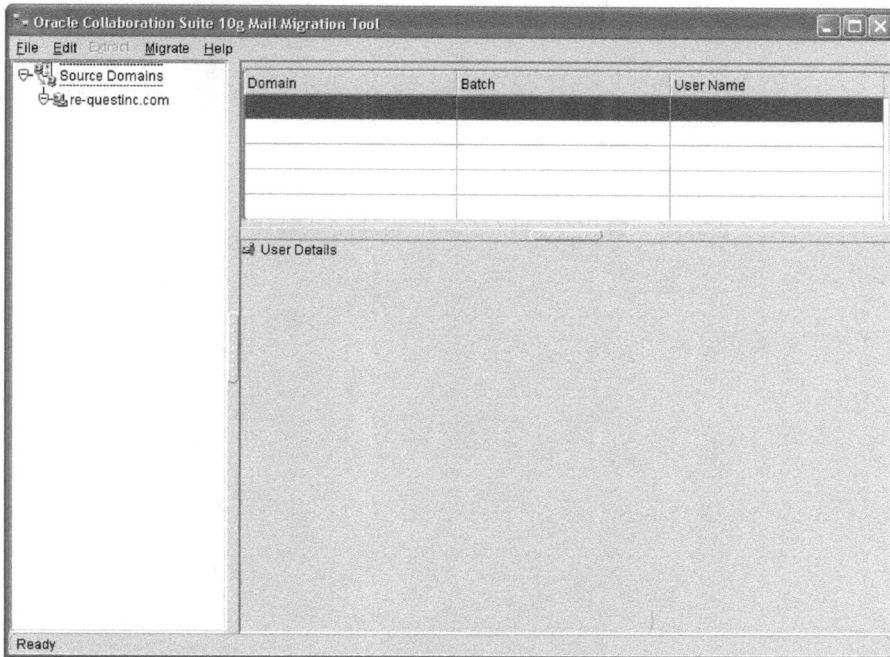

FIGURE 7-16.   *Returning to the Main Email Migration screen after completing the wizard*

correct set of values for the migration process, you could choose the Clear Migration Parameters option off of the Edit menu and start from scratch (trust me, this has value).

The next step is to load the list of users into the Email Migration tool. If you recall, we had to tell the wizard first whether we wanted to provision the users back in the Email Migration tool Wizard Mail System Objects window (shown earlier in Figure 7-9), and then what the information source for the user definitions would be, either the legacy LDAP or a user profiles file (shown earlier in Figure 7-10). If you chose the User Profiles File option in the Migration Setup Wizard, now is the time to create the file and put it in the location where the Email Migration tool expects to find it. The Email Migration tool expects to find it in the $ORACLE_HOME/oes/migration/files directory, and it must be named user_profiles.ldif. An example of the file is shown in an editor window in Figure 7-17. If you are going to use an LDAP

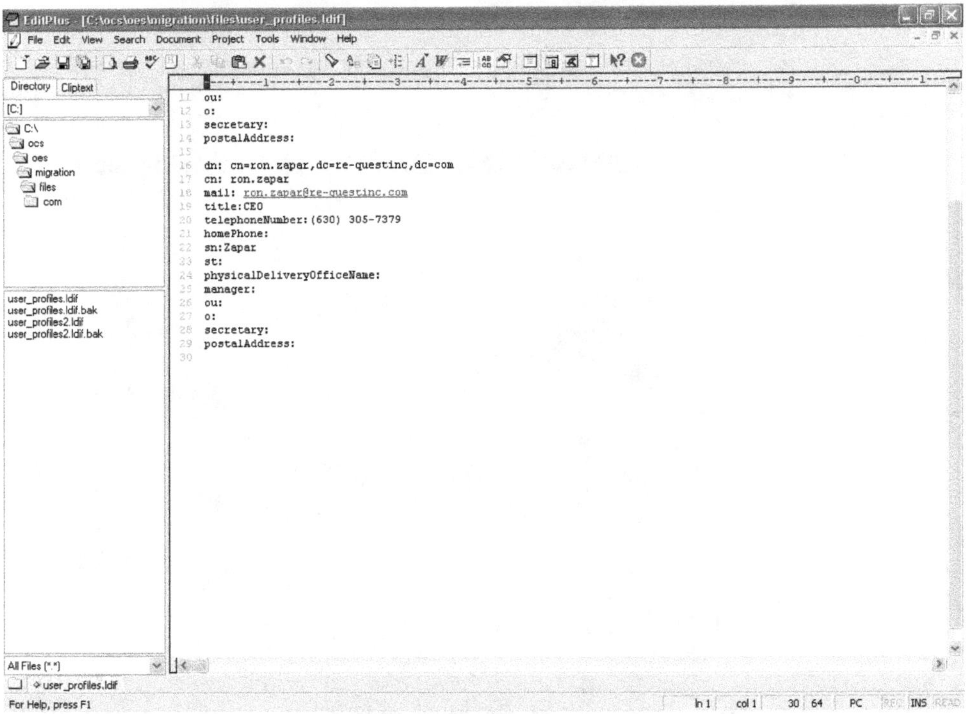

FIGURE 7-17. *user_profiles.ldif file content example*

Server, you need to make sure it is accessible and you have the appropriate Administrator userid and password to log in and access the required LDAP information.

Once you have the users defined in the user_profiles.ldif file or have appropriate access to the legacy LDAP Server, you can choose the Load Users option from the File menu on the main Email Migration tool menu as shown in Figure 7-18.

You will be prompted with the pop-up message shown in Figure 7-19 "Users will be populated into the repository. Do you want to continue?" Choose OK to load the user list into the Email Migration tool repository.

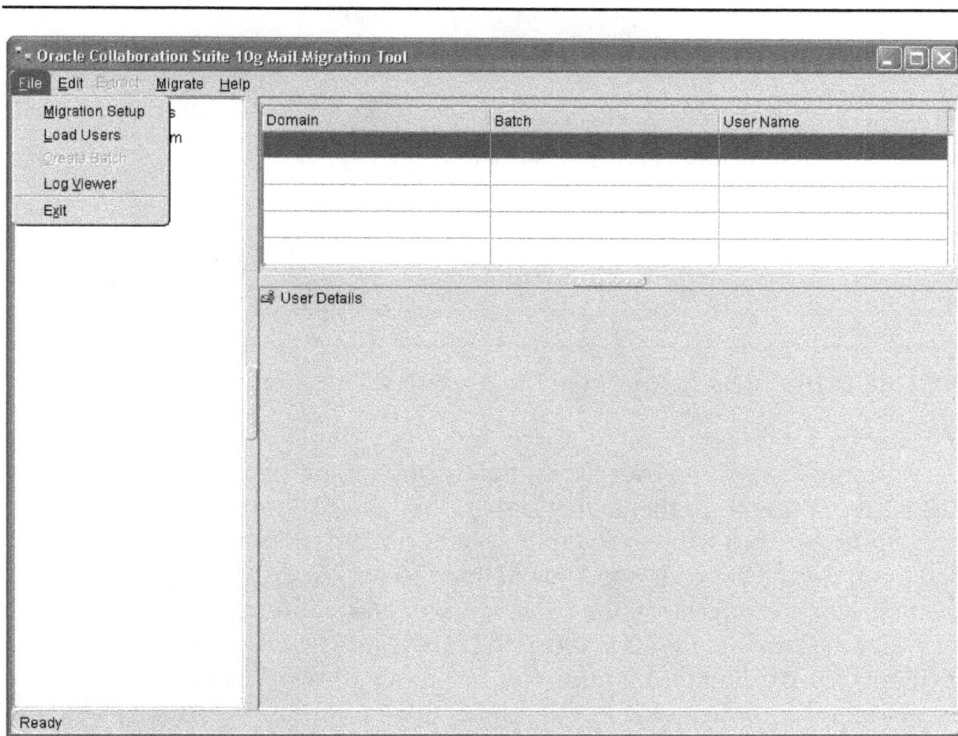

FIGURE 7-18. *Email Migration tool Load Users menu option*

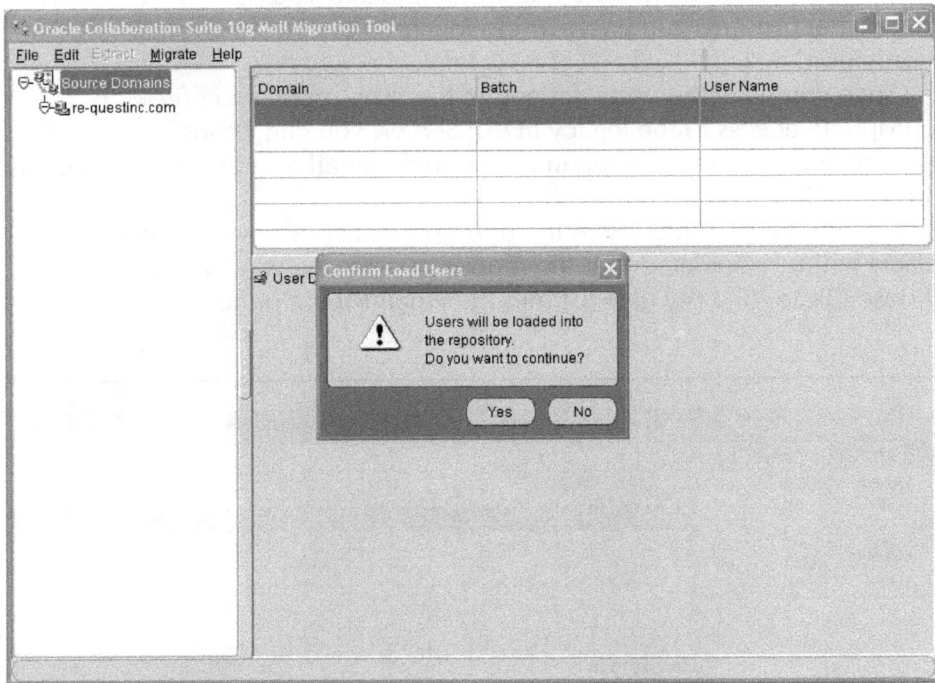

FIGURE 7-19. *Load Users Into The Repository prompt*

With the load of the user list complete, the migration repository now has a list of users from the legacy system that you can perform migration operations on from within the Email Migration tool. In order to migrate any data, you must have user accounts defined to accept the migrated data, so the first step is to provision the users in Oracle Collaboration Suite 10*g*.

From the Migrate menu, choose the Provision Users option as shown in Figure 7-20. The Email Migration tool will now attempt to create all the users in the list (or from the LDAP connection) and provision them in Oracle Collaboration Suite 10*g* Identity Management. A pop-up window with a

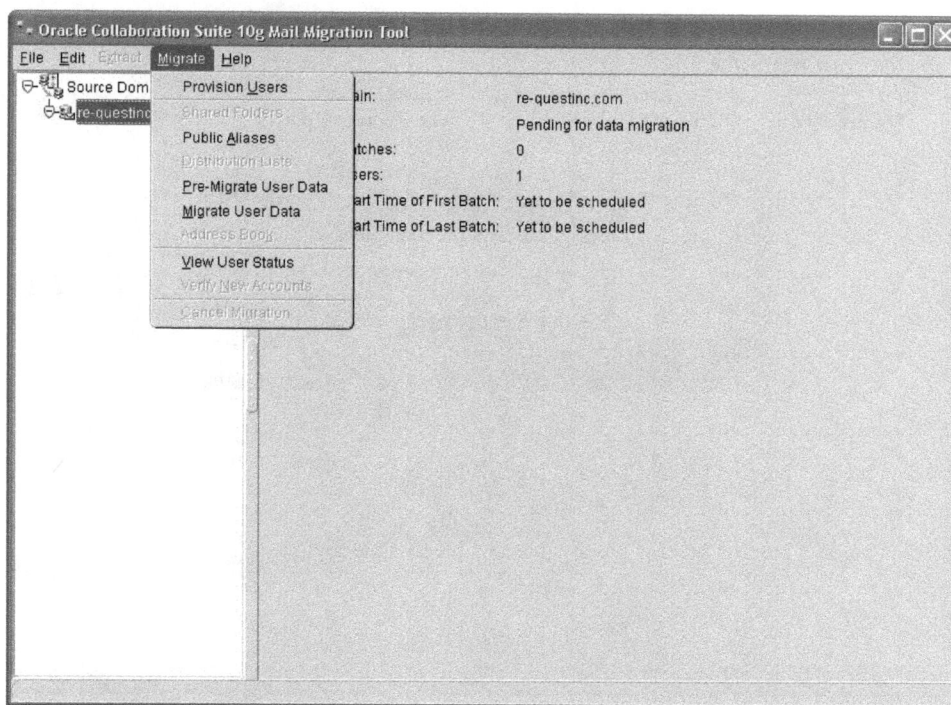

FIGURE 7-20.   *Email Migration tool Migrate menu | Provision Users option*

slide showing progress will be displayed until all user provisioning has been completed. Then a success message like the one shown in Figure 7-21 will pop up.

If you are continuing on to migrate data in addition to provisioning users, you should now choose the Create Batch option from the File menu in the Email Migration tool as shown in Figure 7-22.

When you choose the Create Batch menu option, a pop-up window like the one in Figure 7-23 will appear asking either for the number of users per batch from the full user list or for the location of where the custom user list for creating batches resides. The former allows the scheduling of random groupings of users in the full list, so if no real pattern to the migration plan has been defined, then choosing that option will work fine. However, if the approach is to manage the migration by, say, specific department or by total amount of data per migration pass, then using the custom user list method is recommended.

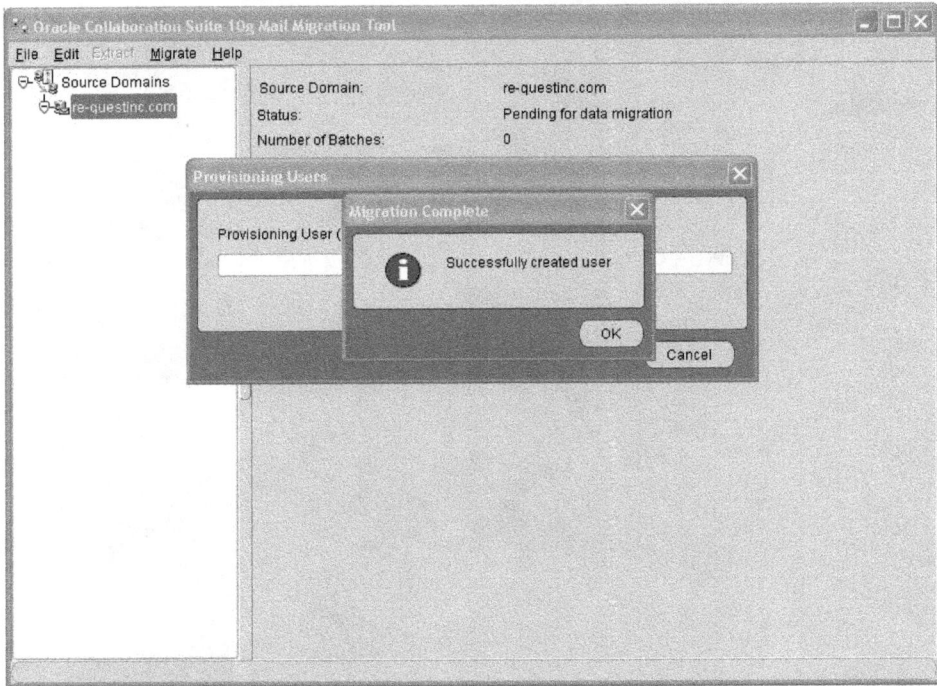

FIGURE 7-21. *Provisioning users completed*

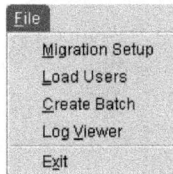

FIGURE 7-22. *Create Batch menu option*

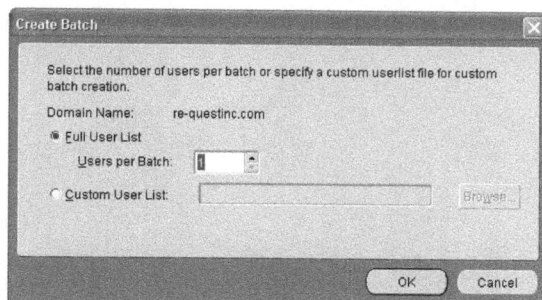

FIGURE 7-23.   *Create Batch options*

Once the batch parameters are defined, the migration tree on the left will reflect the batches created from the user list based upon the match parameters entered. It is possible to drill down on each batch to see what specific users are defined in the batch, as well as to schedule the batch for when the user data is to be either pre-migrated or migrated. Figure 7-24 shows the migration directory tree after two batches are created, with one user in each batch.

Now that users are loaded and provisioned and batches of users to be migrated have been created and scheduled, the migration process can begin. Again, pull down the Migrate menu and choose either the Pre-Migrate User Data or Migrate User Data option as shown in Figure 7-25. Remember, the option of completing the data migration in a two-step process or in a single migration step is available. A two-step process provides the advantage of extracting the information from the legacy system one time and saving a copy of it on the migration machine. This way, if the second step of the migration from the staging file on the migration machine into Oracle Collaboration Suite 10*g* doesn't work, all a migration person needs to do is simply reset the target and re-run the migration. The downside to this approach, however, is that enough space on the migration machine needs to be available to hold all the staged information for a given batch of users migrated at one time—the migration process for additional users might have to be halted if there are issues with one user in a batch that has already been staged. The downside of the one-step approach is that the legacy system must be accessed each and every time a user or set of users is migrated, which impacts everyone still running on the legacy system. I recommend

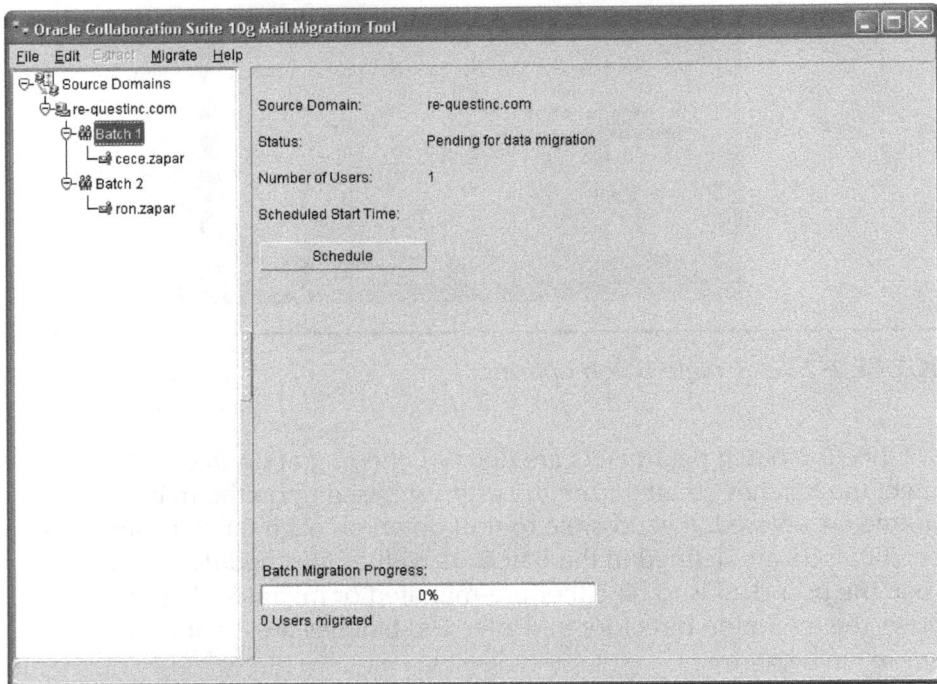

FIGURE 7-24. *Batch creation complete*

using the two-step approach, since you will most likely want to focus on a set of users at a time and can easily re-run migrations for users that have issues. In addition, by doing the pre-migrate process, you do not create routing rules between the two environments that you have to undo if there are issues. Once there is a comfort level that the migration will run correctly, you can execute the full migration and create the routing rules.

Assuming you are taking my advice (otherwise, why would I write the book and you buy it, right?), I will choose the Pre-Migrate option from the Migrate menu. This will bring up the prompt shown in Figure 7-26, which states that message migration will be started, but mail re-routing and notifications will not be enabled yet and this will not migrate Private Folders.

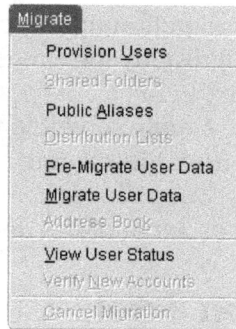

FIGURE 7-25.   *Migrate menu options*

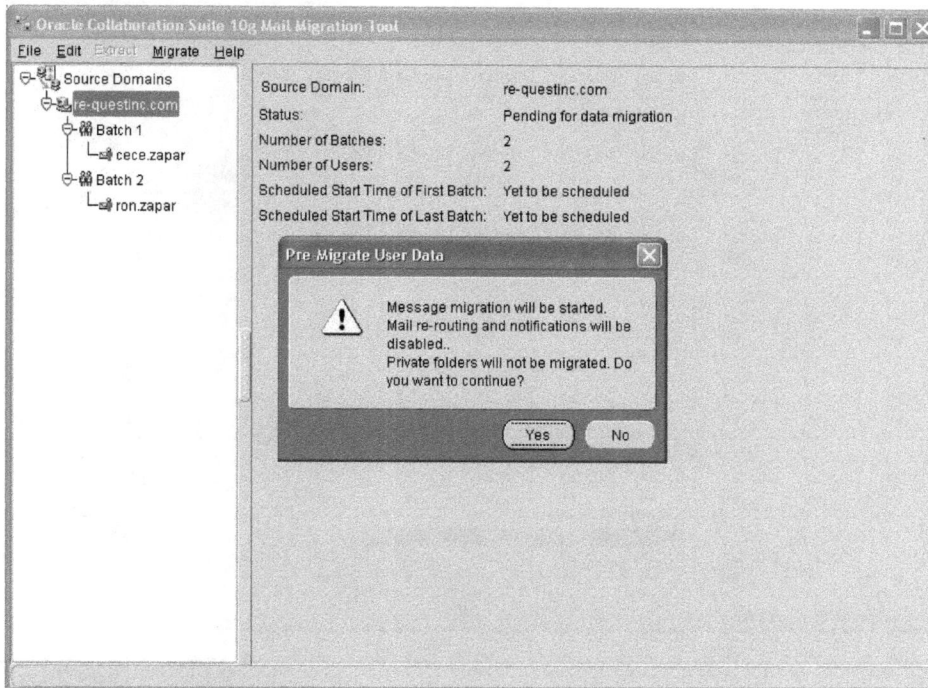

FIGURE 7-26.   *Pre-Migrate User Data prompt in the Email Migration tool*

Clicking Yes here will start the pre-migration process for all scheduled batches where the scheduled migration time is current or past. When complete, the main screen will display the status of the particular batch highlighted as shown in Figure 7-27.

To complete the migration, simply schedule the batch again and choose the Migrate User Data option from the Migrate menu; this will turn off the re-routing and notifications between the two environments and move the pre-migrated data into the user's account in Oracle Collaboration Suite 10*g*.

Calendar Migration Tools

Migrating calendar entries can either be very straightforward or challenging to varying degrees, depending upon what source system you are migrating from.

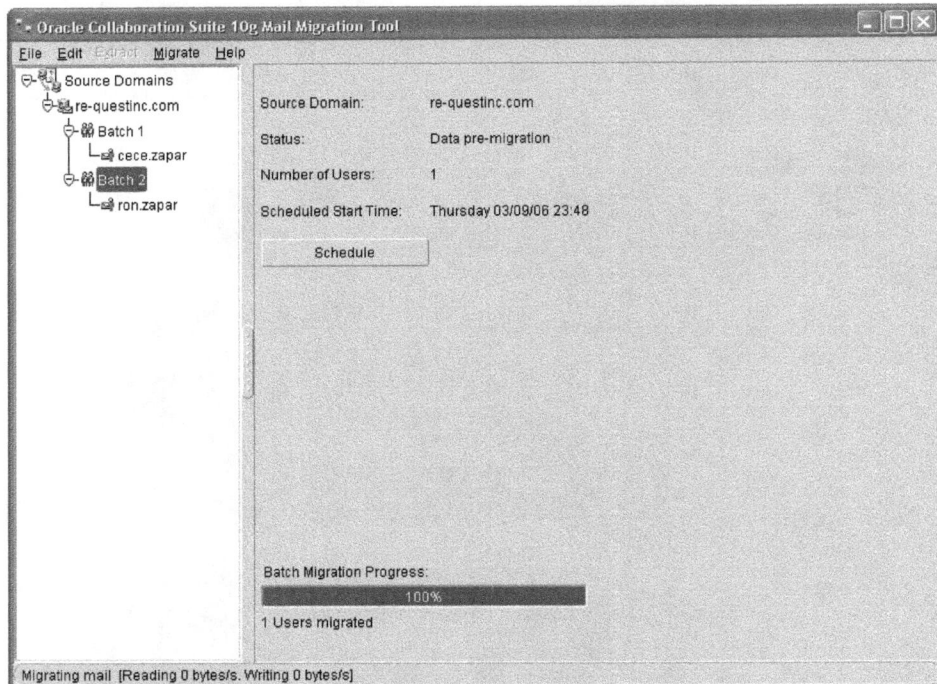

FIGURE 7-27. *Completed migration batch status*

Oracle has defined specific utilities and/or methods for migrating from Microsoft Exchange, MeetingMaker, and Netscape Calendar. All other calendar source systems must be able to produce iCalendar-formatted text files in order for migration to be possible. By far, the most common migrations are from Exchange Calendar– and iCalendar-formatted files, so I will concentrate on those two types in detail in this section.

Oracle has created a command-line migration utility, *unimmimpsrv,* to assist if you are migrating from MeetingMaker. You tell the *unimmimpsrv* utility what MeetingMaker data to migrate by populating the *unimmimpsrv.ini* parameter file with information on the specific MeetingMaker files you wish to migrate.

Netscape Calendar actually requires an intermediate step of migrating into CorporateTime first, then from CorporateTime into Oracle Calendar.

If you are coming from Microsoft Exchange, then you can simply migrate calendar data using the same Email Migration tool (ExMigrate) used for migrating email as previously described.

If you are coming from another legacy system not specifically mentioned previously, then you must extract the calendar data into a text file in iCalendar file format and use the command-line *uniical* utility to upload the calendar entries into Oracle Calendar.

Using Email Migration Tool for Calendar Entries

In order to use the Email Migration tool for migrating calendar data from a Microsoft Exchange server to Oracle Calendar, you need to execute the following steps:

1. Create an ExMigrate migration server environment. This includes installing the ExMigrate tool (if it wasn't already installed for email migration), installing the Outlook Connector (again if not already done for email migration), and setting the configuration files up for your migration (defining variable values and options is done manually in the case of migrating calendar data, by contrast with using the interface as described previously).

2. Create the Oracle Calendar target users that you will migrate the calendar entries to that are extracted from Exchange Calendar.

3. Execute the ExMigrate tool once all values in the configuration files have been defined and the Oracle Calendar users have been created.

4. Review the results and address any anomalies or issues that may be present.

For the sake of brevity I will assume you have already completed the install portion of creating the ExMigrate migration environment as described in the previous section "Email Migration Tool (ExMigrate)," which means the ExMigrate software and the Outlook Connector have already been installed, environmental variables defined, Java Home created, etc. Therefore, the remaining tasks for creating the migration environment center on defining the various configuration files for the ExMigrate tool to be able to connect to Exchange and migrate the correct information for the users.

All configuration files should be placed in the migration subdirectory (this would be C:\ocs\oes \migration if you follow the example for the ExMigrate tool given earlier in the chapter) of your Email Migration tool directory structure. The first configuration file you need to create there is an ExMigrateConfig.ini file. The ExMigrateConfig.ini file must have information in the [ExchangeServer] section regarding the Exchange server environment you are migrating from and the appropriate settings in the [OracleCalendar] section for the target Oracle Calendar environment. In addition you can also populate the [IMAP4] section of the file with email migration information (although that is only necessary if migrating email and calendar entries together in the same ExMigrate run), the [UsersFiles] section with values representing locations for Master and migration subset user and password list files, and the [Options] section, which tells ExMigrate how to deal with certain types of calendar entries such as those that have been deleted, or those that have links to attendees.

In order to populate the [ExchangeServer] section of the ExMigrateConfig.ini file, you will need an Exchange Administrator user with a mailbox and administrative rights (not all user administrators have administrative privileges). You will also need a hint profile that has both Exchange Message Service configured and administrative rights to the Exchange server. A default profile is usually available, but I would suggest having the Exchange Administrator provide one. In my example, I will name mine reqexadmin. You will now have to run the ExMigrate tool on the migration server with the hint profile to gain the necessary information to populate the [ExchangeServer] section of the ExMigrateConfig.ini file as follows (assuming you have a cmd window available on your migration server with the appropriate environment variables set):

```
Exmigrate /hint reqexadmin
```

You will need the organizational unit, or value of ou, as well as the domain, the server name, the admin profile name (the same one you used to run the exmigrate /hint command), and the default domain (the default value on Exchange for this variable is "First Administrative Group").

The next section to be populated in the ExMigrateConfig.ini file is the [OracleCalendar] section. This section provides the ExMigrate tool with all the information necessary for what to migrate, as well as the server name, node, and port to find the Oracle Calendar target environment in. Setting Migrate=1 tells ExMigrate to actually migrate the calendar data (as opposed to just testing connectivity); AllNodes=1 says to migrate to Oracle Calendar Node 1 (this could be a list of several Oracle Calendar nodes, each separated from the next by a semicolon, if we were migrating to a multinode Oracle Calendar environment). The DefaultServer and Default NodeID provide the names of the default Oracle Calendar server and node to migrate to (this can be overridden in the user profiles with the /N value). The remaining variables that begin with *Migrate---* tell ExMigrate what information to migrate from the Exchange Calendar data, including Tasks, Notes, Contacts, and of course Calendar entries themselves.

If you want to migrate email, you can populate the [IMAP] section of the ExMigrateConfig.ini file. If not, then just set the variables to 0 or leave the section blank. I like to provide the variables just in case there is some change in default values from version to version of the ExMigrate tool, or the variable names change (at a minimum you will get an error, rather than just running blind).

For the [UserFiles] section you must provide the "absolute" path names for the ExMigrateUsers.ini file (MasterList, MigrationSubset variables in the [UserFiles] section) and the ExMigratePassword.ini file (UsersPasswordFile, SysOpPasswordFile variables in the [UserFiles] section).

In the [Options] section, you can set several variables like the MaintainLinks, CalendarTimeRange, and KeepOrphanMeetings variables shown in the example that follows. By setting the MaintainLinks variable to a value of 1, you tell ExMigrate to preserve the integrity of the information associated with a given calendar entry, such as data regarding meetings and the status of attendees. CalendarTimeRange has a valid range of 0–12, which is the number of months you want to go back to begin calendar entry migration and therefore limits calendar entries from being migrated that were entered prior to that earliest month (the default is to migrate everything for a given user). By setting the KeepOrphanMeetings variable to 1, you tell ExMigrate to create a private copy of every meeting where the user being migrated is an attendee but the organizer of the meeting is not in the group of users that has been or is currently being migrated.

The [Logging] section allows you to control the level of logging that is captured on the console and in the log file for a given migration run by ExMigrate, as well as tell ExMigrate where to write the log file (and what filename to use). The possible values for both the LogLevelFile and LogLevelConsole variables are none, error, warning, and journal. One configuration is to set the LogLevelConsole value to error while you set the LogLevelFile to journal, so that you will see errors on the screen as they occur but all activity of ExMigrate is captured in the log file for later, detailed review.

Here is an example of a fully populated ExMigrateConfig.ini file:

```
[ExchangeServer]
Organization=tst
Domain=testdomain.com
Server=exch1
ExchangeAdmin=reqexadmin
DefaultExchangeMailboxDomain=EXCHANGE_DOMAIN
[OracleCalendar]
Migrate=1
DefaultServer=ocs-1.testdomain.com
DefaultNodeID=1
AllNodes=1
1=ocs-1.testdomain.com
Port=5730
MigrateCalendar=1
MigrateJournal=1
MigrateNotes=1
MigrateContacts=1
MigrateTasks=1
MigrateOnlyMainFolders=1
[IMAP]
Migrate=0
Server=0
Port=0
[UserFiles]
```

```
MasterList=C:\Program Files\Oracle\OCFO\ExMigrateUsers.ini
MigrationSubset=C:\Program Files\Oracle\OCFO\ExMigrateUsers.ini
UsersPasswordFile=C:\Program Files\Oracle\OCFO\ExMigratePasswd.ini
SysOpPasswordFile=C:\Program Files\Oracle\OCFO\ExMigratePasswd.ini
[Options]
MaintainLinks=1
CalendarTimeRange=6
KeepOrphanMeetings=1
[Logging]
LogFile=C:\Program Files\Oracle\Outlook Connector\ExMigrateLog.txt
LogLevelFile=journal
LogLevelConsole=error
```

The ExMigrateUsers.ini file must be populated in order to tell ExMigrate what users you will migrate overall, as well as what users you want to migrate in this particular execution of the ExMigrate tool. Assuming you wish to migrate a large number of users, you first populate the [MasterList] section of the file with the information of all the users that are going to be migrated to Oracle Calendar (you also want to set MaintainLinks to 1 in the [Options] section of the configuration file to maintain data integrity between the users while subsets of the list are migrated). Then you can copy a portion of the users defined in the [MasterList] into the [MigrationSubset] section of the file.

The format for the user definitions in the ExMigrateUsers.ini file is as follows:

```
/E=ExchangeUser1/M=IMAP4User1/U=OCSUser1
```

The /E is the Exchange username where the calendar data is coming from, the /M is the email username (only necessary if migrating email and Calendar data at the same time), and /U is the Oracle Collaboration Suite 10*g* username you are migrating the calendar data into. The /D=1 value will be added to the beginning of a user definition line in the [MigrationSubset] section once a user has been successfully migrated (you can also add this manually to ignore a user in the subset list for a given ExMigrate execution). Figure 7-28 shows an example ExMigrateUsers.ini file.

The final configuration file that needs to be defined is the ExMigratePassword.ini file. The ExMigratePassword.ini file holds the encrypted password for the Oracle Calendar SuperUser, SysOp, as well as the encrypted password(s) for all users in the [MigrationSubset] section of the ExMigrateUsers.ini file being migrated. Now, you first must retrieve

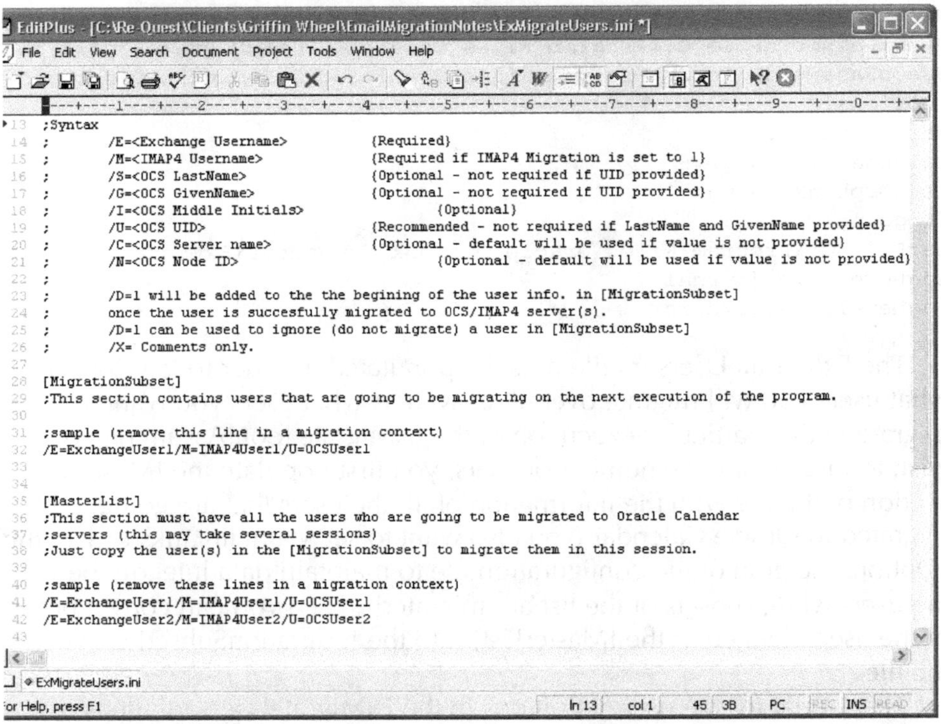


```
;Syntax
;       /E=<Exchange Username>          {Required}
;       /M=<IMAP4 Username>             {Required if IMAP4 Migration is set to 1}
;       /S=<OCS LastName>               {Optional - not required if UID provided}
;       /G=<OCS GivenName>              {Optional - not required if UID provided}
;       /I=<OCS Middle Initials>                {Optional}
;       /U=<OCS UID>                    {Recommended - not required if LastName and GivenName provided}
;       /C=<OCS Server name>            {Optional - default will be used if value is not provided}
;       /N=<OCS Node ID>                        {Optional - default will be used if value is not provided}
;
;       /D=1 will be added to the the begining of the user info. in [MigrationSubset]
;       once the user is succesfully migrated to OCS/IMAP4 server(s).
;       /D=1 can be used to ignore (do not migrate) a user in [MigrationSubset]
;       /X= Comments only.

[MigrationSubset]
;This section contains users that are going to be migrating on the next execution of the program.

;sample (remove this line in a migration context)
/E=ExchangeUser1/M=IMAP4User1/U=OCSUser1


[MasterList]
;This section must have all the users who are going to be migrated to Oracle Calendar
;servers (this may take several sessions)
;Just copy the user(s) in the [MigrationSubset] to migrate them in this session.

;sample (remove these lines in a migration context)
/E=ExchangeUser1/M=IMAP4User1/U=OCSUser1
/E=ExchangeUser2/M=IMAP4User2/U=OCSUser2
```

FIGURE 7-28. *Sample ExMigrateUsers.ini file*

these passwords in encrypted format from Oracle Collaboration Suite 10*g*. To retrieve the encrypted SysOp and Oracle Calendar user(s) passwords, you use the following ExMigrate commands respectively:

```
exmigrate /e OCS_NODEID plaintext_OCS_SysOp_password
exmigrate /e Exchange_Username plaintext_OCS_password
```

An example ExMigratePassword.ini file with one user to be migrated looks like this:

```
;----------------------------------------------------------------------------
; Settings
;----------------------------------------------------------------------------
 [SysOpPasswords]
; This section contains all the node ids and their encrypted SysOp passwords.
1={STD}VcvgXqsP0Bx8TYTagY5JNTzEI5795DYRLIht9/MHofcbn/4mxmjaQA==
```

```
[UsersPasswords]
; This section contains all the users to be migrated and their encrypted
passwords
ocsusr0={STD}0PK12+iEE/xWLnsQHT8UdM+YzltqR8Z/MzILRMIc0i/or5GMrDQ==
```

The next step—although considered optional—is to create the Oracle Calendar users. Now if you have already provisioned your users as discussed in the earlier section "Migrating User Definitions," then chances are you provisioned Calendar up front. However, I would suggest using the Oracle Identity Management Provisioning Console either to verify that the Calendar application has been provisioned or to provision it to the users you plan on migrating calendar data for. If you have a large list of users, Oracle provides the uniuser command-line utility to provision Calendar users. Simply log in to the Applications Tier, source the appropriate environment, go to the $ORACLE_HOME/ocal/bin directory and run:

```
uniuser -ex <filename>
```

The <filename> can be anything you want, but it needs to have entries for each user that have the following format:

```
A DID=cn=James Smith, ou=tst, o=testdomain, c=US
```

The "A" at the beginning indicates to uniuser to add the user to Oracle Calendar.

The next step, after users have been created and the ExMigrate tool configuration files have been set up, is to run the migration. I do so by creating a .cmd file with the following syntax:

```
exmigrate /C ExMigrateConfig.ini /F ExMigrateConfig.ini
```

This way, I only edit the configuration files and don't have to retype the complete command every time. By the way, I would suggest copying the ExMigrate setup (exmigrate.cmd, configuration files, etc.) into the Outlook Connector directory and executing from there so that ExMigrate finds everything in its path that it needs to run successfully.

Once each ExMigrate run is completed, you should review the log files generated to ensure there are no unknown issues with each subset migration. Remember, we told ExMigrate where to put the log file and what to call it in the [Logging] section of the ExMigrateConfig.ini file. The log file format is a text file, so any standard Windows editor will work fine.

iCalendar Migration

If you are migrating from a legacy calendaring system that is not specifically supported by an Oracle tool, it is still possible to migrate to Oracle Calendar in a bulk load manner. You must, however, be able to get your existing calendar entries in a text file in iCalendar—or iCal—format. The iCalendar format is a standard format used to export or import calendar data from any application to any application. Oracle Calendar provides a command-line function, *uniical,* to read iCal-formatted files and load them into the Oracle Calendar target node. Here is an example of the minimal syntax required to create an iCal-formatted calendar entry:

```
BEGIN:VCALENDAR
BEGIN:VEVENT
SUMMARY:Basic Calendar Event
DTSTART:20061003T083000Z
DTEND:20061003T110000Z
END:VEVENT
END:VCALENDAR
```

However, the most common iCal export file entry looks like this:

```
BEGIN:VCALENDAR //must be used for START and END
METHOD:PUBLISH VERSION:2.0
PRODID:Oracle/Calendar
BEGIN:VEVENT
CLASS:PUBLIC
PRIORITY:5
STATUS:CONFIRMED
DTSTART:20061003T160000Z
DTEND:20061003T200000Z
SUMMARY: export //Subject(email) or action on object
UID:29b#400#233b7zzz&0002Yy0yMjA4.. //Unique identifier
END:VEVENT
END:VCALENDAR
```

Once the iCalendar-formatted file is created, run the uniical utility at the operating system prompt of the Oracle Calendar Applications Tier with the following syntax:

```
uniical -import -f <iCalendar-formatted filename>
```

Files/Content Services Migration

There are several ways to move your files-based content into Oracle Content Services from traditional file servers. One way is to use protocols such as FTP, where you connect to the Oracle Content Services server via FTP and transfer files into the defined file folder hierarchy, much the way you would use the traditional FTP protocol between Windows and/or Unix/Linux servers. Another is to use the WebDAV protocol by installing Oracle Drive and dragging and dropping files from your legacy storage location into a WebDAV-mounted drive on your PC using standard Windows Explorer.

There is more information available in Chapters 13 and 14 about Content Services functional and technical architecture, including additional information related to Oracle Drive.

End-User-Implemented Migration

One migration approach that can be pretty painless if managed correctly is to have each individual user move his or her own email (and possibly calendar entries as well if they happen to be using Outlook currently for their email and calendar interface) from the old system to Oracle Collaboration Suite 10*g* using Microsoft Outlook. Of course this assumes a few important but probable things: 1) the users have Outlook on their desktop (or you are willing to install it or have them install it), 2) they currently access their legacy email account through Outlook (POP or IMAP, either one is fine), and 3) detailed instructions can be provided on how to download and install the Outlook Connector for Oracle Collaboration Suite 10*g* (or have someone from the migration team do it for them). If these three things are acceptable in the environment, then the steps in the following example will show the users how to execute a "do-it-yourself" migration. The assumption is that the users have all been provisioned in the new Oracle Collaboration Suite 10*g* environment and the users can access both the new system (complete functionality) and the data from their old email system in the form of Personal Files (.pst files) in Outlook that they have saved their legacy system email messages into in preparation for this migration (a user can only be connected to one profile at a time in Outlook but has access to all the Personal Folders regardless of what account he or she is connected to at any time). In addition, the Oracle Collaboration Suite 10*g* environment must be accessible through the Web Client, the user must have the Outlook Connector installed on their desktop, and Outlook needs to be configured to connect to Oracle Collaboration Suite 10*g*.

To begin the setup and migration process, users need to log in to Oracle Collaboration Suite 10*g* through the Web Client and choose the Email option from the available Links Portlet. This will bring up the Email interface. They will see a folder tree on the left hand side of the screen, with the root being Oracle Mail. They right-click that (or highlight it and choose New from the menu icons) and create a new Folder under Oracle Mail using the Create Folder option. Figure 7-29 shows the operation in the Web Client.

When users click New Folder, the pop-up dialog shown in Figure 7-30 comes up for naming the new folder. They should call it Migrated Emails or something creative like that so that they know exactly where the migrated email is going. Now this can probably be done directly through the Outlook Connector as well, but I found that doing it this way guarantees creating the folder correctly and quickly with no synchronization from the desktop necessary. Figure 7-31 shows the new folder under Oracle Mail in the folder tree in the Web Client.

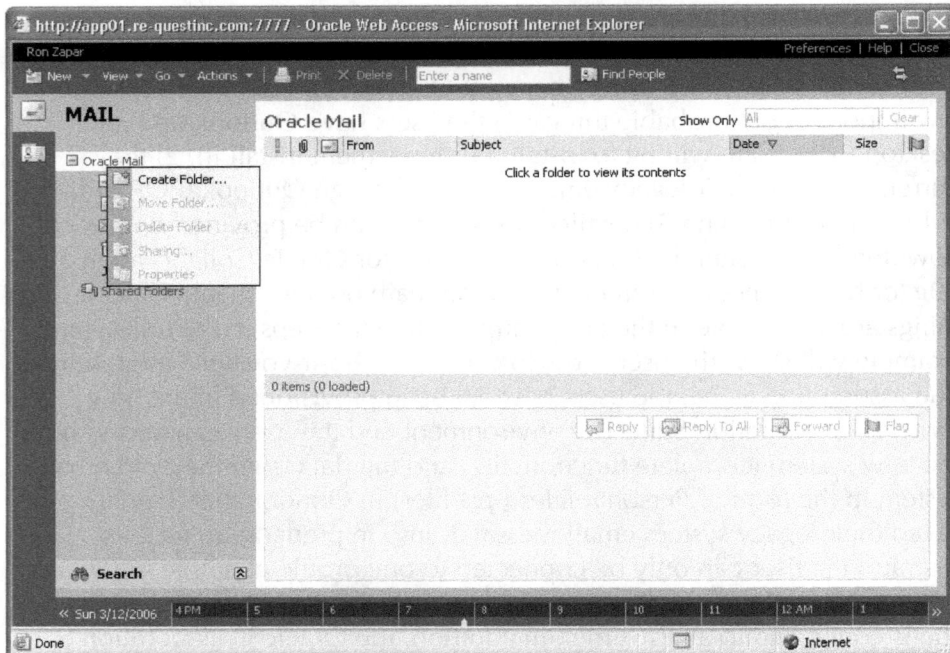

FIGURE 7-29. *Create Migration Folder in the Oracle Collaboration Suite 10g Email Web Client*

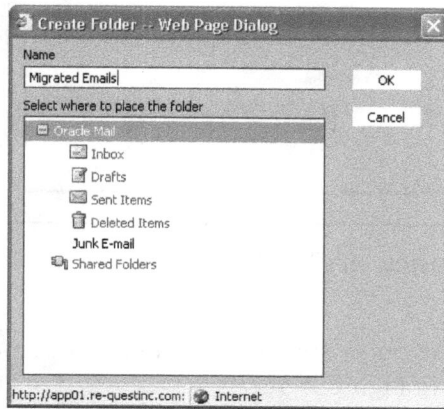

FIGURE 7-30. *New Folder Naming dialog*

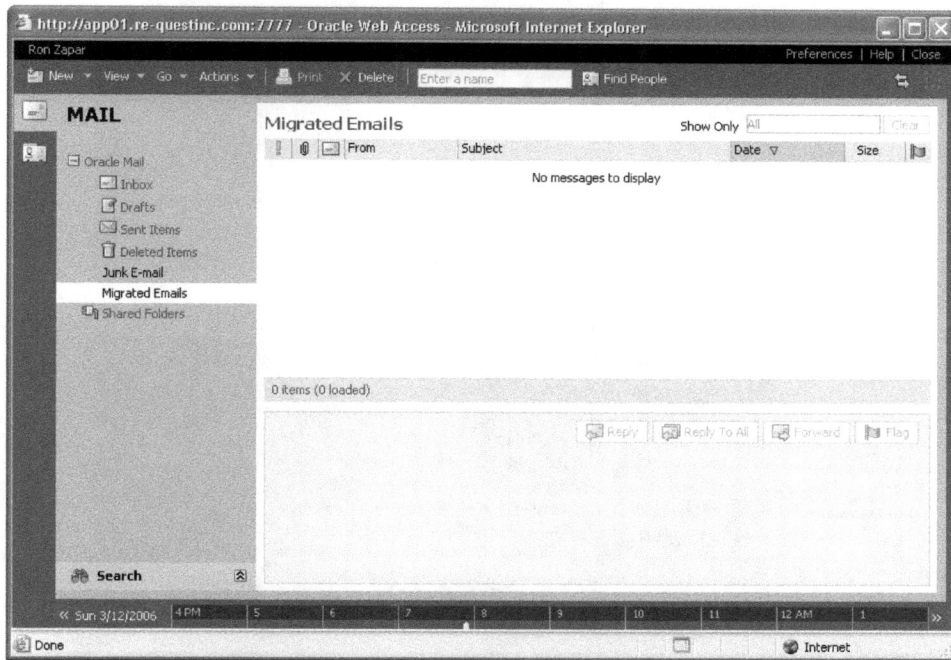

FIGURE 7-31. *New folder appears under Oracle mail folder tree in Web Client*

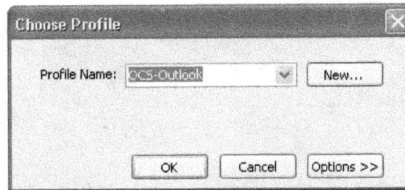

FIGURE 7-32. *Choosing an OCS Profile in Outlook*

Now have them log out of the Web Client and open up the OCS profile in Outlook as shown in Figure 7-32.

Once logged in through Outlook, they should see the new folder they created in the same spot in Outlook as it was created in the Web Client. Figure 7-33 shows the new folder in the Outlook folder tree.

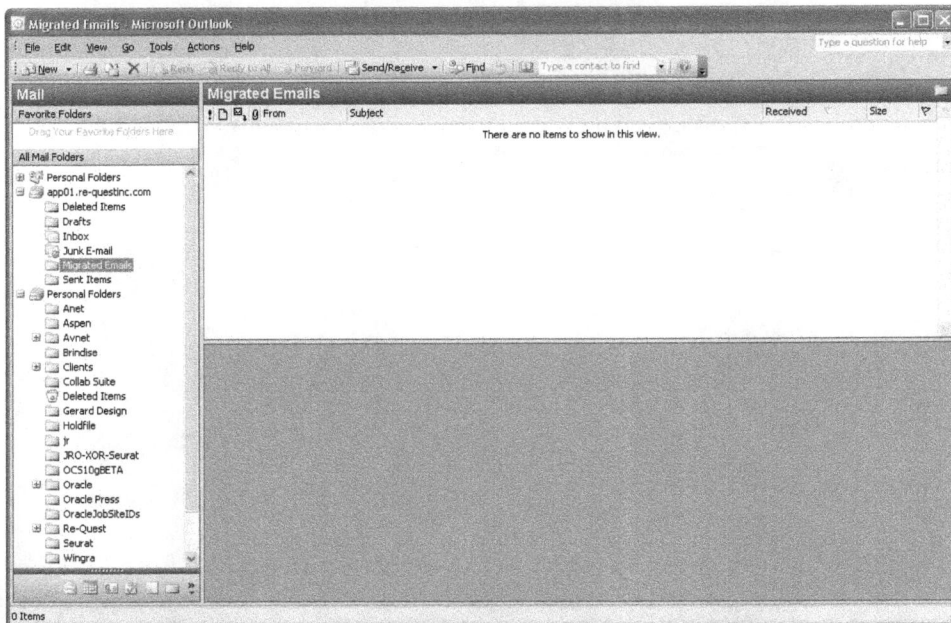

FIGURE 7-33. *New folder in Outlook folder tree*

Now they can open their Personal Folders and select emails to move to the new folder as shown in Figure 7-34. The user can highlight the required emails from their personal folders and drag and drop them into the new Migrated Emails folder in Oracle Mail. Figure 7-35 shows the emails moved to the Migrated Emails folder.

Now to complete the task, users need to again log out of Outlook and log in to the Oracle Collaboration Suite 10*g* Web Client. Figure 7-36 shows the email in the newly created folder accessible from the Web Client. From here, they can move it around in Oracle Collaboration Suite 10*g* Email as much as they want, including moving to their Inbox if they like (which couldn't be done initially through the Outlook client, since the emails did not originate in Oracle Collaboration Suite 10*g*).

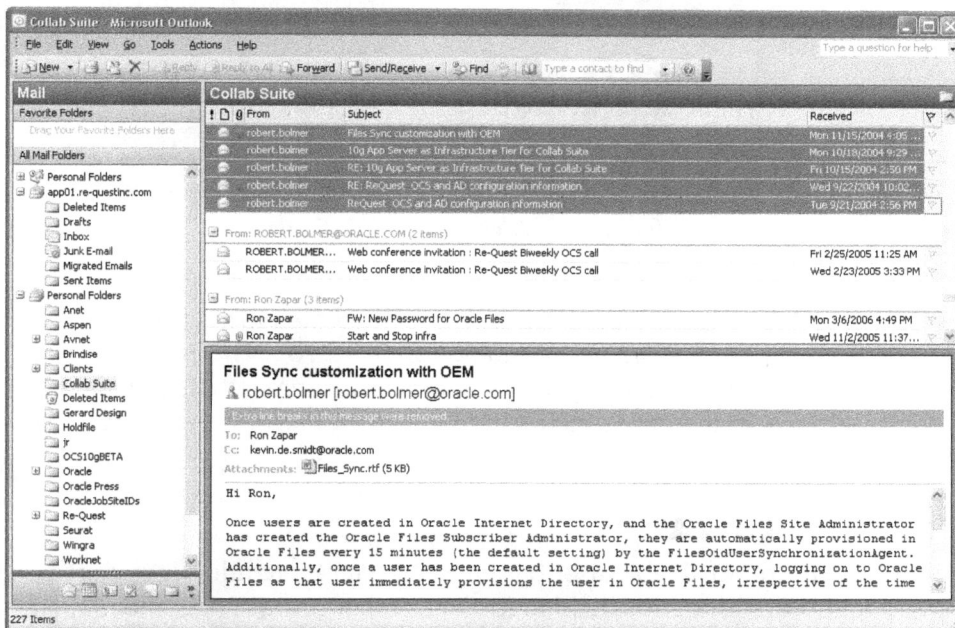

FIGURE 7-34. *Highlighted emails in personal folders to move to migration folder*

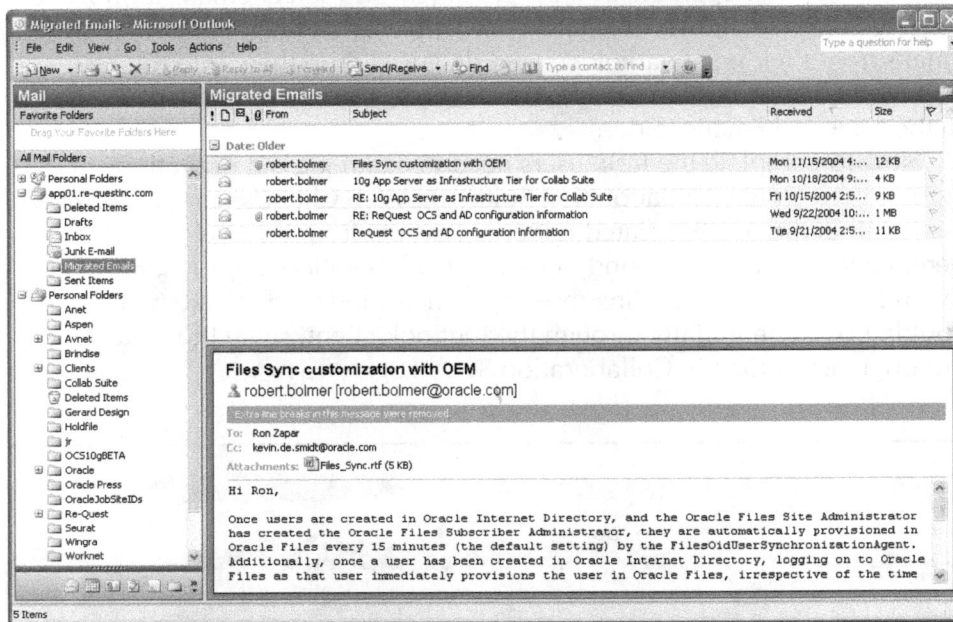

FIGURE 7-35. *Emails moved to Migrated Emails folder*

The users should continue this process until all the emails they wish to migrate are moved into Oracle Collaboration Suite 10*g*. They can do this in iterations as well, taking certain folders or emails at a time, then placing them where they want in the new system, and then going back for more later.

Coexistence

If there is any sort of sizable user base and an email migration is required, you should probably seriously plan for a period of coexistence, meaning a period of time where there will be some users on the old email system and some users on the new system. In terms of email this is pretty straightforward, and the Email Migration tool will set up the forwarding rules from Oracle Collaboration Suite 10*g* to the legacy system. However, the calendar is not that straightforward. One thing the users can do is to extract calendar entries from their current production calendars and email them as attachments to users on the other system; i.e., Oracle Collaboration Suite 10*g* users can

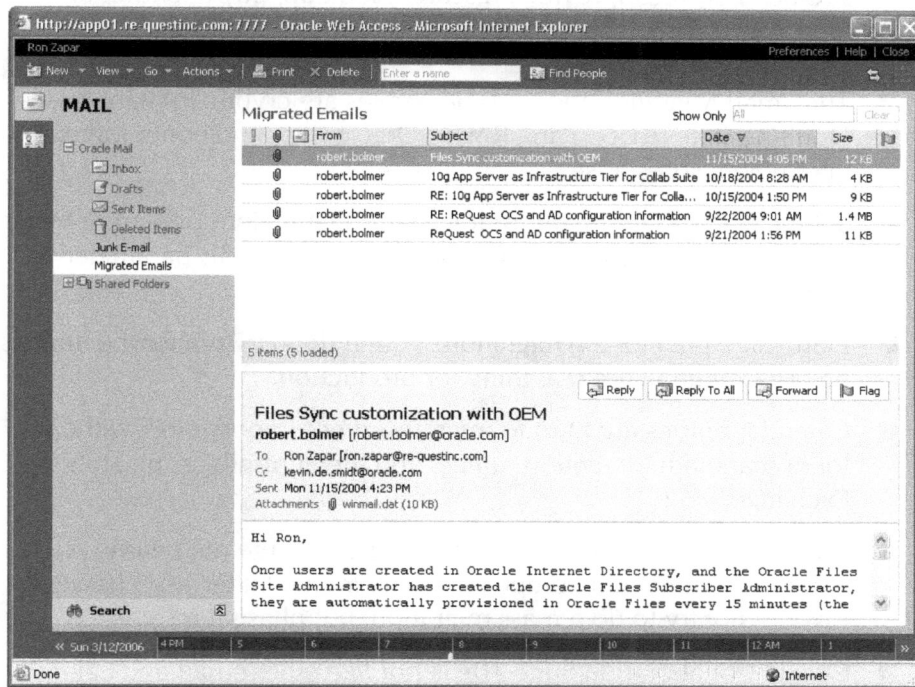

FIGURE 7-36. *Migrated email available in web client*

extract their meeting invitations to an iCalendar file format and email to the legacy users they want to invite to a meeting and vice versa. The issue here is that the users need to know who is on what system and be savvy enough to execute that process every time. However, it is the only choice for calendar entries, and many people use this approach today when sending meeting invitations to users outside their own email and calendaring system.

Tips and Techniques

I would say that the migration process can be extremely challenging, especially for an Oracle person who is not necessarily familiar with core LDAP and email technical architectures and tools. Some of the things I learned along the way I tried to discuss in the preceding examples, but in general a list of things to remember, recall, review, research, look up, pay attention to, etc., follow:

- The Email Migration tool error messages are cryptic in many cases. Don't hesitate to open an SR with Oracle Support sooner rather than later when issues arise.

- Set the System Parameter for logging to Debug in the Migrate Menu System Parameters option. The default value for this parameter is Notification.

- Plan, plan, plan for the migration . . . and do a dry run for the timings before executing the real thing for production.

- Calendar entries are hard to migrate—if not impossible—without a lot of manual intervention, unless you are currently using Steltor or Exchange.

- Multiple migration machines are a must for large migrations that need to be done in a compressed time frame. Either way, however, I would not try to do a mass migration, but phase it in.

- Oracle Collaboration Suite 10*g* is *not like* other email and calendar systems from an Administrative perspective. Do not expect to be able to manage this migration process—or production for that matter—without some Oracle knowledge and hands-on support.

- Use the defaults!!!!!! Every time I have had a customer attempt to "create a user *like* the Administrator", the migration fails . . . until they get religion and realize this is precise stuff and won't work— unless set up completely correctly from the beginning.

- Read the Metalink Notes, Tips, product documentation, etc., before trying this the first time. I have done this more times than I like to think about and a) I have *never* gotten it right on the first try (I believe there is a bolt of lightening waiting for anyone who in fact does that) and b) have never had it work the same way twice.

- Don't be shy. Have the Administrator(s) for the current legacy email and file solutions available to assist during the migration planning and execution to jump in if there are any issues with the old environment that require quick response and Administrative abilities. If you are an Administrator of the current legacy system, then take the same advice regarding Oracle assistance.

Summary

As in many migration efforts, planning and familiarity are the keys to a successful migration from any legacy application into Oracle Collaboration Suite 10g. There are a matrix of choices and options involved in a migration, and it is extremely important to review each of them for how it will impact—positively as well as negatively—your specific migration effort. Finally, as with all IT solutions, remember that success is not measured by how much data is migrated, but rather if the correct information is migrated for the user community to be satisfied.

PART
III

Managing Your
OCS Environment

CHAPTER
8

User Provisioning and Management

Be alert to give service. What counts a
great deal in life is what we do for others.

—Anonymous

N ow that all of the topics related to installation and migration have been presented in detail, it is time to begin discussing the management requirements of the Oracle Collaboration Suite 10*g* environment. As with any other enterprise software product, the key to long-term success of Oracle Collaboration Suite 10*g* in any company is for the Administrators to be proactive in terms of managing and maintaining the key components of the environment. In addition to system maintenance tasks, there are also certain functions that an Administrator needs to perform, such as adding and deleting users, controlling passwords and quotas, and provisioning access to specific application components of the product. I am going to cover the different user creation and maintenance requirements here in this first chapter of Part III since without users none of the rest of the maintenance and administration of the Oracle Collaboration Suite 10*g* environment would be necessary. Darn users, can't live with 'em, can't get rid of them without making your job obsolete at the same time!

User Provisioning Options

Since the need for actually having users in the environment to more or less start the requirement for a maintenance life cycle has been established, I will begin everything in this chapter by discussing the provisioning, or creation, of users in the Oracle Collaboration Suite 10*g* environment. Now, as I discussed in the preceding chapter, there are several mechanisms and ways of executing those mechanisms that can be used to provision users in Oracle Collaboration Suite 10*g*. Some of the ways to provision users are best when creating users a few at a time, while others are best when creating large numbers of users in a single pass. I will go through an exercise with each tool and let the specific situation decide which one is best.

Identity Management User Provisioning Console

The most straightforward way to create a user is through the Oracle Collaboration Suite 10*g* Identity Management Self-Service Console, which will be populated on the Infrastructure tier when installing the Oracle Collaboration Suite 10*g* product. However, this is also the most manually intensive interface for creating users, so it is usually reserved for creating only a few users at a time. Generally, Administrators will use this interface only for one-off user creation after they have created the majority of their user profiles via one of the bulk load processes I will explain a little later in the chapter.

The Oracle Collaboration Suite 10*g* Identity Management Self-Service Console is a web-based interface that walks Administrators through the process of creating users in the Oracle Internet Directory and provisioning Oracle Collaboration Suite 10*g* application components to them. The Self-Service console is the most straightforward way to provision users, since Administrators don't need to know any of the syntax for ldif files or know any ldap-specific commands to load users into the Oracle Internet Directory. Figure 8-1 shows

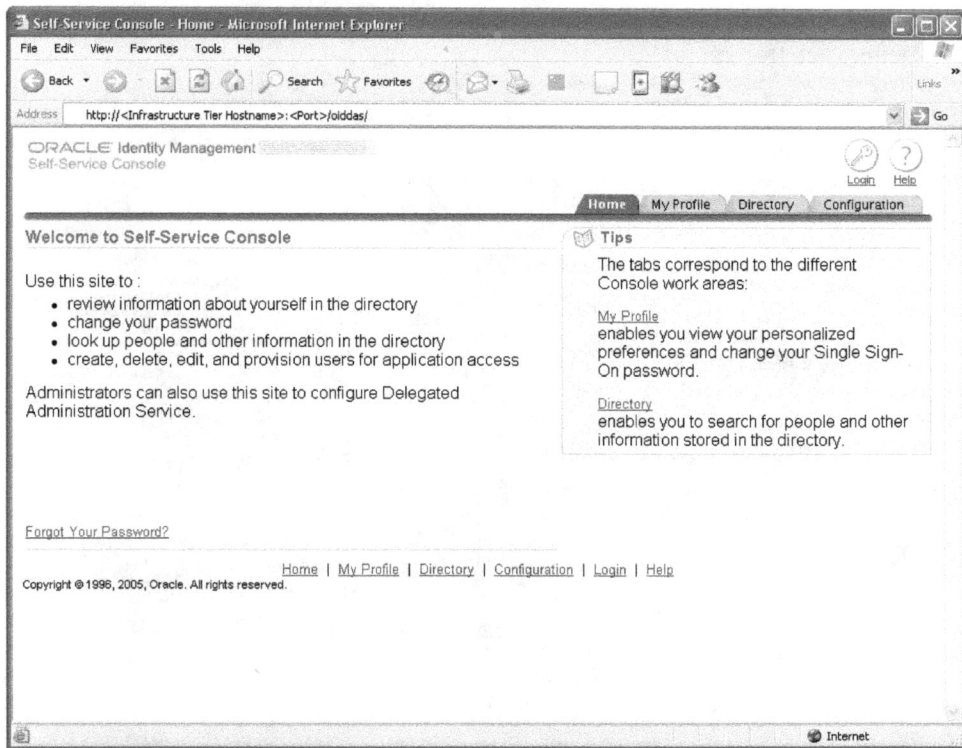

FIGURE 8-1. *Identity Management Self-Service Console access*

how to access the Oracle Collaboration Suite 10*g* Identity Management Self-Service Console from a browser. The Identity Management Self-Service Console page can also be accessed from the Oracle Collaboration Suite 10*g* Welcome page by clicking the Provisioning Console link near the top on the left-hand side of the page.

Admittedly, it can be a bit confusing to figure out how to start on this page for the first-time visitor, but actually it is very simple to navigate, since there is really only one choice on the page at this point. Although a bit inconspicuous, the Login icon/link in the upper right-hand corner is the only thing that you can choose at this time. Well, actually, that isn't 100 percent true. You can in fact click any of the tabs—Home, My Profile, Directory, Configuration—or the links on the page, but regardless of what you click, you will wind up in the same place as if you click the Login link . . . the Single Sign-On page pictured in Figure 8-2.

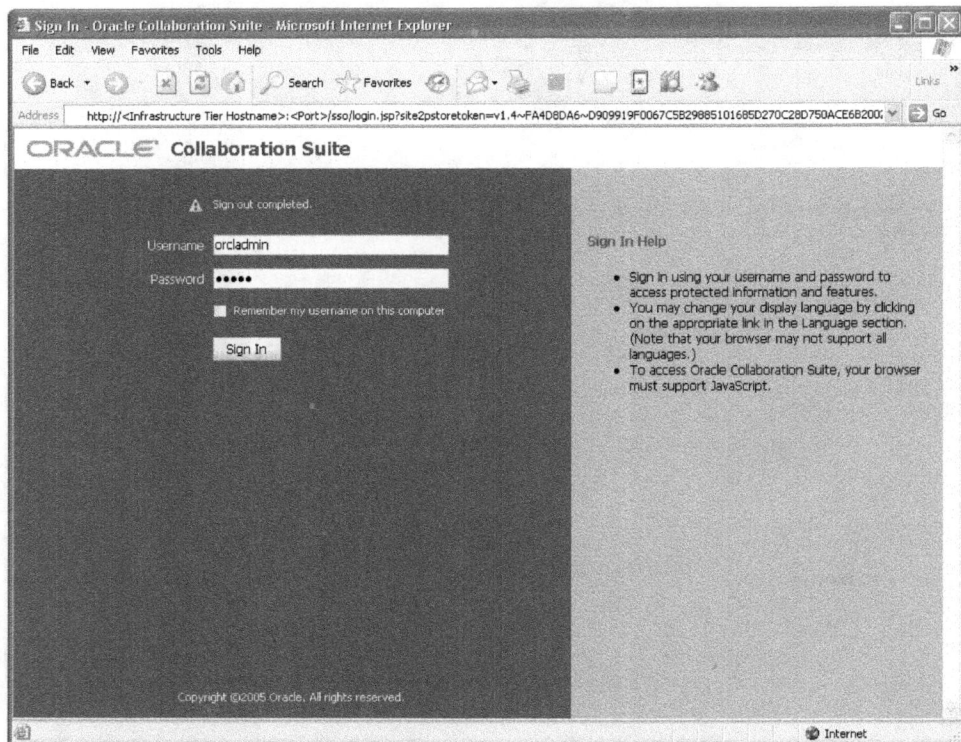

FIGURE 8-2. *Identity Management Self-Service Console single sign-on page*

In order to perform user provisioning and administration functions, you must sign in here as an Identity Management Administrator such as orcladmin (or any user created by orcladmin as an Identity Management Administrator after installation) as shown here in the example. Once you are signed into the Self-Service Console, the main page comes back up, but you can navigate to the other areas of functionality now that sign-on has occurred. Figure 8-3 shows the page once you return from a successful sign-on. The only real aesthetic difference is that the link in the upper right-hand corner now reads Logout instead of Login.

Once here, you can click the Directory tab to begin the user provisioning process. Figure 8-4 shows the initial image of the Directory page when the tab is clicked.

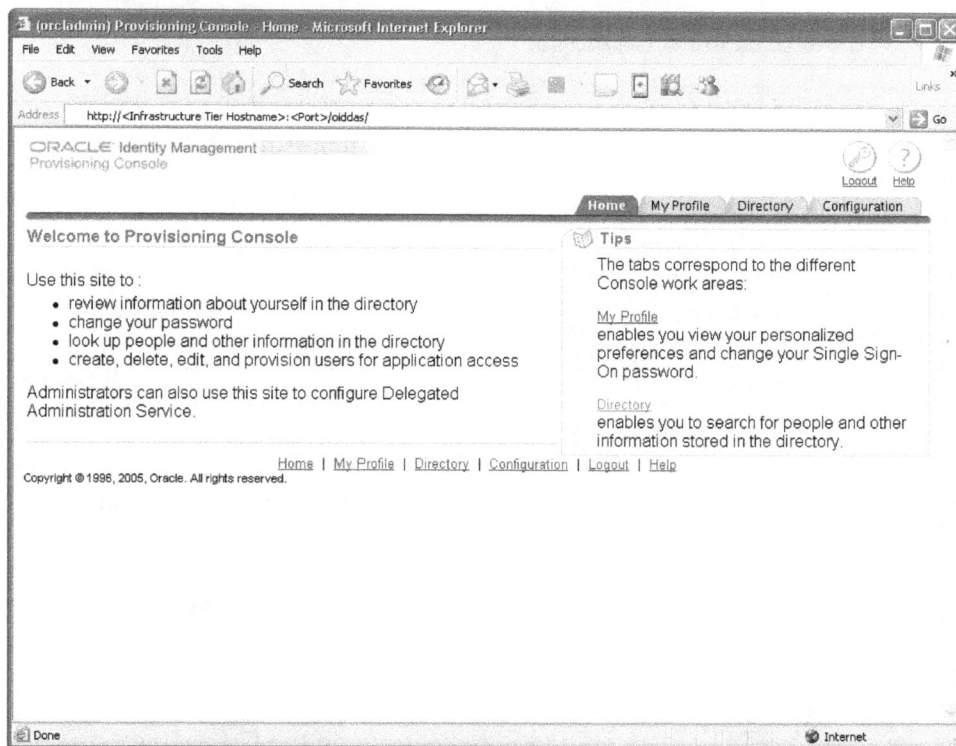

FIGURE 8-3.   *Identity Management Home page after login*

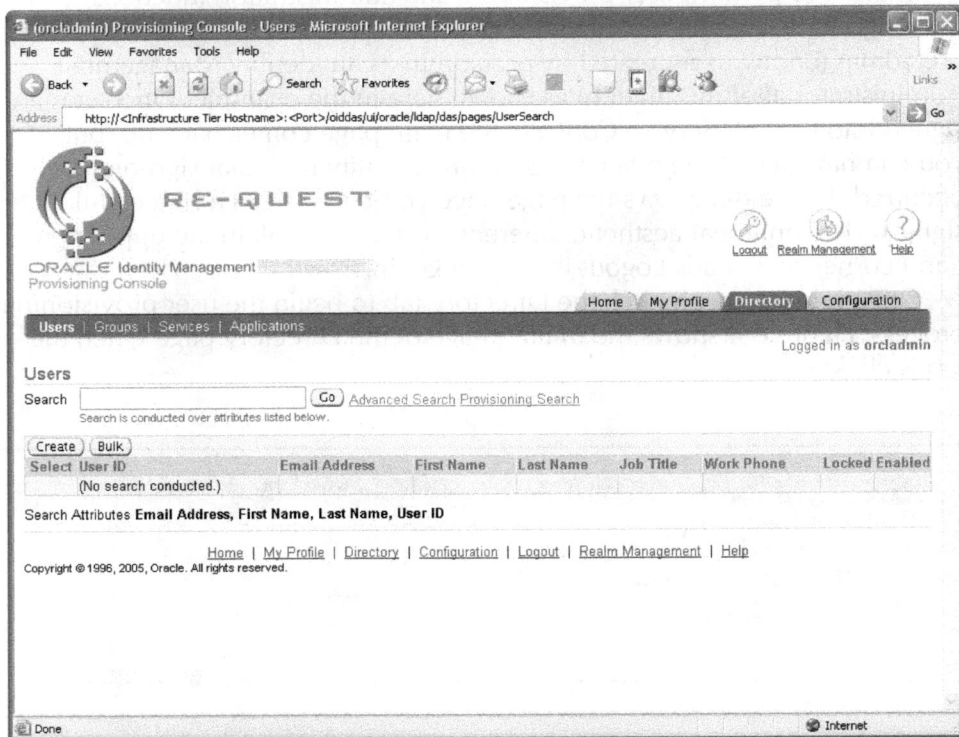

FIGURE 8-4. *Directory tab in Provisioning Console*

The Users section comes up by default when the Directory page first displays. Notice there are no existing users listed, just a blank page with the ability to search for existing users, along with a Create or Bulk button for provisioning new users. I will cover the search function later on in the chapter when I discuss user maintenance, but the search allows the Administrator to bring up a subset of the entire Oracle Collaboration Suite 10*g* user population, or even a single user if the search criteria are narrow enough. Once the user has been identified, that user's profile can be selected for editing.

For now, however, I am going to concentrate on the Create button and its associated functionality. Clicking the Create button located in the middle of the blank Provisioning Console main page brings up the first of several pages for entering in necessary information for creating a new Oracle Collaboration Suite 10g user. This first Provisioning Console page is where general, but very important information is entered for the new user being created. Figure 8-5 shows this General information page for the Create User process with a sample user profile beginning to take shape.

Notice the particular fields identified by the *. This means those particular fields are mandatory, and user provisioning will not be allowed to continue without populating those fields. Last Name, User ID, Password and Confirm Password, and Email Address are the only mandatory fields, but it is recommended to populate as much of this information as is available for each user, since this data will be captured into the user's Oracle Internet Directory profile and be visible to other users of the Oracle Collaboration

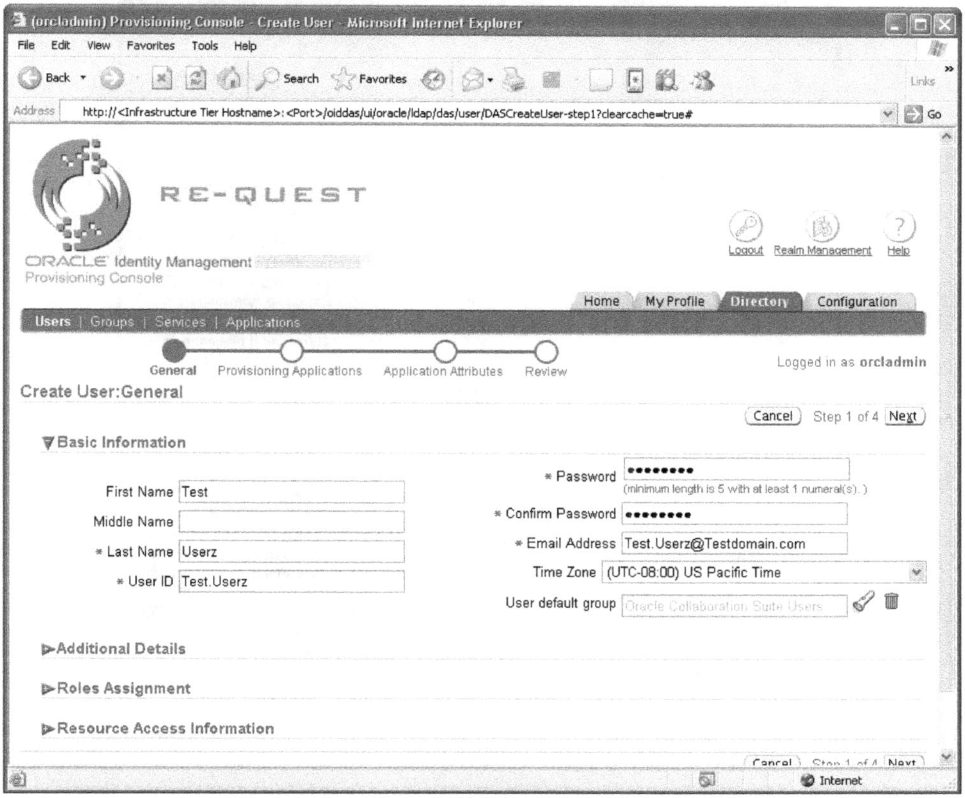

FIGURE 8-5. *General information page*

Suite 10g product. The more information available, the more effective an Oracle Internet Directory search can be as well. Notice that one of the non-mandatory fields I populated in this example is the User default group field. I selected the value from the pop-up list shown in Figure 8-6 that is accessible by clicking the flashlight icon to the right of the entry field. The actual group is called OCS_PORTAL_USERS, but the display name of Oracle Collaboration Suite Users is what populates the field when it is selected from the list.

Once satisfied with the information entered into the General page, an Administrator moves to the next area of user creation, Application Provisioning, by clicking the Next button in the upper or lower right-hand corner of the page. The Application Provisioning page, as shown in Figure 8-7, displays

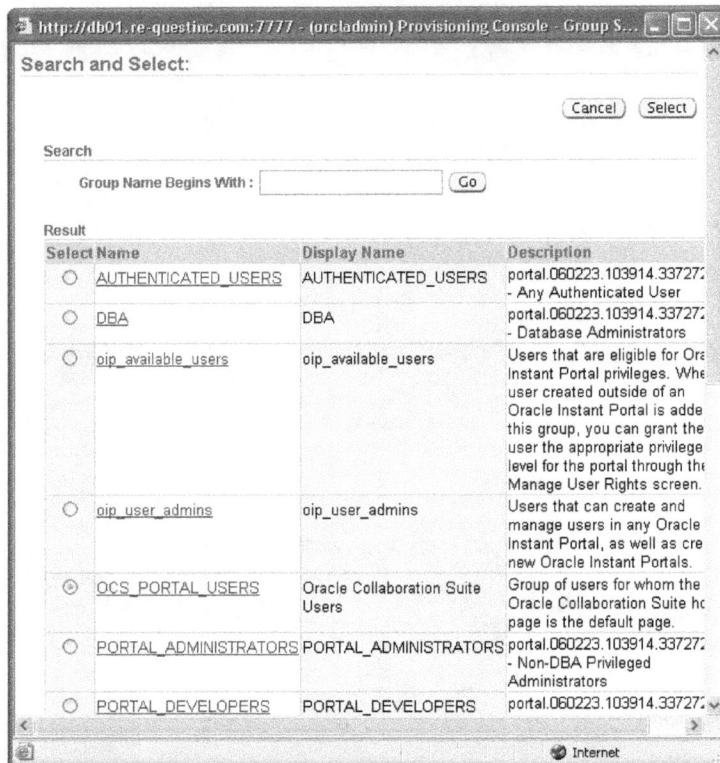

FIGURE 8-6. *Default Group Selection pop-up list*

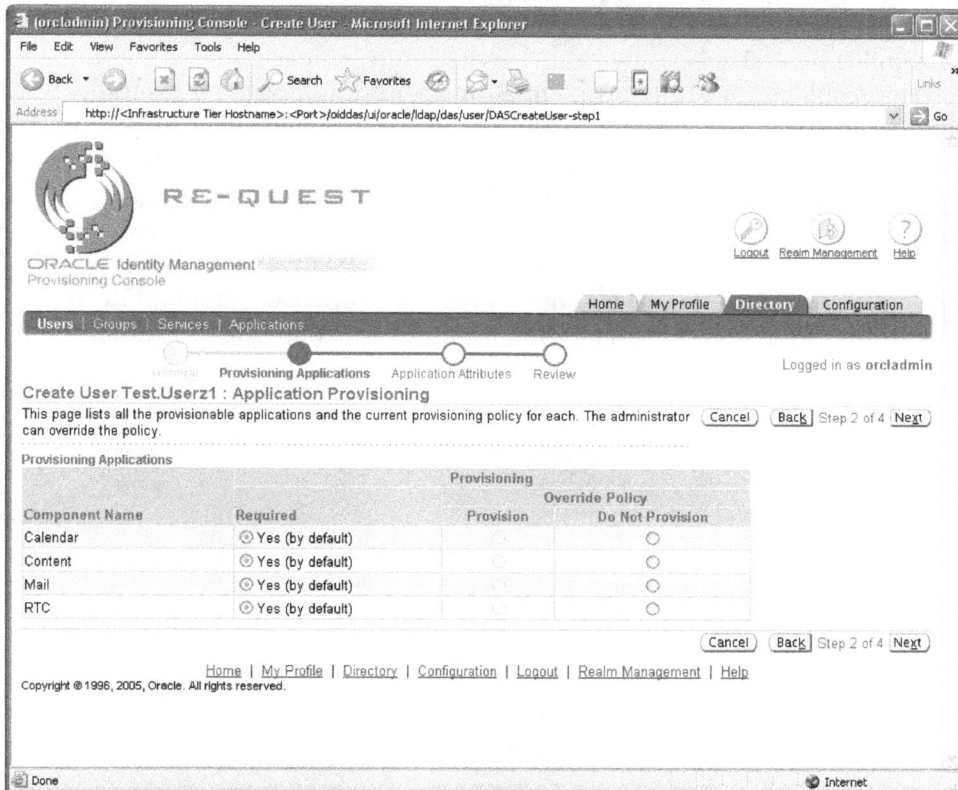

FIGURE 8-7.   *Identity Management User Creation Application Provisioning page*

all applications and their default provisioning rules as available for this installation of the Oracle Collaboration Suite 10*g* product.

Since I installed all the component applications in this example installation, all components are available for provisioning by default. As an Administrator, you may choose to override the default policy at this point. For example, let's say an outside contractor comes on board for a project and the only access he/she should have is Real-Time Collaboration. You may choose to override the default policy and not provision Email and/or Content Services to that particular user—you can do so by clicking the appropriate radio button in the Do Not Provision section of the Application Provisioning page.

Once all the application provisioning rules have been set appropriately for the user, clicking Next brings up the Application Attributes page, pictured here in Figure 8-8.

The Application Attributes page allows an Administrator to define specific attributes such as user role (user versus administrator), quotas, and expiration dates, for the specific applications being provisioned to the user being created. The available attributes will be different depending upon the application, and some of the attributes are modifiable by users themselves if they log in to the Self-Service console (they have access to all non-Administrative attributes to change for their specific user profile), but some call for special attention. For example, setting an Email Quota is important,

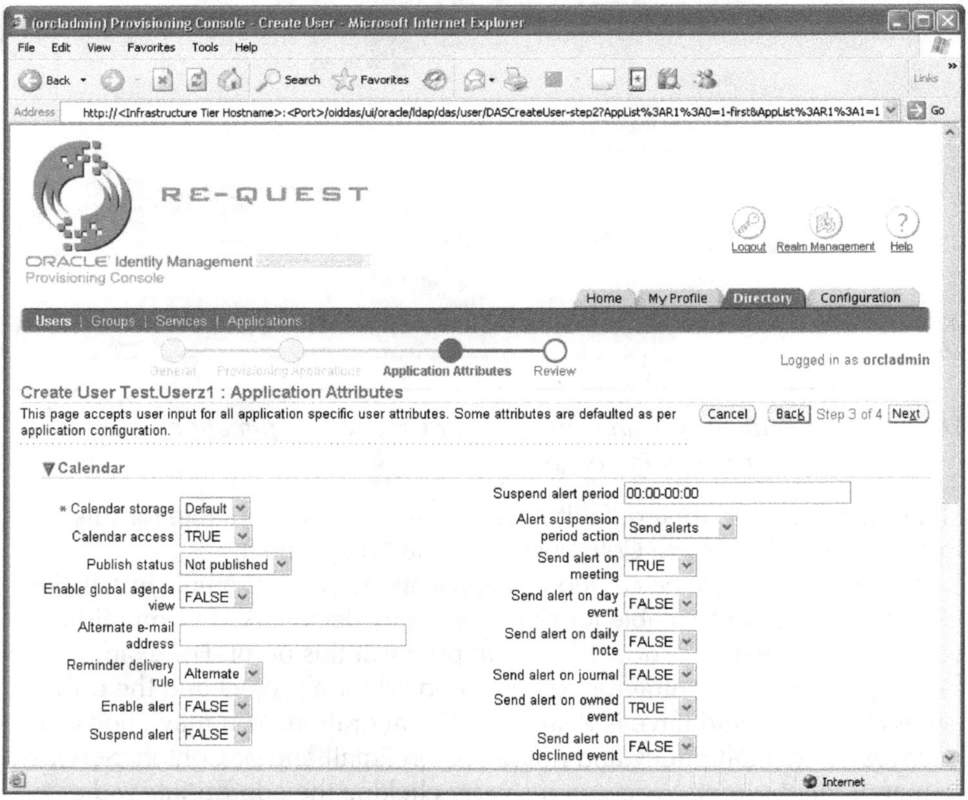

FIGURE 8-8. *Identity Management Provisioning Console Application Attributes page*

especially if a user might consume a large amount of space during the migration process. By setting the quota now, when the user is first created, excess space consumption can be prevented before any email—migrated or received—is allowed to consume space. Another important attribute to set is Email User Role. This attribute defaults to User, but it is important to set at least one user up as the System Administrator so that the user can manage the particulars of the Email environment later on. Archive Policy is important as well if in fact you set up a policy for moving email off to archive. Most of these attributes I am discussing here are related to the Email application, so I have included Figure 8-9 to show you all the attributes for that application. Some applications, such as Real-Time Collaboration (shown at RTC), have no attributes to be populated.

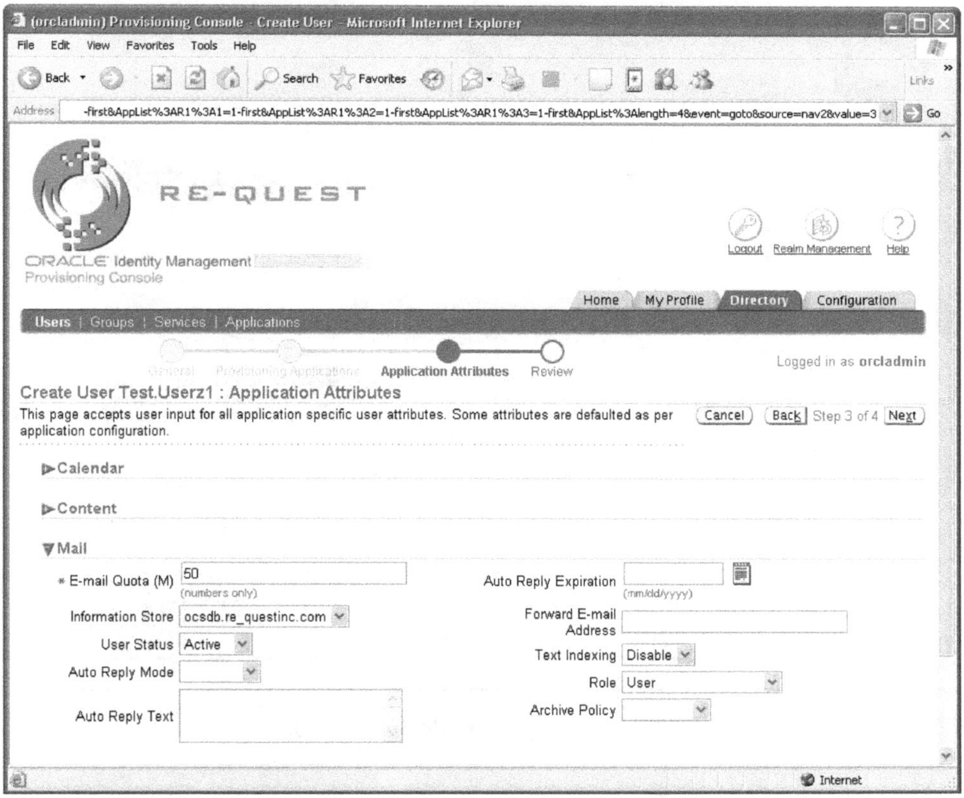

FIGURE 8-9. *Email application attributes in Provisioning Console*

Once you are comfortable with the settings for all modifiable attributes for all applications for this user, you can click Next to move to the Review page. As shown in Figure 8-10, this page summarizes everything defined in the provisioning process for the user on a single page.

Application-specific attributes are displayed on the second half of the page. An example of that section of the page is pictured in Figure 8-11.

If any values entered for this user do not look right here, now is the time to make the corrections. Simply use the Back button to move back to the

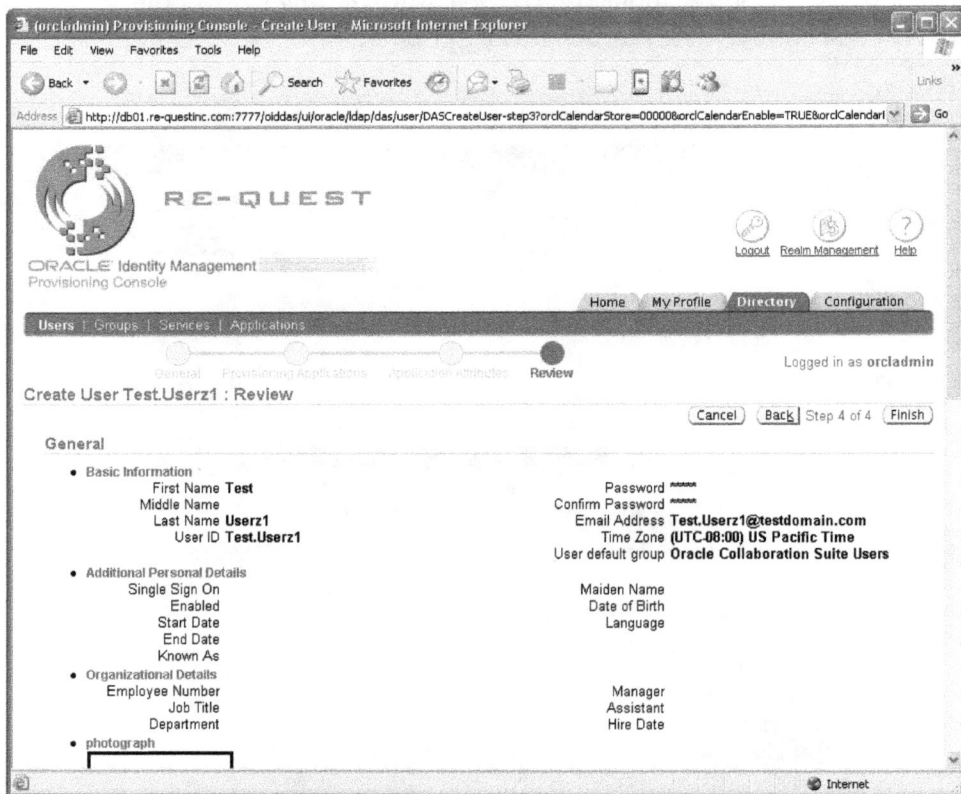

FIGURE 8-10. *User Provisioning Console Review page*

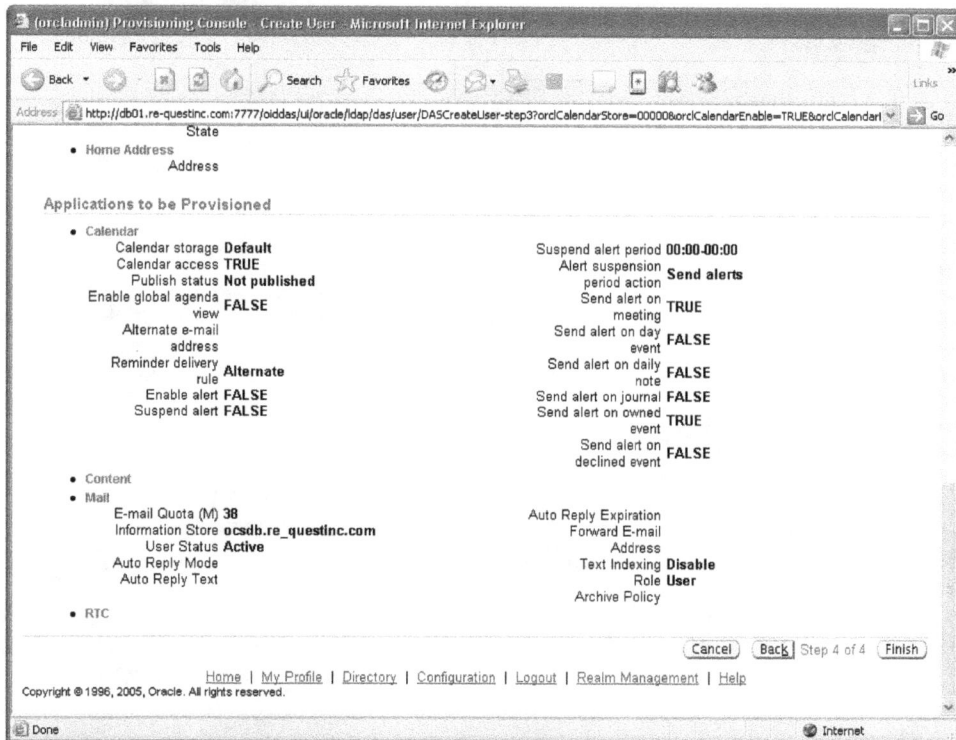

FIGURE 8-11. *User Provisioning Console Review page application attributes*

page in the User Provisioning Console where the attribute to be changed exists and update the value. Then use the Next button to again move forward to the Review page. Once satisfied with everything on the Review page, click Finish to provision the user just defined. If the provisioning process is successful, you are returned to the beginning of the Directory provisioning page and the Confirmation message shown in Figure 8-12 is displayed.

This covers the process for provisioning one user at a time through the Provisioning Console. Now let's discuss using this same interface for provisioning users a group at a time using this same mechanism and interface.

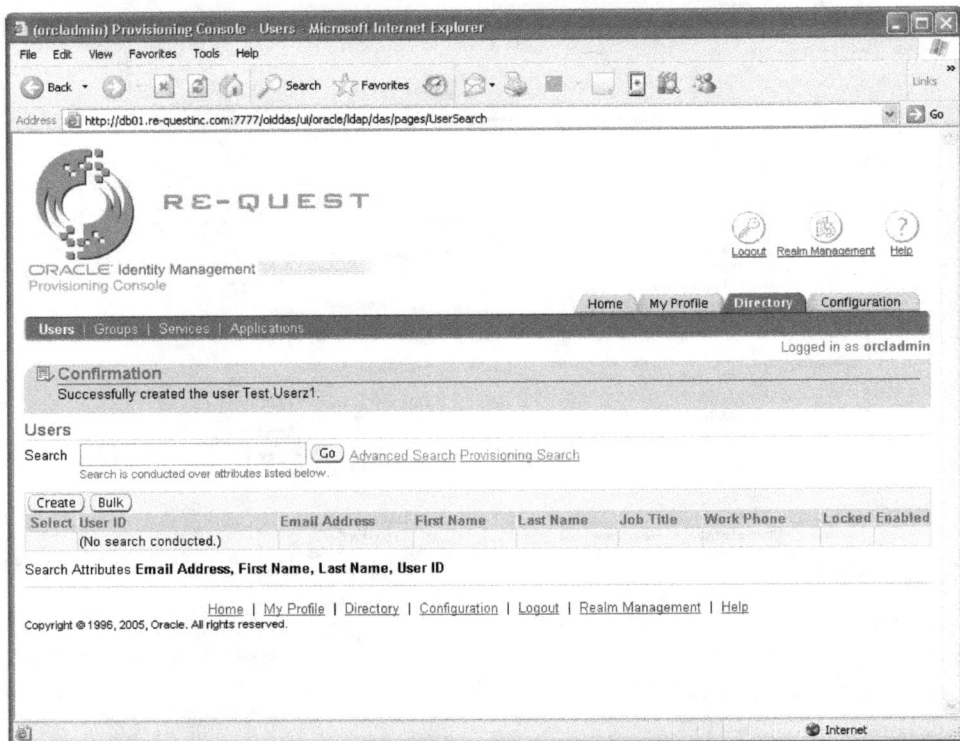

FIGURE 8-12. *User provisioning success message*

Identity Management Provisioning Console Bulk Load

Another way the Identity Management Provisioning Console can be used to create users in Oracle Collaboration Suite 10*g* is to perform the user provisioning through the available bulk load feature. This feature allows an Administrator to create multiple users in bulk or batch format.

The biggest difference between the single-user provisioning you completed in the preceding section and the Provisioning Console bulk load feature is that you must predefine your user profile information in an ldif-formatted flat file prior to running the bulk load function. Figure 8-13 shows an example of a user profile definition in an ldif-formatted flat file that can be used to create users through the bulk load feature of the Provisioning

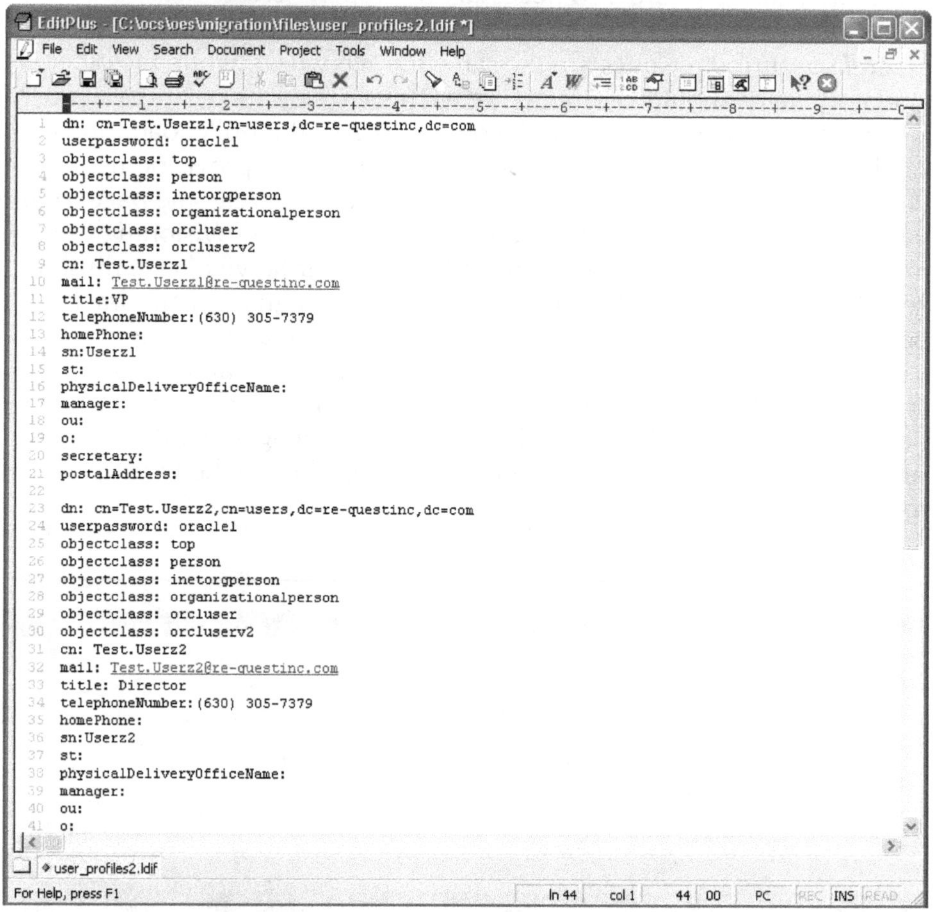


```
dn: cn=Test.Userz1,cn=users,dc=re-questinc,dc=com
userpassword: oracle1
objectclass: top
objectclass: person
objectclass: inetorgperson
objectclass: organizationalperson
objectclass: orcluser
objectclass: orcluserv2
cn: Test.Userz1
mail: Test.Userz1@re-questinc.com
title:VP
telephoneNumber:(630) 305-7379
homePhone:
sn:Userz1
st:
physicalDeliveryOfficeName:
manager:
ou:
o:
secretary:
postalAddress:

dn: cn=Test.Userz2,cn=users,dc=re-questinc,dc=com
userpassword: oracle1
objectclass: top
objectclass: person
objectclass: inetorgperson
objectclass: organizationalperson
objectclass: orcluser
objectclass: orcluserv2
cn: Test.Userz2
mail: Test.Userz2@re-questinc.com
title: Director
telephoneNumber:(630) 305-7379
homePhone:
sn:Userz2
st:
physicalDeliveryOfficeName:
manager:
ou:
o:
```

FIGURE 8-13. *Example LDIF-formatted file for bulk load*

Console. Several attributes are mandatory, which by the way will mirror the fields that were mandatory in the General section of the individual user provisioning we just went through. These include the ***dn:*** attribute at the top of each definition, which defines the ldap tree distinguished name for the new user; the ***userpassword:*** field, which is of course the password the user starts off with; the ***cn:*** attribute, which is the username field; the ***mail:*** attribute for the email address; and finally the ***sn:*** attribute, which is the Last Name attribute for the user whose definition is being created. The various *objectclass:* attributes are also necessary to properly create these users as Oracle Internet Directory users, but as you can see from the figure, these *objectclass:* attribute values are the same for every user, while the other mandatory fields should be unique for each user.

Once the file has been created, you can access the Bulk Load function in exactly the same way you accessed the individual user provisioning function in the process I just described. Simply start out at the Welcome page for the Oracle Collaboration Suite 10*g* product and select the Provisioning Console link on the left-hand side of the page. Once the Self-Service page displays, click either the Directory tab or the Login link and sign in as an Oracle Internet Directory Administrator. Again, I just use orcladmin, since it exists by default in every Oracle Internet Directory installation and has all necessary privileges to complete the user provisioning tasks. Once signed in as orcladmin, you will be placed in the Identity Management Provisioning Console, where choosing the Directory tab will bring up the Users page as shown in Figure 8-14.

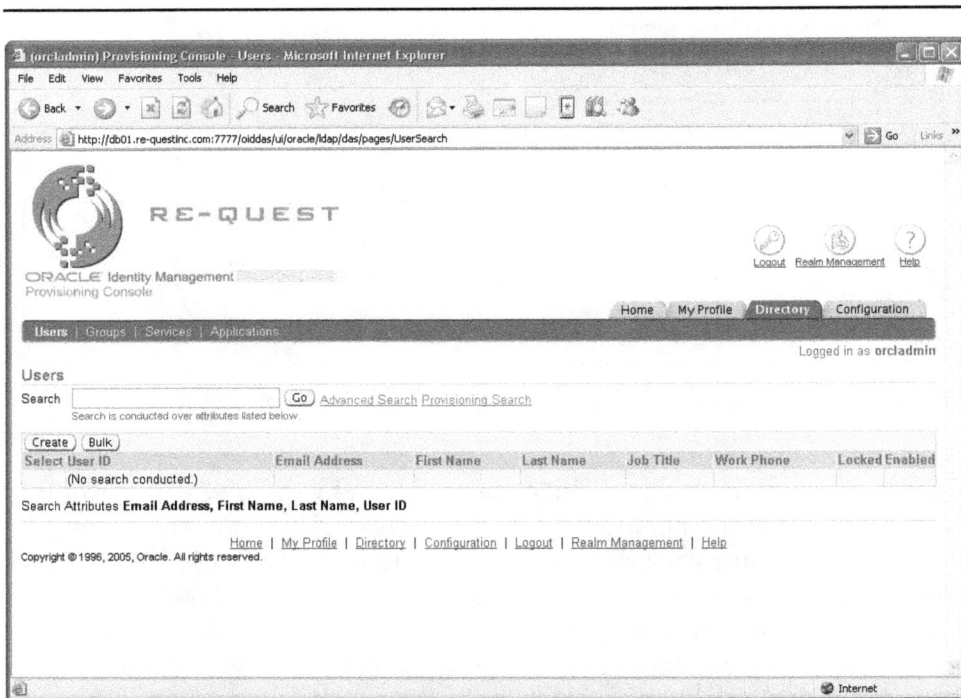

FIGURE 8-14. *Provisioning Console Directory Tab Users page*

Notice the Bulk button just to the right of the Create button that was chosen in the single-user provisioning exercise you just completed. Clicking Bulk will begin the Bulk user load process. You are placed in the Bulk page, where the location and name of the pre-created ldif file is entered (the Browse button can be used to locate the file as well). As Figure 8-15 shows, I choose the Ignore Failed Users check box so that the Bulk Load process actually runs through the entire file, rather than stopping on the first error. The bulk load process will create a log file of the execution, which will be named <ldif-filename>.ldif.log, as well as a file to hold any users that fail to get created during the execution, which is named <ldif-filename>.ldif.failed.

Once the location and name of the ldif file have been populated in the LDIF File field, click OK to begin the bulk user provisioning process. The progress bar shown in Figure 8-16 will move from left to right as the users are created. Once the entire bulk load process completes, the status of each step in the execution can be reviewed in the Details section at the bottom of the page, which includes timestamps for each of the steps the process

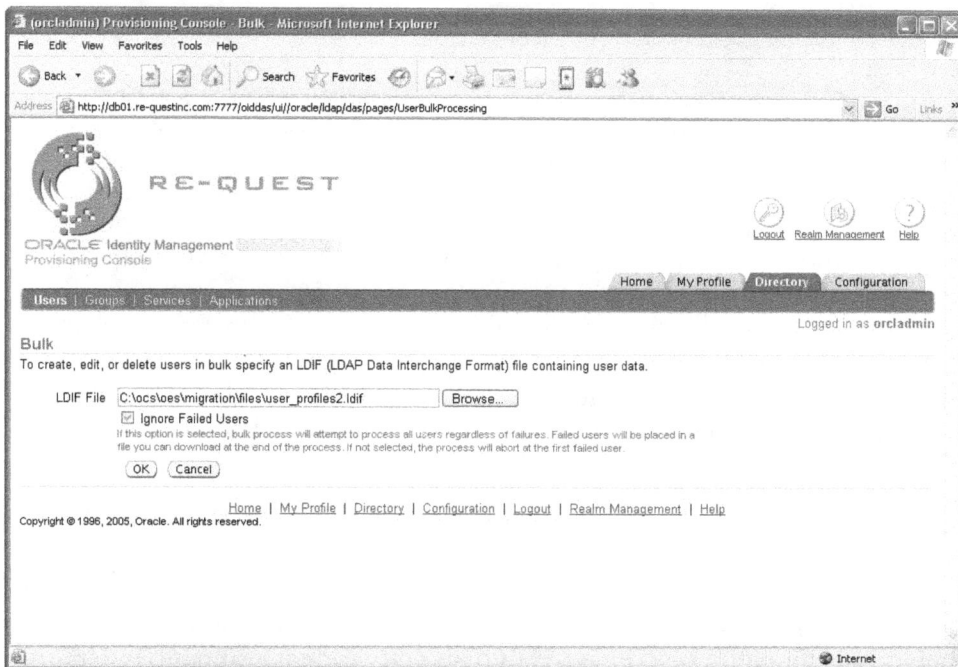

FIGURE 8-15. *Provisioning Console Bulk User Load page*

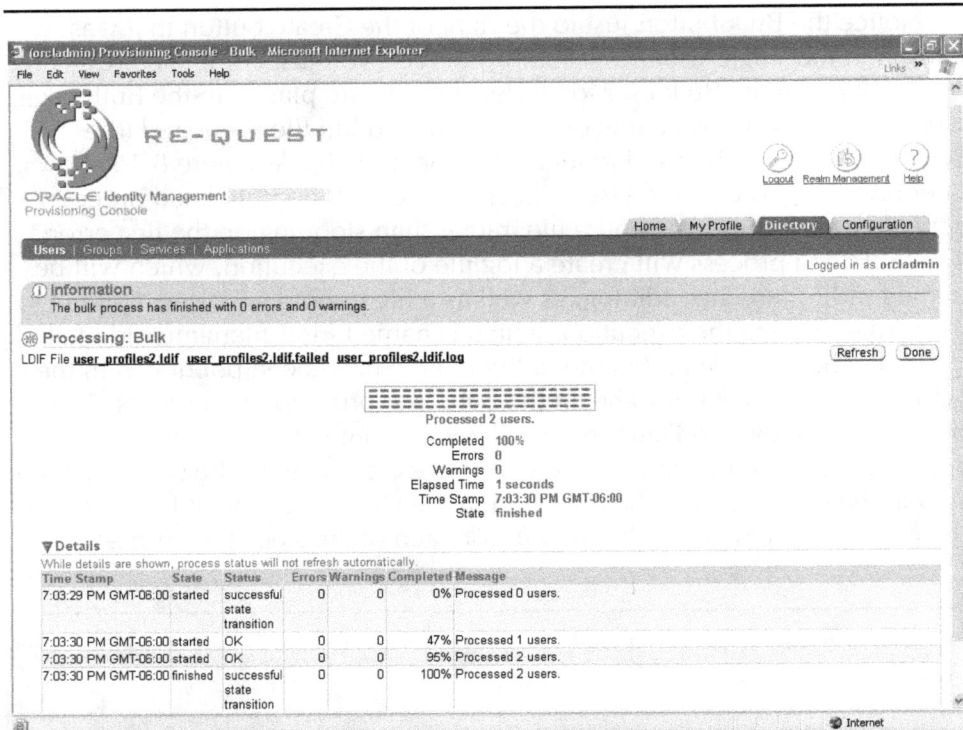

FIGURE 8-16. *Bulk Load Processing and Status page*

executes, the status of the step, a count of the errors and warnings that occurred during the step, and its percentage complete. If everything completes successfully as in my example in Figure 8-16, this given batch is complete. If there are errors, the log file and the failed file need to be reviewed and possibly corrected and re-run until all users in the batch have been successfully created.

Provisioning Users via LDAP Commands

Standard LDAP commands can also be used to bulk-load users into the Oracle Collaboration Suite 10g Identity Management. A simple ldif file can be extracted from a legacy system, for example, or defined manually, and that ldif file can then be converted into an entry format compatible with the

Oracle Collaboration Suite 10g Identity Management by running the LDAP command *ldifmigrator* provided in the $ORACLE_HOME/bin directory for the Infrastructure tier against the ldif file. Once converted, the ldif file can finally be loaded into the Oracle Collaboration Suite 10g Identity Management using LDAP command *ldapadd,* also provided in the $ORACLE_HOME/bin directory of the Infrastructure tier Oracle Home ($ORACLE_HOME/bin where $ORACLE_HOME=/<mount-point>/<infrastructure tier oracle directory>/).

Email Migration Tool

The Email Migration Tool also uses an ldif flat-file format to load users in batches into the Oracle Collaboration Suite 10g Identity Management. The Email Migration Tool expects the user profile information to be defined in a file named user_profiles.ldif, which must be placed in the <Drive Letter>:\ ocs\oes\migration\files directory before running the Email Migration Tool to provision users. Since I covered this approach in the Chapter 7, I am going to simply direct you to the section in Chapter 7 on migrating user definitions using the Email Migration Tool, since the process for migrating users from a legacy system and creating them from scratch using this tool is identical.

Additional User Requirements

In addition to user provisioning, Administrators also have other management and maintenance requirements to be concerned with around the Oracle Collaboration Suite 10g user community they manage. Administrators need to concern themselves with such things as granting and revoking access to, and managing quotas for, each of the Oracle Collaboration Suite 10g components for each user.

Additional Component Provisioning

In some cases when a user is first created, that user may only be provisioned for a subset of the available Oracle Collaboration Suite 10g components. In some instances additional components will need to be provisioned at a later time. Fortunately, the Oracle Collaboration Suite 10g Identity Management Provisioning Console provides for such functionality out of the box.

To provision additional Oracle Collaboration Suite 10*g* components to a user, you must first log in to the Provisioning Console as you did to create a new user. Then navigate to the Directory tab and either retrieve the entire list of users or conduct a search as shown in Figure 8-17 to narrow the list to include the user that needs the additional component provisioned.

Simply enter a portion of the username for the user you wish to modify along with the wildcard % and click Go. This will bring up all users that matched the search criteria entered. In this example, for the sake of simplicity, I narrowed the search such that it brought up only a single user, as shown in Figure 8-18.

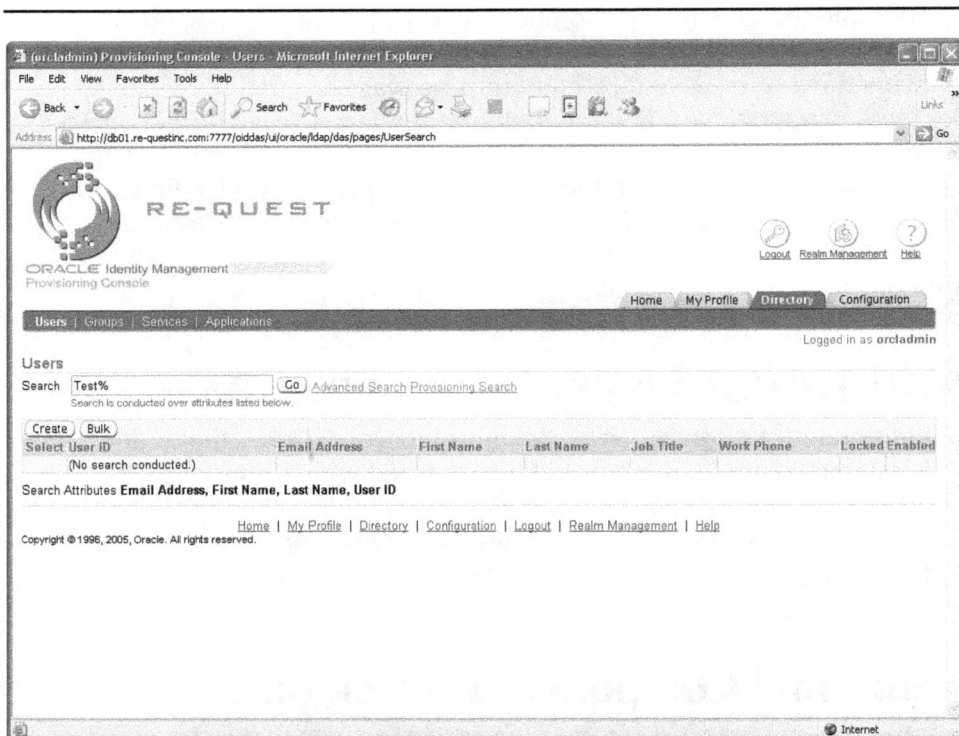

FIGURE 8-17. *Identity Management Provisioning Console user search*

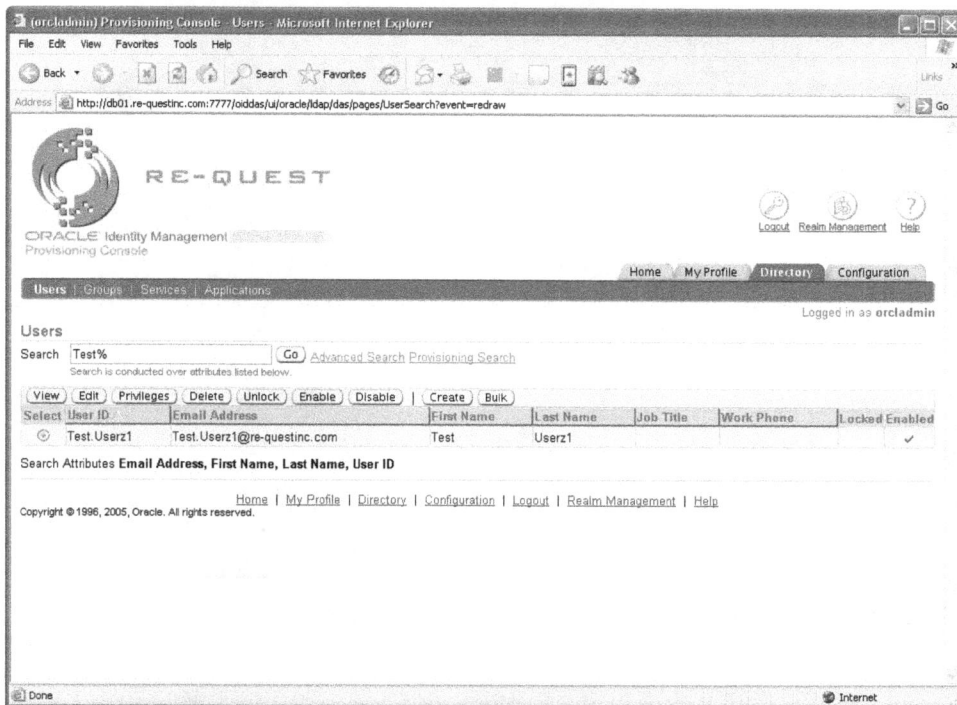

FIGURE 8-18. *Search list returned in Provisioning Console*

From here select the radio button to the left of the user record to be modified and click Edit. This will place you in edit mode on that particular user and begin the edit session on the General page as shown in Figure 8-19 (similar to where you were placed to create the user as discussed in the earlier part of this chapter).

Clicking Next from here will move you to the Application Provisioning page of the Provisioning Console user edit session as pictured in Figure 8-20.

Any applications not currently provisioned for the user being edited will show up on the bottom of the page, and the Yes radio button will be selected (by default) to provision the application for this user. You must select No for any applications that should not be provisioned for this user, but any Yes radio buttons left selected will cause the associated Oracle Collaboration Suite 10g component(s) to be provisioned. By clicking Finish

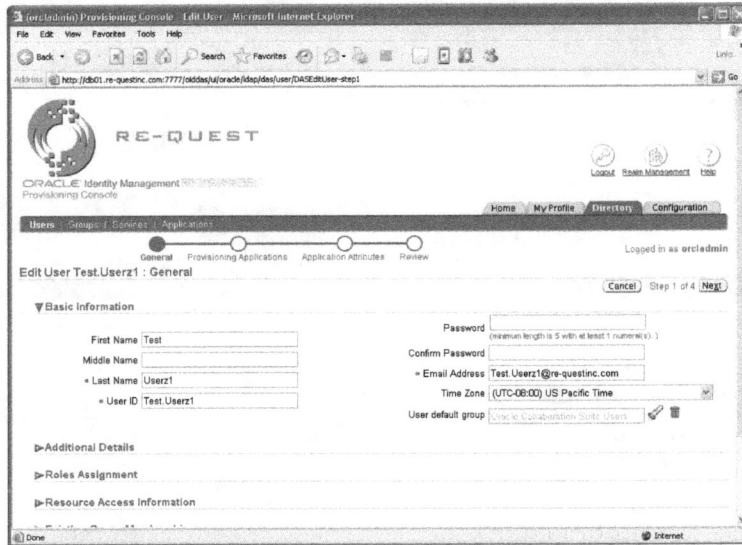

FIGURE 8-19. *Provisioning Console User Edit General page*

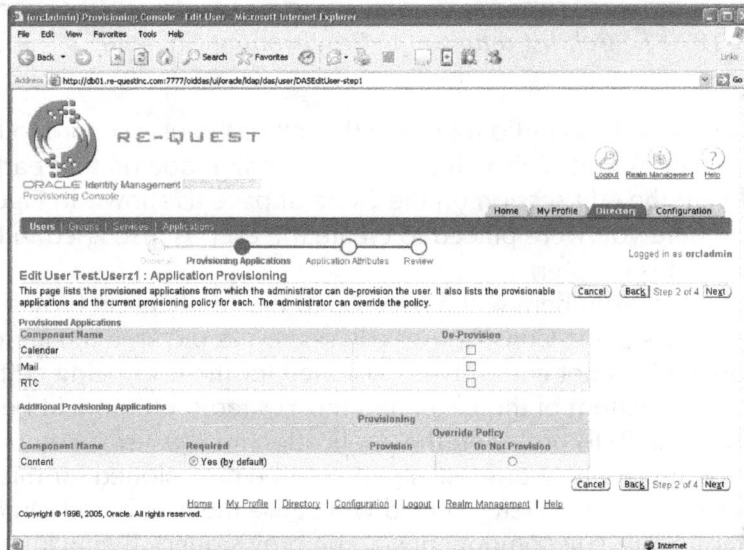

FIGURE 8-20. *Provisioning Console User Edit Application Provisioning page*

once all sections of the edit session have been completed, the user is modified and the selected application(s) provisioned. You must therefore pass through the Application Attributes section and click the Finish button on the Review section pictured in Figure 8-21 to provision the additional component(s) to this user.

When you click Finish, the Provisioning Console returns you to the General page and displays the confirmation message: "Successfully modified the user <Username>," as shown in Figure 8-22 (similar to the way it displayed the confirmation message "Successfully created user <Username>" when the initial provisioning was completed).

Quota Setting

As I mentioned in Chapter 7, when discussing the management of space consumption, it is better to establish quotas up front in the life cycle of the

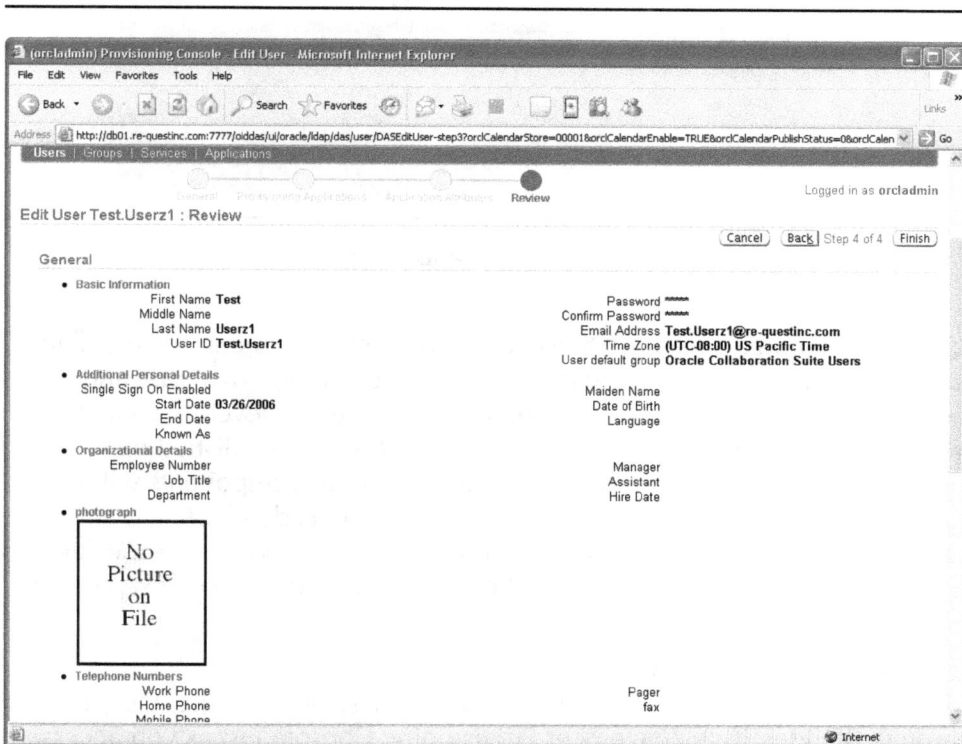

FIGURE 8-21. *Provisioning Console User Edit Review page*

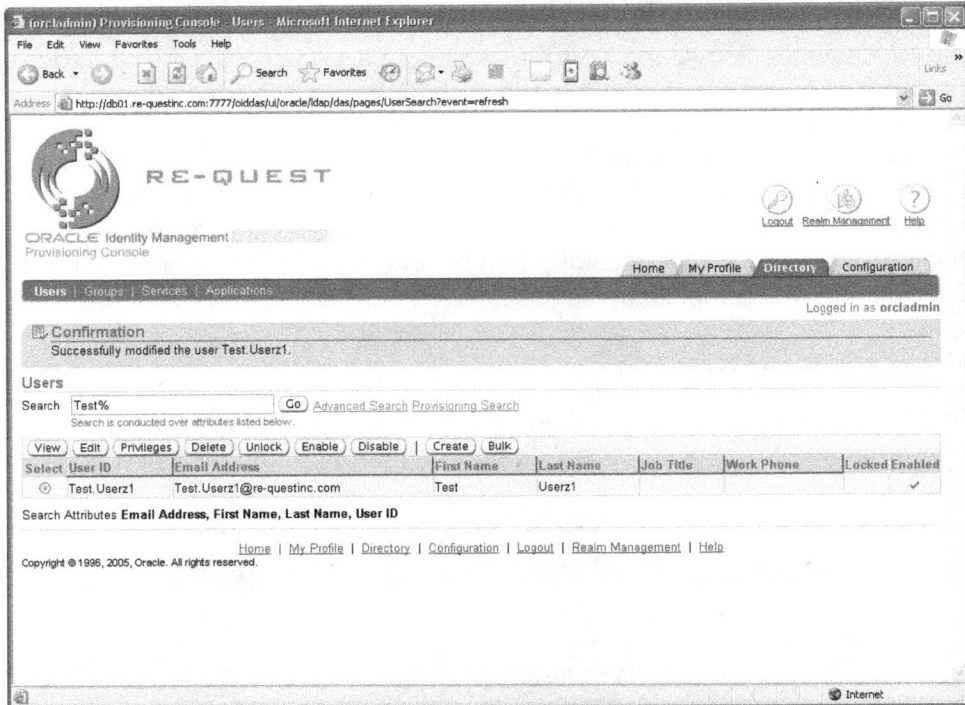

FIGURE 8-22. *Successful user modification message*

Oracle Collaboration Suite 10g rollout than to attempt to enforce them after users have had an opportunity to consume space at their own rate and establish their own "policies" (in other words store whatever they want whenever they want!). However, whether quotas are established up front or not, there will be times when user quotas for certain components will need to be adjusted. The main components where quota is definable are Email and Content Services. Each has its own way to set or update quota values, so I will navigate you through locating the quota values for each one separately.

Email Quota Setting

The Email quota is the more straightforward quota setting because it is accessed through the Identity Management Provisioning Console just as you accessed it to create the users. As you may recall, one of the pages in the provisioning workflow is the Applications Attributes page. There the Administrator (and to a lesser extent the users themselves) could set/modify attributes for the individual applications, specifically Calendar and Email. Referring back to Figures 8-8 and 8-9, the modifiable attributes for Calendar and Email are pictured respectively. Looking closely at Figure 8-9, you can see the quota parameter is defined there for the email application. So, using the access path to this page defined in the previous section "Provisioning Users via LDAP Commands," you should navigate to this page for the user(s) you wish to modify the Email quota value for and change it. Remember to click Next all the way through and then click the Finish button to have the changes take effect.

Content Services Quota Setting

Setting quotas for Content Services is a bit different than setting Email quotas in that quotas are not managed strictly on a user-by-user basis in Content Services, but rather by content storage "unit." First, a quota is assigned to the Content Services site itself, a term that describes the virtual organizational grouping of users that can collaborate on content. A site is associated with a given Identity Management realm (domain). Users in one site cannot access the content of users in another site. In most Oracle Collaboration Suite 10*g* installations a site is an instance of Content Services. Usually a given implementation of Oracle Collaboration Suite 10*g* will only have a single realm (domain) and therefore only one Content Services site. Next, because multiple users are usually assigned to manage and use documents stored in a particular library, a quota is allocated to libraries in Content Services rather than to individual users. If you think about it, if a user accesses documents across multiple libraries in Content Services that have been uploaded, created, modified, etc., by other users, then how can the quota amount be assigned to any one user? This way, libraries, or groups of users, must conform to a quota for the grouping of documents. So your question is, what does this mean to you as an Administrator, correct? (I could hear it coming.) Well, what it means is that there are several places to manage quota amounts: one for the site and then one for each library defined in Content Services.

Let's start with the site-level quota amount:

1. To access this quota value, go into the Oracle Collaboration Suite Control site (Enterprise Manager). This is accessible by clicking the link on the upper left-hand side of the Welcome page, as shown in Figure 8-23, or by typing the Enterprise Manager URL into your browser (I recommend the first choice).

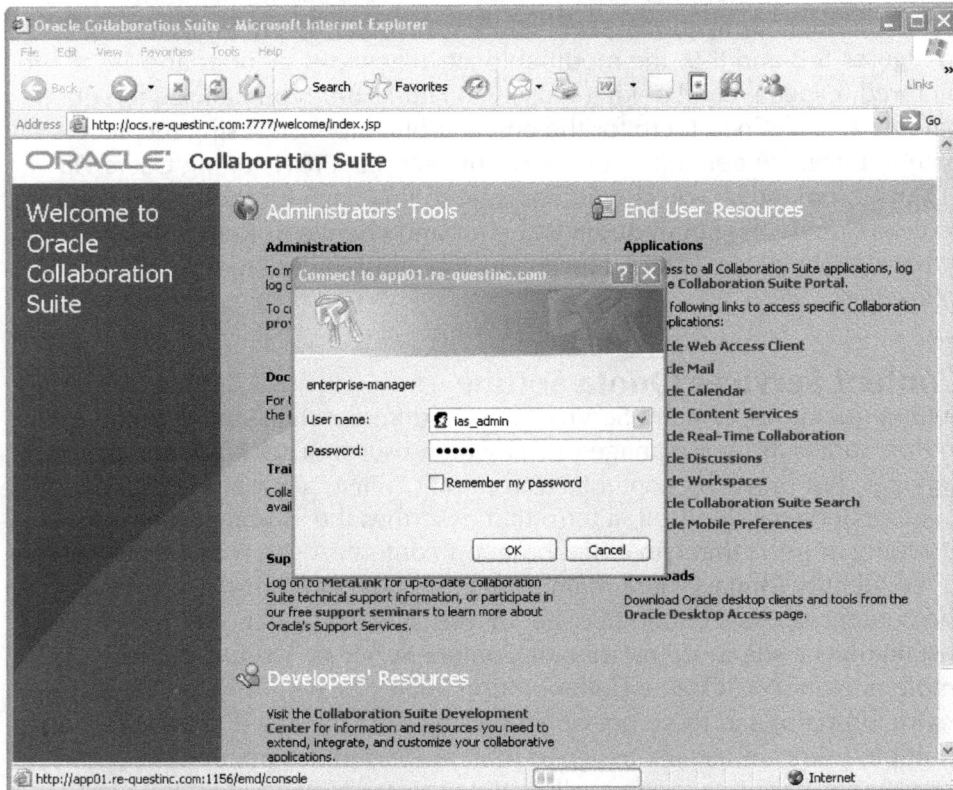

FIGURE 8-23. *Oracle Collaboration Suite Control link on the Welcome page*

   2. Click the Control link. The sign-on box for the Enterprise Manager
      site pops up as shown in Figure 8-23, asking for the Enterprise
      Manager Administrator username and password. I use the default
      username created during the install, ias_admin.

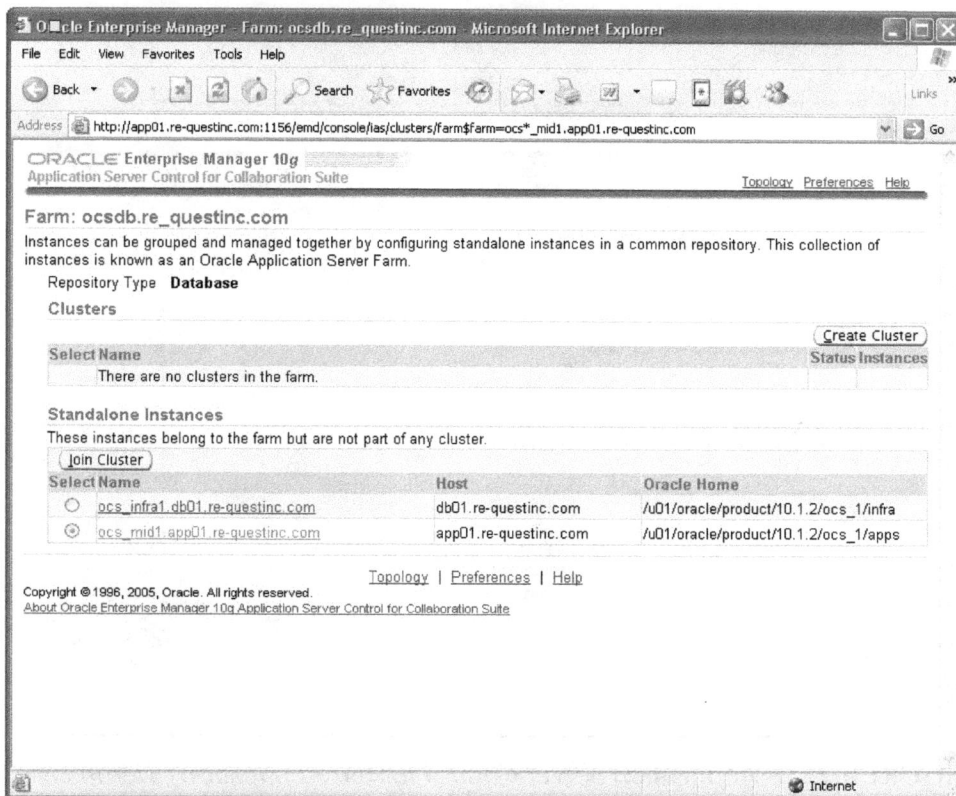

FIGURE 8-24. *Select the Middle Tier in Enterprise Manager*

3. Since you are administering application-level parameters in this case, navigate to the Applications Tier of the Oracle Collaboration Suite 10*g* installation, shown here by the selected radio button in Figure 8-24, by clicking the link. This brings up the Applications Tier processes and associated information in Enterprise Manager as pictured in Figure 8-25.

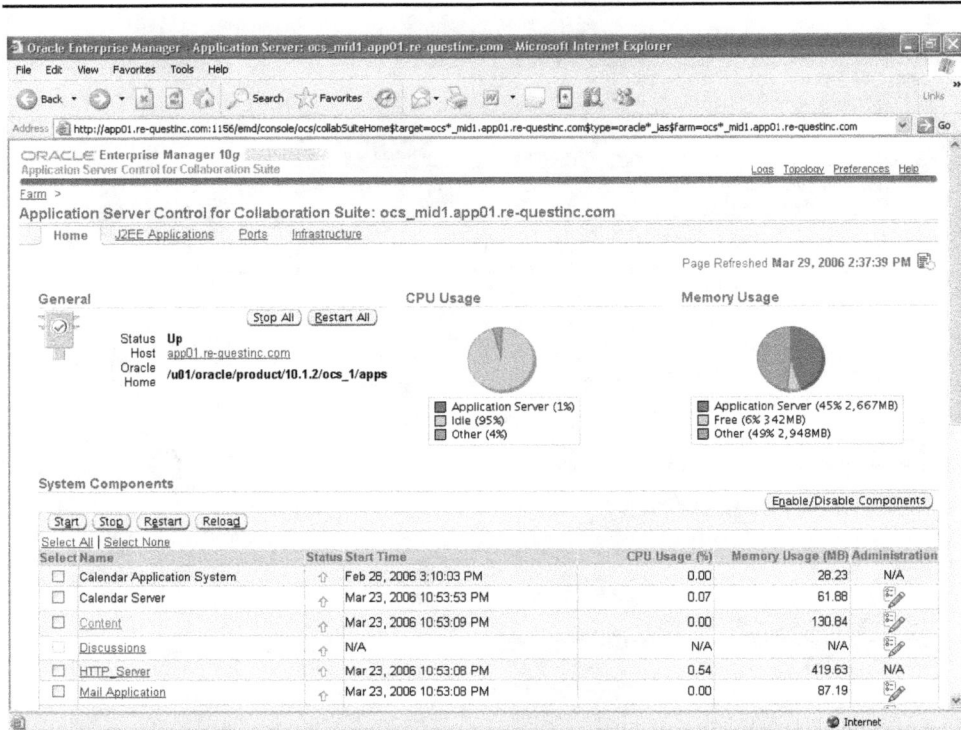

FIGURE 8-25. *Application Server Control for the Applications Tier in EM*

4. Click the Content link to bring up a summary page of information in Enterprise Manager for the Content Services component of the Applications Tier, shown in Figure 8-26.

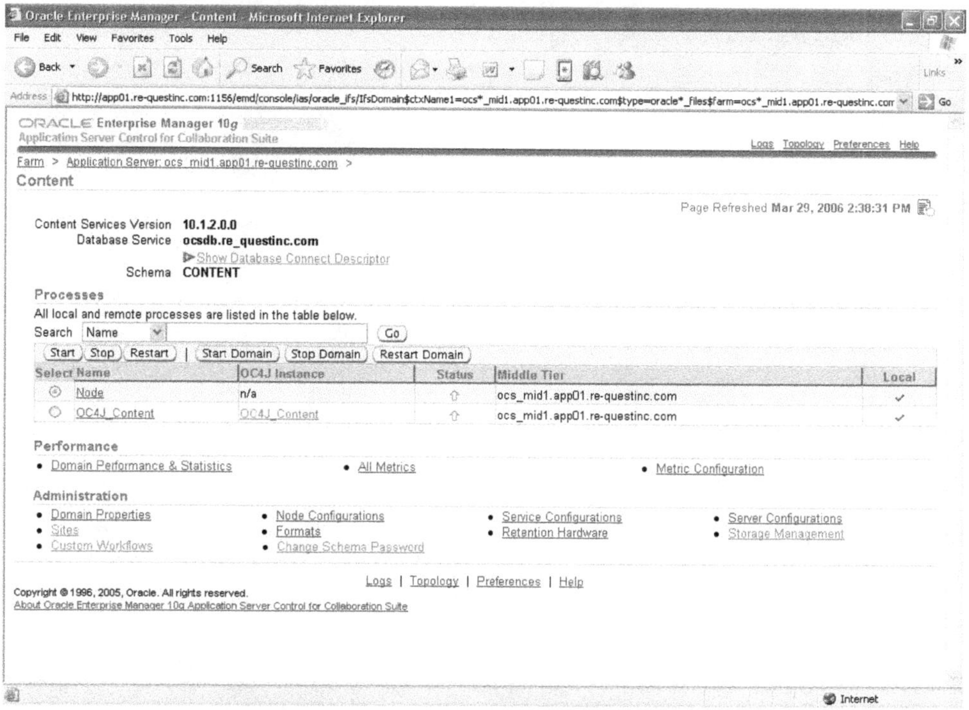

FIGURE 8-26.   *Content Services page in EM*

5. Click the Sites link in the Administration section at the bottom of the page to bring up the list of sites for this implementation of Content Services. Notice I only have one site in my implementation, pictured in Figure 8-27.

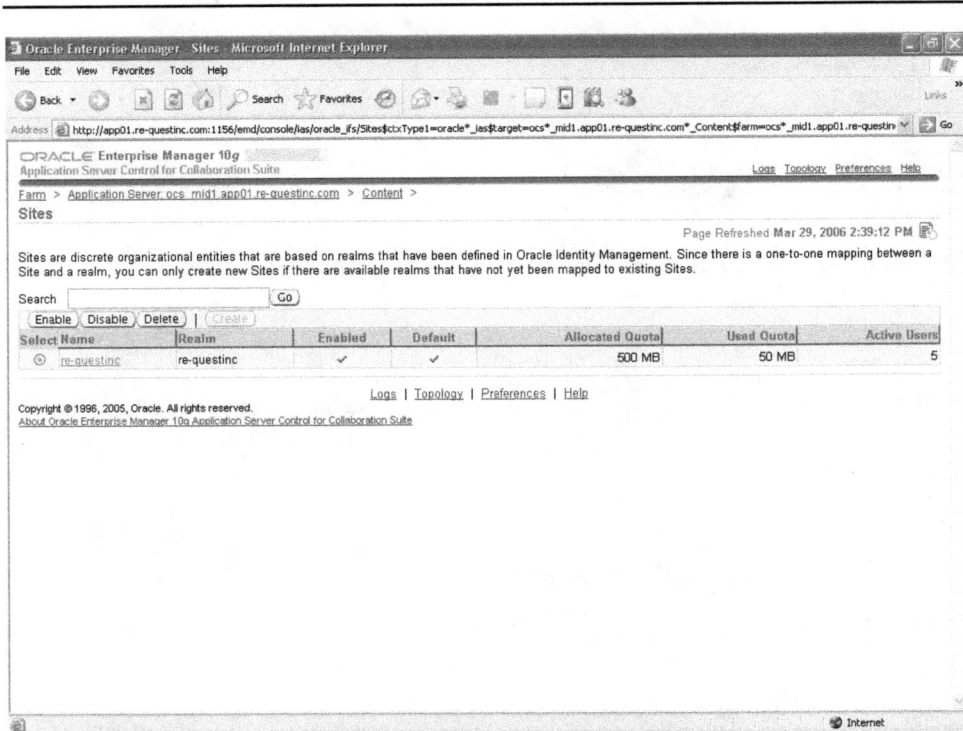

FIGURE 8-27. *Sites List page for Content Services*

6. Click the site name to edit the quota value as shown in Figure 8-28.

7. Once the value is changed as in Figure 8-29, click OK.

The message "Site <site name> has been successfully modified" is displayed, and you are returned to the Sites list page, shown here in Figure 8-30.

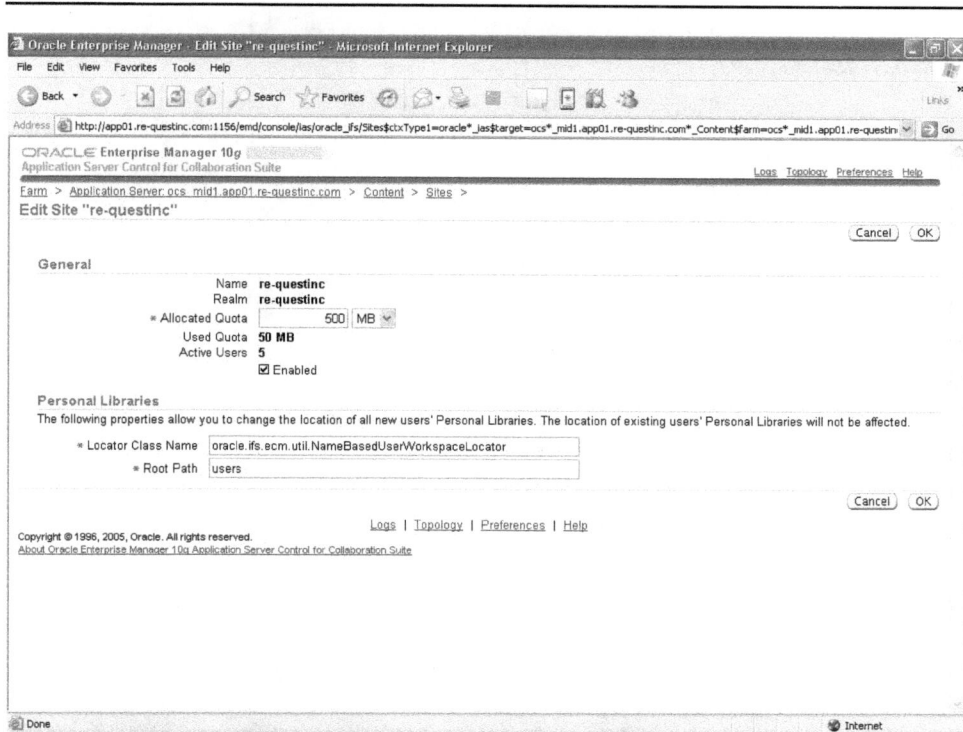

FIGURE 8-28. *Site detail for changing quota value*

Now I will walk you through modifying quota values for libraries in Content Services. This requires you to log in to Content Services directly.

1. To do so, go to the Collaboration Suite Welcome page and choose to log into either the Portal or directly into Content Services via the links on the right-hand side of the page. If you choose Content Services, you will be brought to the Content Services Launch page pictured in Figure 8-31.

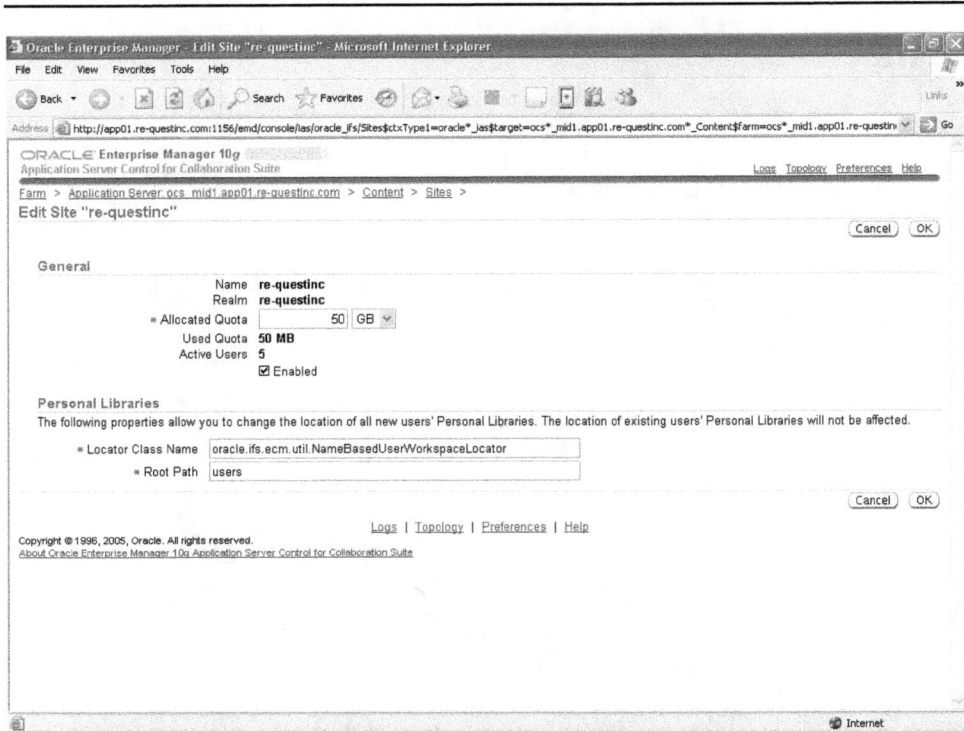

FIGURE 8-29. *Modified quota value for the site in Content Services*

2. Click Launch to be directed to the Single Sign-On page. Remember, you are going to need Administrator access, so log in as orcladmin (there are other administrative users that can be created, but orcladmin has everything) as shown in Figure 8-32.

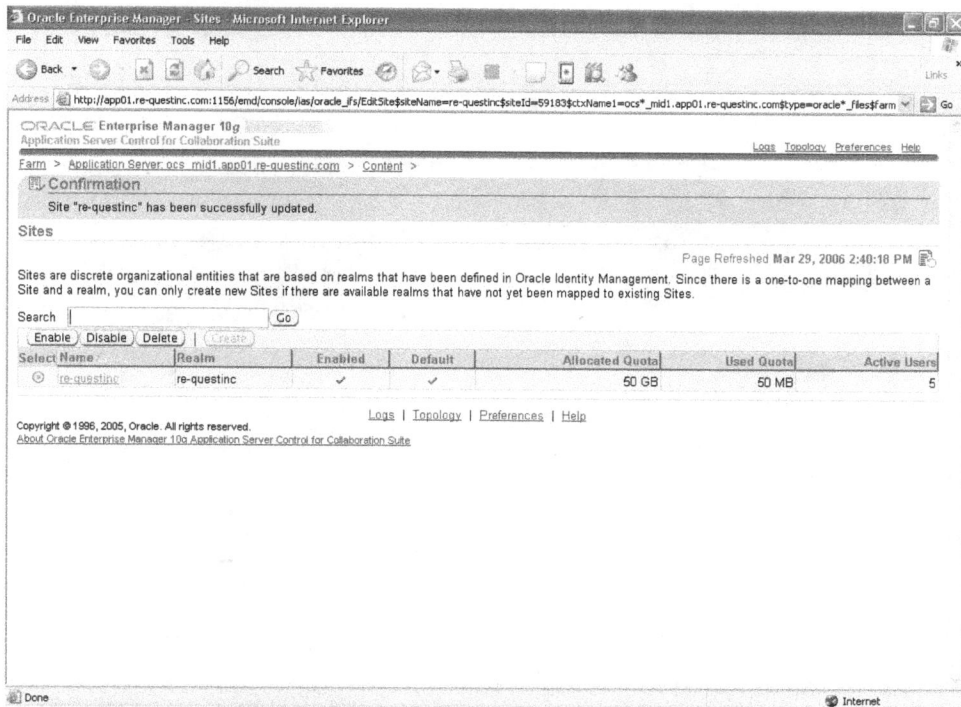

FIGURE 8-30.   *Quota successfully modified*

3. When first signing in, you are put in "User" Mode. You must explicitly change to Administrator Mode by clicking the Switch to Administration Mode link, which is present in the upper right-hand corner and is highlighted in Figure 8-33.

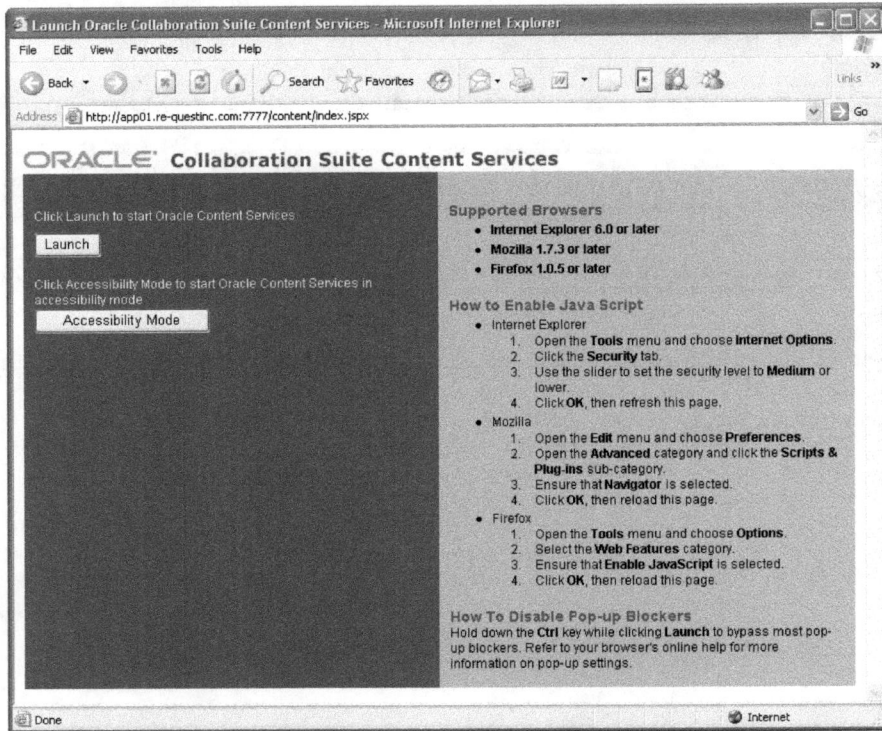

FIGURE 8-31. *Content Services Launch page*

4. Once you are in Administrator Mode, the menu on the left-hand side of the page changes, and one of the options is Quota Settings. Click Quota Settings to bring up the Quota settings currently in place. This shows the default quota assigned for any new library created. You can change the value and click Save Changes, and from then on any new library created in this Content Services site will be given that quota. Figure 8-34 shows the Quota Settings page.

5. This takes care of any new library created, but any library already created needs to be adjusted individually. To do that, while still in Administrator Mode, click the File icon on the left-hand side of the page to display the current library folder tree for the site. By right-clicking any library, you can access the Properties option from the pop-up as shown in Figure 8-35.

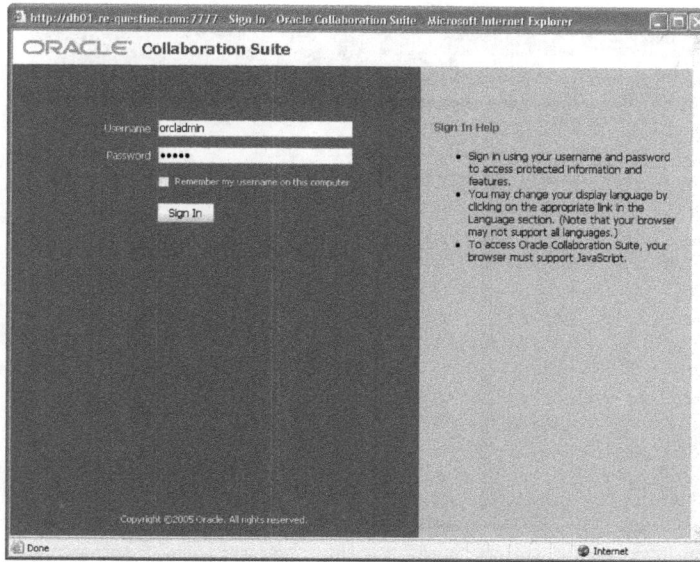

FIGURE 8-32. *Content Services single sign-on*

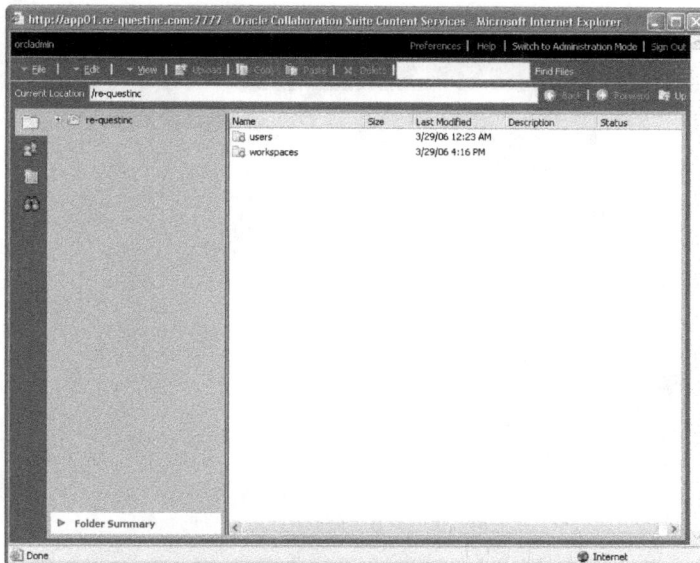

FIGURE 8-33. *Content Services Administrator Mode link*

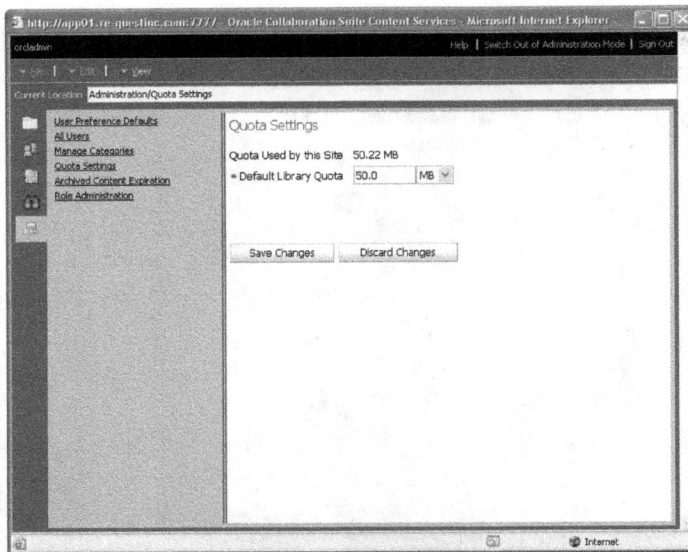

FIGURE 8-34. *Content Services Quota Settings*

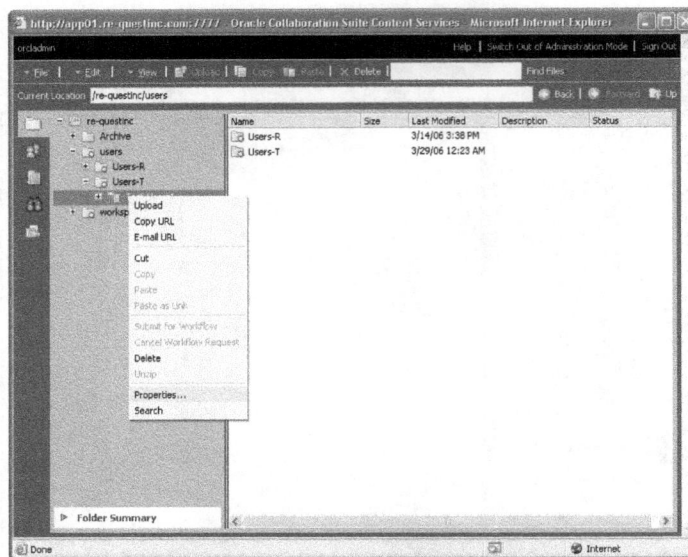

FIGURE 8-35. *Content Services Library Quota Administration*

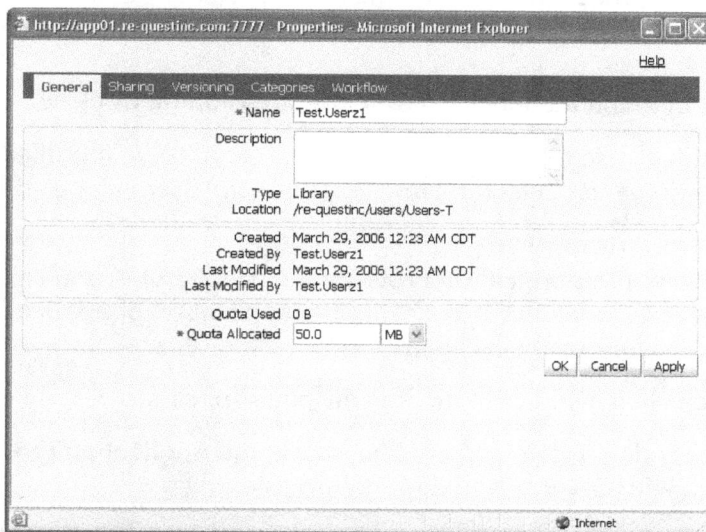

FIGURE 8-36.   *Library Properties page*

6. Click the Properties option to display information about the particular library, including the current quota value. An example of a Properties page is pictured in Figure 8-36. The quota can be changed here for this library.

Deleting/Disabling Users

The last section of this chapter deals with disabling user access to Oracle Collaboration Suite 10g components, or removing them from access to the entire suite altogether. In many cases Administrators must manage someone out of an environment rather than into it, so it is important to know how to disable access for a user, or remove a user completely.

De-Provisioning Components

We are going to start with partial removal of a user and work up to complete deletion. The first type of user removal is to de-provision a user from a component of Oracle Collaboration Suite 10g. This is accomplished through the exact same process as provisioning a component of Oracle Collaboration Suite 10*g* after a user has been created:

1. Log in to the Identity Management Provisioning Console.

2. Conduct a search to find the user that needs to be modified, select the user, and click Edit. Note that only one user can be edited at a time.

3. Move to the Application Provisioning page (2 of 4) and select the De-Provision check box next to the application or applications you wish to remove from the user.

4. Click Next again until the Review page appears.

5. There, click Finish. Figure 8-37 shows the Application Provisioning page with Email selected for de-provisioning.

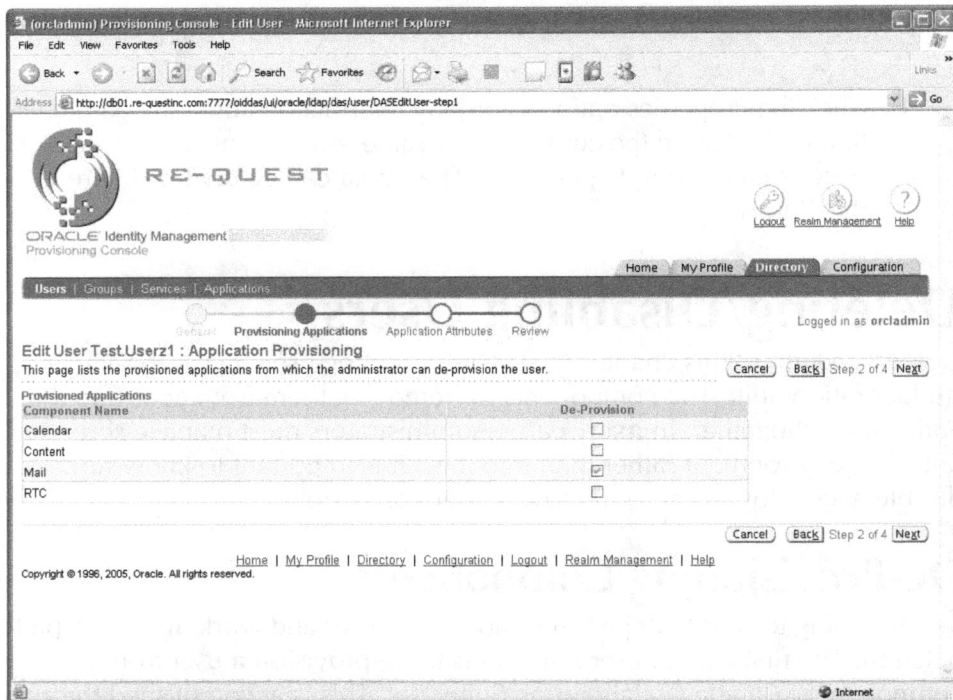

FIGURE 8-37. *Application de-provisioning example*

Password Expiration and User Lockout

Password expiration is another form of user disablement to consider. Basically, password expiration allows an Administrator to provide only current users—those using the system regularly—with valid passwords. Users who do not access the system for long periods of time will not have active usernames out there that others might get a hold of and use. Password expiration also allows for password policy changes to be enforced for everyone over time. For example, suppose you change your password policy to be more complex for security purposes—say, make the password a minimum of seven characters long with two numbers instead of the original five characters with one number. If you do not force periodic password changes, you could still have users out there with passwords that are easier to guess or steal.

Password policy is controlled by the Oracle Identity Management component of Oracle Collaboration Suite 10g. To access the Oracle Directory Manager, you need to go out to the server where the Infrastructure Tier is installed and run the oidadmin tool from there. The administrative userid for the Identity Management tool is cn=orcladmin. Once logged in, navigate to the Password Policy Management branch of the Internet Directory tree and highlight the policy for your implementation. Figure 8-38 shows the detail for the active password policy in my system. Notice the Password Expiry Time attribute, entered in seconds. This determines how long a password can be used before expiring. Shortening this time will obviously cause more frequent expirations and therefore more frequent password changes. Additional attributes such as Number of Grace Logins After Password Expiration and Password Expiration Warning (also entered in seconds) can give users a heads up on password expiration and not force an immediate password change the next time they log in after the password expires.

Another lockout attribute, Global Lockout Duration, shuts down a user's access for a period of time if the user incorrectly enters a password more than a certain number of times—determined by the attribute "Password Maximum Failure." Both values are modifiable by an Administrator and are

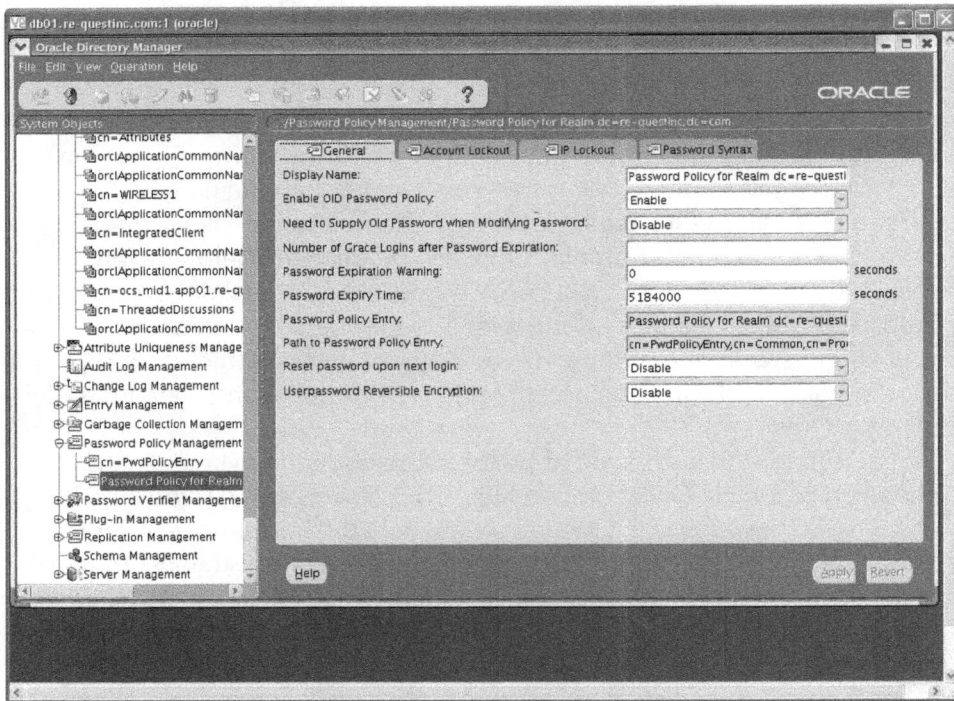

FIGURE 8-38. *Oracle Directory Manager Password Policy General tab*

found on the Account Lockout tab of the Password Policy for the realm shown in Figure 8-39.

The Global Lockout Duration (again defined in seconds) determines how long a user is locked out after having incorrectly entered a password the number of times indicated by the Password Maximum Failure attribute value. It is important to understand that this number is cumulative—yes, I said cumulative—which means that the user doesn't have to enter their password incorrectly this number of times in a row, just this number of times since being provisioned, before being locked out.

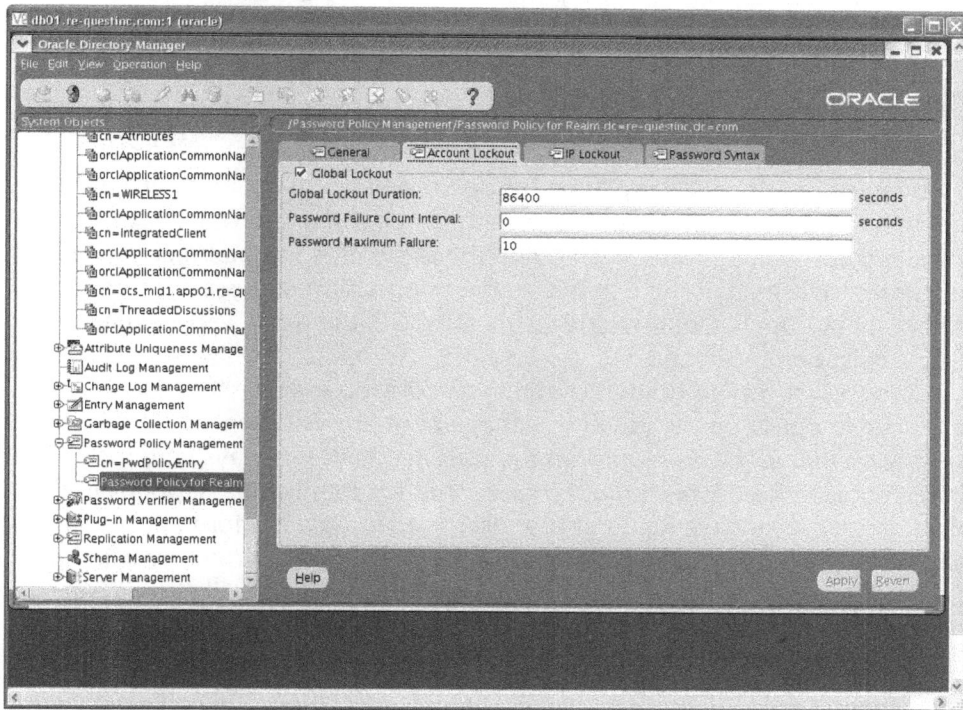

FIGURE 8-39.   *Oracle Directory Manager Password Policy Account
Lockout tab*

Disabling or Deleting Users

Users can be Disabled or Deleted through the Identity Management
Provisioning Console in the same manner that they are created or edited.
Figure 8-40 shows the options for user administration in the console.

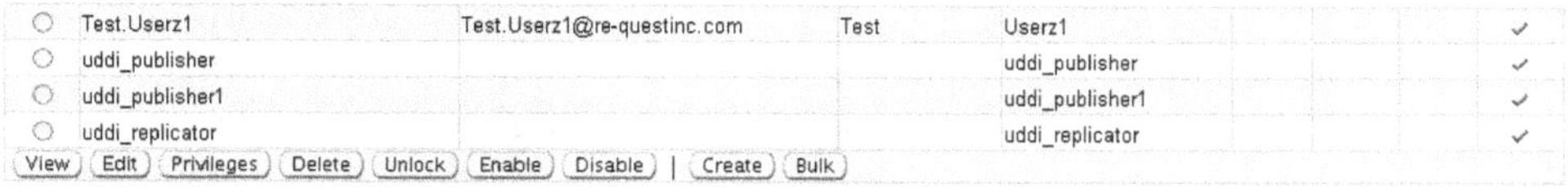

FIGURE 8-40.   *Identity Management Provisioning Console user
modification choices*

Selecting a user and choosing the Disable or Delete button will either disable login for that user or delete the user completely.

Managing Content for Removed Users

In many cases the content owned by a particular user is still of benefit to the company even though the person himself or herself may not be around anymore. Security policy says this user must be removed from access to sensitive company information, but at the same time the organization does not want to lose anything of value in the information that user has under his or her ID in Oracle Collaboration Suite 10*g*. So, the data—email, files, etc.—must be preserved.

The easiest way to do that is to first disable the user, either by choosing the disable option in the Identity Management Provisioning Console or by simply changing the password on the user account. (I always vote for the latter, since that ensures the old user cannot log in, nothing happens to the data, and I can always log in as that user to manipulate information.) Then you can move the email from that account to another account by using the Outlook Connector in much the same way you learned in Chapter 7, moving the messages to local personal folders in Outlook while logged in as the disabled user. You can then upload them to the account of another user by changing the connection and copying the local folder messages to an online folder created in Oracle Collaboration Suite 10*g*.

In terms of Content Services, since almost all of the content is stored in shared libraries, it will still be accessible to the other members of the library. In terms of private or personal folders, again logging in as that user is the easiest way to deal with it, or the Administrator (for instance, orcladmin) has complete control over those files in the account being removed and can do whatever is necessary with them.

Summary

I hope this chapter is helpful in presenting the options and processes available to facilitate the creation, management, and deletion of users within the Oracle Collaboration Suite 10*g* environment. User provisioning and management is a critical component to the administration of the product, and it should be understood thoroughly before the solution is moved into the production environment.

CHAPTER
9

Managing the Collaboration Suite Component Server Processes

Technology is dominated by two types of people:
those who understand what they do not manage,
and those who manage what they do not understand.
                                    —Archibald Putt/Putt's Law

As you can probably tell from the content of the book so far, I am very big on process. I am especially big on defining repeatable processes for anything I do. If something is proved to be effective—read: it works—then it should be thoroughly documented as well as defined in scripts, configuration files, executables, etc., so that it can be reused over and over again to achieve what is sometimes a very novel idea in this business of technology . . . expected results! I cannot tell you how many customers I have worked with in the past that insist on reinventing the wheel each and every time they go through a particular set of tasks, whether that be an Oracle install, a server upgrade, configuring a backup process, or defining users (had to throw a plug in for the previous chapter, sorry). They insist upon struggling to remember the steps, the commands, the setup, and the end result . . . *every time*! It drives me nuts, to be quite honest. And to be even more honest, much of my company's success has been derived from being able to figure something out once in a project, or an operations process or support setting, document how we got there, and then position that solution as a repeatable offering.

To that end, one of the most important repeatable tasks that eludes pretty much everyone regarding Oracle Collaboration Suite 10*g,* especially those who are not familiar with the Oracle Application Server architecture, is the method of properly stopping and starting the background processes from every tier in the Oracle Collaboration Suite 10*g* architecture, and in the correct order. In reality, more Oracle Collaboration Suite installations have been "abandoned" because application components could not be restarted after a server reboot or unplanned termination, than for any other reason. If only the System Administrator or the Oracle Collaboration Suite 10*g* Administrator had understood the interdependencies between the individual tiers as well as their processes, they could have avoided failure. Okay, to be brutally honest, if they would have just understood that the install does *not* put the necessary entries in the rc.d files in any Unix/Linux environment to stop and start the Oracle Collaboration Suite 10*g* processes on server shutdown and restart respectively, they could have avoided the perceived disaster. I say "perceived" because in most cases they could have salvaged the installation by doing a little research. Because you care enough to read this book, you are going to effectively avoid the disaster that tripped up your unenlightened brethren by using the information provided in this chapter to a) prevent bad things from happening when bringing a server down, and b) understand the appropriate order and interdependency between all the tiers and associated background processes of those tiers in an Oracle Collaboration Suite 10*g* environment.

There are two ways to manage these processes: command-line commands and the Enterprise Manager Application Server Control Console for Oracle Collaboration Suite 10*g*. I will discuss both methods in this chapter, as both have their place and value in managing and administering an Oracle Collaboration Suite 10*g* environment. I will start with the command line, since that is how I first learned how to manage Oracle Collaboration Suite in previous releases and then carried it over to Oracle Collaboration Suite 10*g*. The command-line approach is also very important when taking the next step and automating the startup and shutdown of Oracle Collaboration Suite 10*g* processes with the shutdown and startup of the server itself. Enterprise Manager Application Server Control Console for Oracle Collaboration Suite 10*g* also comes in handy when manipulating individual processes, reviewing log files, etc., during startup and shutdown, so I will spend some time on the access to and usage of that tool as well. Enterprise Manager Database Console also allows the management of the Oracle Database 10*g* instance through the web interface.

Command-Line Tools

Command-line management of any software may seem like old school in this day and age of web-based tools available for managing environments. But command-line execution is very effective when it comes to starting and stopping components of the Oracle Collaboration Suite 10*g* product. Given the dependency between the processes within the individual tiers, as well as between tiers of the Oracle Collaboration Suite 10*g* architecture, a scripted command-line approach to starting things up and shutting things down has some real value. The command-line-scripted process can even be taken one step further and put into the startup and shutdown steps of the server to ensure that Oracle Collaboration Suite 10*g* processes never get taken down out of order or incorrectly.

Environmental Variable Settings

Before any commands to manage Oracle Collaboration Suite 10*g* processes can be run, it is imperative to set the required environmental variables for the particular tier you are working in. Setting appropriate environmental variables for the specific tier allows Administrators to execute commands without the need for knowing specifically what executables reside in which directories, or having to be in a particular directory to execute them. Environmental variables are also necessary to make sure the correct version of an executable is run for a particular tier, and the correct configuration files for all processes to be managed are available. In addition, especially with the database environment, there are certain environmental variables that need to be set for the administrative commands to find message files, database names, etc., in order to execute properly.

The easiest way to define the environmental variables is to put them in the appropriate profile file for the operating system shell you are running. I recommend the bash shell when installing Oracle Collaboration Suite 10*g* on Linux, so I define the environmental parameters in the .bash_profile file for the oracle Linux user. The variables can also be defined in /etc/profile, in which case they will be defined for every user logging in to the server (or you can target specific users with if-then logic). However, this only works effectively if each tier of the Oracle Collaboration Suite 10*g* environment is running on its own server. If more than one tier are running on the same server, then presetting variables in the profile files can create issues, since they will have to be reset, overwritten, etc., each time an Administrator needs to switch the tier they are managing. The PATH variable specifically causes issues. The first time the PATH variable is reset to add the Oracle bin directories (Ex: $ORACLE_HOME/bin: $ORACLE_HOME/opmn/bin), everything is fine. However, if an attempt is made to reset it after Oracle paths have already been added to it, the next reset simply "stacks" Oracle paths in front of those already set, which could lead to issues of running incorrect executables and is, at a minimum, confusing. In the case of more than one Oracle tier running on a single server, the best solution I found is to set up .env files for each tier and execute them manually based upon which tier an Administrator wishes to manage.

I will leave the choice of where to specifically set the environmental variables for your specific installations up to you, but I usually set things up in .env files in /home/oracle so that I can easily find them, and I can set the environmental variables explicitly, when I want, for whatever tier I want. I set up one for each tier, so I create an infra.env file and an ocs.env file, each setting ORACLE_HOME, ORACLE_BASE, ORACLE_SID, LD_LIBRARY_PATH, and PATH, as well as something I like to use to resolve the issues with the resetting of the PATH variable, which I named ORIGINAL_PATH. I set ORIGINAL_PATH to the explicit value returned by echoing the $PATH variable after first logging in to the server as the oracle user. I then use ORIGINAL_PATH when setting PATH in any .env files I create from that point forward. This way, regardless of how many times I source any individual .env files or switch between environments, I always get only the original value of $PATH along with the Oracle paths for just the tier I am working with at the time. The following example shows a typical infra.env file that I set up for setting the Infrastructure Tier environmental variables:

```
export ORIGINAL_PATH=/usr/kerberos/bin:/usr/local/bin:/bin:/usr/bin:
/usr/X11R6/bin:/home/oracle/bin
export ORACLE_HOME=/u01/oracle/product/10.1.2/ocs_1/infra
export ORACLE_BASE=/u01/oracle/product/10.1.2/ocs_1
export ORACLE_SID=ocsdb
export LD_LIBRARY_PATH=$ORACLE_HOME/lib: $ORACLE_HOME/network/lib
export PATH=$ORACLE_HOME/bin:$ORACLE_HOME/opmn/bin:$ORIGINAL_PATH
```

This next example shows a typical ocs.env file that I set up for setting the Applications Tier environmental variables:

```
export ORIGINAL_PATH=/usr/kerberos/bin:/usr/local/bin:/bin:/usr/bin:
/usr/X11R6/bin:/home/oracle/bin
export ORACLE_HOME=/u01/oracle/product/10.1.2/ocs_1/apps
export ORACLE_BASE=/u01/oracle/product/10.1.2/ocs_1
export LD_LIBRARY_PATH=$ORACLE_HOME/lib: $ORACLE_HOME/network/lib
export PATH=$ORACLE_HOME/bin:$ORACLE_HOME/opmn/bin:
$ORACLE_HOME/dcm/bin:$ORACLE_HOME/ocas/bin:$ORIGINAL_PATH
```

Note that in the Applications Tier .env file I do not set the ORACLE_SID variable, since that variable does not need to be set in order to access the database through the Middle Tier processes. If however, you wanted to test connectivity to the database through SQL*Plus and SQL*Net, you would set that variable as well. Additionally, instead of setting ORIGINAL_PATH to an explicit value, you could move the setting of this variable to the /etc/profile with the following line:

```
export ORIGINAL_PATH = $PATH
```

This avoids setting an explicit value in the .env files for something that is determined by the operating system and not the Oracle install.

Once the environmental variables are set properly, you can begin using the various commands available to start, stop, and status individual background components of Oracle Collaboration Suite 10*g* tiers. There are specific commands for starting, stopping, or checking the status of specific background processes, depending upon which tier's components you are manipulating. In addition to the individual commands, there are usually groups of commands—starting and/or stopping an entire tier, for example—that will need to be executed together and in a specific sequence. For those purposes you can create scripts to run the groups of commands in a particular order and with a single execution from the command line.

Starting and Stopping the Applications Tier Components

The Applications Tier is actually the easiest tier in the Oracle Collaboration Suite 10*g* environment to start up, shut down, and monitor. There are basically three main sets of background processes that provide all the services in the Applications Tier, each controlled with its own command. There are the Application Server processes, the Application Server Control Console processes, and the Email Listener processes.

Starting/Stopping Application Server Processes

The Application Server processes are all the processes associated with the actual Oracle Application Server 10*g* platform, along with the Oracle Collaboration Suite 10*g* application components and subcomponents, running on the application server Middle Tier. Each application component has several component and subcomponent processes associated with it, so if the entire suite of applications is installed, the list of processes running on the Middle Tier can be fairly lengthy. Oracle provides OPMN (Oracle Process Manager and Notification) as a means for starting and stopping the Applications Tier component and subcomponent processes. OPMN also monitors the processes and handles things like auto-restart of the processes on failure, notification between dependent components, and statistics gathering. To get a list of the processes running on the Oracle Collaboration Suite 10*g* Applications Tier, an Administrator uses the following command (assuming the appropriate environmental variables and path are sourced as described previously):

```
opmnctl status
```

Figure 9-1 shows what the list of OPMN processes looks like for a fully installed Oracle Collaboration Suite 10*g* Applications Tier environment when running the opmnctl status command.

If as an Administrator you want additional information regarding the OPMN processes running on the Middle Tier, you can use the following command:

```
opmnctl status -l
```

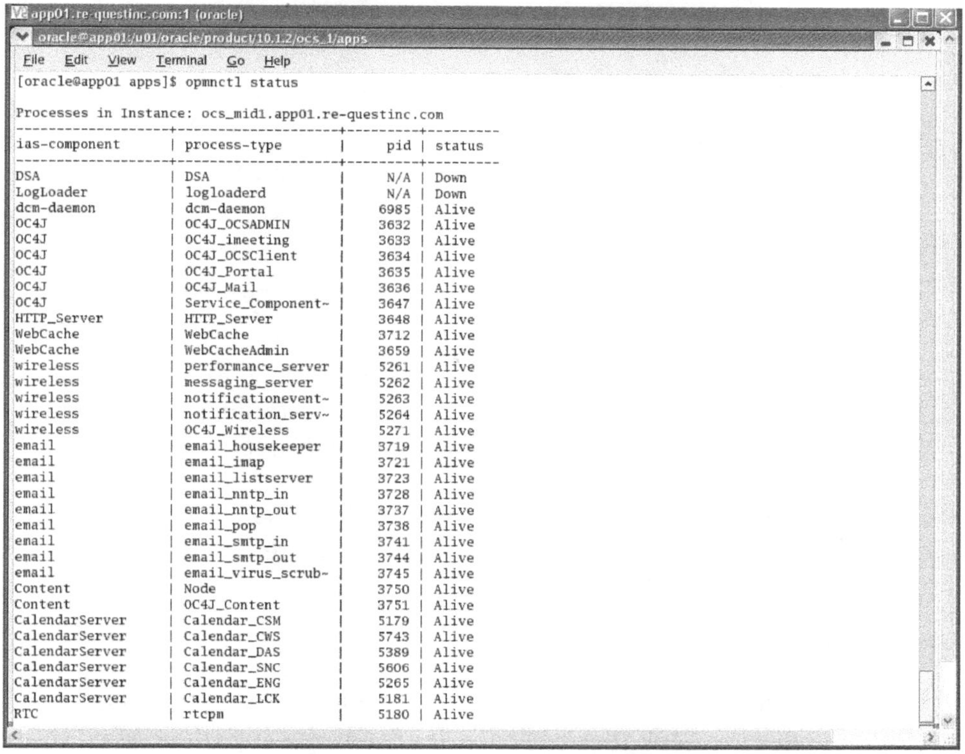

FIGURE 9-1.   *Applications Tier processes*

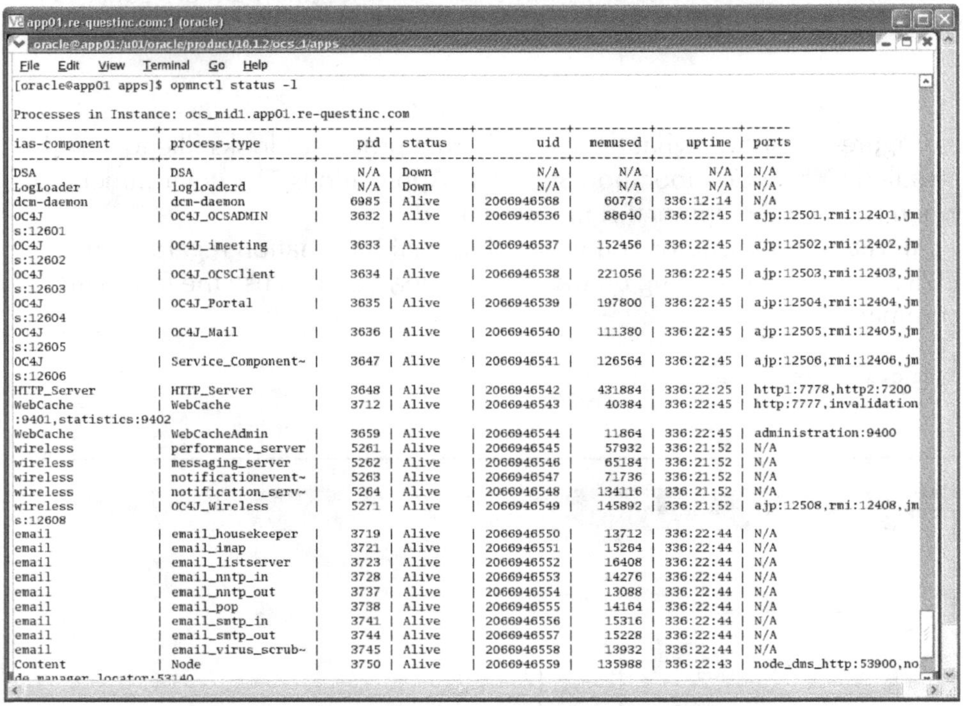

FIGURE 9-2. *Applications Tier processes viewed with the –l parameter*

Figure 9-2 shows the additional detail displayed when the –l parameter is used with the opmnctl status command. Additional information available through the –l parameter includes things like memory used and uptime.

In addition to reviewing status, the opmnctl command can be used to start and stop all Applications Tier processes, or individual components and subcomponents as well. To stop everything that is currently configured on the Applications Tier, enter the following:

```
opmnctl stopall
```

This command not only stops all the Applications Tier components and subcomponents, it also stops OPMN itself. This means the entire Middle Tier is shut down. To start everything back up, enter

```
opmnctl startall
```

or

```
opmnctl start
opmnctl startall
```

which first starts OPMN stand-alone with no Applications Tier components running, and then starts all the Applications Tier component and subcomponent processes under OPMN.

There are two ways to use the opmnctl command to start and stop components and subcomponents. You can either start the entire component using

```
opmnctl <startproc/stopproc> ias-component=<component name>
```

or start and stop a particular process within a component using

```
opmnctl <startproc/stopproc> process-type=<process name>
```

The different component and subcomponent/process names can be seen by referring to previous Figure 9-1, which shows the opmnctl status command results. Notice there are ias-components on the right-hand side of the table and each ias-component has one or more associated process-types listed in the middle column. So, to stop all OC4J processes at once, use

```
opmnctl stopproc ias-component=OC4J
```

But, if you only wanted to stop the OC4J_Mail java container—a process-type or sub-component of the OC4J component—use

```
opmnctl stopproc process-type=OC4J_Mail
```

It is extremely critical to note that the names must be entered on the command line *exactly* as they are displayed in the opmnctl status table, as they are case-sensitive. The opmnctl command gets its information regarding the components and subcomponents that should be available for management with the opmnctl command by reading the opmn.xml file, which is located in the $ORACLE_HOME/opmn/conf directory of the Applications Tier Oracle install directory. Components and subcomponents can be added, changed, and removed from the Applications Tier configuration via modifications to the opmn.xml file, which can be modified using

Application Server Control Console by clicking the Process Management link at the bottom of the Oracle Application Server instance home page. The OPMN server does not need to be restarted after you edit the opmn.xml file because Application Server Control Console automatically reloads the updated opmn.xml file after you edit the file. We will cover additional information related to this file in Chapter 12.

The opmn.xml file can also be manually edited (I actually do it this way all the time), but then the following command must be run on the command line:

```
opmnctl reload
$ORACLE_HOME/dcm/bin/dcmctl updateConfig
```

The dcmctl updateConfig command reads the updated opmn.xml file and updates the configuration repository with the manually made changes.

In addition to starting the Applications Tier OPMN processes, the Oracle Collaboration Suite 10g Calendar components needs to be started as well (the Calendar processes are not yet 100 percent integrated with the Applications Tier OPMN environment as of this writing). To start and stop the Calendar processes, you need to either be in the $ORACLE_HOME/ocas/bin directory or have it sourced in your PATH variable so that you can run the following commands:

```
ocasctl -start
ocasctl -stopall
```

Failure to do so will result in the Calendar function not being accessible to the users when they log in to the Oracle Collaboration Suite 10g Portal.

Starting/Stopping Application Server Control Console Processes

The Application Server Control Console itself has processes that run on the Applications Tier server and that must be stopped and started whenever the server is rebooted. To start and stop the Application Server Control Console, the following commands are necessary:

```
emctl start iasconsole
emctl stop iasconsole
```

Starting/Stopping the Email Listener Process

Finally, if the Applications Tier is running the Oracle Collaboration Suite 10*g* Email component, an Email Listener must run in order for the standard email protocols such as SMTP, POP, and IMAP to be available. Because these standard emailprotocols run on secured ports (port numbers below 1024), this Email Listener—named listener_es—must be started and stopped by the root operating system user. First, log in to the server as the oracle user and source the Applications tier environment. Then execute the following set of steps/commands to start the Email Listener as root:

```
cd $ORACLE_HOME/bin
su (log in as root but keep oracle user environment set)
<enter root password>
env | grep ORA (check environment to make sure variables are set)
./tnslsnr listener_es -u <oracle user uid> -g <oracle install group gid> &
<Enter> on a blank command line (just trust me on this one)
```

If the oracle user was set up the way I recommend in Chapter 3, the values for oracle user uid and oracle install group gid should be 500 and 501 respectively. I usually check the values anyway by doing an "id" command as the oracle user, or an "id oracle" command as root just before beginning the preceding sequence of commands just to verify the oracle user uid and group gid values.

If the command terminates when you hit the <Enter> on the blank line (didn't I tell you to trust me), you can check the listener_es.log file located in the $ORACLE_HOME/ network/log directory. However, most of the time the issue is related to the fact that sendmail is currently running on the machine. Executing the following quick check command will show if sendmail is running:

```
ps -ef | grep send
```

If sendmail is running, then connect as root and execute

```
kill -9 <pid> - OR - killall sendmail
```

on the sendmail process (and remove from the system startup steps later). The sendmail process can also be gracefully shut down, again as root, by executing

```
sudo -s - OR - msu -
/etc/init.d/sendmail stop
```

You can then attempt the preceding tnslsnr command again to start the Email Listener. If it still doesn't start, then I would definitely suggest reviewing the listener_es.log file for the error messages, or checking the ports for some of the other protocols such as 110 for POP, 143 for IMAP, or 119 for NNTP. I have had situations where the Email Listener seems to error out or not start, but then when I attempt to start it again it produces an error message saying it is already running (ports in use message). In this case I run

```
lsnrctl status listener_es
```

to see if it is up, and if so, I stop and start it again. You can do all of this as root, since the environment is available to root if you followed the preceding instructions to get to this point. The stop command for the Email Listener looks like this:

```
lsnrctl stop listener_es
```

Starting and Stopping the Infrastructure Tier Components

Oracle has simplified the architecture of the Oracle Collaboration Suite product for the average installation with the 10*g* release because now the Infrastructure Tier and the Datastore Tier can be combined and managed together. In older releases of the product you were required to run two database instances, a DSTOR and an INFRA, for the Infostore and Oracle Internet Directory/Metadata Repository components respectively. Now in the 10*g* release of the Collaboration Suite product those two instances are combined into one by default, so there is only one database instance to manage in the architecture, and it can be clustered using Oracle's RAC technology (in prior versions of Collaboration Suite only the Infostore instance could be RAC'd). I strongly recommend keeping things this way unless there is a compelling reason for the databases to be separated, such as using an already existing infrastructure database for the Oracle Collaboration Suite 10*g* installation. In addition, there are fewer possible issues with startup/shutdown timing and order if they are in a single instance, since now the database components can all be shut down together as the last step of the shutdown process and brought up together as the first step in restarting the Oracle Collaboration Suite 10*g* environment.

Starting/Stopping the Database

As I mentioned, the database is the last component to be shut down and the first component to be started up in the Oracle Collaboration Suite 10*g* architecture. The startup and shutdown commands are pretty straightforward as long as the environmental variables have been properly set. To start the database, execute the following set of commands while logged in as the oracle user to the Infrastructure Tier server where the database lives (don't forget to source the proper environment first):

```
sqlplus "/ as sysdba"
SQL> startup;
SQL> exit;
```

Figure 9-3 shows an example of starting up the database for an Oracle Collaboration Suite 10*g* instance.

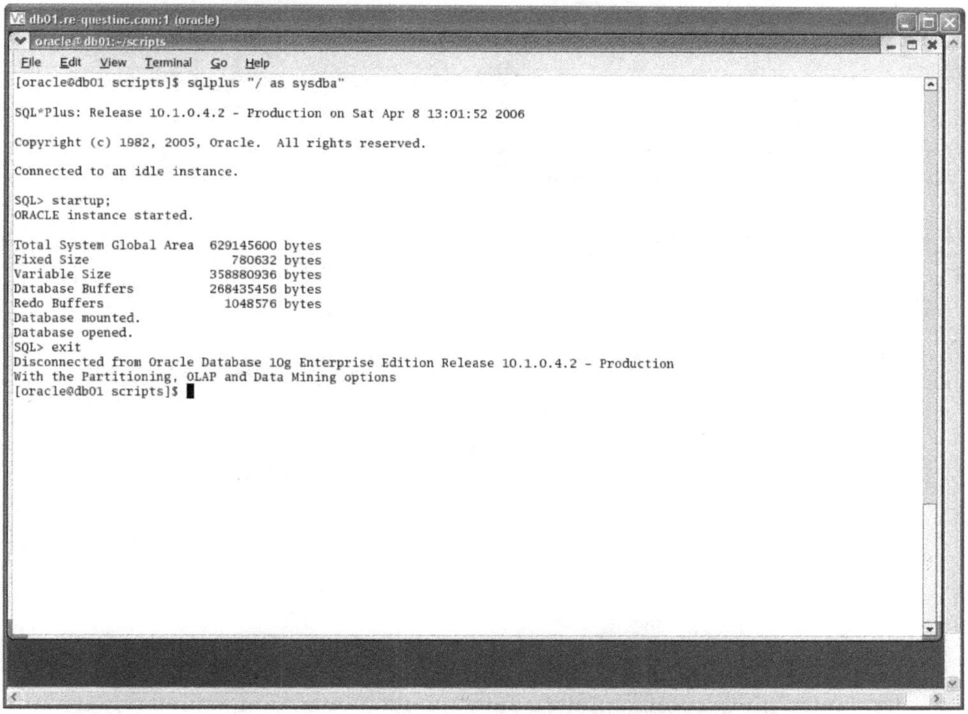

FIGURE 9-3. *Oracle Collaboration Suite 10g database instance startup*

To shut down the database instance, execute the following commands:

```
sqlplus "/ as sysdba"
SQL> shutdown immediate;
SQL> exit;
```

Using the shutdown immediate command—as opposed to a simple shutdown—disconnects any idle/dormant connections to the database rather than waiting for them to log out (which may never happen). Figure 9-4 shows an example of a successful shutdown of an Oracle Collaboration Suite 10*g* database.

Starting/Stopping the Database Listener

The Infrastructure Tier has a Database Listener that manages the communication between the various Oracle Collaboration Suite 10*g* Applications Tier and Infrastructure Tier processes and the database. This Listener is a common

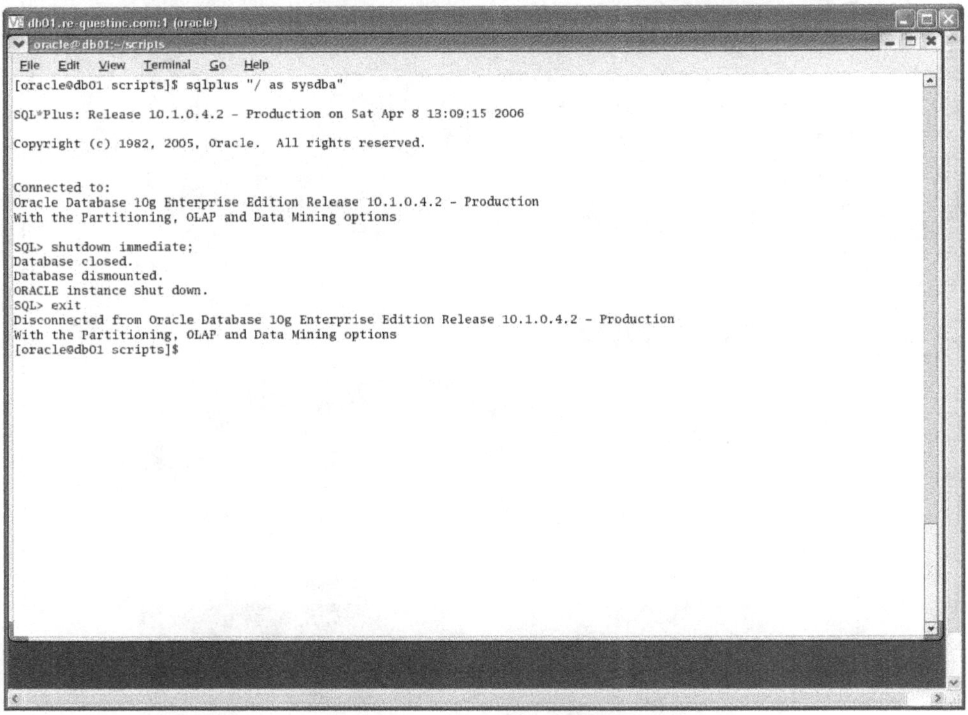

FIGURE 9-4. *Oracle Collaboration Suite 10g database instance shutdown*

component of any Oracle Database 10g architecture and has actually been the method of communication to any Oracle database instance for a very long time. To start the Database Listener, you must log in to the Infrastructure Tier server as the oracle user where the Listener is installed, source the proper environment, and run the following:

```
lsnrctl start
```

Figure 9-5 shows the results of a typical Database Listener startup in an Oracle Collaboration Suite environment. Notice it tells you what host and port it connects to in order to facilitate communication with the Oracle database instance.

The command to stop the Database Listener is

```
lsnrctl stop
```

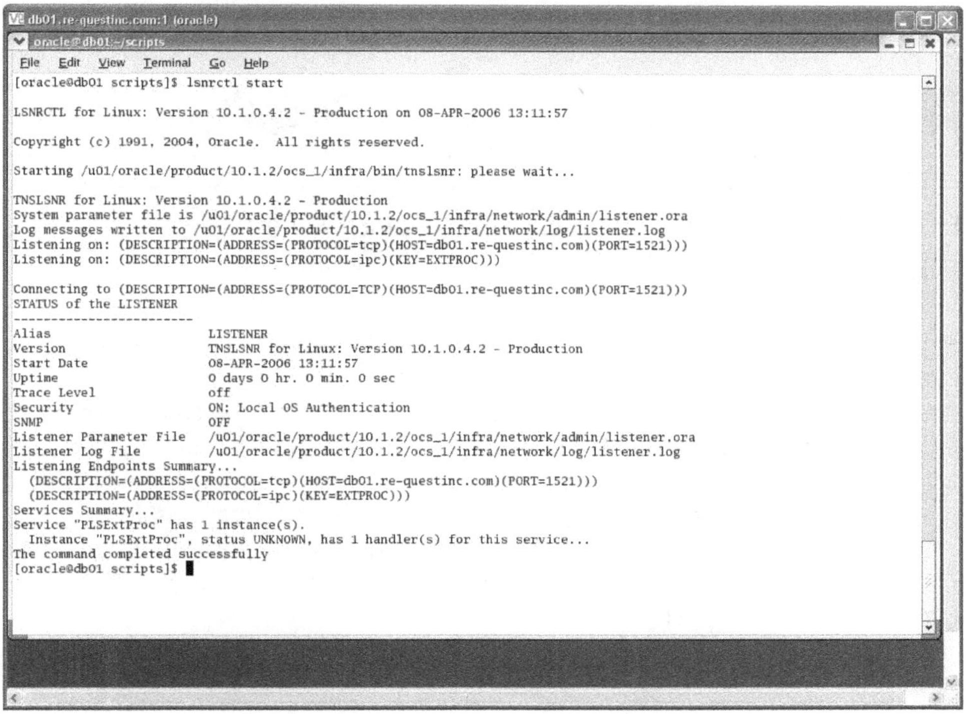

FIGURE 9-5. *Starting the Oracle Collaboration Suite 10g Database Listener*

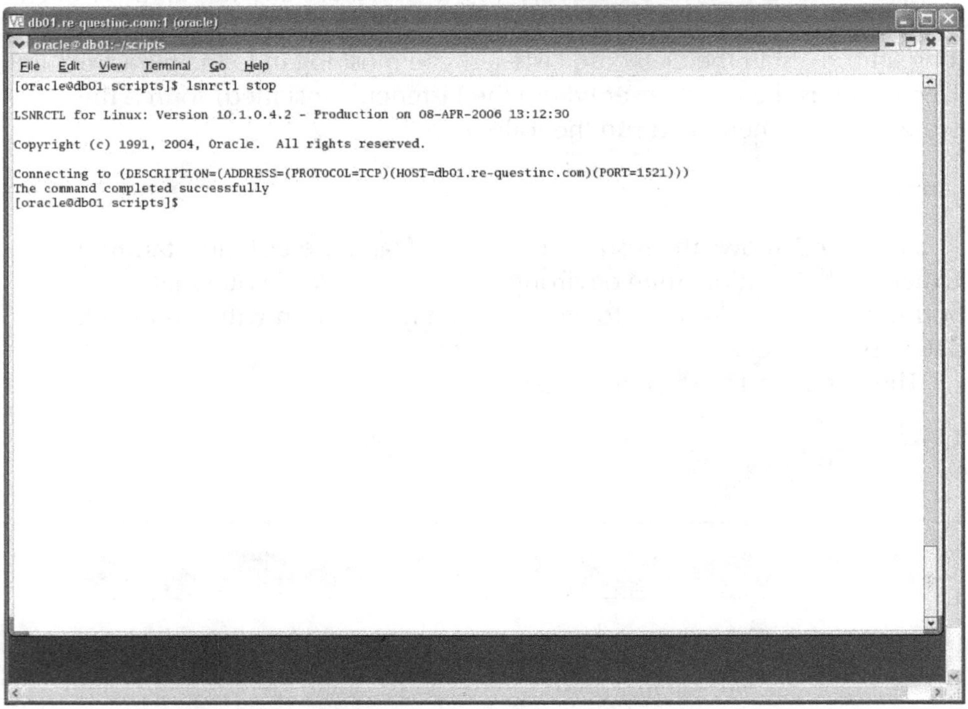

FIGURE 9-6. *Stopping the Oracle Collaboration Suite 10g Database Listener*

Figure 9-6 shows the results of a successful Database Listener stop command.

It is important to note that the Database Listener must be started for any of the remaining components of the Oracle Collaboration Suite 10g environment to come up successfully. Recalling the information from earlier chapters, all Infrastructure Tier processes as well as Applications Tier processes rely on the database for holding process status information (Oracle Internet Directory entries), as well as Oracle Collaboration Suite 10g content (email, files, lists, etc.).

Starting/Stopping the Infrastructure Tier Components

The Infrastructure Tier is where the Oracle Internet Directory and Identity Management processes run, and those processes are managed by using OPMN commands just like the Applications Tier processes. To start the Infrastructure Tier processes, log in to the Infrastructure Tier server as the oracle user, source the Infrastructure environmental variables, and run

```
opmnctl startall
opmnctl status
```

Alternatively, you can optionally run opmnctl start to start opmn separately from the OPMN processes, then opmnctl startall.

Figure 9-7 shows the results from an opmnctl status command when everything starts successfully on the Infrastructure Tier. Notice specifically that the HTTP_Server, OC4J_Security, and OID process types must be

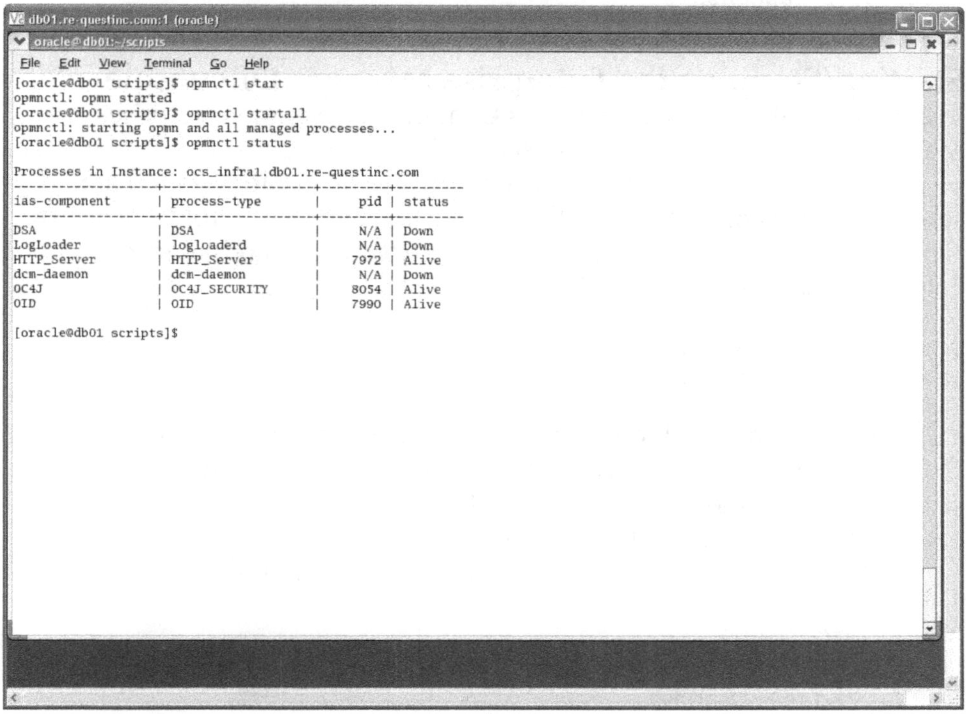

FIGURE 9-7.   *Successful Infrastructure Tier startup*

started (the other process types are part of a standard Oracle Application Server 10g Infrastructure Tier installation but are not necessary for Oracle Collaboration Suite 10g).

Starting/Stopping Application Server Control Console Processes

The Application Server Control Console gives the Administrator the ability to manage the various components and subcomponents of the Applications Tier through a web-based graphical interface. I will discuss the Control Console functionality further in the second half of this chapter. The Control Console itself has processes that run on the Applications Tier server and that must be stopped and started when the server is rebooted. To start and stop the Application Server Control Console, the following commands are necessary:

```
emctl start iasconsole
emctl stop iasconsole
```

Starting/Stopping the Enterprise Manager DBconsole

In addition to the Application Server Control Console, the Enterprise Manager Database Console also needs to be started so that the database can be monitored. The Enterprise Manager Database Console is started and stopped in the same manner as the Application Server Control Console, by running emctl commands. The following are the commands to start/stop the Enterprise Manager Database Console:

```
emctl start dbconsole
emctl stop dbconsole
```

This covers the detail commands to start and stop all components of the Oracle Collaboration Suite 10g architecture. I recommend scripting the setting of environmental variables and the start and stop of the processes, each by tier. The order of things is as follows:

To start the Oracle Collaboration Suite 10g environment,

1. Source the Infrastructure Tier environmental variables.

2. Start the database.

3. Start the Database Listener.

4. Start the Infrastructure Tier opmn processes.

5. Start the iasconsole.

6. Start the dbconsole.

7. Source the Applications Tier environment.

8. Start the Applications Tier opmn processes.

9. Start the Calendar processes.

10. Start iasconsole.

11. Start the Email Listener (as root).

To stop the Oracle Collaboration Suite 10*g* environment,

1. Source the Applications Tier environment.

2. Stop the Applications Tier opmn processes.

3. Stop the Calendar processes.

4. Stop iasconsole.

5. Stop the UM Listener (as root).

6. Source the Infrastructure Tier environmental variables.

7. Stop the Infrastructure Tier opmn processes.

8. Stop the iasconsole.

9. Stop the dbconsole.

10. Stop the database.

11. Stop the Database Listener.

I personally like to create a /scripts subdirectory under the /home/oracle directory for the oracle user and put a start_<tier> and stop_<tier> script in there that puts the necessary commands in the previously described order.

I also make them executable files. I then either navigate to this directory and run them, or better yet, add this directory to my PATH variable when I source it in my .env file for the tier, so that I can run them wherever I am on the server, as long as my environment is sourced.

Application Server Control Console/Enterprise Manager

Now that we have covered using command-line commands to manage the Oracle Collaboration Suite 10g components and subcomponents, I will discuss using the web-based tools to do the same thing. The Enterprise Manager Application Server Control Console is much more robust in the Application Server 10g architecture, so it makes sense for that to carry over into the Oracle Collaboration Suite 10g management approach. I used to do everything from the command line in the previous releases of Oracle Collaboration Suite, but now I use the Control Console for quite a few things. The next few sections will take you through the Control Console and Enterprise Manager (for the database) and how to use them for managing the components and subcomponents of Oracle Collaboration Suite 10g.

Application Server Control Console

Let's will walk through the Application Server Control Console first. In order to use the Application Server Control Console, it must be running. Executing a status command as follows will verify that the console is up and running:

```
emctl status iasconsole
```

The same command will work on both the Infrastructure Tier and the Applications Tier. Figure 9-8 shows the result of the preceding status command if the Control Console is indeed up and running.

This information also tells you what URL you need to use to access the Control Console from your browser. Pay particular attention to the port value at the end of the URL, as different installations can have different port values, depending upon whether other processes were already using a default port prior to the Oracle Collaboration Suite 10g installation process, whether it is a single-server install, etc.

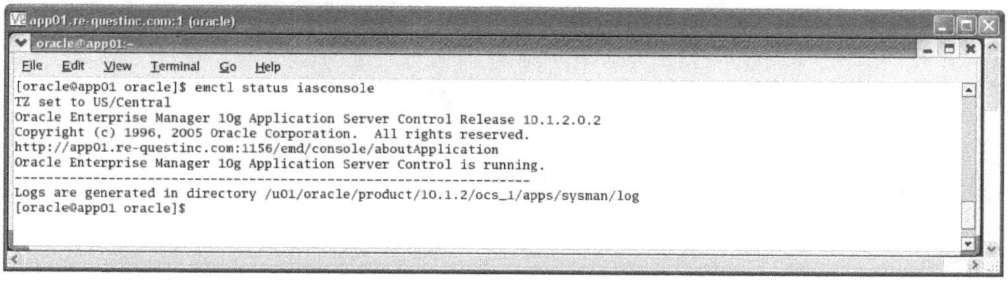

```
app01.re-questinc.com:1 (oracle)
oracle@app01:~
File  Edit  View  Terminal  Go  Help
[oracle@app01 oracle]$ emctl status iasconsole
TZ set to US/Central
Oracle Enterprise Manager 10g Application Server Control Release 10.1.2.0.2
Copyright (c) 1996, 2005 Oracle Corporation.  All rights reserved.
http://app01.re-questinc.com:1156/emd/console/aboutApplication
Oracle Enterprise Manager 10g Application Server Control is running.
--------------------------------------------------------------------
Logs are generated in directory /u01/oracle/product/10.1.2/ocs_1/apps/sysman/log
[oracle@app01 oracle]$
```

FIGURE 9-8. *Application Server Control Console Status*

Take that URL from the status command results and enter it into a Microsoft Internet Explorer browser. Oracle Application Server 10*g* has a requirement to use Microsoft Internet Explorer with the Control Console and Enterprise Manager. It is the *only* supported browser for these tools at this time. Other may work (for example, I use the Mozilla browser from the Linux KDE desktop on the servers all the time), but if there is an issue IE is the only one that is actually supported. You should be prompted for a username and password to sign in with as shown in Figure 9-9. You can also navigate to the Control Console by using the Oracle Collaboration Suite Control link on the upper left-hand side of the Collaboration Suite Welcome page.

The ias_admin user and associated password should be used to sign in here. Once you are signed in, the Application Server Control Console Farm page displays. The Farm page shows any clusters of servers that are in the server farm, along with any individual servers in the farm (a farm of servers is a group of servers deployed into the same Oracle Application Server 10*g* environment). Figure 9-10 shows a Farm page for an Oracle Collaboration Suite 10*g* environment running two servers—one Infrastructure and one Applications—in its farm.

From here you can now navigate to either the Infrastructure Tier server or the Applications Tier server simply by clicking the server name in the farm list of servers. You will now go into the Applications Tier first to show the options for managing the individual components or subcomponents of the Applications Tier.

FIGURE 9-9. *Application Server Control Console sign-on*

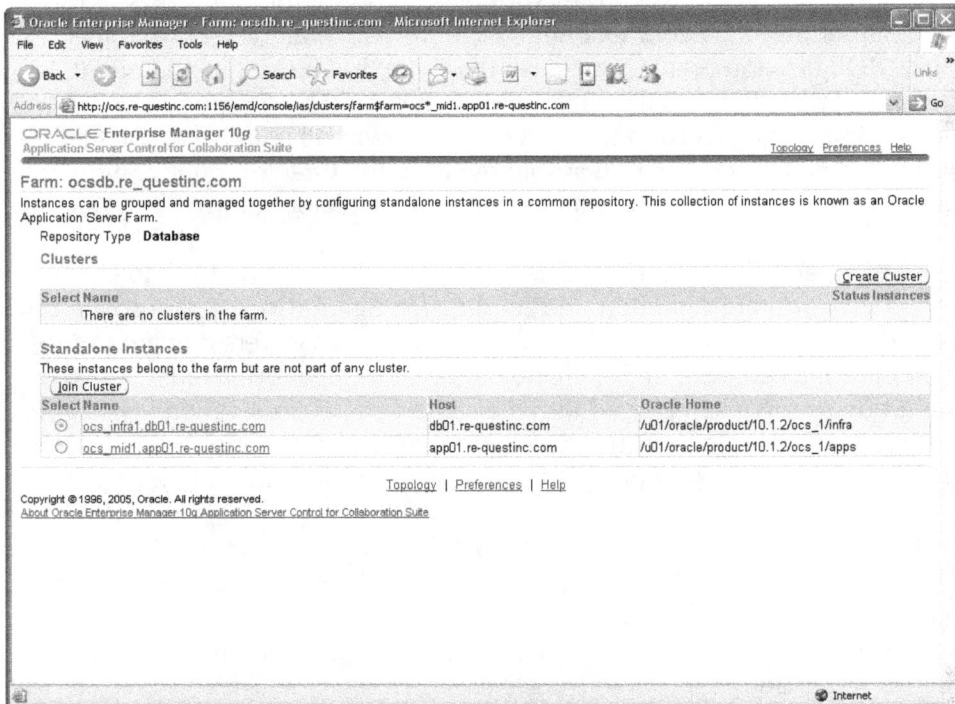

FIGURE 9-10. *Application Server Control Console Farm page*

Applications Tier

By clicking the Applications Tier name on the Farm page, you move to the Application Server Control Console for the Applications Tier shown in Figure 9-11.

Note the ability to stop all and restart all with the buttons in the General section of this page. There is also some resource utilization information graphically displayed in the top section of the page as well. The System Components section of the page contains all the components and subcomponents of the Applications Tier processes. Figure 9-12 shows an example of the complete System Components section of the page. Notice how the list of components and subcomponents looks a lot like the list displayed when you ran the opmnctl status command. That's because the

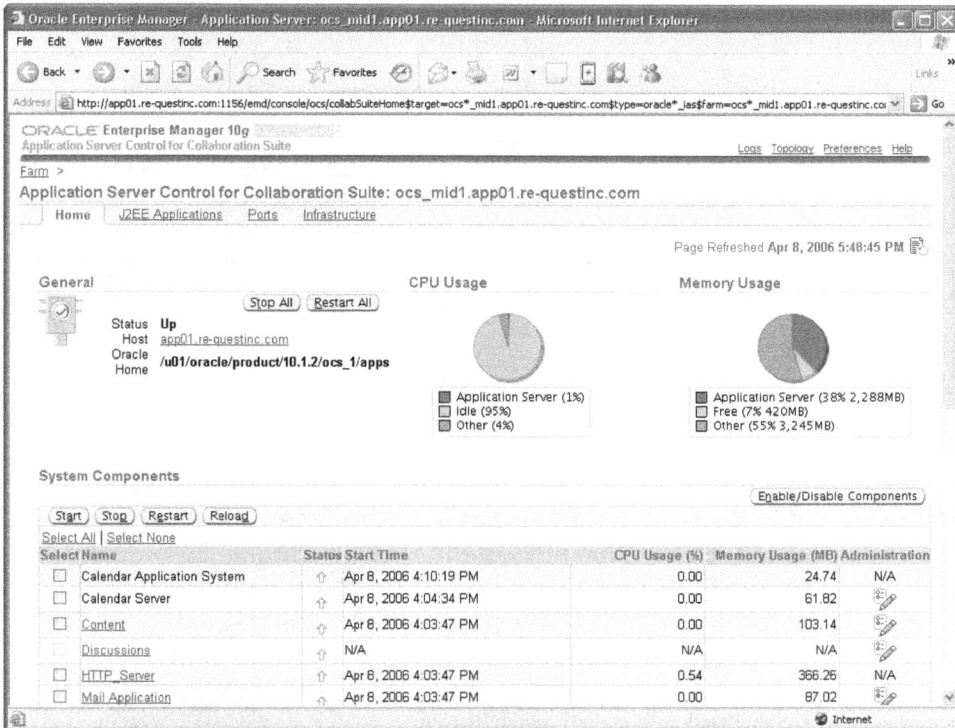

FIGURE 9-11.   *Application Server Control Console for Oracle Collaboration Suite 10g Applications Tier*

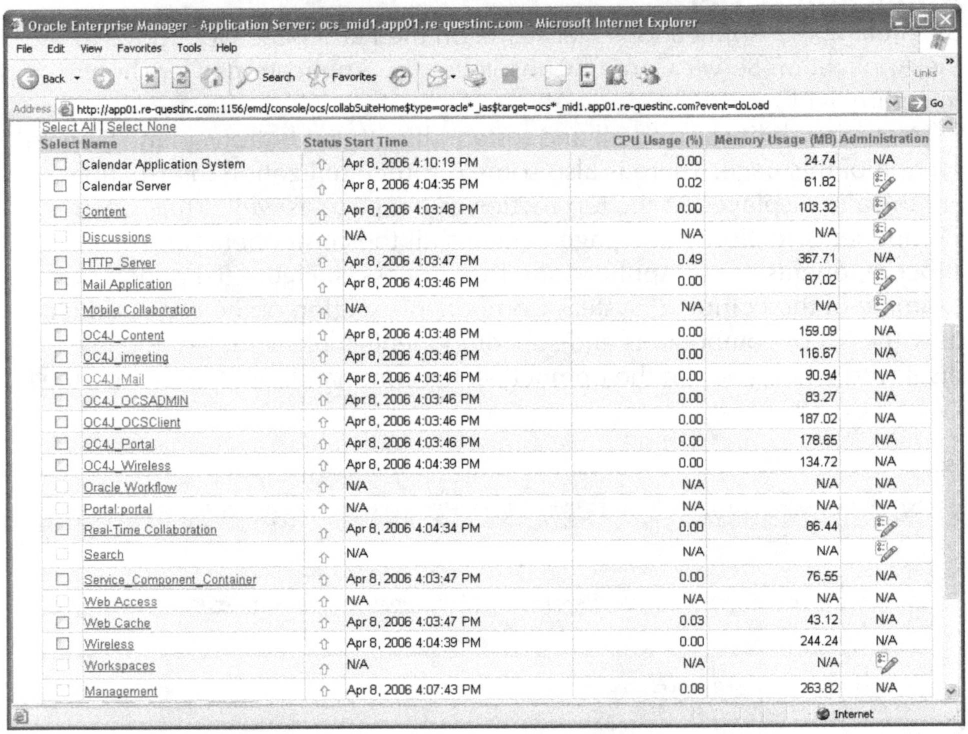

Select	Name	Status	Start Time	CPU Usage (%)	Memory Usage (MB)	Administration
☐	Calendar Application System	⇧	Apr 8, 2006 4:10:19 PM	0.00	24.74	N/A
☐	Calendar Server	⇧	Apr 8, 2006 4:04:35 PM	0.02	61.82	
☐	Content	⇧	Apr 8, 2006 4:03:48 PM	0.00	103.32	
☐	Discussions	⇧	N/A	N/A	N/A	
☐	HTTP_Server	⇧	Apr 8, 2006 4:03:47 PM	0.49	367.71	N/A
☐	Mail Application	⇧	Apr 8, 2006 4:03:46 PM	0.00	87.02	
☐	Mobile Collaboration	⇧	N/A	N/A	N/A	
☐	OC4J_Content	⇧	Apr 8, 2006 4:03:48 PM	0.00	159.09	N/A
☐	OC4J_imeeting	⇧	Apr 8, 2006 4:03:46 PM	0.00	116.67	N/A
☐	OC4J_Mail	⇧	Apr 8, 2006 4:03:46 PM	0.00	90.94	N/A
☐	OC4J_OCSADMIN	⇧	Apr 8, 2006 4:03:46 PM	0.00	83.27	N/A
☐	OC4J_OCSClient	⇧	Apr 8, 2006 4:03:46 PM	0.00	187.02	N/A
☐	OC4J_Portal	⇧	Apr 8, 2006 4:03:46 PM	0.00	178.65	N/A
☐	OC4J_Wireless	⇧	Apr 8, 2006 4:04:39 PM	0.00	134.72	N/A
☐	Oracle Workflow	⇧	N/A	N/A	N/A	N/A
☐	Portal:portal	⇧	N/A	N/A	N/A	N/A
☐	Real-Time Collaboration	⇧	Apr 8, 2006 4:04:34 PM	0.00	86.44	
☐	Search	⇧	N/A	N/A	N/A	
☐	Service_Component_Container	⇧	Apr 8, 2006 4:03:47 PM	0.00	76.55	N/A
☐	Web Access	⇧	N/A	N/A	N/A	N/A
☐	Web Cache	⇧	Apr 8, 2006 4:03:47 PM	0.03	43.12	N/A
☐	Wireless	⇧	Apr 8, 2006 4:04:39 PM	0.00	244.24	N/A
☐	Workspaces	⇧	N/A	N/A	N/A	
☐	Management	⇧	Apr 8, 2006 4:07:43 PM	0.08	263.82	N/A

FIGURE 9-12. *Full list of system components in Control Console for the Applications Tier*

Application Server Control Console is displaying the same information, but in a web-based graphical manner.

From this section of the page you can check one or more of these processes and Start, Stop, Restart, or Reload them (a reload actually re-reads the configuration files from the file system before restarting the process). This is exactly the same functionality available through the various opmnctl startproc/stopproc commands I've explained, but again through a much more elegant interface. The Control Console will understand the dependencies between the various processes just as OPMN does, and it will process accordingly. You can even drill down into the various processes to review all the detail behind how the processes were defined and configured, including all the Java applications associated with a particular container (OC4J process), parameters and environmental variables set when the processes are started in the background, memory minimum and maximum values set on the command line when starting the processes, etc.

One example I will show here is the Mail Application system component. If you drill down on that particular process, you access all the subcomponents associated with the Oracle Collaboration Suite 10g Email protocols. Figure 9-13 shows the list of service targets for the protocols displayed when you click the Mail Application name.

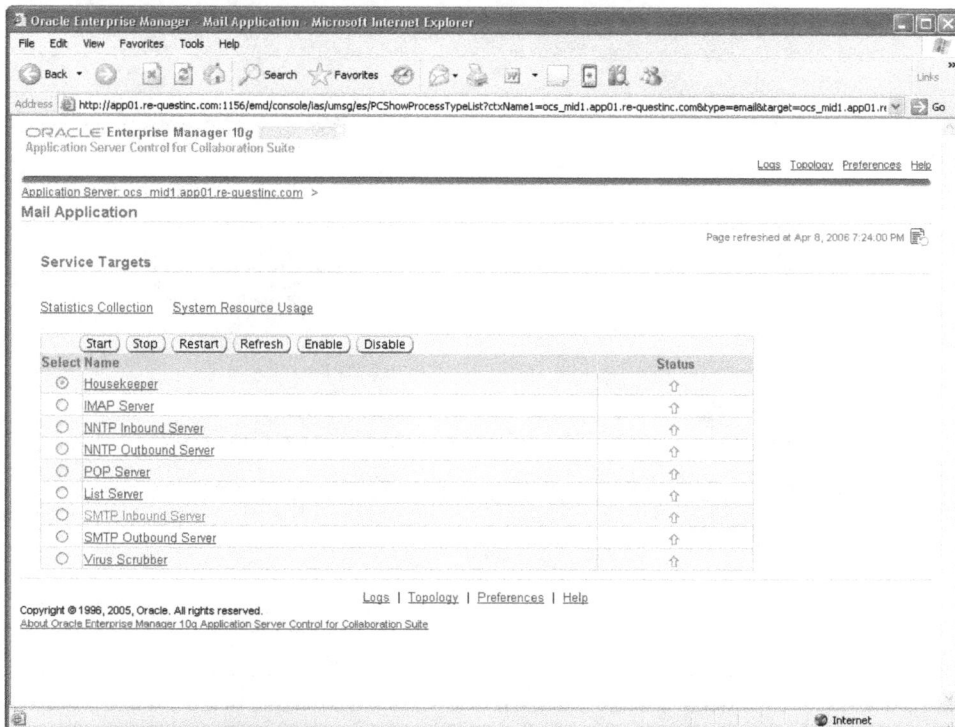

FIGURE 9-13. *Mail Application service targets*

Drilling further into a particular service target, in this case SMTP Inbound Server, you will see the actual process instances running for that service target (you can have more than one instance of a given service target running at a time). Figure 9-14 shows the single process instance running for SMTP Inbound Server.

At any level, whether it is the complete tier, or all the way down to the individual process instances for a given service target, you have the ability to start and stop the component for maintenance purposes.

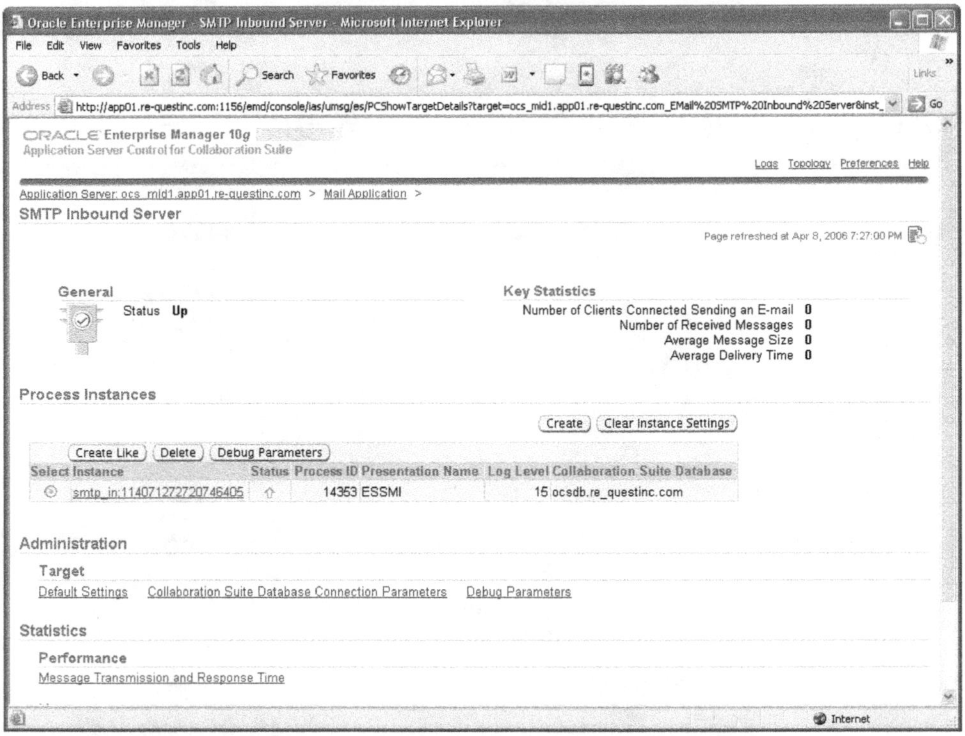

FIGURE 9-14. *SMTP Inbound Server Process Instances page*

Infrastructure Tier

If you go all the way back to the Farm page displayed in Figure 9-10 and click the name of the Infrastructure instance, you can now review the processes associated with the Infrastructure Tier of Oracle Collaboration Suite 10g. Figure 9-15 shows an example Control Console page for the Infrastructure Tier.

This page looks identical to the same page displayed for the Applications Tier in Figure 9-11, but the system components list is obviously much smaller. Again, just as with the Applications Tier, the system components list

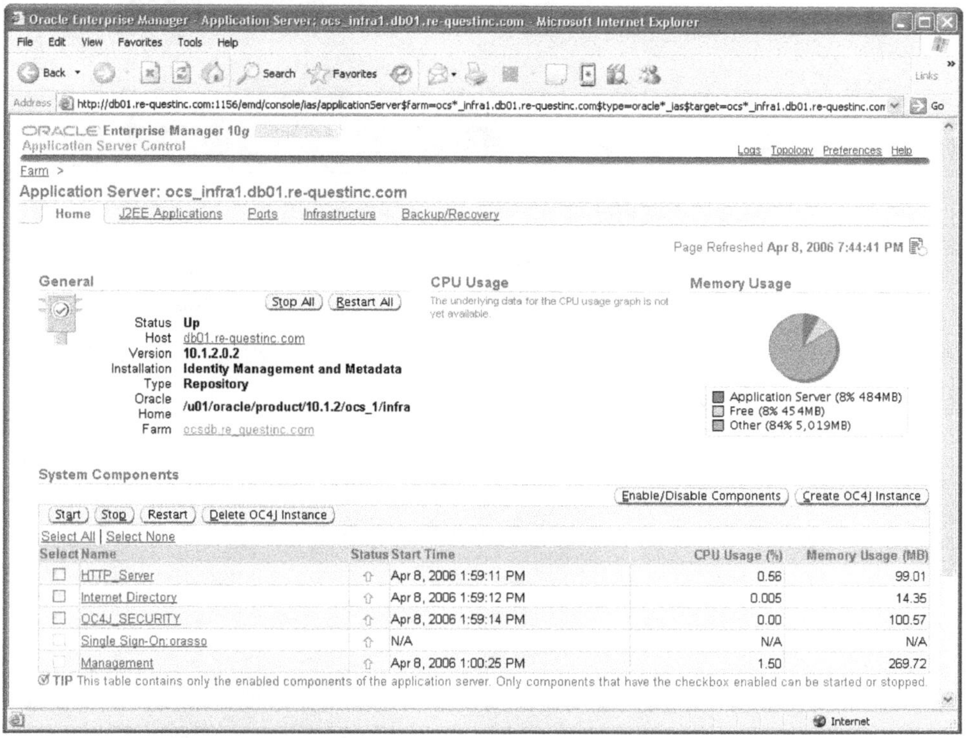

FIGURE 9-15.   *Application Server Control Console for Oracle Collaboration Suite 10*g *Infrastructure Tier*

looks like that displayed when the opmnctl status command was run. And just as for the Applications Tier, these components can be started, stopped, and managed from this page just as they can through the various opmnctl commands described in the earlier section "Command-Line Tools."

Enterprise Manager Database Console

The Enterprise Manager Database Console can be used to start and stop the Oracle Collaboration Suite 10*g* database instance, as well as to perform Database Administration functions and set alerts for proactive monitoring. To access Enterprise Manager Database Console, you need two things: a Microsoft Internet Explorer browser and the URL to access the console, including the port it is running on. You get the latter by performing an emctl status dbconsole command from the command line as shown in Figure 9-16.

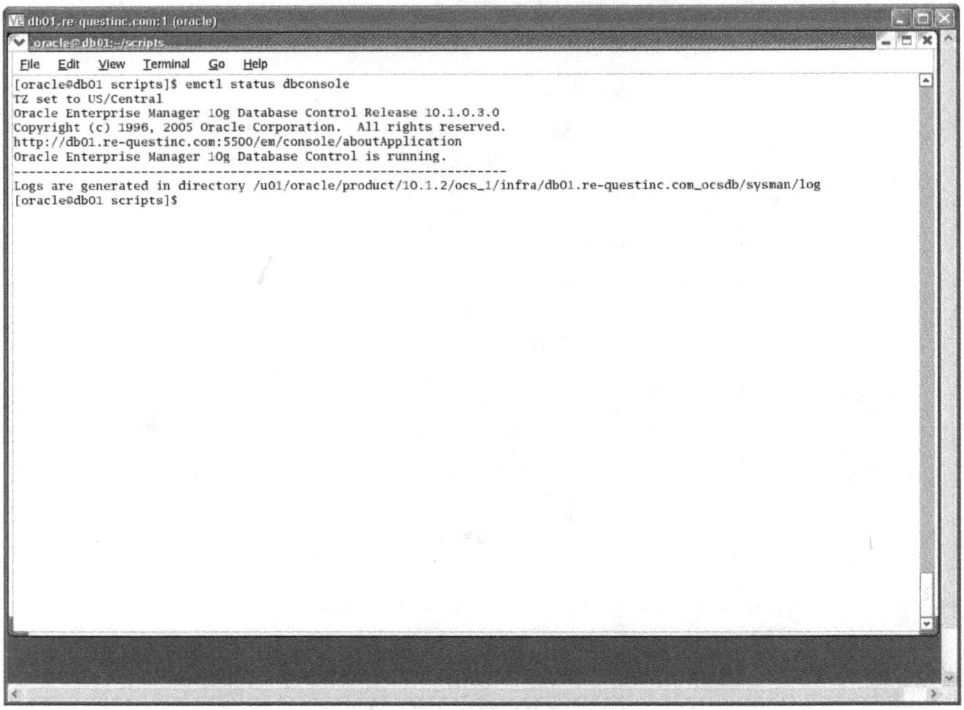

FIGURE 9-16. *emctl status dbconsole command*

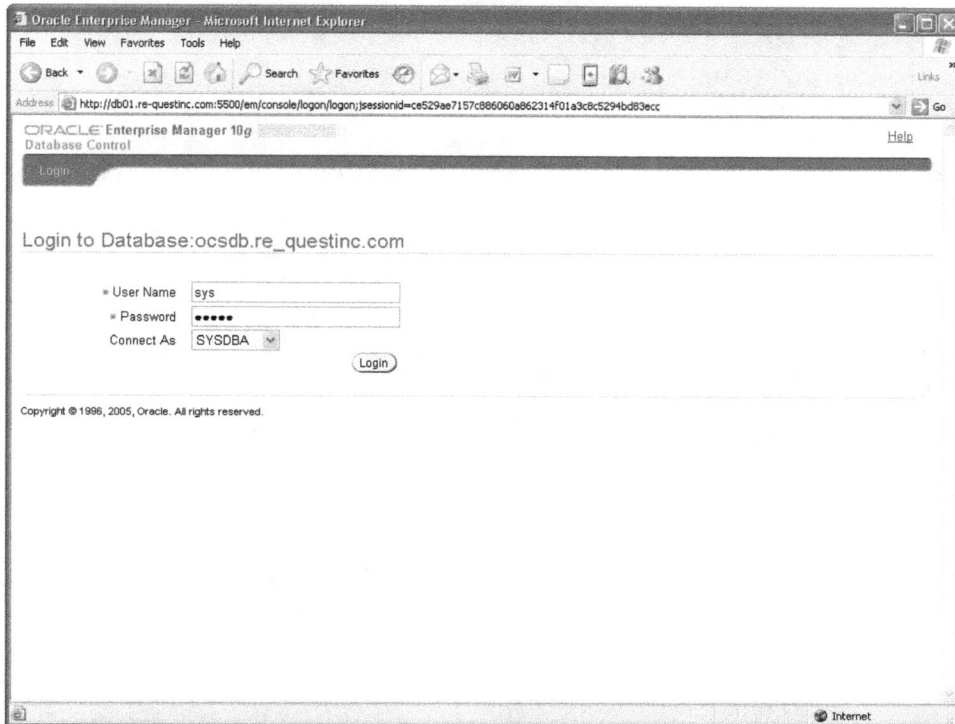

FIGURE 9-17.   *Enterprise Manage Database Console sign-on screen*

You enter that URL in your browser and get prompted for a User Name and Password and Connect As parameter. I use SYS, although SYSTEM would work as well, and so would SYSMAN. I always choose the SYSDBA Connect As value. The sign-on page is shown in Figure 9-17.

Clicking Login takes you to the main page for the Database Console. From here you can shut down and restart the instance, as well as access all the various Administrative tools you need to manage the database instance. You can even click the Listener Name displayed in the Listener field in the General section of the page and manage the listener just as you did from the command line with the lsnrctl stop command. The Listener detail page is shown in Figure 9-18.

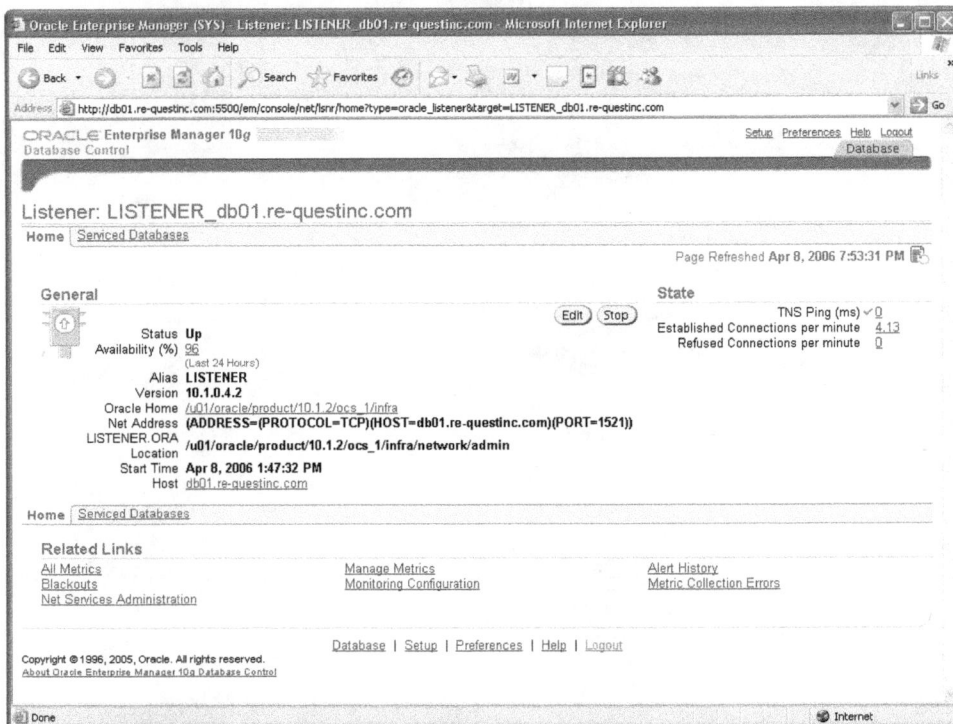

FIGURE 9-18. *Enterprise Manager Listener Detail page*

Summary

This completes the chapter on managing the processes, components, and subcomponents of the Oracle Collaboration Suite 10*g* Infrastructure and Applications tiers. One thing I want to emphasize is that whether you control things from a command-line interface or the Enterprise Manager Browser interface, you must always be conscious of the order of processing between the components of a tier, as well as between the tiers themselves. So, for example, you need to know that you have shut down the Applications Tier completely before you can shut down the Infrastructure Tier processes, and everything needs to be down before you can shut down the Datastore. Just because you use the Enterprise Manager Database Console to shut down the Datastore does not mean the tool itself will manage the dependency that the Applications Tier and other Infrastructure Tier components be shut down first. Keep overall dependency in mind when managing the individual components and subcomponents of the Oracle Collaboration Suite 10g environment.

Next we will discuss backup strategies for the Oracle Collaboration Suite 10g environment.

CHAPTER
10

Backup and Recovery

*Life is inherently risky. There is only one big risk you
should avoid at all costs, and that is the risk of doing nothing.*
                                                        —Denis Waitley

Backup and recovery is one of the most fundamental
responsibilities of any database administrator (DBA) and/or
system administrator (SA). In the traditional Oracle Database
realm, backups are as old as the earth and sky. And while the
necessity of taking backups has been with us from the
beginning—and there have been huge evolutionary strides made by Oracle
in the tools provided—the topic is still large and intimidating to new users of
Oracle's products. The documentation set for the current version on the
database includes four documents containing over 800 pages of material—
and that only covers the database backups. Backups of the Application
Server and Oracle Collaboration Suite 10*g* are additional topics with entire
books of supporting documentation in their own right. Where should one
begin? What's recommended? This chapter will attempt to cull the key
elements from all of the relevant documents to give you a foundational
introduction to backup and recovery for Oracle Collaboration Suite 10*g*
environments based upon practical experience.

The focus will be on identifying what needs to be backed up, how to
configure and run the backups, and also how to manage them on an ongoing
basis. Special emphasis will be placed on understanding what is being
backed up and what mechanisms are performing what parts of the process.
And while the intent is to provide you with a road map for implementing
complete backups for Oracle Collaboration Suite 10*g* to enable recovery
from virtually any type of failure/data loss, it is outside the scope of this
chapter as well as redundant to Oracle's own documentation to present
step-by-step guidance for each possible recovery scenario. If the goal of
helping you to set up and understand your backups is accomplished, you'll
be well prepared to consult the appropriate manuals (and work with Oracle
Support) in order to deal with any recovery situation—confident in the
knowledge that the backups necessary to any successful recovery effort exist.

What Needs to Be Backed Up?

There's a simple answer to that question: "Everything." So let's identify the
different types of data and/or information that should be protected before

examining the tools and techniques for taking the backups. Here are the major categories:

- **Operating system install/configuration**   This includes such fundamental information as the base OS version, non-default kernel parameter settings, installed patches, hostname, IP address, and user and group definitions. While not necessarily Oracle-specific, the server hardware and operating system configurations are important foundational components.

- **Oracle product install/configuration**   As in the case of the OS-level information, you should always maintain good records of what Oracle products are installed, their exact version numbers, patches applied, and configuration settings (such as instance names, networking port assignments, and URLs). This information is always available, initially, in the Oracle Installer log files. It should, however, also be maintained over time as patches and upgrades modify your environments.

- **Oracle product binaries**   These are the actual Oracle executable programs and all of their associated resources. This is typically the $ORACLE_HOME location on each node that makes up your Oracle Collaboration Suite 10*g* installation.

- **Oracle Database control files, redo logs, and data files**   In an Oracle Collaboration Suite 10*g* environment, this refers to the database(s) hosting the Identity Management, Infrastructure, and Oracle Collaboration Suite 10*g* Datastores. Depending upon your needs, this may be a single database or there may be more than one. For the purposes of this book we assume that all database-based storage resides in a single Oracle database.

- **Middle Tier configuration**   In an Oracle Collaboration Suite 10*g* environment this includes configuration information about the base Application Server's components as well as those additional components that make up Oracle Collaboration Suite 10*g*. Beyond pure configuration information, and included in this category for convenience, are the Oracle Calendar data files and externally stored Oracle Content Services BFILE data.

Now, let's examine, step-by-step, the process of implementing backups of all of those resources. We'll follow the chronology of installing and making Oracle Collaboration Suite 10g ready for use, and we'll discuss what should be done at each step of the process. For purposes of discussion we will assume that your Oracle Collaboration Suite 10g installation is distributed across two servers: an "infrastructure" node to host the database and identity management components and another "Middle Tier" (or "Mid-Tier") node to host the remaining non-database components of the Application Server and Oracle Collaboration Suite 10g proper.

Documenting the Installation

Before any of the Oracle software is even installed, you'll acquire and prepare one or more servers to host Oracle Collaboration Suite 10g. And while the installation documentation provides a list of minimum prerequisites for computers and operating systems hosting Oracle Collaboration Suite 10g (including operating system release levels, kernel parameter settings, patch levels, RPM levels, quantity of memory, and speed of CPUs), you should record the actual values for those resources in your environment. Chapter 1 of your environmental configuration document should describe the makes and models of your servers; how much memory, disk, and CPU are installed on each machine; base operating system release levels; etc. Beyond the base install, your configuration decisions should also be documented in this section for future reference. Some examples include hostnames, IP addresses, username and group membership of the OS account that will "own" the Oracle software, file system mount points, and (perhaps) SAN LUN definitions. This is also a good time to make sure that all hardware and software licensing and maintenance agreements are in order.

Once the hardware and operating system have been prepared, while running the Oracle Installer, you'll be prompted to choose a name and location for the Oracle Software homes, networking ports, database names, SIDs, domains, and passwords. All of that information should also be documented during the installation process. Call this Chapter 2, if you like. Should it ever be necessary to rebuild a server from scratch (in preparation for some restore/recovery operation), you should be able to consult the configuration documentation and be assured of reproducing the original configuration precisely. This is a very important step but is also easily overlooked during a first-time installation of Oracle Collaboration Suite 10g.

If that's the case, I wouldn't panic. All of this environmental information is available in the form of Oracle Installer log files, Oracle Enterprise Manager web pages, and/or OS configuration files.

Whether you capture your configuration information during the installation process or after the fact, the important thing is to gather and maintain it over time. If you upgrade your operating system, update your documentation to reflect it. Add another file system or another disk? Update the docs. Apply a patch? Update the docs. The point is that a foundational element of any backup and recovery strategy is to understand what it is—exactly what it is—that you are trying to protect. And while there are tools that will make copies of your data and configurations, there is no substitute for having your environment documented for future reference. It will also, incidentally, come in handy should you find yourself working with Oracle Support. Often, half of the challenge of opening a new Service Request (SR) lies in accurately describing your environment. If you take the time to capture and maintain your configuration information, then you won't be scrambling to locate it later (when, possibly, the database or server nodes are down and cannot be consulted).

Configuring the Database for Backups

With the 10*g* releases of Oracle Collaboration Suite 10*g*, the default installation creates a single database to host the Oracle Identity Management, the Infrastructure Tier Metadata Repository, and the Oracle Collaboration Suite 10*g* Datastore. Once the Oracle Installer session is complete, all database, Oracle Application Server (iAS for short), and Oracle Collaboration Suite 10*g* services will be up and running and you'll have a fully functional Oracle Collaboration Suite 10*g* environment. What's missing is any sort of meaningful fault tolerance vis-à-vis the ability to recover the database. And since the Oracle database is the most significant underlying technology stack component supporting the Oracle Collaboration Suite 10*g* product, we'll begin our task of setting up our programmed backups with a look at the Recovery Manager (RMAN) tool.

The Recovery Manager Tool

RMAN isn't really a separate tool. Strictly speaking, it is a part of the Oracle database itself. And it has, at this point, been around for so long and become so sophisticated and reliable that it is hard to imagine that DBAs ever had to perform backups and recoveries without it. So what, in a nutshell, *is* RMAN anyway? Recovery Manager is a set of programs that understands, at a very detailed level, the architecture of the Oracle database, how to back up the database, how to keep track of those backups, and finally, how to use those backups to restore and recover a damaged database. RMAN is, essentially, a backup wizard for the database, and it works well. In fact, with the 10*g* release of the Oracle database RMAN can now do some truly amazing things. Beyond taking online (i.e., "hot") backups while the database is up, open, and active, RMAN can now perform fast incremental backups of only those parts of the database that have changed since the last backup, do transparent software compression of data to save space, and also use and manage the new Flash Recovery Area (FRA) of the 10*g* database. Let's look at some of the configuration that we'll need to do (beyond the default database configuration provided by the Oracle Installer) in order to take advantage of some of these features.

By default the Oracle Collaboration Suite 10*g* database is configured to run in NOARCHIVELOG mode—which is to say that the only options for recovering from a damaged database would be to restore the most recent cold backup. By today's 24 × 7 Internet-era standards, that doesn't seem reasonable. First of all, it isn't likely that you'd want to tolerate long periods of downtime to take cold backups. But even if that were acceptable, you probably wouldn't want to accept the loss of all changes to the database between the last good cold backup and the time of the failure. So obviously, Oracle's default is meant to be changed in every production installation. The product is shipped in this NOARCHIVELOG mode (presumably) because there are so many possible ways to configure backups that it is pointless to attempt any default beyond "none." So enabling ARCHIVELOG mode is one of the first things that you'll need to do. But once you do so, you'll need to specify a location to hold the archived online redo log files. These archive logs are essentially change-by-change records of what occurs in the database. Since they are created continuously as the database is in use, they can be applied to a backup of the database ("hot" or "cold") to recover from failures right up to the last "commit" statement issued before the failure—a much more effective and desirable capability. Let's opt to use the Oracle 10*g* database's Flash Recovery Area to hold both your archive logs and your RMAN backups.

Oracle 10*g* Database Flash Recovery Area

To make database configuration changes you'll need to open a terminal session to "source" the operating system environment file (see Chapter 9), shut down all Infrastructure and Mid-Tier nondatabase services (using the opmnctl utility), and then to launch the SQL*Plus tool and issue the following commands:

```
sqlplus "/ as sysdba"
alter system set db_recovery_file_dest =
'/u01/oracle/orabackups/flash_recovery_area' scope=both sid='*';
alter system set db_recovery_file_dest_size = 15g scope=both sid='*';
alter system set db_flashback_retention_target = 60 scope=both sid='*';
shutdown normal;
startup mount;
alter database archivelog;
alter database enable block change tracking;
alter database flashback on;
alter database open;
exit;
```

Look at what's happening here. First off, you're specifying a location for the DB_RECOVERY_FILE_DEST database parameter. This is the directory location the database will use as the Flash Recovery Area (FRA). You should ensure that the directory exists before executing this ALTER SYSTEM command. The next statement specifies an upper limit on the amount of disk space that the database may consume in the FRA. In this example you're saying that only 15 gigabytes may be used to store all of the archive logs and the RMAN backups. You'll see a little later on how the database and RMAN keep the FRA from exceeding that quota. But for the moment you should plan to use a value that is large enough to hold a full backup of your database, and also all of the archive logs that will be generated between backups. This can best be determined through trial and error and close monitoring. In any case, those two parameters are all that is required to define a FRA for the database. So what are the remaining commands doing? Setting the DB_FLASHBACK_RETENTION_TARGET parameter sets a time-based quota (in minutes) on the use of space in the FRA for the Flashback Database option, which will be discussed later. Notice that all of those SQL statements were issued with the database up, open, and running in normal mode. But you're not done yet, and the remaining steps must be performed in a somewhat more restrictive mode.

The next step is to perform a normal shutdown of the database (so that all datafiles are consistent when the database is restarted) and then to restart the database to the mount point. Now we'll issue several ALTER DATABASE statements to change the options in effect. The first (i.e., ALTER DATABASE ARCHIVELOG;) turns on archiving of the online redo log files and enables online RMAN backups. The second instructs the database to maintain a bitmapped index to changed database blocks, which enables very fast incremental RMAN backups. The third enables the Flashback Database option. And finally, the ALTER DATABASE OPEN; statement returns the database to normal service. (The exit; command simply exits the SQL*Plus tool.) You may now restart all nondatabase services using opmnctl. We still haven't taken a backup yet, but the database has now been configured to support RMAN backups. And though you'll soon see that you won't need to interact with RMAN directly, it is instructive to see and understand how RMAN works. To that end, you might wish to perform a full hot RMAN backup of the database right now in order to get a feel for how it works. Still using the same terminal session that was used to run SQL*Plus, invoke RMAN and perform the backup using the following commands:

```
rman target /
configure retention policy to redundancy 2;
configure controlfile autobackup on;
configure controlfile autobackup format for device type disk clear;
backup as compressed backupset database plus archivelog;
exit;
```

That's pretty simple, but now walk through it line by line just to make sure that you understand what you're seeing here. The first line launches the RMAN command line interface—notice that your prompt immediately becomes "RMAN>" to signify that RMAN command input is now expected instead of operating system commands. The next three commands are backup configuration commands that only need to be run once. After that RMAN will remember your directives. In this case you're saying that no more than two backups need be maintained in the FRA at any given time (i.e., "redundancy 2,"), that the database's control file should be automatically backed up whenever you do any RMAN backup, and finally, that you wish to let RMAN choose a format for the control file backup's name. Because you're using a FRA for the database, RMAN can (and will) make all the right decisions for you with no more information than you've provided here.

Okay, finally, the "meat and potatoes," the command BACKUP AS COMPRESSED BACKUPSET DATABASE PLUS ARCHIVELOG is instructing RMAN to perform a full hot backup of the database and all archivelog files, to compress the backup files as they are being created, and to write the backups into the FRA. The final exit command simply exits the RMAN command-line interface. And that's it. That is all it takes to take a full backup of the database! It hardly seems worth so many words to describe the setup, and it might make you wonder why Oracle doesn't provide for this setup as the default, "out of the box" configuration. The answer is that we've made certain assumptions that Oracle cannot make for all customers.

The most significant assumption is that enough disk space is available for a FRA (i.e., disk-based RMAN backups). And while it might seem, at first glance, that the FRA would actually require more disk space than the database itself, that isn't necessarily true. First of all, RMAN has never backed up empty database blocks (which is to say portions of the pre-allocated database data files that have never been used before—or, in DBA parlance, "above the high-water-mark"). Second, notice the "as compressed backupset" clause of the RMAN backup command. This invokes software compression of the backups that can result in backups of 1/3 the normal size (or even better) at the expense of longer backup times and more CPU consumption. But given all of the advantages of using a FRA—along with ways to mitigate the costs—the use of a FRA is recommended as a best practice (and a core design element for our illustrations in this chapter). Clearly, however, the use of a FRA is *not* a requirement. The RMAN documentation set doesn't extend to over 800 pages for nothing. There is a way to meet virtually any set of constraints, if necessary. But in terms of leveraging some of Oracle's newest and best capabilities around backup and recovery, the FRA is highly recommended.

Climbing the Techstack: iAS Backup Configuration

If you've purchased Oracle Collaboration Suite 10g primarily for its headline features (i.e., Email, Web Conferencing, Content Services, Calendaring, etc.), it might not be immediately apparent to you that you've also purchased iAS, which includes such foundational components as the Apache web server, an LDAP directory server, and a SingleSignOn (SSO) capability—not to mention J2EE containers and a number of Oracle-proprietary development tools. And while it might have been obvious that the Oracle database was a foundational technology stack component for Oracle Collaboration Suite 10*g*, you might not have realized that between the database and Oracle Collaboration Suite 10*g* lies (for many, if not all, Oracle Collaboration Suite 10*g* features) iAS. We've just seen that the RMAN capability provides us with a highly sophisticated "expert" backup and recovery wizard for ensuring that the database is properly backed up and/or recovered. After all was said and done, we were able to back up the entire database with one simple command. Surely the same must be true of the Application Server. For the most part, yes! Oracle has supplied you with the tools to support the proper backup and recovery of their Application Server, but unlike RMAN, which is a part of the database itself, these tools are in the form of perl and command scripts.

Unlike the Oracle database, which is a single large, complex, but coherent product, the application server is, in many ways, a heterogeneous collection of products and services that—taken together—have been branded as an "application server." This "collection of tools" nature presents a real challenge in terms of backup and recovery, since (unlike in the case of the database) the number, types, and locations of each component's configuration, deployment, and/or data stores are nonuniform. For example, the Apache server uses an httpd.conf file (among others) to control its operation. That file should be backed up in order to protect the Apache service. The OC4J J2EE containers have no httpd.conf files but do have a host of other configuration files that need to be protected. Each component—and each deployed application—may have unique backup requirements. So what's the solution? Answer: $ORACLE_HOME/backup_restore. Huh?

The iAS Backup and Recovery Tool

Recall that the Oracle Home is the directory location on your servers where the Oracle software is actually installed. In the case of Oracle 10*g* Application Server installations, the backup_restore directory contains the iAS equivalent of what RMAN is to the database (i.e., a program—and associated resources— to manage the backup and recovery of all of the configuration files for the iAS components). Below the backup_restore directory is a config directory that contains a large number of inp (or backup input) definition files.

The files are iAS component–centric—which is to say that there's one for Apache, one for SSO, etc., and each file, in turn, contains a set of directives that identify which file system locations should be copied from or to as part of backup and recovery operations. In addition to the component-specific inp files, there is also a "master inp file" named config.inp, which contains parameters that control all subsequent backup and restore operations. This is very similar in concept to the RMAN "configure" commands. Beyond specifying things like backup and log file destinations, Oracle home, DBID, and Database SID, the config.inp file also names all of the other inp files that should be included by reference during backup runs.

So then, you can see that Oracle's approach is quite flexible and allows for a consistent backup and recovery approach over time as components are added, removed, or modified within the iAS umbrella. The config.inp file itself must be customized/completed before performing iAS backups or restores, and this may be done via the command line or via the Oracle Enterprise Manager console. Before explaining how to do that, there's something else to understand about the iAS backups. Not only do they use the inp files to copy the iAS component configuration information for safekeeping, they also run your RMAN backups for you at the same time!

Just as you've learned how to set up and run RMAN manually, you've now learned that the iAS backup tool handles that for you, right? Yes, but there's a catch. The iAS backup and restore tool *will* handle your backups for you correctly only *if* it is correctly configured to do so—and there's some gotchas lurking here for the uninitiated. But because you understand the approach to the RMAN backups, you're also in a good position to make good configuration decisions at this point. Begin by taking a closer look at some of the files in the $ORACLE_HOME/backup_restore directory. More specifically, look at all of the files with a .tmpl extension. These are all templates of RMAN scripts. What's an RMAN script? Well, you saw one earlier. It contained CONFIGURE and BACKUP commands. And, it turns out, given that you're using a Flash Recovery Area, the RMAN scripts don't need to be very complicated. In fact, the RMAN script templates provided by Oracle are actually *too* complicated. They don't accommodate the use of a FRA, and they contain configuration commands that would attempt to place backups outside of the FRA! This isn't really a problem, though. Once again, Oracle's approach is very flexible and easily customized. You can simply comment out any CONFIGURE commands that attempt to set nondefault control file autobackup formats. If you also remove the FORMAT clause from all ALLOCATE CHANNEL xx TYPE DISK commands, then by default, all disk backups will go to the Flash Recovery Area defined for the database—which is exactly what you want. You might wish to create copies of the original template files before editing them (for future reference). Test your changes ahead of time using the RMAN command-line interface, if you wish.

Now that you've customized the RMAN template files, you're ready to use them to create the actual RMAN scripts that will be used by the iAS backup and recovery tool. That's right, RMAN doesn't use the templates directly. Only during the process of setting up the config.inp file are the templates read, customized, and then written out as the RMAN scripts that will be used from that point on. So then, how do you set up the config.inp file? Simply navigate to the $ORACLE_HOME/backup_restore/config/ directory and edit the config.inp file (with, for example, vi) and replace the VALUE_NOT_SET strings with the requested values. Once you've saved your changes, you'll need to generate all of the RMAN configuration files using the same tool that you'll use to perform the actual backups and restores: bkp_restore.sh. This is a simple wrapper shell script that calls a perl script that does the actual work of doing backups and restores. Here's the command to process the config.inp file:

```
$ORACLE_HOME/backup_restore/bkp_restore.sh -m configure
```

This process is very much like running the root.sh script during an Oracle Installer session in that it only needs to be run once (unless you wish to change the stored values), not as part of each backup or restore run. Once the configure run is complete, the customized config.inp file will supply the stored values to all future backup and restore runs.

Again, as in the case of the RMAN discussion, it seems like a lot of words to explain something that is, essentially, a few keystrokes—and that's true. Executing the iAS backups is even more trivial than the simple manual RMAN backup that we ran. For example,

```
$ORACLE_HOME/backup_restore/bkp_restore.sh -m backup_instance_
online -v
```

would perform a full hot RMAN backup and also a backup of all of the iAS component resources identified by the inp files that config.inp is aware of. Note that such a backup command only makes sense on the Infrastructure

Tier (where the Oracle database is running). To back up a Middle Tier node, you'd use a different parameter value to just process the inp files (but not call RMAN), thus:

```
$ORACLE_HOME/backup_restore/bkp_restore.sh -m backup_config -v
```

In both cases, the –v switch instructs the script to send "verbose" output to the terminal—and you should run the backups that way (at least once) to see all of what is being done. You're getting closer to a full backup and recovery solution for Oracle Collaboration Suite 10*g*, but you're not there yet. Recall that while both the database and iAS are foundational components to Oracle Collaboration Suite 10*g* (and at this point you're doing backups of both of them), Oracle Collaboration Suite 10*g* is a superset of iAS. You're still missing backups of the very heart and soul of Oracle Collaboration Suite 10*g*.

Oracle Collaboration Suite 10*g* Backup Configuration

Strictly speaking, you didn't need to run the bkp_restore.sh script at all in order to set up the Oracle Collaboration Suite 10*g* backups. In fact, if you read the Oracle Collaboration Suite 10*g* Backup and Recovery documentation carefully, you'll note that they actually tell you *not* to configure or run the iAS backups from the Oracle Enterprise Manager web page. So why bother to learn about the shell script, the perl script, the RMAN templates, the inp files, etc.? The answer to that question will become obvious in very short order. Let's jump right into the Oracle-provided backup and restore scripts and resources for Oracle Collaboration Suite 10*g*. They're delivered in the $ORACLE_HOME/backup_restore directory (just as for the Application Server). They're driven by inp files (just as they are for the Application Server—including using config.inp as the master configuration file). The config.inp file must be customized and the configure command issued using the following command:

```
$ORACLE_HOME/backup_restore/ocs_bkp_restore.sh -m configure
```

The script operates exactly like the iAS script does—except that it also displays any existing configuration options while prompting you to (optionally) supply new values. But again, the config.inp file stores your responses for use in all future backup and restore operations. Are you seeing a pattern here? There's more. Once you've customized the config.inp file, you can run your new Oracle Collaboration Suite 10*g* backups for Infrastructure Tier nodes like this:

```
$ORACLE_HOME/backup_restore/ocs_bkp_restore.sh -m
backup_instance_online -v
```

and like this for Middle Tier nodes:

```
$ORACLE_HOME/backup_restore/ocs_bkp_restore.sh -m backup_config -v
```

Obviously, the similarities are visible. So, what's going on here? Well, the good news is that Oracle has done something very logical here. Just as the iAS backup script backs up the resources related to the Application Server components (as identified by their inp files) and then proceeds to call RMAN to back up the database, the Oracle Collaboration Suite 10*g* backup script is doing the same thing. Which is to say that it is backing up the Oracle Collaboration Suite 10*g*–specific resources according to a list of Oracle Collaboration Suite 10*g*–related inp files, and then it is calling the iAS backup script. The iAS backup script does its own job as before and also calls RMAN as before. So the Oracle Collaboration Suite 10*g* backups are layered in a stack of supporting infrastructure in exactly the same way that the product depends upon iAS and, in turn, the database. The approach is very logical and well thought-out. That said, it is very important to run the ocs_bkp_restore.sh script with the -m configure command even if you've previously run the bkp_restore.sh script in configure mode. The reason is that only the Oracle Collaboration Suite 10*g* version of the script will include the Oracle Collaboration Suite 10*g*–specific inp files in the config.inp configuration file. This is, no doubt, why the Oracle documentation warns against running the iAS EM Backup/Recovery Wizard. If you do so in an environment already configured for Oracle Collaboration Suite 10*g* backup and restore operations, you will cause the config.inp file to revert to an iAS-only version. Is that it? Are you now backing up "everything"? Almost, but not quite.

While most Oracle Collaboration Suite 10*g* content is stored inside the Oracle database (and therefore has been backed up with RMAN), there is an exception to that rule that you should consider. Oracle Content Services stores content, inside the database, as LOB (i.e., "Large Object") columns—basically an entire binary document stored as the column of a table row.

And while this has the advantage of making the content searchable using all of the facilities of the database, the size (and cost) to maintain these tables may become prohibitive at some point. Therefore Oracle Collaboration Suite 10*g* provides for a mechanism to archive older data outside of the database using the BFILE mechanism. When using BFILEs, only a pointer to the documents is maintained inside the database proper, while the data itself is stored on the file system outside of the database's normal data files. And while from an Oracle Collaboration Suite 10*g* user's functional perspective this may be fairly transparent, RMAN backups don't save and restore the external BFILEs. So you need to ensure that some other part of your Oracle Collaboration Suite 10*g* backup and recovery strategy handles this. One way would be to add the directory location of the BFILEs to an inp file so that the normal Oracle Collaboration Suite 10*g* backups will "pick them up." This is easily accomplished by retrieving the location of the BFILEs from the database using the following SQL statement:

```
select distinct(BASEBFILEPATH) from content.odm_media;
```

The file system location returned could then be included in the following inp file:

```
$ORACLE_HOME/backup_restore/config/config_misc_files.imp
```

The ocs_bkp_restore.sh script would then know where to find the BFILEs. Another option would be to simply ensure that the file system location of the BFILEs is backed up to tape by your operating system backups. Given the potential size of the BFILEs, that is actually the preferred solution.

Once you've run the ocs_bkp_restore.sh –m configure command in every $ORACLE_HOME that makes up your installation, your Oracle Collaboration Suite 10*g* backup configuration is finally complete. The challenge now lies in the execution and management of the backups.

Running and Managing Your Backups

After all of that configuration work, it would seem that running your Oracle Collaboration Suite 10*g* backups boils down to a single simple command per $ORACLE_HOME location, for example, for an Infrastructure Tier home:

```
ocs_bkp_restore.sh –m backup_instance_online
```

It hardly seems that there could be anything more to be said about it—and yet that's not really the case. There are still a number of important issues to be considered.

Synchronize Your Oracle Collaboration Suite 10g Backups

Because you may have installed Oracle Collaboration Suite 10g on multiple servers (most likely two or more), you'll need to configure and run your Oracle Collaboration Suite 10g backups in multiple locations. It is important to schedule these jobs to run as concurrently as possible, since the configuration information for some Oracle Collaboration Suite 10g components is distributed among the different computer nodes. So, for example, you might decide to use the unix/linux cron daemon to schedule and run your backups each night at midnight. If so, be sure that the crontab file on each host is set to run the ocs_bkp_restore.sh script at the same time. Using another tool like Oracle Enterprise Manager's Job Scheduling facility or Maestro is okay too, but be sure that whatever tool you choose gives you as much control as possible over start times. Another option that would involve some shell scripting would be to use secure shell (ssh) to submit the backups on all nodes from a central location. The advantage would be that changes to start times (or ad hoc backup submissions) would always be consistent. It seems likely that future releases of Oracle's ocs_bkp_restore.sh script will provide built-in support for multiple $ORACLE_HOME (and multiple server) coordination of these backups—or perhaps it will end up being managed by Enterprise Manager Grid Control. But in the near term you'll need to plan to manage this manually.

Move Your Backups to Tape

RMAN backups to a Flash Recovery Area have a number of important advantages over backups directly to tape (including faster recovery from failures), but they will not protect you against the loss of an entire server (or disk storage array). Likewise, since the Oracle Collaboration Suite 10g (and iAS) backups are really nothing more than disk-based copies of selected files (stored as.jar archive files), by themselves they only represent a partial solution. In order to completely protect your Oracle Collaboration Suite 10*g* environment against all types of failures, it is important to move the RMAN and Oracle Collaboration Suite 10*g* backups off of your servers and onto tape.

The good news is that this is very simple to accomplish if you're already using a network backup utility like Veritas NetBackup or HP's Data Protector—both of which offer integration directly to Oracle's RMAN capability. In fact, virtually all of the major "media management" vendors support RMAN because Oracle is such a dominant player in the database market. Unfortunately, while support for RMAN is fairly universal, the products themselves are quite different. It is, therefore, outside the scope of our discussion to describe the setup of tape backup solutions and their integration with RMAN. You should consult the Oracle Database Backup and Recovery Advanced User's Guide's discussion of "Configuring RMAN to Make Backups to a Media Manager" for details on the integrating RMAN with your specific tape management product.

Once your tape backup/tape media management product is installed and configured for use with RMAN, there are a number of DO and DO NOT hints to help ensure complete and useful backups of your servers:

- DO ensure that all operating system directory locations are being backed up.

- DO ensure that the backup directory location and backup log file directory location specified when running the ocs_bkp_restore.sh –m configure command are being backed up.

- DO write a new RMAN script that allocates a channel to SBT (System Backup to Tape) and then performs a BACKUP RECOVERY AREA; command. This RMAN job should run after the nightly ocs_bkp_restore.sh jobs have already run. It will copy the RMAN backups and archive logs from the Flash Recovery Area to tape and—and this is very important—record the fact that it has done so. Accordingly, should the database need to "make space" in the Flash Recovery Area in order to respect the disk space quota set by the DB_RECOVERY_FILE_DEST_SIZE parameter, it can and will remove backups that have already been copied to tape.

■ DO ensure that the Oracle Content Services BFILE location is being backed up.

■ DO NOT back up the live database data files without RMAN. Since they are open files and constantly being written to, any such non-RMAN backups would be "smeared" and useless. It would be a waste of time and tape. What's more, if such copies were ever restored to disk from tape, they would automatically damage the database and cause you to have to perform media recovery!

■ DO NOT elect to take non-RMAN backups of the Flash Recovery Area instead of an RMAN BACKUP RECOVERY AREA; backup. If you do so, the backups will not necessarily be smeared, but RMAN will not know that the FRA contents have been copied to tape and may not, therefore, be able to reuse space as aggressively as necessary.

Purge the Oracle Collaboration Suite 10*g* Backup Directory

If you're performing daily Oracle Collaboration Suite 10*g* backups, you'll soon notice that the backup destination location will continue to grow without bounds. Unlike a Flash Recovery Area, the Oracle Collaboration Suite 10*g* backup destination is not "system managed" to a disk quota. In order to keep disk usage to a reasonable amount (and prevent the file system from filling completely), you should write a shell script to remove old Oracle Collaboration Suite 10*g* backups and run that script from any job scheduler, preferably Oracle Enterprise Manager Jobs control.

Create and Retain Cold Baseline Backups

While the focus of this chapter has been on setting up and running regularly recurring backup processes, you should also plan to create and retain (on tape, perhaps) a full cold backup of your entire Oracle Collaboration Suite 10*g* installation (both Infrastructure and Middle Tiers, as well as all database content) immediately upon successful installation or upgrade of the product. In those rare circumstances where even the facilities needed to perform a restore (using your nightly backups) are lost or damaged, having a full cold backup of your installation can save precious time and trouble, since the alternative (in the absence of baseline cold backups) could be re-installing the software from original media before being able to restore/recover using normal backups. Again, such circumstances may be rare, but they can occur. Better safe than sorry.

Further Reading and Recovery Options

As Oracle customers we are truly blessed with very high quality documentation—and plenty of it, too. In fact, the only complaint may be that even while Oracle's products become more and more sophisticated (and easy to use), behind the scenes they are still very complex. This becomes apparent the first time one attempts to navigate the full documentation library for a product like Oracle's database and, to a lesser degree, Oracle Collaboration Suite 10g. That being said, the Oracle Collaboration Suite Administrator's Guide chapter titled "Backing Up and Recovering Oracle Collaboration Suite" should be consulted for a full discussion of the various options and parameters available when invoking the ocs_bkp_restore.sh script—while doing both backups and/or restores. Beyond the online (hot) backups that have been illustrated, it is also possible to easily run incremental (hot or cold) backups. An option even exists for rolling back the entire database to a point in time before logical corruption (read: "user error") occurred via the Flashback Database option (which, you may recall, you enabled). Becoming familiar with these options before you face a recovery situation will pay dividends in the future.

Summary

If you've read this chapter sequentially and performed all of the setup/ configuration tasks as they were presented, then at this point you should have a useful set of backups being taken on a nightly basis. Beyond the end result, you also have some level of understanding for how those backups work (what is being backed up and by what mechanisms). You're not an expert yet, but you've got a solid baseline of understanding to continue to refine the Oracle Collaboration Suite 10g backups to fit your environment.

You might, for instance, determine that your installation is simply too big to support using a Flash Recovery Area and that your RMAN backups must go directly to tape. Given what you know about how the Oracle Collaboration Suite 10*g* backup script uses RMAN templates to configure your backups, you'd have no problem making that change. Similarly, should you find yourself in a recovery situation, you'll have all of the environmental information at your fingertips so that you can quickly and effectively engage Oracle Support (if you needed to—or choose to—open an SR). Finally, any exploration of the official Oracle documentation sets should now yield a sense of déjà vu and confidence as you expand your competence beyond the foundational material presented here.

CHAPTER
11

Monitoring and Managing Log Files in the Collaboration Suite Environment

That men do not learn much from the lessons
of history is the most important of all the lessons
that history has to teach us.

—Aldous Huxley

O ne of the most important areas of administration for the Oracle Collaboration Suite 10*g* architecture is the series of log files generated throughout the environment. There are log files associated with each tier of the Oracle Collaboration Suite 10*g* product, as well as with each of the individual application components. These log files contain important messages related to events that occur in the environment (such as startup and shutdown of a tier or component) and access and error data related to HTTP requests, as well as warnings and errors generated when issues are encountered either by users or the system itself (such as Java exceptions in the OCS WebClient). In addition to the application component and Application Server log files, there are also log files generated on the Oracle Datstore Tier that contain information similar to that just described for the Application Server Tier but specifically related to the database itself.

The fact that there are so many log files in so many places, along with their various naming conventions, formats, and content, makes proactive management and monitoring of the log files and their content mandatory in order to maintain a healthy Oracle Collaboration Suite 10*g* environment. One of the primary responsibilities of an Oracle Collaboration Suite 10*g* Administrator is to routinely monitor and maintain the log files produced within the environment for critical errors indicating issues with one of the tiers or application components. In addition, these log files must be purged and recycled so that they do not grow to an unmanageable size, or even halt the Applications Tier. If these log files are not routinely reviewed for errors and managed for space consumption and size, some very bad things happen in the Oracle Collaboration Suite 10*g* environment.

In this chapter, I will provide a foundational Best Practices understanding of the log files, where they are located, and how they are formatted, along with some effective tools and procedures that can be used to review and maintain them.

Application Server and Application Component Logs

By far the largest number and most diverse set of logs to manage in the Oracle Collaboration Suite 10*g* environment are those that are generated on the Applications Tier for both the Oracle Application Server 10*g* environment and the individual Oracle Collaboration Suite 10*g* application components. They come in many shapes and sizes and contain a wide range of information regarding access, application messages, process management information, and error codes. Although this release of Oracle Collaboration Suite has gotten much better at standardizing the locations, naming conventions, and content of the log files, there is still some inconsistency, especially for someone who is not familiar with managing applications running in an Oracle Application Server 10*g* environment.

Log Structure(s) and Locations

Some of the Oracle Collaboration Suite 10*g* components as well as some application components use a specific log file structure known as Oracle Diagnostic Logging ("ODL"), which encompasses both the file naming convention and standard content written in XML format.

An ODL log is actually a set or group of log files that includes the currently active log file in the group, which is usually named log.xml, along with any ODL Archives, also known as segment files (if they exist). Log rotation is enabled by setting parameters within the component logging configuration files, such that when log files reach a defined size, they are renamed to log*n*.xml, where *n* is an incremental segment number starting at 1 (and then a new log.xml is established). The actual size of any given log file is not always exactly equal to the maximum segment parameter value. Log files may be slightly larger or smaller than the defined maximum value when rotation occurs, since individual log entries are not split across files. The first list that follows shows all the ODL-based log files locations in the Oracle Collaboration Suite 10*g* Applications Tier. Similar locations will exist for the Infrastructure Tier Application Server components as well, specifically for the Apache and dcm components, as well as the j2ee home and OC4J_SECURITY applications components. The second list shows the log file locations for the Infrastructure Tier for Oracle Collaboration Suite 10*g*.

Locations of ODL-Based Logs in the Applications Tier

./Apache/modplsql/logs/
./dcm/logs/dcmctl_logs/operations/
./dcm/logs/dcmctl_logs/
./dcm/logs/daemon_logs/operations/
./dcm/logs/daemon_logs/
./dcm/logs/emd_logs/operations/
./dcm/logs/emd_logs/
./wireless/logs/
./j2ee/home/log/operations/
./j2ee/home/log/home_default_island_1/oc4j/
./j2ee/OC4J_Content/log/OC4J_Content_default_island_1/oc4j/
./j2ee/OC4J_imeeting/OC4J_imeeting_default_island_1/oc4j/
./j2ee/OC4J_Mail/log/OC4J_Mail_default_island_1/oc4j/
./j2ee/OC4J_OCSADMIN/log/OC4J_OCSADMIN_default_island_1/oc4j/
./j2ee/OC4J_OCSClient/log/OC4J_OCSClient_default_island_1/oc4j/
./j2ee/OC4J_Portal/log/OC4J_Portal_default_island_1/oc4j/
./j2ee/OC4J_RM/log/OC4J_RM_default_island_1/oc4j/
./j2ee/OC4J_Wireless/log/OC4J_Wireless_default_island_1/oc4j/
./j2ee/Service_Component_Container/log/Service_Component_
Container_default_island_1/oc4j/

Locations of ODL-Based Logs in the Infrastructure Tier

./Apache/modplsql/logs/
./dcm/logs/dcmctl_logs/operations/
./dcm/logs/dcmctl_logs/
./dcm/logs/daemon_logs/operations/
./dcm/logs/daemon_logs/
./dcm/logs/emd_logs/operations/
./dcm/logs/emd_logs/
./j2ee/home/log/operations/
./j2ee/home/log/home_default_island_1/oc4j/
./j2ee/OC4J_SECURITY/log/OC4J_SECURITY_default_island_1/oc4j/

The ODL log files have a specific structure, defined in XML so that they can be displayed by either the Collaboration Suite Control Console or other tools that display XML formatted files. Each ODL message written to a log file includes a HEADER element that holds information about the message, an optional CORRELATION_DATA element that contains information used in correlating messages across the various Oracle Collaboration Suite 10g components, and a PAYLOAD element that contains the actual message text along with any associated values and optional arguments. An example ODL message, including the optional CORRELATION_DATA section, is shown in Figure 11-1.

In addition to the ODL-based log files just described, many other log files are generated within the Oracle Collaboration Suite 10g architecture. Some log files are standard in the sense that they will always exist in the environment, with the same naming conventions. A good example of this is the list of log files that exists for each J2EE application deployed in the Oracle Application Server 10g environment. Under the $ORACLE_HOME/j2ee/OC4J_

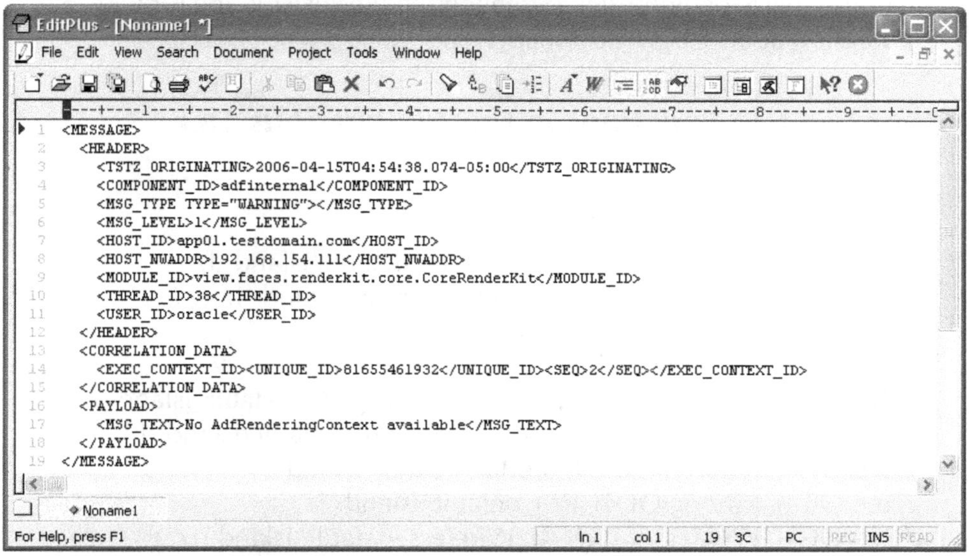

FIGURE 11-1. *Example ODL message*

<InstanceName>/log/OC4J_<InstanceName>_default_island_1/ directory there will always be the following log files: global-application.log, server.log, default-web-access.log, rmi.log and jms.log. (Note that these log files are specific to Java architecture standards that are not part of the subject matter of this book. Additional information can be found in product documentation related to Java application development and deployment in the Oracle environment.) It is important to understand that these particular log files can also be ODL enabled by modifying their respective xml configuration files for the particular OC4J instance in which ODL logging is desired. I will discuss enabling ODL messaging in the later section "Configuring the Logging Function." Other examples of text-based logging are the OPMN process logs located in the $ORACLE_HOME/opmn/logs/ directory and the Apache error and access logs located in the $ORACLE_HOME/Apache/Apache/logs/ directory, all of which need to be closely monitored and managed in an Oracle Collaboration Suite 10*g* environment for error information as well as size considerations. By modifying the log definition entries in the opmn.xml and httpd.conf file, log rotation can be enabled for the respective components. The following list shows the log file directories where the non-ODL formatted log files exist in the Oracle Collaboration Suite 10*g* environment.

Other Log File Locations in the Applications Tier

./j2ee/home/log/operations/
./j2ee/home/log/home_default_island_1/
./j2ee/OC4J_Content/log/OC4J_Content_default_island_1/
./j2ee/OC4J_imeeting/OC4J_imeeting_default_island_1/
./j2ee/OC4J_Mail/log/OC4J_Mail_default_island_1/
./j2ee/OC4J_imeeting/applications/imeeting/imtapp/logs/
./j2ee/OC4J_OCSADMIN/log/OC4J_OCSADMIN_default_island_1/
./j2ee/OC4J_OCSClient/log/OC4J_OCSClient_default_island_1/
./j2ee/OC4J_Portal/log/OC4J_Portal_default_island_1/
./j2ee/OC4J_RM/log/OC4J_RM_default_island_1/
./j2ee/OC4J_Wireless/log/OC4J_Wireless_default_island_1/
./j2ee/Service_Component_Container/Service_Component_Container_default_island_1/

```
./j2ee/OC4J_Portal/applications/jpdk/jpdk/apidoc/oracle/portal/log/
./jlib/log/
./network/log/
./ldap/odi/log/
./ldap/log/
./upgrade/log/
./sysman/j2ee/log/
./sysman/log/
./dsa/log/
./sso/log/
./oes/log/
./chgip/log/
./bibeans/log/
./um/log/
./ocsclient/install/log/
./ocsclient/log/
./content/log/
./ocal/log/
./imeeting/im/log/
./diagnostics/logs/
./backup_restore/logs/
./Apache/Apache/logs/
./Apache/modplsql/logs/
./opmn/logs/
./iaspt/logs/
./portal/logs/
./javacache/admin/logs/
./dcm/logs/
./wireless/logs/
./wireless/pimap/logs/
./webcache/logs/
./ocas/logs/
./ocsprovs/logs/
./workspaces/logs/
./discussions/logs/
./imeeting/install/logs/
./imeeting/logs/
```

Configuring the Logging Function

Administrators responsible for managing Oracle Collaboration Suite 10*g* environments need to review and set the available logging options so that they know where the logs produced are located, as well as how much or how little information is written to those logs. In addition, parameters for rotating log files and managing the overall amount of space log files consume should also be reviewed and adjusted accordingly. Generally speaking, unless there is some type of problem that an administrator is trying to resolve, log levels can be set to produce the minimal amount of information available. If and when a problem arises that requires additional detail for debugging purposes, log configuration parameters can be modified to produce additional logging information.

To turn ODL logging on for the HTTP Server within the Oracle Collaboration Suite 10*g* Applications Tier, you must follow two main steps. First, a subdirectory called *oracle* must be created under the $ORACLE_HOME/Apache/Apache/logs/ directory tree to store the ODL message logs. Next, the OraLogMode parameter must be set to *oracle* and the OraLogSeverity set to *message-type:message-level* in the httpd.conf file located in the $ORACLE_HOME/Apache/Apache/conf/ directory. The *message-type* value must be one of the following: INFORMATION, INTERNAL_ERROR, ERROR, WARNING, NOTIFICATION, or TRACE. The *message-level* value must be an integer between 1 and 32, where 32 is the least verbose and 1 is the most verbose, meaning that more detailed messages will be produced if the message-level is set to 1 than if it is set to 32. The httpd.conf file can either be modified via the Oracle Collaboration Suite 10*g* Control Console (HTTP_Server Administration Advanced Server Properties page) or by simply editing the file at the command prompt and then stopping and restarting the HTTP Server for the Applications Tier. My only suggestion is that you enter the parameters before any LoadModule statements are issued (which are usually at the end of the file anyway). So, an example setting looks like this:

```
OraLogMode oracle
OraLogSeverity INFORMATION:10
```

To turn ODL logging on for an OC4J application component, simply uncomment the ODL reference in <log> section of the various configuration files located in the $ORACLE_HOME/j2ee/<OC4J_Component>/config/ directory. Figure 11-2 shows the before and after syntax in the configuration

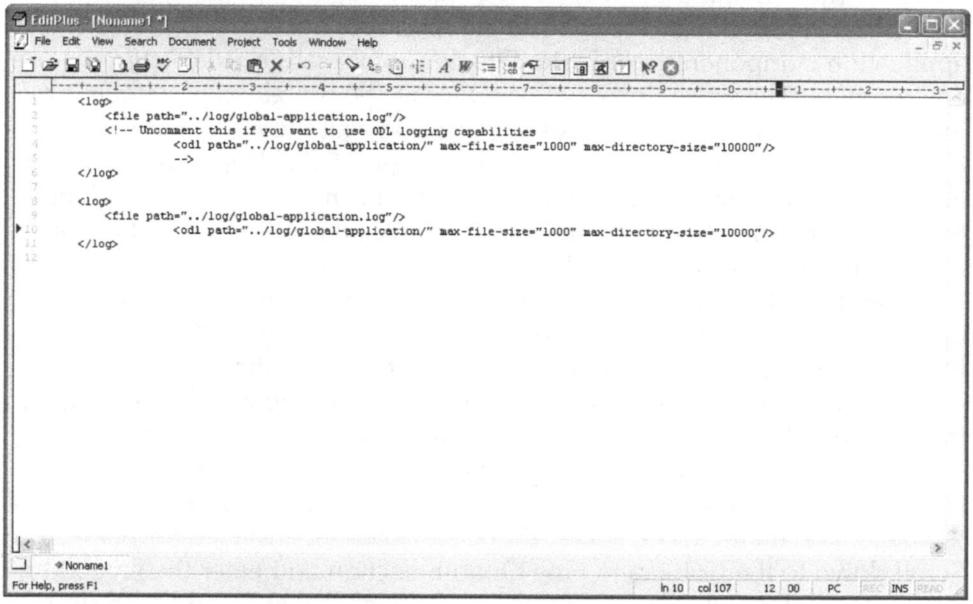

FIGURE 11-2.   *ODL enabling in the OC4J configuration files*

xml files for enabling the ODL messaging. The first section shows the lines
with the comments; the second section shows the syntax with the comments
removed (ODL logging enabled).

Note that in the ODL enabling line of the configuration file you tell the
log writer the location you want the log files written to, how big you want
each log file to get before rotating and archiving occur, and how big you
want the entire ODL log set to get before files are overwritten. The log level
is determined by the *level* variable set in the j2ee-logging.xml file, which is
the place for setting OC4J-specific logging directives.

Text-based logging and ODL-based logging can be enabled at the same
time, which might not be practical in terms of space utilization but can
create more diagnostic information as it relates to the specific application
component. Use the information provided here to set up logging to best fit
the particular situation at any given time.

The Oracle Collaboration Suite 10*g* application components that support ODL also support the ability to correlate messages across and between application components within the Oracle Collaboration Suite 10*g* environment. The Execution Context ID, or ECID, is a globally unique identifier associated with a thread of execution as it moves across Oracle Application Server 10*g* and Oracle Collaboration Suite 10*g* OC4J application components in the environment. This makes it easier to identify the component or application that first generates a problem so that it can more quickly and easily be analyzed at its root cause.

To enable ECID generation for an OC4J instance, the Java command-line option "–Doracle.dms.transtrace.ecidenabled=true" must be set. To enable the variable, it must be added to the command line for the OC4J container through the Oracle Collaboration Suite Control Console as follows: Log in to the Oracle Collaboration Suite Control Console, and choose the Applications Tier from the instances available. Then click the OC4J instance for which ECID enablement is desired. Choose the Administration tab at the bottom of the page, and then choose Server Properties from the Instance Properties list. Scroll down to the Command Line Options section and enter the preceding parameter at the end of the Java Options field, click Apply, and then stop and restart the OC4J instance. Figure 11-3 shows the parameter entered in the Java Options field of the Command Line Options.

Reviewing the Logs

There are several options for reviewing the content of the log files generated in the Oracle Collaboration Suite 10*g* environment. Depending upon how sophisticated the logging setup is and how much activity occurs in the

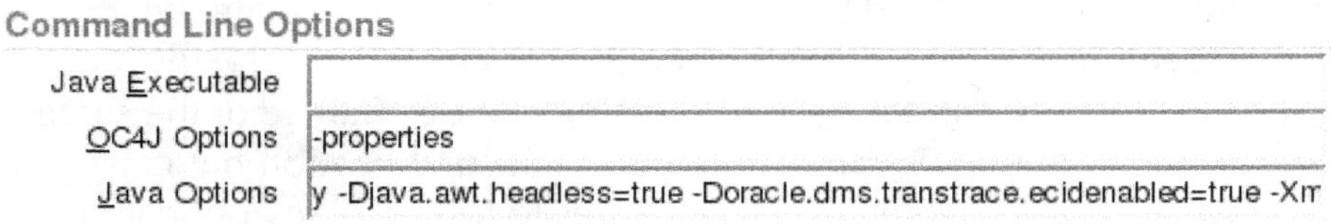

Command Line Options

Java Executable	
OC4J Options	-properties
Java Options	y -Djava.awt.headless=true -Doracle.dms.transtrace.ecidenabled=true -Xm

FIGURE 11-3. *ECID Parameter Set in Command Line Java Options field*

environment that will generate log messages, a method that best suits the situation can be chosen. Also, different circumstances can determine that one review method is better than another. For example, if the environment is stable and an administrator is just doing proactive monitoring, using one of the search engines will work fine. However, if there is a known issue with a specific Oracle Collaboration Suite 10*g* application component, reviewing the logs by using the Oracle Collaboration Suite 10*g* Control Console GUI, an XML reader (for the ODL-enabled messaging files), or even just diving right into the log file by hand is probably the better choice.

Reviewing the log files manually is pretty straightforward. The log files reside in the directory structures described in the section "Log Structure(s) and Locations" earlier in the chapter. Simply log in to the server as the oracle software owner operating system ID, set the Oracle environment, and change directories into the log directory for the particular component whose log files need to be reviewed. Use the local editor (vi in Linux, for example) or a file viewer to open the file and review it.

Inside the Oracle Collaboration Suite 10*g* Control Console, you can review the log files through the GUI interface. To review the log files, you can either search through available components for their respective log files or drill down into a specific Applications Tier component—say OC4J_ Content—and review the logs from the Control Console page for that component. To complete a search through the entire set of application components and their logs, choose the instance for the Applications Tier from the main page of the Control Console after signing in as the Administrator (ias_admin). In either the upper right-hand corner as shown in Figure 11-4 or the center at the bottom of the page as seen in Figure 11-5 you will find a Logs link that will take you to the Logs function of the Collaboration Suite Control Console.

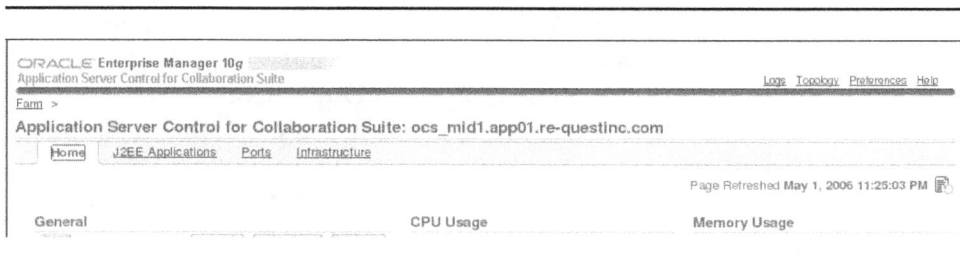

FIGURE 11-4. *Logs link on top of instance page of Control Console*

FIGURE 11-5. *Logs link on bottom of instance page of Control Console*

There are two tabs to choose from on the Log function page. One allows for viewing the logs as they reside on the server; the other lets you search through a Log Repository. I will cover how to set up a Log Repository later in this chapter, so for now let's concentrate on how to view logs on the first tab.

Basically, the idea in the Log Files tab is to choose the components whose logs need to be reviewed from the available components list on the left and move them to the selected list on the right. Once all the components you want to review the logs for are selected, click Search. The View Log tool goes out to the operating system and pulls up a list of all available log files for all the components in the selected components list. Figure 11-6 shows an example of searching for the logs for the Content component.

From the displayed list, you can then click a specific log and review it online through the GUI tool.

Log Repository and Log Loader

Another way of managing and reviewing the log files for Oracle Collaboration Suite 10g is by setting up a Log Repository and configuring the Log Loader process to take the various logs from the operating system directories for the Applications Tier and load them into the Log Repository on a scheduled basis. Using a Log Repository consolidates the log information from the various components of an Oracle Collaboration Suite 10g environment and provides an easy method to search all the log files in one place to help expedite the problem analysis and resolution process.

The first requirement in configuring this type of log review environment is to create the Log Repository itself. There are two options for creating and

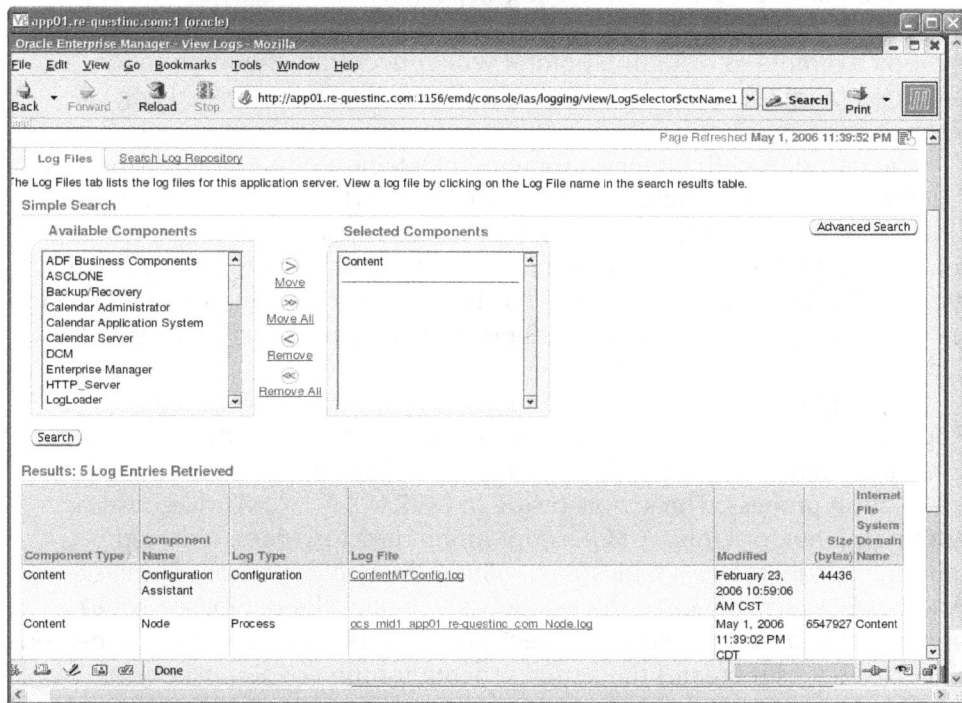

FIGURE 11-6. *View Logs page example*

configuring a Log Repository. The first is to use a file- or directory-based repository where the log files are collected and stored in a directory on the server. By default a directory named $ORACLE_HOME/diagnostics/ repository is created when Oracle Collaboration Suite 10*g* tiers are installed. The second—and recommended—option is to use an Oracle Database instance as the Log Repository. The advantages of using a database-based Log Repository are similar to the advantages identified for using the Oracle Collaboration Suite product itself for managing files. Coordination and search of log files, management of the space and performance, and access through the Control Console GUI for all log files from all tiers of the Oracle Collaboration Suite 10*g* environment are all reasons that a database Log Repository makes more sense than a directory/file-based Log Repository.

Since the directory/file-based Log Repository is basically set up by default via the install, or is at a minimum easily configured with that out-of-the-box example as a starting point, I will concentrate the information provided in this section on creating the Oracle Database–based Log Repository.

You can start with either an Oracle 9*i* Database or an Oracle 10*g* Database as the host database, but since we are discussing the Oracle Collaboration Suite 10*g* environment, I would recommend implementing at least a 10*g*R1 database as the Log Repository host. For this writing, I will assume that the database instance has been created by an Oracle DBA and named LOGREP and is created independently from the existing Oracle Collaboration Suite 10*g* Datastore.

A set of SQL scripts to create and manage the database-based Log Repository is deployed to the Oracle Home directory structure when the Oracle Collaboration Suite 10*g* environment gets laid down during the installation process. The scripts reside in $ORACLE_HOME/diagnostics/ admin in Linux or Unix. A SQL script in the directory named dmrep_ tablespace.sql creates a tablespace to hold the Log Repository objects. Another SQL script named dmrep_user.sql creates the database user to own the database schema and objects, and last but not least a script named dmrep_create.sql creates the actual schema for the Log Repository.

The first step in the Log Repository creation after the initial Log Repository host database instance has been created is to create the tablespace for holding the Log Repository schema objects. The dmrep_ tablespace.sql script must be run as an Administrator account (one that has SYSDBA privileges) such as SYS or SYSTEM and requires two SQL command-line parameters when executed: tablespace name and tablespace data file name. I would suggest using DMREP as the tablespace name (creative I know). I would precreate the directory structure on the mount point where I wanted the tablespace data file to be created, and name it, for example, /u02/oracle/product/10.1/ oradata/LOGREP/. Figure 11-7 shows the actual SQL syntax for creating the Log Repository tablespace.

So, the execution of the dmrep_tablespace.sql script looks like this:

```
[oracle@logrep u02]$ sqlplus "/ as sysdba"
SQL> @$ORACLE_HOME/diagnostics/admin/dmrep_tablespace.sql dmrep /u02/oracle/
product/10.1/oradata/LOGREP/dmrep01.dbf
Tablespace created.
SQL> exit
```

```
Rem
Rem Copyright (c) 2004, Oracle Corporation.  All rights reserved.
Rem
Rem    NAME
Rem      dmrep_tablespace.sql - create a tablespace for the diagnostic
Rem      message repository.
Rem
Rem    DESCRIPTION
Rem      This script creates a tablespace for the diagnostic message repository.
Rem      Use of this script is optional, an existing tablespace can also be
Rem      used for the diagnostic message repository.
Rem
Rem      This script requires two arguments:
Rem      1. The name of the tablespace to be created.
Rem      2. The path for the tablespace datafile.
Rem
Rem    NOTES
Rem      You must connect to a database as an administrator in order to execute
Rem      this script.
Rem
Rem      Sample usage:
Rem        SQL> connect sys as sysdba
rem        ....
Rem        SQL> @ORACLE_HOME/diagnostics/admin/dmrep_tablespace.sql dmrep
Rem              'ORACLE_HOME/diagnostics/repository/dmrep.dbf'
Rem
Rem    MODIFIED    (MM/DD/YY)
Rem    mjgoncal    04/22/04 - project 11706
Rem    mjgoncal    03/08/04 - Created
Rem

CREATE TABLESPACE &1
LOGGING
DATAFILE '&2' SIZE 50M
EXTENT MANAGEMENT LOCAL
SEGMENT SPACE MANAGEMENT AUTO;
```

FIGURE 11-7. *Log Repository tablespace create syntax*

Once the tablespace is created, the next step is to create the user to own the Log Repository schema. The dmrep_user.sql script requires the name of the user, the password for the user, and the default tablespace for that user to create objects in. I recommend using dmrepadmin for the user, dmrep as the password (change it to something that matches internal password patterns), and dmrep for the tablespace created previously.

Now that the tablespace for holding the schema objects is in place and the user to own the schema has been created, it's time to actually create the Log Repository schema. So, while logged in to SQL*Plus as the dmrepadmin user, run the dmrep_create.sql script. This script requires no parameters. Remember to review the messages that are returned from running this script to ensure the Log Repository objects got created successfully. Please note that this script creates raw database objects and not database objects that have been refined in terms of storage parameters, initial and next extent values, etc. If this lingo makes no sense to you, contact your Oracle DBA for assistance. If you don't have an Oracle DBA, you will need to review the syntax for setting storage parameters either as defaults for the tablespace or on an object by object basis.

Now that the database-based Log Repository has been created, you need to start the Log Loader opmn process to initially load the Log Repository and then periodically refresh it with newly generated log files from the environment. But before starting the LogLoader, you need to modify the logloader.xml file repository element to reflect the change to using a database-based Log Repository. The logloader.xml file is located in the $ORACLE_HOME/ diagnostics/config/ directory. Using vi or some other native editor, locate the <repository> element, uncomment the <database_repository ....> sub-element, and modify the url and user parameters to reflect the specific environment information for the database-based Log Repository. Figure 11-8 shows the BEFORE and AFTER information for the repository element of the logloader.xml file.

Please note that in the figure, db02.testdomain.com is the host server running the dmrep database, 1521 is the SQL*Net port the listener for that database instance is listening on, and dmrep is the database instance name.

The next step is to store the password for the dmrepadmin database user in the wallet for the Log Repository located in the LogLoader directory. To do this, execute the following:

```
[oracle@logrep]$ $ORACLE_HOME/diagnostics/bin/logloader -storePassword -user
dmrepadmin -pwd dmrep
```

Finally, start the LogLoader process by using either the Oracle Collaboration Suite 10g Control Console or the command opmnctl startproc ias-component=LogLoader. The opmnctl command can be run at the operating system prompt as I have shown before. However, to start the Log Loader via the Control Console you have to do a little bit of digging. Start up the Control Console in the browser, sign in as ias_admin, and choose the Applications Tier link from the instance farm list. From the main processes page for the instance, note the Logs link in the upper right-hand corner of the page. Clicking that takes you to the View Logs page, which has two tabs.

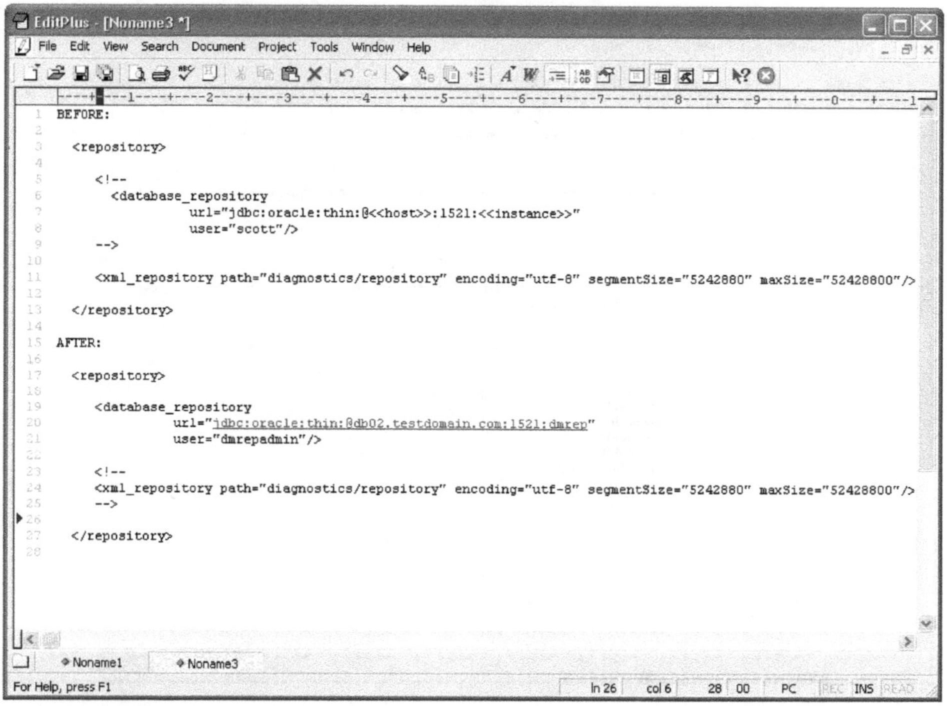

FIGURE 11-8. *Before and After values in the logloader.xml file*

The first tab is one you saw earlier to do limited log views and searches from the directory structure. The second tab is the Search Log Repository tab, which you can click to begin a search through the Log Repository. If the Log Loader opmn process is not running, you will get a message across the top of the page telling you exactly that, with a button/link to the Log Loader page where you can start it. Click the button to see the Log Loader process page shown in Figure 11-9. Then click Start and the process starts successfully. Now the Log Loader process begins to gather the logs and populate the Log Repository with the log messages as determined by your configuration.

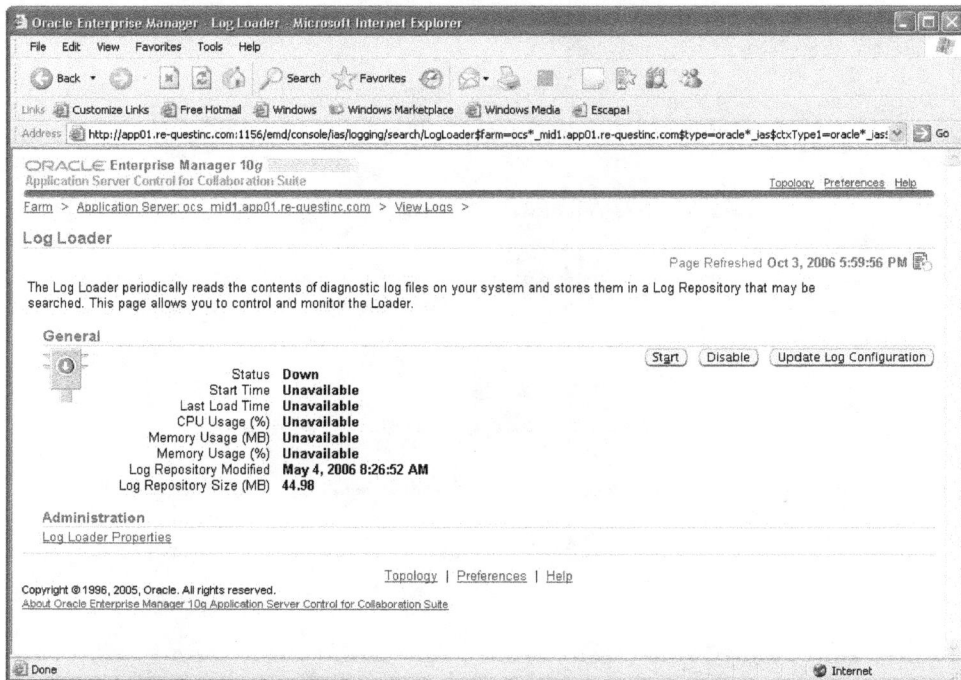

FIGURE 11-9. *Log Loader Process page in Control Console*

I want to emphasize the fact that like any robust data solution, the Log Repository will need to be managed in and of itself to maintain proper performance and availability. It is another database instance in the environment and therefore needs to be treated as such in order to continue to function properly.

Log Search

Once the Log Repository has been created, the log information can be searched through the Oracle Collaboration Suite Control Console. Log in to the Control Console as ias_admin, and from the farm listing choose the tier where you want to review the logs (I usually go to the Applications Tier) and

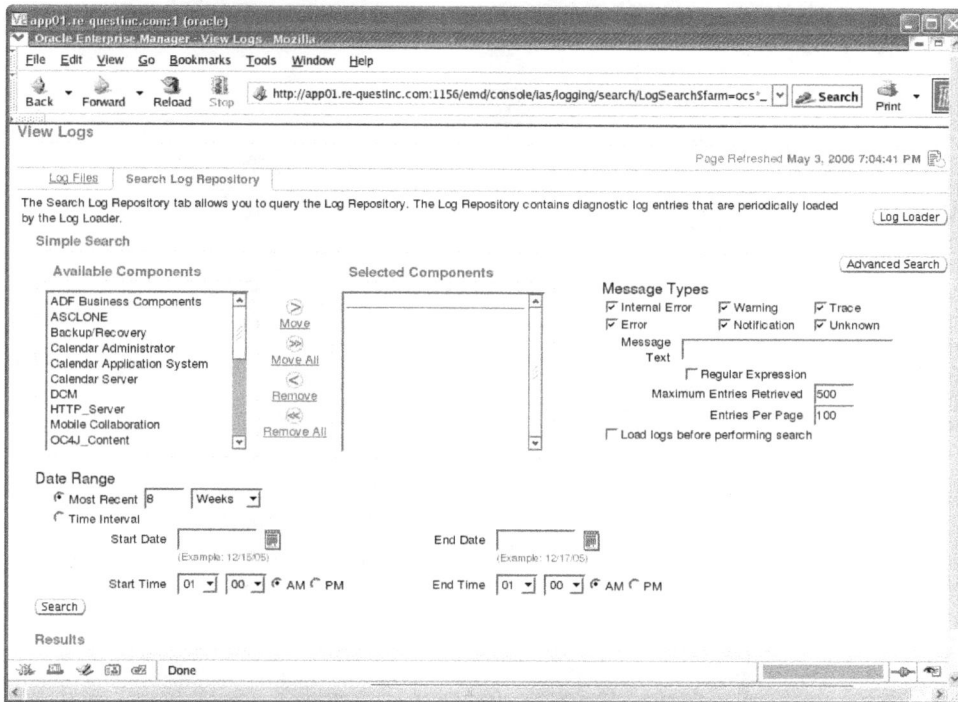

FIGURE 11-10.   *Search Log Repository tab in the View Logs page of Control Console*

click the Logs link at the top right of the tier page, shown earlier in Figure 11-4. This will bring up the View Logs page, where you select the Search Log Repository tab, which is shown in Figure 11-10. From here, you can run several search options against the Log Repository. For example, you can define the types of messages—error, internal error, trace, etc. You can also search for specific message text and limit the message time by interval or by a time to go back as shown in the figure.

When all of the search criteria have been defined, click Search and the processing page will display as shown in Figure 11-11. Once the search is completed, you can review the results on the Results page as shown in Figure 11-12.

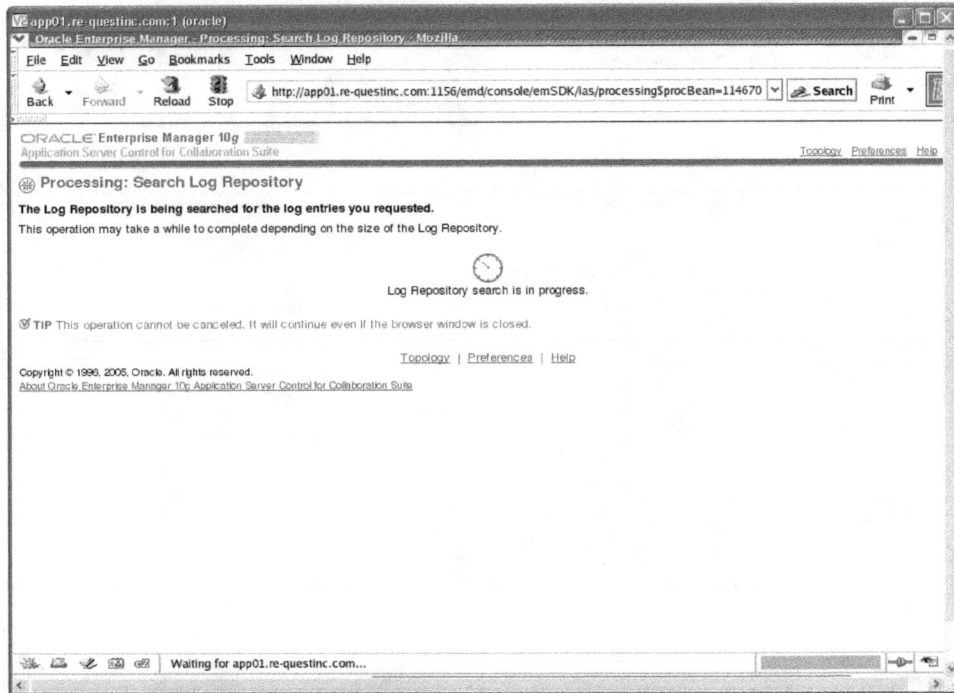

FIGURE 11-11. *Processing search logs request*

You can then review the summary level results and drill down by selecting the check box next to the message(s) you want to review further and click the View Detail button. A detailed page of content on the selected message will display as shown in Figure 11-13.

Managing the Application-Level Logs

Obviously, given the capabilities of the Log Repository and ODL, there is a great advantage in configuring these options to manage themselves in terms of removing log data and making it available for quick and useful searches. However, a portion of the logging in Oracle Collaboration Suite 10*g* still needs to be manually managed. For example, I can set up the Apache access_log and error_log files for rotation so that an individual file does not

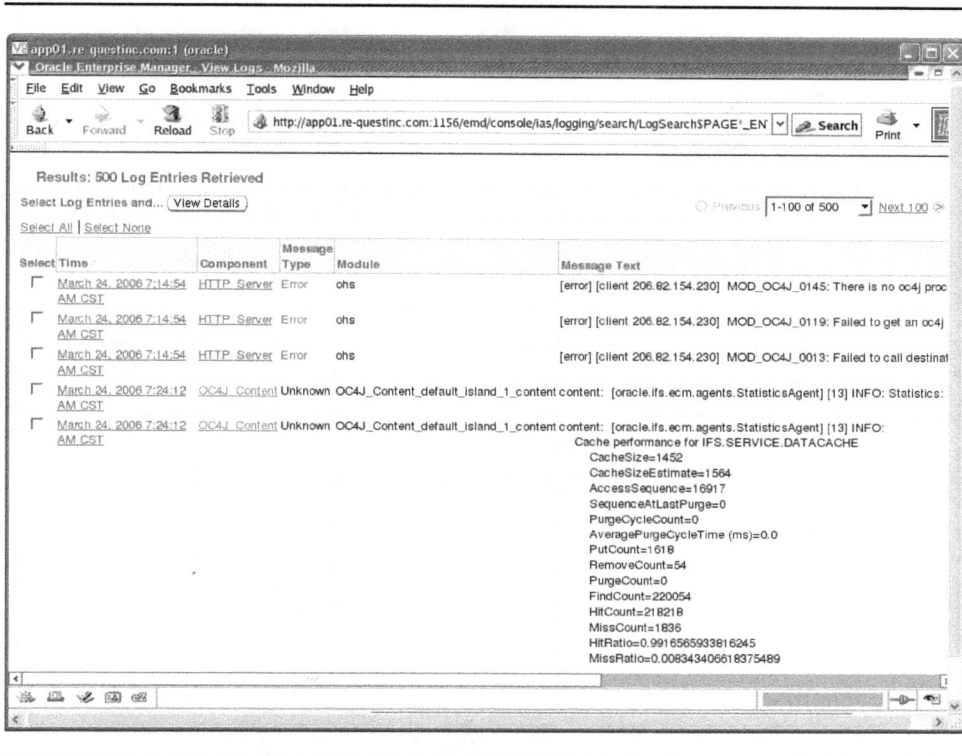

FIGURE 11-12. *Search Log Repository results*

get too large, but they don't get managed through the Log Repository and are not ODL compliant, so the log archives need to be managed with a different process. I have seen many Oracle Application Server and Oracle Collaboration Suite 10*g* implementations, and my company has a general approach to dealing with the types of logs that aren't managed "automatically" by the product infrastructure itself.

First off, as you've seen, each log must be "rotated" or "rolled over" on a periodic basis to prevent any given OS file from becoming too large. And by "too large" I mean both too large to be easily referenced (i.e., perhaps too big to open with the vi editor, etc.), but also in terms of the OS's hard limit on the size of any file. Once the hard limit has been reached, any processes attempting to write to a maxed-out log file will either "freeze" or fail—a bad situation in either case. So how does one "rotate" or "roll over" a particular

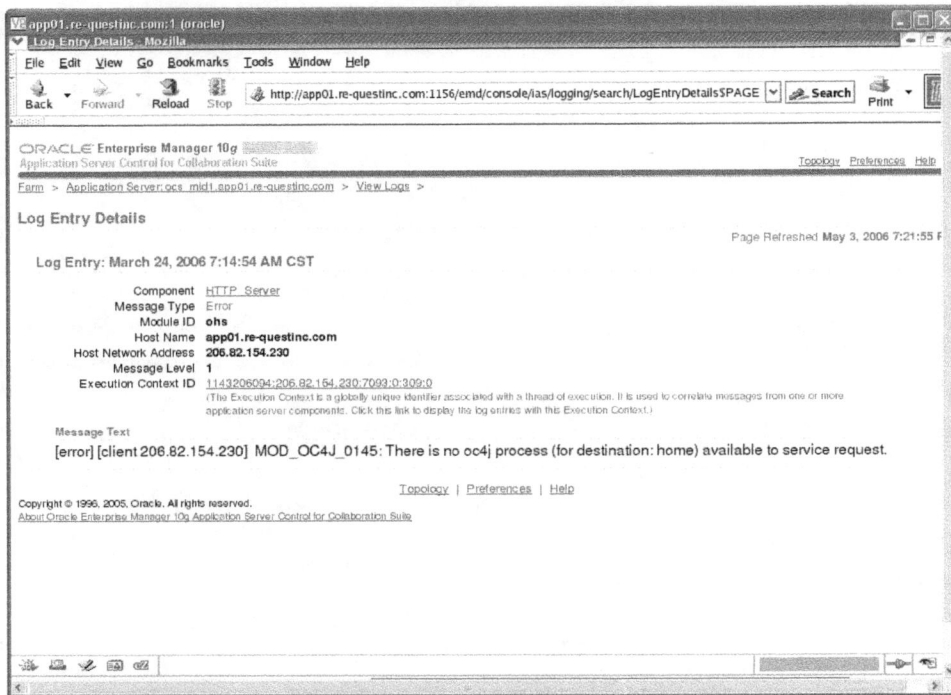

FIGURE 11-13. *Log Message Detail display*

non-ODL-compliant log file? The answer, unfortunately, is component-specific. For Middle Tier webcache logs, for instance, the Enterprise Manager iAS console may be used to specify a rollover interval in a very declarative manner (i.e., select your options as a drop-down list box on a web page), while for Apache logs you might need to specify the log rotation interval as the number of seconds between the generation of new log files. In still other cases we'll write simple OS command scripts (run on a regular basis via a job scheduler) to automate the rotate/rollover. The rule of thumb is to *always* use any Oracle-provided mechanism before writing your own script. But regardless of how you manage to periodically end one log file and begin the next, it is the function that is important (not the form).

Once your non-ODL log files are being rotated/rolled over, you've protected yourself against any one file becoming too large to use (or too large to write to), but each log directory will still continue to grow in size. Are many smaller log files really better than a single large file? Yes. Don't they both consume the same *total* amount of space? Not necessarily. It all depends on what we do next and how we handle the archival and purge components of our strategy. Assume for the sake of discussion that you roll over your webcache logs once per week and that, on average, you wouldn't expect to consult a log file after two weeks. But at the same time, it might be useful to retain the files on disk for up to three months. So then, your retention policy looks like this:

- **Week 1**   Current webcache log file being written to by the live Oracle process.

- **Week 2**   Information from week 1 has been rolled over and exists in a separate, uncompressed file on disk.

- **Weeks 3–9**   Information that was rolled over one week ago is now compressed (using gzip, pfzip, compress, etc.) and retained on disk.

- **Beyond Week 9**   Compressed rolled-over log files more than seven weeks old are removed from disk (i.e., purged).

In this example, we've rotated/rolled over our logs on a periodic basis (based on time, not size), defined and implemented noncompressed and compressed retention periods, and defined and implemented a purge. And that closes the loop. Once the process has been in place and operating for as long as it takes to purge the first log file, your disk usage should become fairly stable (allowing for natural growth and extraordinary processing exceptions, of course). Any significant increase or decrease in space consumption beyond that point is, itself, something that should be investigated.

Here's a Linux/Unix-based example of commands to implement the policy that I've sketched out. The logs being processed are from the webcache, and the "live" log file is named "access_log." Once Enterprise Manager rolls the log over, the new filename will contain a datestamp component (for instance, "access_log.20060410_1102"). Given those inputs, we begin by compressing any rolled-over log file that is more than seven days old:

```
find $ORACLE_HOME/webcache/logs -name "access_log.*" -a ! -name
"access_log.*.gz" -mtime +7 -exec gzip {} \;
```

Yes, that's all one command in Linux/Unix. If read aloud, it would be described as follows: "Find files in the webcache log directory that are named beginning with 'access_log.' (which, by virtue of the trailing '.' excludes the active log file) but are not already compressed (i.e., end with the gz extension) and have not been modified in the last seven days. Pass each file that matches those rules into the gzip utility to be compressed." So much for the archival process. Now let's examine the purge process:

```
find $ORACLE_HOME/webcache/logs -name "access_log.*.gz" -mtime +76 -exec rm
{} \;
```

Yep, that's right, another single command to implement the purge rule. Since you've got some experience looking at complex "find" commands, the meaning here should be obvious: "Find compressed access_log files in the webcache log directory that have not been modified in 76 days (7 days in the live log file + 7 days rolled over in an uncompressed state + 76 days as compressed logs = 90 days of retention) and then remove them."

Executing the two commands in the preceding example on a regular basis (perhaps on a weekly basis after the webcache log file rollover occurs) is a complete solution for one specific log file. And while you could write a specific script for each log file to be managed, it probably makes more sense to write a more sophisticated, parameter-driven script that can handle any number of log files that match the processing pattern but differ only in terms of retention periods, locations, and filename patterns. And, of course, any production archive/purge script should also generate logs of its own activities (including clearly listing files compressed and/or deleted). If driven by a parameter file (with one row for each log to be managed), all of your archive/purge processing might be executed on a nightly basis with a single invocation from the cron scheduler. But that's the "holy grail." Start small. Build complexity and sophistication into your code little by little (carefully unit-testing it as you go along.)

Oracle Database Logs

Ironically, even though the database logs have been around for a lot longer than the Application Server logs, there is actually *less* in the way of infrastructure in place to manage the database logs. And since the database is *the* most significant technology stack component underlying all of Oracle Collaboration Suite 10*g*, database log types (and their management) deserve special attention.

The Alert Log

First off, and strictly speaking, there is only one true database log file, known as the *alert log*. The alert log is written to the "background dump destination" (i.e., "bdump") by the database at startup and shutdown times, when online redo log switches occur, when deadlocks are detected, when requested space is not available, when sessions crash due to bugs—to name just a few of the automatic and configurable types of information that may appear in the database's alert log. The alert log is never rotated or rolled over by the database or by Enterprise Manager. And while it isn't managed actively in that respect, it may be removed (or renamed) at any time—even while the database is up and running—without adverse consequences. Accordingly, it is very easy to write our own rollover, archive, and purge processing for the database alert log (modeled on the approach outlined for non-ODL-managed Application logs). In fact, all that's missing from our prior example is a command to rename the active alert log to a rolled-over name, thus:

```
mv alert_PROD.log alert_PROD.log.$(date '+20%y-%m-%d_%H:%M:%S')
```

This command is just a simple renaming of the active alert log file to include a datestamp value. Then, the next time the database needs to write to the alert log, it will create a new log (once again named alert_<SID>.log). If we add find commands for the compress and purge stages, we once again have a complete solution for the database alert log.

Trace Files

Written to both the "bdump" and the "user dump" (i.e., "udump") destinations, the database creates "single-use" log files known as *trace* files. And while all trace files end with a trc filename extension, they may be generated in different ways and under different circumstances. For example, user-requested session traces and ad hoc requests to back up database control files are sent to the "udump" destination, while internal database errors (i.e., "ORA-00600" errors) will automatically write a trace file to the "bdump" destination. And while the circumstances that initiate the creation of trace files vary (as does the content and location), all trace files have some things in common. First, they are named for the OS process that creates them; their sizes may be (but are not required to be) limited by configurable database parameters; and they are not reused/rotated/rolled over in any way by the database.

They also tend not to have a very long useful lifetime (generally speaking). Trace files serve as detailed information (backing up and expanding upon what is in the alert log) or as sources of detailed performance tuning data. When working with Oracle Support to resolve errors, you might be asked to upload your alert log and specific trace files. You might process a trace file with the tkprof utility in order to generate a SQL tuning report. But in most cases (99 percent of the time), a trace file more than one week old is unlikely to be useful for anything. And yet they may be generated quite frequently—and they can be quite large.

Left unmanaged, trace files can (over time) consume vast amounts of disk space. Fortunately, trace files are easy to manage. Since each is unique, there is no need to rotate them or roll them over. Simply apply compress (i.e., archive) and purge policies against them. Compressing after one week and purging after one month is reasonably conservative, assuming periodic review by your DBA.

Core Dumps

Unlike alert logs and trace files, *core dump* files are not human-readable text files. They are, instead, binary images of memory written to the "core dump destination" (i.e., "cdump") disk location at the time of a severe error. The only people who will ever be able to make use of the core dump files are some of the folks at Oracle Support. But even they only ask for you to send core dump information in very specific circumstances. These files are, however, like trace files in the sense that they are "one-off" logging mechanisms and they are also capable of consuming large quantities of disk space. This would suggest that you'd want to archive and purge them in the same way as you handle trace files, except that compressing a binary file isn't going to generate much of a savings in space, and so you should probably just remove the core dumps on the same purge schedule as for the trace files.

Audits

Audit logs are, again, single-use log files that the database generates automatically whenever the database is started, stopped, or accessed by someone using SYSDBA (or "superuser") privileges. In the latest versions of the database these files are created in the "audit dump destination" (i.e., "adump"), while in older DB versions the files are created in $ORACLE_HOME/rdbms/audit directory. In both cases, the files are small and end with an aud extension. If left unmanaged over a long period of time, many thousands of these files can accumulate—with both inode and space consumption becoming significant. The recommended approach is to not bother archiving (i.e., compressing) these files, because they are, individually, so small, but to remove them from disk after 90 days. If longer-term retention is required to meet internal or external audit requirements, backups to tape prior to purge are preferable to allowing these files to consume ever-increasing amounts of disk space.

DataPump Dumps and Logs

The latest versions of the 10*g* database also create, by default, an additional dump destination known as the "datapump dump destination" (i.e., "dpdump"), which is where database export dump files (logical backups) are written. These DataPump exports are only performed on demand (never automatically), but even so, it might be a good idea to include the dump files (files with a DMP extension) and log files (files with a LOG extension) from the "dpdump" location in your archive and purge strategy. As exports are ad hoc objects, there are no best-practice guidelines in terms of retention policies (aside from periodically purging old exports and their log files).

Summary

Virtually all database-related log files are located within the $ORACLE_ HOME/ admin/<SID>/ directory structure (assuming an Oracle-standard organization). The different types of logs are organized into subdirectories just below that level (i.e., "adump," "bdump," "cdump," "dpdump," and "udump"), and while there are minor differences to their management, in all cases you should put a management process into place to ensure that log files on all tiers do not become too large and/or do not consume excessive amounts of inode and disk space resources. A single (fairly simple) shell script—run via the cron scheduler on a nightly basis—is all it takes to prevent database log–related problems. Use the examples provided in this chapter to develop scripts to implement your own rollover/archive/purge policies and procedures.

CHAPTER
12

Collaboration Suite 10g Component Application Administration

*Where there is the necessary technical skill
to move mountains, there is no need for
the faith that moves mountains.*

—Eric Hoffer

U p until this point in the book you have read about installation, configuration, management, and administration at the overall Oracle Collaboration Suite 10*g* environment level. I have described the overall architecture of an Oracle Collaboration Suite 10*g* environment, migration to the suite, and how to start and stop the environment on the various tiers. This chapter is designed to take a deeper dive around the individual application components themselves, understanding their architecture, how they work, how to deal with their individual background processes, and what areas require special attention. I am going to specifically concentrate on Email, Calendar, and Real-Time Collaboration in this chapter, since a later chapter is devoted exclusively to the newest addition to the Oracle Collaboration Suite 10*g* family of functionality, Content Services. So in the famous words of the late, great Jackie Gleason, " . . . and away we go!"

Email Component Administration

The chapter starts with the Email application because a company that implements Oracle Collaboration Suite 10*g* Mail is implementing one of the most robust Email applications available today. But along with capability comes some complexity as well as administrative requirements. For example, the good news is that all email messages within the Email application are stored and managed in an Oracle 10*g* database. The flip side is that in order to manage the Oracle Collaboration Suite 10*g* Mail application, one needs some Oracle Database Administration skills . . . and Email Administrator skills . . . and Network Administration skills. So, for the average "Oracle Guy" (I love that generic descriptor) the Oracle part of this is easy . . . *but* does he know the first thing about the SMTP protocol, IMAP functionality, or POP email access? Also, remember that email is by far the most dynamic unstructured data source in any enterprise, so the growth and management of just the data alone can be overwhelming at times. So, I will take you down the path of understanding Oracle Collaboration Suite 10*g* Mail . . . from an "Oracle Guy's" perspective. Ready?

Mail Application Architecture

To effectively understand the *how* of managing the Oracle Collaboration Suite 10g Mail application, one must first understand the *what* of the application. Oracle Collaboration Suite 10g Mail has all the same components of any standard email solution, except that the Oracle database plays such a large part in the architecture, and the application components are delivered to the end user via the Oracle Application Server 10g platform. Let's examine the architecture of the Oracle Collaboration Suite 10g Mail application.

The architecture of the Oracle Collaboration Suite 10g Mail application consists of several components that run on the Oracle Application Server 10g platform. Users logging in to Oracle Collaboration Suite 10g are authenticated using Single Sign-On and Oracle Identity Management. The entire set of Oracle Collaboration Suite 10g functionality is then delivered to the end user on the web via the Oracle Portal and OC4J engine. Email specifically is a Java application managed by the Oracle Process Monitor tool (OPMN) and is delivered either as a portlet with robust desktop application–like functionality via the Oracle Collaboration Suite 10g Portal, or as a thin WebClient from a URL on the Welcome page of the Oracle Collaboration Suite 10g product. There are also a set of background OES processes that provide the standard email protocols of SMTP for sending and receiving email, as well as POP3 and IMAP4 protocols for receiving email via desktop programs developed on those standard protocols. Figure 12-1 depicts the Oracle Collaboration Suite 10g Mail architecture and displays the components that run on the Applications Infrastructure Tier.

The Single Sign-On (SSO) and Oracle Identity Management (OIM) components talk to the Oracle Internet Directory for user authentication and email address information stored there, and the email protocols and user interfaces manage the email information inside the Mail Store database (in most installs the OID and the Mail Store exist in the same Oracle Database 10g instance as depicted in Figure 12-1). The email clients that are available for users to access Oracle Collaboration Suite 10g Mail can be browser-based, thick desktop tools such as Outlook and Thunderbird, and wireless tools such as Pocket PCs, Blackberrys, and Treos.

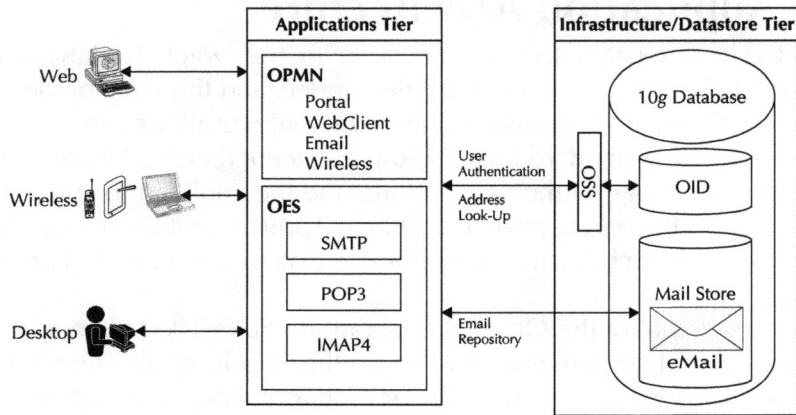

FIGURE 12-1. *Oracle Collaboration Suite 10g Mail architecture*

Email Process Management

To effectively manage the Oracle Collaboration Suite 10*g* Mail application, you must be able to manage all the components shown in Figure 12-1. You must manage the OPMN and OES processes on the Applications Tier, the SSO/OIM processes on the Infrastructure Tier, and the database instance(s) containing the Infrastructure and Mailstore data.

Let's start with the SSO/OIM, OPMN, and OES processes, which can be managed either from the command line on the server or from Collaboration Suite 10*g* Control Console. SSO/OIM processes run on the server where the Infrastructure Tier was installed. They are also OPMN managed, so they can be started, stopped, and statused with the *opmnctl startall/stopall/status* command at the server command prompt. Figure 12-2 shows the commands being executed and the associated results. You start out with an *opmnctl status* command to see where the processes are in terms of being up or down. Notice that the DSA and LogLoader processes are down; they will be that way normally unless you have the LogLoader process running to populate a Log Repository (see Chapter 11 on log file management). The main processes we are concerned about are the HTTP Server, the OC4J_ SECURITY, and the OID processes. If any one of those processes is not running, the Single Sign-On function will not work.

```
db01.re-questinc.com:1 (oracle)
oracle@db01:~/scripts
File  Edit  View  Terminal  Go  Help
[oracle@db01 scripts]$ opmnctl status

Processes in Instance: ocs_infra1.db01.re-questinc.com
----------------------+--------------------+---------+---------
ias-component         | process-type       |   pid | status
----------------------+--------------------+---------+---------
DSA                   | DSA                |   N/A | Down
LogLoader             | logloaderd         |   N/A | Down
HTTP_Server           | HTTP_Server        | 16397 | Alive
dcm-daemon            | dcm-daemon         |  9315 | Alive
OC4J                  | OC4J_SECURITY      | 16411 | Alive
OID                   | OID                |  9223 | Alive

[oracle@db01 scripts]$ opmnctl stopall
opmnctl: stopping opmn and all managed processes...
[oracle@db01 scripts]$ opmnctl start
opmnctl: opmn started
[oracle@db01 scripts]$ opmnctl status

Processes in Instance: ocs_infra1.db01.re-questinc.com
----------------------+--------------------+---------+---------
ias-component         | process-type       |   pid | status
----------------------+--------------------+---------+---------
DSA                   | DSA                |   N/A | Down
LogLoader             | logloaderd         |   N/A | Down
HTTP_Server           | HTTP_Server        |   N/A | Down
dcm-daemon            | dcm-daemon         |   N/A | Down
OC4J                  | OC4J_SECURITY      |   N/A | Down
OID                   | OID                |   N/A | Down

[oracle@db01 scripts]$ opmnctl startall
opmnctl: starting opmn and all managed processes...
[oracle@db01 scripts]$ opmnctl status

Processes in Instance: ocs_infra1.db01.re-questinc.com
----------------------+--------------------+---------+---------
ias-component         | process-type       |   pid | status
----------------------+--------------------+---------+---------
DSA                   | DSA                |   N/A | Down
LogLoader             | logloaderd         |   N/A | Down
HTTP_Server           | HTTP_Server        | 22501 | Alive
dcm-daemon            | dcm-daemon         |   N/A | Down
OC4J                  | OC4J_SECURITY      | 22588 | Alive
OID                   | OID                | 22518 | Alive

[oracle@db01 scripts]$
```

FIGURE 12-2. *OPMN Server command-line commands*

You can also use the Collaboration Suite 10*g* Control Console, which is installed automatically with the Oracle Collaboration Suite 10*g* environment, to access the Infrastructure Tier instance and manage the SSO/OIM processes through a web interface rather than from the command line (10*g* Grid Control is also a tool that can be used for managing the Oracle Collaboration Suite 10*g* environment, but it must be installed and configured stand-alone). You can go in and start, stop, and status the entire Infrastructure Tier as well as the individual processes from the Control Console. Figure 12-3 shows the main page from the Control Console for the Infrastructure Tier.

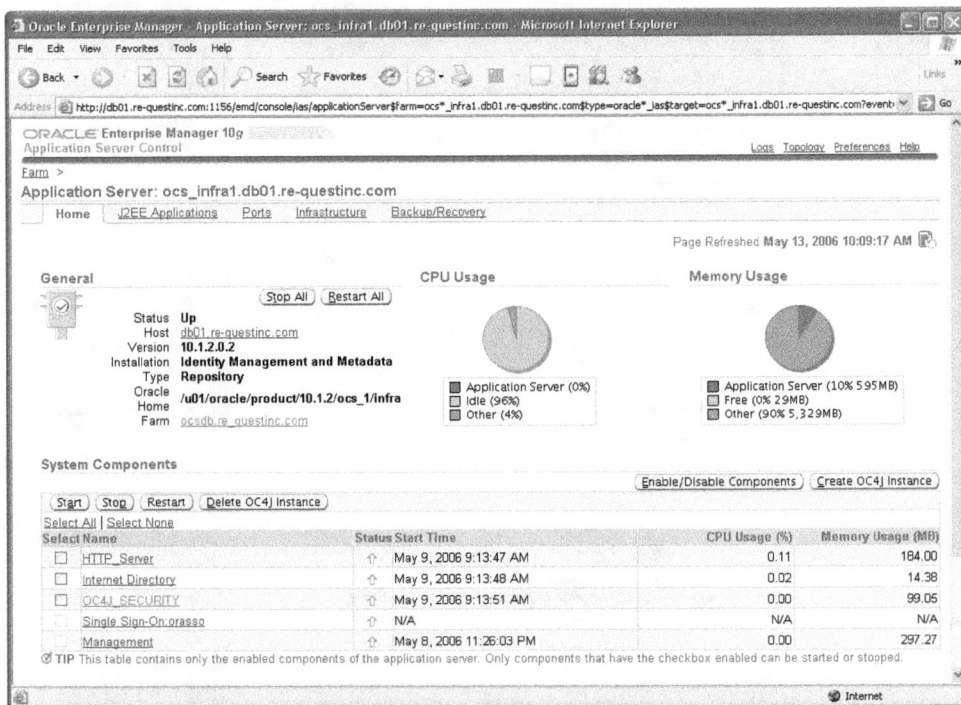

FIGURE 12-3. *Infrastructure Tier Control Console*

To manage a process, you can either select the check box to the left of the process and use the Stop, Start, or Restart button (please do *not* select the Delete OC4J Instance button for any of the Infrastructure processes!), or you can click the process name itself and get the detail page for that process from the Control Console and manage it from there. Figure 12-4 shows the detail page for the OID process.

Now we'll move on to the OPMN and OES Email processes, all of which run on the Applications Tier. You can use the same command-line tools and Control Console functions to start and stop the Applications Tier Email applications and processes as you used to manage the SSO/OIM processes. Besides the opmnctl commands for managing the email services, there are various oes (Oracle Email Server) commands that provide an Administrator with the ability to manage Email users, groups, server-side rules, and distribution lists, as well as gather and present statistics about the mail server.

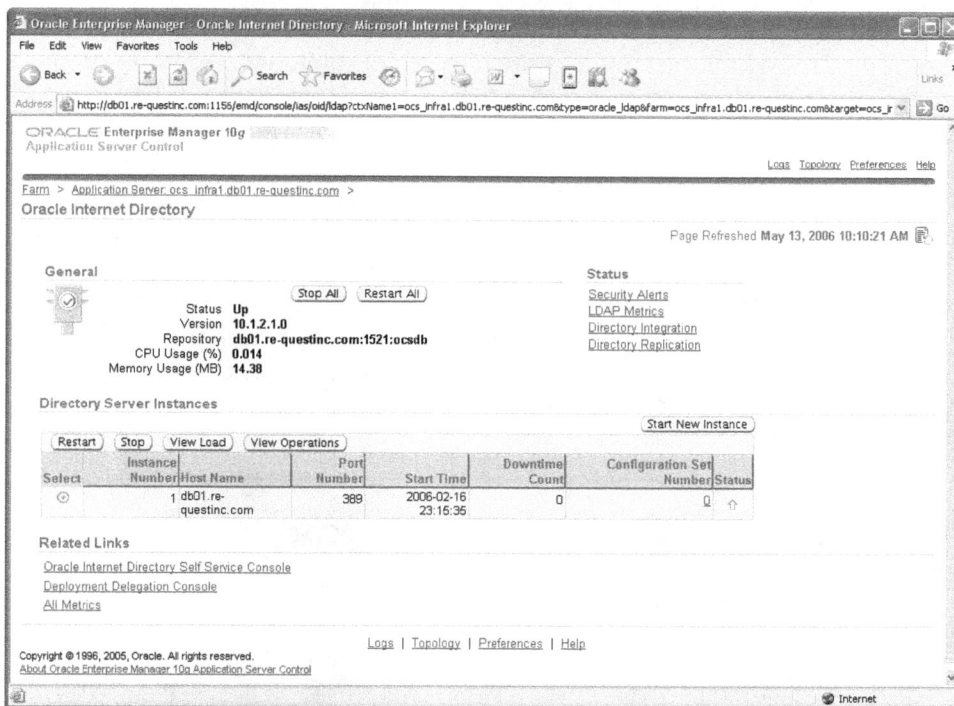

FIGURE 12-4. *OID Process Detail Control Console page*

We'll start with the opmn processes and the available options for managing them. Basically, as far as the commands themselves, opmnctl (with the start, startall, startproc, stop, stopall and stopproc options) is the command-line tool for managing the Oracle Collaboration Suite 10*g* Mail processes. The biggest difference between the opmn processes on the Applications Tier and the opmn processes on the Infrastructure Tier, which we already covered, is the sheer number of opmn processes that run on the Applications Tier to support the functionality provided by the various Oracle Collaboration Suite 10*g* Applications. Whereas the Infrastructure Tier has only the OID and OC4J_SECURITY processes to support Identity Management and Single-Sign-On, the Applications Tier supports all opmn processes and subprocesses for every Oracle Collaboration Suite 10*g* application component installed and running. Since we are focusing on the email function in this section, I will take this opportunity to show the opmn commands for managing components and subcomponents (referred to as process types) of the Mail application. Figure 12-5 shows the results of an *opmnctl status* when the Applications Tier is completely down (no opmn processes running).

Now we attempt to bring up just the Applications Tier components necessary for supporting the Mail application and its access. Note that instead of issuing an *opmnctl startall* command, here, we use the *startproc ias-component* option of the *opmnctl* command to bring the Applications Tier components up one at a time. First, bring up the core Applications Tier components of the HTTP Server and WebCache. Next, bring up the opmn OC4J component, since the Portal and WebClient for Email are in the OC4J component. Next, bring up the opmn component itself, which contains all the actual email functions—SMTP, IMAP, POP, etc. Figure 12-6 shows the

```
[oracle@app01 oracle]$ opmnctl status

Processes in Instance: ocs_mid1.app01.re-questinc.com
--------------------+--------------------+---------+---------
ias-component       | process-type       | pid | status
--------------------+--------------------+---------+---------
DSA                 | DSA                 | N/A | Down
LogLoader           | logloaderd          | N/A | Down
dcm-daemon          | dcm-daemon          | N/A | Down
OC4J                | OC4J_OCSADMIN       | N/A | Down
OC4J                | OC4J_imeeting       | N/A | Down
OC4J                | OC4J_OCSClient      | N/A | Down
OC4J                | OC4J_Portal         | N/A | Down
OC4J                | OC4J_Mail           | N/A | Down
OC4J                | Service_Component~  | N/A | Down
HTTP_Server         | HTTP_Server         | N/A | Down
WebCache            | WebCache            | N/A | Down
WebCache            | WebCacheAdmin       | N/A | Down
wireless            | performance_server  | N/A | Down
wireless            | messaging_server    | N/A | Down
wireless            | notificationevent~  | N/A | Down
wireless            | notification_serv~  | N/A | Down
wireless            | OC4J_Wireless       | N/A | Down
email               | email_housekeeper   | N/A | Down
email               | email_imap          | N/A | Down
email               | email_listserver    | N/A | Down
email               | email_nntp_in       | N/A | Down
email               | email_nntp_out      | N/A | Down
email               | email_pop           | N/A | Down
email               | email_smtp_in       | N/A | Down
email               | email_smtp_out      | N/A | Down
email               | email_virus_scrub~  | N/A | Down
Content             | Node                | N/A | Down
Content             | OC4J_Content        | N/A | Down
CalendarServer      | Calendar_CSM        | N/A | Down
CalendarServer      | Calendar_CWS        | N/A | Down
CalendarServer      | Calendar_DAS        | N/A | Down
CalendarServer      | Calendar_SNC        | N/A | Down
CalendarServer      | Calendar_ENG        | N/A | Down
CalendarServer      | Calendar_LCK        | N/A | Down
RTC                 | rtcpm               | N/A | Down

[oracle@app01 oracle]$
```

FIGURE 12-5. *opmnctl status command on the Applications Tier*

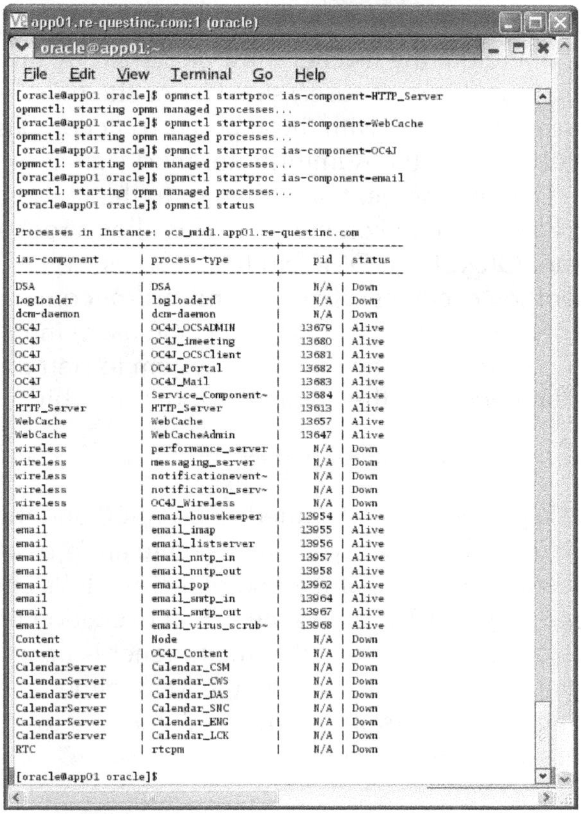

```
app01.re-questinc.com:1 (oracle)
oracle@app01:~

File   Edit   View   Terminal   Go   Help
[oracle@app01 oracle]$ opmnctl startproc ias-component-HTTP_Server
opmnctl: starting opmn managed processes...
[oracle@app01 oracle]$ opmnctl startproc ias-component-WebCache
opmnctl: starting opmn managed processes...
[oracle@app01 oracle]$ opmnctl startproc ias-component-OC4J
opmnctl: starting opmn managed processes...
[oracle@app01 oracle]$ opmnctl startproc ias-component-email
opmnctl: starting opmn managed processes...
[oracle@app01 oracle]$ opmnctl status

Processes in Instance: ocs_midi.app01.re-questinc.com
-----------------+--------------------+---------+--------
ias-component    | process-type       |   pid  | status
-----------------+--------------------+---------+--------
DSA              | DSA                |   N/A  | Down
LogLoader        | logloaderd         |   N/A  | Down
dcm-daemon       | dcm-daemon         |   N/A  | Down
OC4J             | OC4J_OCSADMIN      | 13679  | Alive
OC4J             | OC4J_imeeting      | 13680  | Alive
OC4J             | OC4J_OCSClient     | 13681  | Alive
OC4J             | OC4J_Portal        | 13682  | Alive
OC4J             | OC4J_Mail          | 13683  | Alive
OC4J             | Service_Component~ | 13684  | Alive
HTTP_Server      | HTTP_Server        | 13813  | Alive
WebCache         | WebCache           | 13657  | Alive
WebCache         | WebCacheAdmin      | 13647  | Alive
wireless         | performance_server |   N/A  | Down
wireless         | messaging_server   |   N/A  | Down
wireless         | notificationevent~ |   N/A  | Down
wireless         | notification_serv~ |   N/A  | Down
wireless         | OC4J_Wireless      |   N/A  | Down
email            | email_housekeeper  | 13654  | Alive
email            | email_imap         | 13655  | Alive
email            | email_listserver   | 13956  | Alive
email            | email_nntp_in      | 13957  | Alive
email            | email_nntp_out     | 13958  | Alive
email            | email_pop          | 13962  | Alive
email            | email_smtp_in      | 13964  | Alive
email            | email_smtp_out     | 13967  | Alive
email            | email_virus_scrub~ | 13968  | Alive
Content          | Node               |   N/A  | Down
Content          | OC4J_Content       |   N/A  | Down
CalendarServer   | Calendar_CSM       |   N/A  | Down
CalendarServer   | Calendar_CWS       |   N/A  | Down
CalendarServer   | Calendar_DAS       |   N/A  | Down
CalendarServer   | Calendar_SNC       |   N/A  | Down
CalendarServer   | Calendar_ENG       |   N/A  | Down
CalendarServer   | Calendar_LCK       |   N/A  | Down
RTC              | rtcpm              |   N/A  | Down

[oracle@app01 oracle]$
```

FIGURE 12-6. *Starting Mail and Web interfaces only*

execution of these commands in this order and the resulting Applications Tier components that were started by issuing an *opmnctl status* command after they are all completed.

After the opmn processes are started, there is one final step involved in completing the startup of the Mail application. Oracle Collaboration Suite 10*g* uses a Listener architecture similar to the one employed for communications to the Oracle database for port communications to Oracle Mail protocols. A listener process, in this case named *listener_es,* must be started in order for communications to inbound and outbound SMTP, as well as POP and IMAP functions, to be enabled. Since the ports that support these functions are below 1024, they are considered protected or secure ports, and therefore the listener must be started by the root user in Linux but on behalf of the oracle user, since he or she must manage the back-end processes associated with those ports. To accomplish the secure startup of the Mail Listener, the Administrator must sign in as oracle, source the Applications Tier environment, and then su to the root user, leaving the environment set like that of the oracle user. This allows root to have access to all the necessary ORACLE_HOME/bin functions as well as message files, etc. The root user then executes a background *tnslsnr* command referencing the specific listener_es name as well as the oracle user Linux ID and the oinstall Group ID, which tells the operating system to start this as root under the oracle user referenced. So the command looks like this:

```
[root@app01 scripts] tnslsnr listener_es -u 500 -g 501 &
```

where the oracle user had been identified as user 500 and the oinstall group has been identified as group 501 (you can execute an *id oracle* command as root to find these values). The & at the end of the line tells Linux to run this in the background. Figure 12-7 shows the actual execution of the command and then a status command to show that the Listener is up and listening on all the proper Mail ports. Just to complete the loop, either the oracle user or root could execute the *lsnrctl stop listener_es* command to stop the Listener when bringing the Mail application down.

NOTE
For the listener to start successfully, ensure that the sendmail process is not running. Sendmail is a process in Linux/UNIX, which by default runs on port 25. Since the SMTP portion of the email listener listener_es runs on this port itself, sendmail needs to be shut down to make this port available to the listener. This can be done by executing the command /etc/init.d/sendmail stop as root.

Now that you have brought up all the necessary Applications Tier components and subcomponents to support the Mail application, you can log in to the Oracle Collaboration Suite 10*g* Portal and see what it looks like.

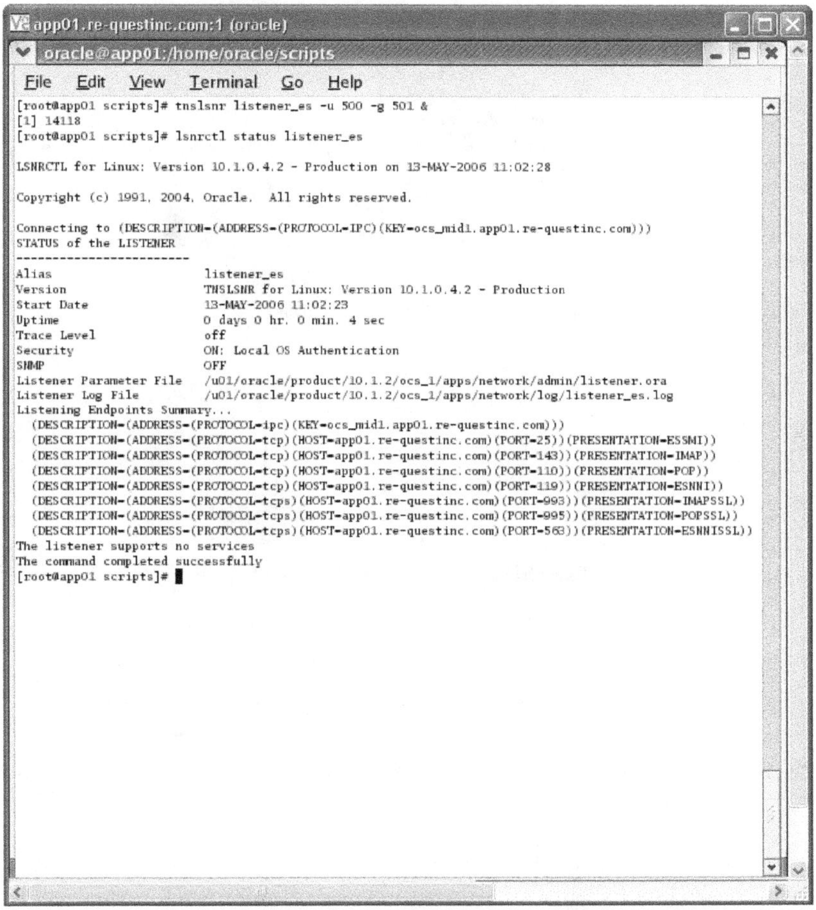

FIGURE 12-7. *tnslsnr command and status*

Remember, since we started the entire OC4J component, we can either use the web interface for Mail directly from the Oracle Collaboration Suite 10*g* Welcome page link or log in to the Oracle Collaboration Suite 10*g* Portal and select the Mail application either from the Links portlet in the upper left-hand corner of the Oracle Collaboration Suite Portal page or from the Mail portlet itself located in the middle of the Oracle Collaboration Suite Portal page. Figure 12-8 shows the Oracle Collaboration Suite Portal page. Notice that all the other applications are unavailable in their respective portlet frames, since we started only the web interface and Mail.

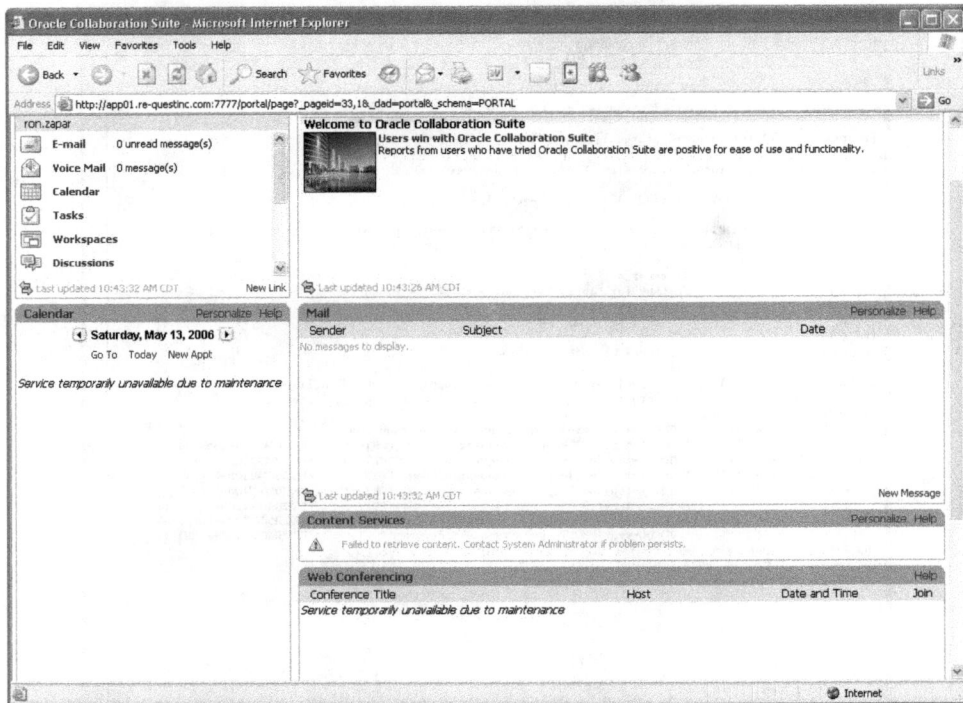

FIGURE 12-8. *Oracle Collaboration Suite Portal page with only Mail available*

In addition to the opmn functions, there are also oes functions that can be used by an Administrator to manage components of the Mail application and environment. The oes functions available are as follows:

- **oesctl**   Commands to control Mail functions

- **oesmon**   Commands to provide a summary of Mail system statistics

- **oesucr**   Commands to create and delete users

- **oesdl**   Commands to add and delete users from distribution lists

- **oesng**   Commands to manage newsgroups

- **oesrl** Commands to create and manage server-side email rules
- **oeschart** Commands to chart statistics provided by oesmon

The *oesctl* command is used to configure and control the various Mail services such as SMTP, POP, and IMAP. The oesctl command provides a subset of the functionality available on Oracle Collaboration Suite 10*g* Control Console pages for Mail but is handy when developing the type of start and stop scripts I outlined in the Chapter 9 or setting the environments up to automatically start and stop Oracle Collaboration Suite 10*g* components through rc.d entries. It also provides a means for managing the environments when circumstances do not provide for browser access (security, network access, server configuration). For example, oesctl can be used to start and stop a Mail service, but it cannot be used to modify its associated parameters (for example, you cannot add a trusted domain value through oesctl). Figure 12-9 shows a series of examples for oesctl commands.

FIGURE 12-9. *oesctl commands and associated results*

In the first command shown in Figure 12-9, I execute an *oesctl show targets* command. This command produces a display of all the Mail services targets configured on the Mail server. With the next command, *oesctl shutdown <target>:<instance>*, I shut down a particular target, the garbage collection process (this process cleans up deleted emails inside the message repository). I then do an *oesctl show status <target>:<instance>* command to verify that the instance is actually shut down. I can then start the gc instance backup using an *oesctl startup <target>:<instance>* command, and again verify it is backed up using the *oesctl show status <target>:<instance>* command. The next command I execute is an *oesctl show processes <target>: <instance>* command against the SMTP_IN Mail service to show how many processes are currently running under the SMTP_IN service. I then execute an *oesctl create instance <target>:<instance>* to create another SMTP_IN process under the SMTP_IN instance. I execute the *oesctl show processes <target>:<instance>* command to display the now two SMTP_IN processes running. I then use the *oesctl delete instance <target>:<instance>* command to delete the second instance of the SMTP_IN process I just created, and verify it is gone with another *oesctl show processes* command.

The next command-line function I want to discuss is *oesmon*. The oesmon command provides a means to obtain raw metric data from the Mail services. Metrics can be used to understand the detail of how an individual Mail service is performing, its workload, thresholds, etc. Each Mail service has its own set of metrics germane to its function. For example, in Figure 12-10, I executed a *oesmon names <target>:<instance>* to display all the names of all metrics for the SMTP_IN service. I found out the names of the *<targets>:<instances>* by first executing the *oesmon targets* command as shown in the figure (similar to the *oesctl show targets* command discussed previously).

Every metric and every managed object has a name. The metric names can only contain alphanumeric characters, including the underscore character, and cannot contain any spaces or the dot character. The metric names are also case sensitive. The output of the *oesmon* command is returned in ASCII character strings, displaying the full name of the metric and its associated value. The metric value itself is always represented in the form of either a string or a number.

FIGURE 12-10. *oesmon targets and oesmon names <target>:<instance> commands*

Every metric is associated with an object called a managed object. Managed objects are associated with other managed objects in a parent-child relationship, forming a hierarchical tree structure of managed objects and metrics. The metrics are always leaves of the tree. The full name of any given object is formed by connecting all the names along the path from the tree root to the object. In this case, the object may be either a metric or a managed object.

A numeric metric represents either a gauge-type value or a counter-type value. A gauge measures the current amount of something and is characterized by a value going up and down. A counter measures an accumulated value and is characterized by the value remaining the same or becoming larger. If the value of a counter goes past the maximum supported number, then the value wraps around to 0.

I think the best way to understand this construct is to display and dissect a couple of examples of executing the command at the command line. Figure 12-11 illustrates an example of running *oesmon get <target>:<instance> <metric_name>* command on three different metrics to display the various

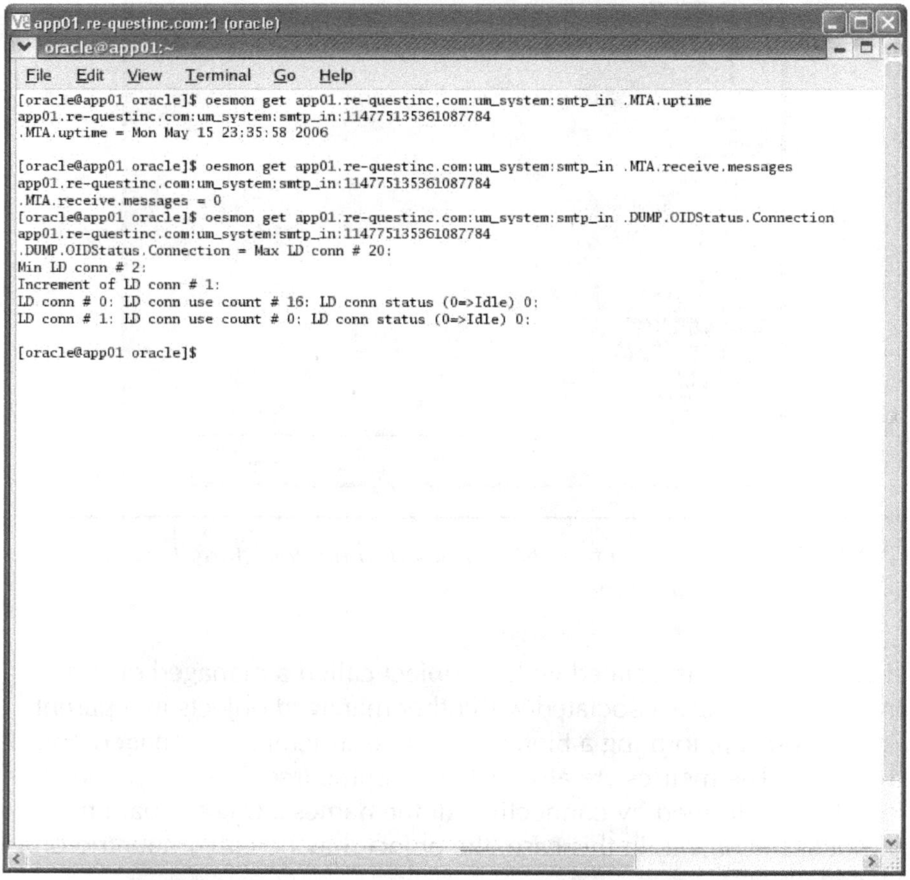

FIGURE 12-11. *oesmon get commands and displayed results*

types of values that can be returned from the command. In the first command .MTA.uptime is displayed, which returns an ASCII character string representing the date and time to the second the target process was last started. In the second command I display a counter value when I complete an *oesmon get* on the .MTA.receive.messages metric. Finally, I display a block of characters showing various values when I complete an *oesmon get* on the .DUMP.OIDStatus. Connection metric to display information about the SMTP_IN target's OID Connection status.

In the next commands, displayed in Figure 12-12, I want to show an example of the hierarchy tree concept. By executing the *oesmon get*

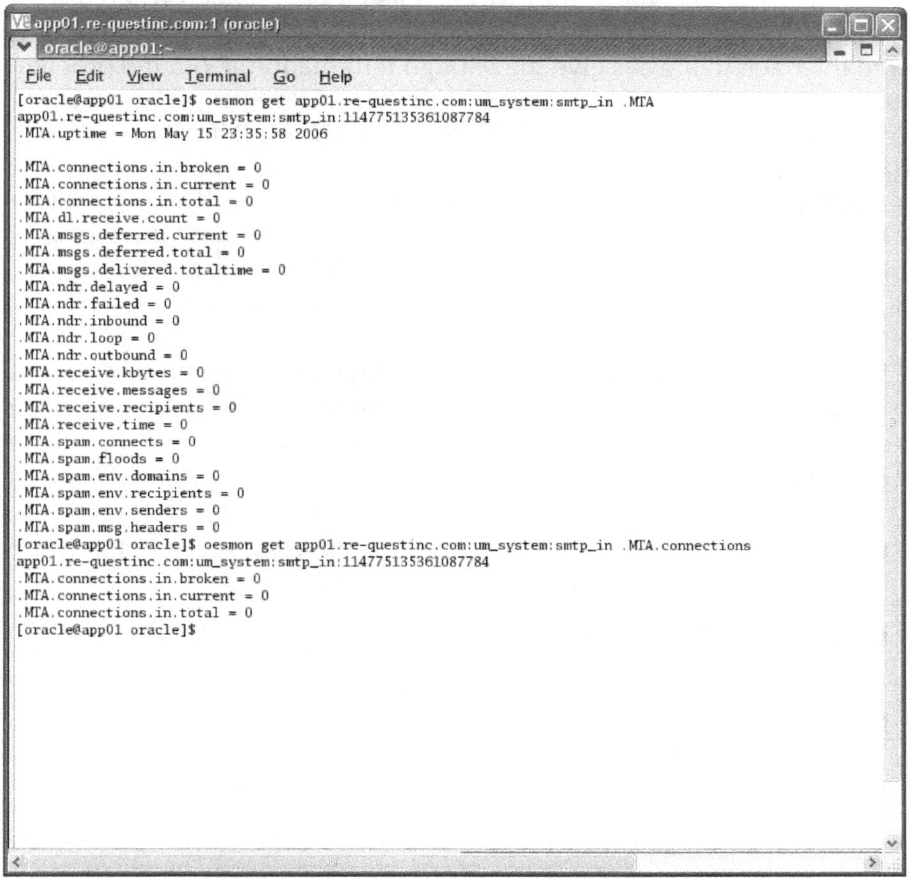

```
app01.re-questinc.com:1 (oracle)
oracle@app01:~

File  Edit  View  Terminal  Go  Help
[oracle@app01 oracle]$ oesmon get app01.re-questinc.com:um_system:smtp_in .MTA
app01.re-questinc.com:um_system:smtp_in:114775135361087784
.MTA.uptime = Mon May 15 23:35:58 2006

.MTA.connections.in.broken = 0
.MTA.connections.in.current = 0
.MTA.connections.in.total = 0
.MTA.dl.receive.count = 0
.MTA.msgs.deferred.current = 0
.MTA.msgs.deferred.total = 0
.MTA.msgs.delivered.totaltime = 0
.MTA.ndr.delayed = 0
.MTA.ndr.failed = 0
.MTA.ndr.inbound = 0
.MTA.ndr.loop = 0
.MTA.ndr.outbound = 0
.MTA.receive.kbytes = 0
.MTA.receive.messages = 0
.MTA.receive.recipients = 0
.MTA.receive.time = 0
.MTA.spam.connects = 0
.MTA.spam.floods = 0
.MTA.spam.env.domains = 0
.MTA.spam.env.recipients = 0
.MTA.spam.env.senders = 0
.MTA.spam.msg.headers = 0
[oracle@app01 oracle]$ oesmon get app01.re-questinc.com:um_system:smtp_in .MTA.connections
app01.re-questinc.com:um_system:smtp_in:114775135361087784
.MTA.connections.in.broken = 0
.MTA.connections.in.current = 0
.MTA.connections.in.total = 0
[oracle@app01 oracle]$
```

FIGURE 12-12. *oesmon managed target metric hierarchy*

<target>: <instance> .MTA command I can show all branches and leaves of the hierarchy for the SMTP_IN .MTA managed target.

Now I will move on to the *oesucr* command. Oracle's best practices suggest that the easiest way to create a few users (say 1 to 10) would be to use the User Provisioning Console, available from the link on the Oracle Collaboration Suite 10*g* Welcome page. However, I am old school (no, do *not* see Rodney Dangerfield in the dictionary . . . although I don't get no respect sometimes either!), and therefore I believe that sometimes doing things manually through command-line execution definitely has its merits. For one thing, in order to use the command-line function, you need to develop a more detailed understanding of what the function is doing, how it is doing it, and what it needs to complete its process successfully. For another, if/when something goes wrong, I feel more enabled when using the command-line function to dig in and resolve the problem rather than relying on the interface to always give me enough information about the problem through error messages and log files to be able to resolve it. The *oesucr* command is used to create Oracle Collaboration Suite 10*g* Mail users from the command line. This tool is only for creating and deleting email users. The corresponding public (OID) users are not created or deleted by the tool. For user creation, the users must exist in OID before running the tool to create the corresponding email users. For user deletion, after running the tool, the users are no longer valid email users, but they are still users in the OID.

The *oesucr* command expects either command-line parameter input or the more commonly used input file containing the attributes for creating a list of users. The *oesucr* command syntax is *oesucr <file> [–v] [–d],* where the options are as follows:

- <file> is the path to the file containing the user records of the users to be created or the list of users to be deleted.

- The –v flag is for verbose and therefore prints out detailed debug messages.

- The –d flag deletes users.

The content of the file defined by the <file> parameter must have the following parameters with values for each Mail user to be created:

- mail = <email address>
- mailhost = <domain>
- orclmailquota = <bytes>
- userpassword = <password>
- baseuserdn =<cn=email,cn=users,dc=oracle,dc=com>

An example looks like this for my Oracle Collaboration Suite environment:

```
mail=test.user1@testdomain.com
baseuserdn=cn=user1,cn=users,dc=testdomain,dc=com orclmailquota=400000000
```

The option to create a user right at the command line without the <file> parameter looks like this:

```
[oracle@app01 oracle] oesucr -cmd mail=test.user1@testdomain.com
baseuserdn=cn=user1, cn=users,dc=testdomain,dc=com orclmailquota=400000000
other_optional_attributes
```

where *other_optional_attributes* are oraclemailstore and userpassword. An example of each is highlighted here:

```
oraclemailstore=cn=mail.testdomain.com,cn=mailstores, cn=UM_SYSTEM,
cn=EMailServerContainer, cn=Products,cn=OracleContext
```

```
userpassword=welcome1
```

The oesucr command can also be used to manage users as well. When users are created and then subsequently deleted, their mailstore artifacts are not removed automatically (this allows for access to a mailbox for a deleted user in the event it contains important information that needs to be retained). The downside of this is that the user cannot be recreated as a Mail user with the same username until these artifacts are cleaned out of the Mail repository. To permanently remove these artifacts from the Mail repository, you must add the clean_user_mailstore_data switch to the oseucr command. Specifically, you can use the switch as follows:

```
[oracle@app01 oracle] oesucr <file> -clean_user_mailstore_data -v
```

where the <file> contains a list of email addresses separated by commas for which the respective artifacts should be permanently cleaned from the Mail repository.

The *oesdl* command is another Mail command-line function used to add and delete users from distribution lists. The syntax is as follows:

```
[oracle@app01 oracle] oesdl <file>
```

The <file> parameter is necessary (whereas it is optional in the case of the oesdl command); it points to the location and name of a file that contains a list of records, each followed by an empty line. Each record must have the name of the distribution list and a list of its users. For adding users to a distribution list, the user type must be indicated, as a regular user, a distribution list, an alias, or a foreign user, as follows:

- U: for a regular user

- F: for a foreign user

- L: for a distribution list

- A: for an alias

Figure 12-13 shows examples of several types of entries to the input file for the *oesdl* command.

The first example shows adding a list of three users to an existing distribution list. The parameters action=add and newlist=n are the key parameters for this particular entry as they indicate the adding of the users to the list and the fact that the list is not new (i.e., not being created in/by this file entry).

The second entry in Figure 12-13 shows adding one distribution list to another already existing distribution list. The parameters action=add, newlist=n, and usertype=L are key in this example, as they say add the user to the existing list; the "user" being added is of type L, or List. . .i.e., another distribution list.

The third example in the input file uses the newlist=y parameter to add the new distribution list right from the input file (versus having already been created prior to running the command this particular time) and add users to it.

The fourth and final example uses two entries in the input file to complete its function. In the first input file, entry the action=delete parameter is used to

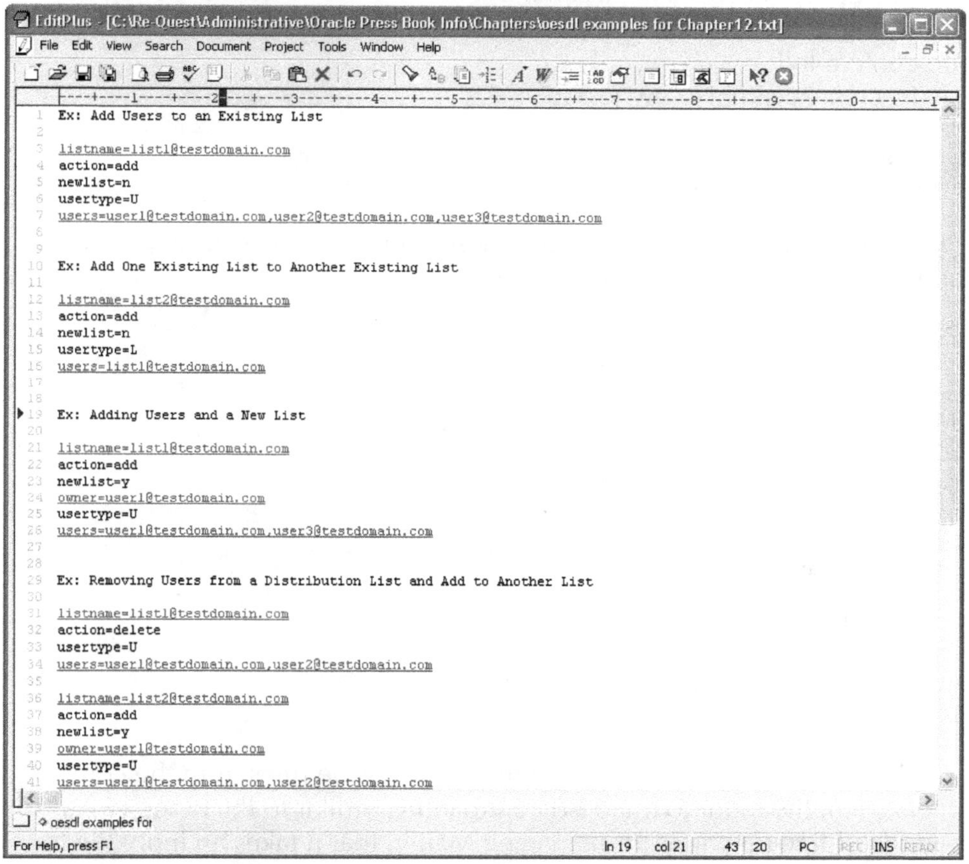

FIGURE 12-13.   *oesdl input file content examples*

delete the users listed from the list1@testdomain.com distribution list. Then the second entry adds those same users to the list2@testdomain.com distribution list.

The *oesng* command is used to create and delete NNTP newsgroups in the Oracle Collaboration Suite 10*g* application. The example syntax is as follows:

```
[oracle@app01 oracle] oesng <file>
```

This utility accepts a file as an input and creates or deletes newsgroups according to the information specified in the file. Some examples of input file content follow.

To create a simple newsgroup,

```
name=simplenewsgroup1
newsstore=db1.testdomain.com
```

To create a publicly moderated newsgroup that allows postings with information posted retained for 30 days,

```
name=pubnewsgroup1
newsstore=db1.testdomain.com
action=create
description=A Public Newsgroup
moderatedgroup=true
moderator=user1@testdomain.com
moderator=user2@testdomain.com
postingallowed=true
retentiondays=30
```

To delete a newsgroup,

```
name=simplenewsgroup1
action=delete
```

The *oesrl* command is used to create server-side rules from the command line. Again, the input to the *oesrl* command is similar to the other command-line functions for managing Mail in that it takes an input file to tell it what rules to create or delete. You can also use the *oesrl* command to list the rules that currently exist for a particular email address, or for the entire domain.

Now, a little about what server-side rules actually are, and how they are used. Server-side rules are rules for managing email messages in different ways directly on the Mail server (versus managing them with rules defined in the desktop client tool). Server-side rules allow the execution of conditional actions based on the properties of a message, or they affect how it is processed by the Mail server. For example, as a Mail Administrator you could implement a server-side rule that says any email message to any email address in your domain with an attachment ending in .exe is rejected. You can also implement server-side rules on a user-by-user basis. For example, you can say any email messages to test1@testdomain.com should be forwarded to test2@testdomain.com. The server-side rules are stored internally within the Oracle Internet Directory but are not meant to be modified directly. Any rule modifications should be made through the published interfaces. Within the OID Directory Information Tree (DIT), rules are stored in their XML format right with the directory element to which they apply. For example, rules created for specific users/email addresses are stored in the Mail server container part of the DIT with the user/person who "owns" the rule. Domain level rules—rules that apply to an entire email Domain versus a single user—are stored in the OID as a subentry of the Mail domain, and system-wide rules reside at the top level of the Oracle Mail DIT.

Many options and combinations of options are available with server-side rules, actually too many to cover completely in this chapter, so I will use this as an opportunity to show some examples of server-side rules and the associated syntax defined in the input file to the *oesrl* command, as well as provide some additional reference points to provide a more thorough understanding of the possibilities when using server-side rules.

First, however, let me discuss using the *oesrl* command to print out existing server-side rules from Oracle Collaboration Suite 10g Mail. Using *oesrl –p <email address>*, you can list out any server-side rules defined specifically for that email address. If you substitute *<domain name>* for *<email address>* using *oesrl –p <domain name>*, you can see all server-side rules defined at the domain level on a Mail server.

Note that, to modify or edit an existing server-side rule, you would use the *oesrl –p* command with either the *<domain name>* or *<email address>* parameter to print out to stdout (screen by default) the rules in XML format for the entire domain or just one user respectively, copy the rules to an .xml file, make any required modifications, and then use the file as input to the *oesrl –x <XML file>* command to overwrite the current definition of the rule stored in the Mail server.

The *oesrl* command will also accept a text property file for creating the rules. Simply use the *oesrl –c <properties filename>* command to create the rules from an XML file.

My first example of a server-side rule creation is a rule that automatically moves email messages that come into an account from a particular email address into a specific folder within the receiving email address on Oracle Collaboration Suite 10g Mail. Figure 12-14 shows the definition of the server-side rule to move any emails that come to my email address from the orclguest@re-questinc.com email address into a folder I created in my account called Discard.

```
 EditPlus - [C:\Re-Quest\Administrative\Oracle Press Book Info\Chapters\oesrl inp...
  File  Edit  View  Search  Document  Project  Tools  Window  Help

   ----+----1----+----2----+----3----+----4----+----5----+----6----+----7----+---
  1  <account qualifiedName="ron.zapar@re-questinc.com" ownerType="user" id="0">
  2
  3     <rulelist event="deliver">
  4
  5        <rule description="mvorclguest" group="all" active="yes" visible="yes">
  6           <condition negation="no" junction="and">
  7              <attribute tag="rfc822from"/>
  8              <operator caseSensitive="no" op="contains"/>
  9              <operand>orclguest@re-questinc.com</operand>
 10           </condition>
 11
 12           <action>
 13              <command tag="moveto"/>
 14              <parameter>/ron.zapar/Discard</parameter>
 15           </action>
 16
 17        </rule>
 18
 19     </rulelist>
 20
 21  </account>
 22

 oesrl input file exa
For Help, press F1                          ln 1    col 1     22   3C    PC    REC  INS  READ
```

FIGURE 12-14.   *Server-side rule for moving emails to a specific folder*

Note the qualifiedName parameter at the top of the rule indicating that
this rule applies to that particular user (versus a domain- or a system-wide
rule). Next notice that the rule eventlist parameter is set to deliver, which
means to execute the rule on the delivery of a message. The rule name value
is set to mvorclguest, which identifies the rule by name when it is put into
the Mail server. Parameters active=yes and visible=yes mean the rule should
be active on the server when created and visible to the user as a rule. The
attribute tag parameter tells the rule to check the from field on the incoming
message for the email address defined in the operand parameter, and the
operator parameters tell it not to be case sensitive and to check for the
operand value in the from field. The action section of the rule tells it to
execute a moveto action and move the email message into the Discard
folder under my username.

The next example involves rejecting emails at the system level based on
content. This will block executables attached to emails as a means for
transporting a virus. Figure 12-15 shows a rule that is defined at the system
level to reject any email message that has an attachment whose name ends
in .exe.

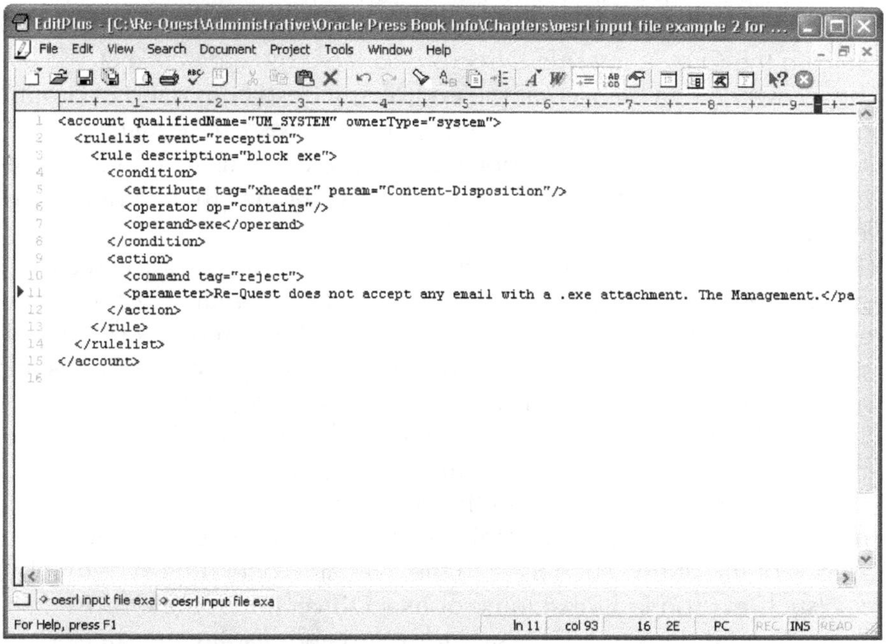

FIGURE 12-15. *Server-side rule example rejecting .exe attachments*

Notice the ownerType parameter at the top is set to system (versus user in the earlier example, in Figure 12-14), which means this rule applies across the board to every user in the system. The rulelist event here is reception (it was delivery in the preceding example), so the email messages can be dealt with when the system receives them, *not* when they have already been moved through the system for delivery (the sooner a potential virus-carrying email message is caught, the better). The <attribute tag= "xheader" param="Content-Disposition"/> section of the rule definition tells the rule to look at the xheader of the message for the content information and, based upon the command tag parameter, reject any message that has an attachment that contains the string "exe" in its name, and to put out the information in the parameter section as a message indicating the email message was rejected because there was a .exe attachment.

I can also perform a verification of all rules for a single user or a given domain by using the *oesrl –r <email address>/<domain name>* to read the rule(s) from the Oracle Internet Directory to see if they are correct.

The –v switch can be used at the end of any *oesrl* command to produce verbose Debug-level output. For example, by using *oesrl –r <email address> –v* you can get a large amount of Debug messages, whereas if you eliminate the –v parameter, you get a single line returned stating "Rule verification successful."

The *oeschart* utility enables an Oracle Mail Administrator to create graphs illustrating the system's current load and performance. Oracle Mail servers track a range of metrics that are periodically stored in a set of mail statistics tables. The *oeschart* command-line function generates charts and images that can be used to publish reports and web pages in order to provide an Oracle Collaboration Suite 10g Administrator with a graphic picture of the status of the Mail system implementation and environment. The images are only created when the command is run. Therefore, to have dynamically updated charts, administrators must schedule periodic executions of the utility, such as with the available operating system job queues (such as cron in Unix/Linux) or as a DBMS job in the Oracle database. Several steps are necessary to set up and display the statistical information.

The first step necessary to configure *oeschart* is to set the collection interval for the statistics of the various Mail server components. The value is stored in the Oracle Internet Directory and can be modified through the Oracle Directory Manager interface (oidadmin). This setting can also be done through the Enterprise Manager Collaboration Suite Control Console. The specific variable in the OID is defined for each of the targets (SMTP, NNTP, POP3, IMAP) and is named orclMailAdminCollectionInterval. The variable starts out as a null value in the out-of-the-box installation and must be set to an integer that equals the number of seconds between collection runs. It is suggested that statistics be collected every ten minutes (600 seconds) for the various email processes, while the garbage collection process can be collected once an hour (3600 seconds). The steps to set the orclMailAdminCollectionInterval value through oidadmin are as follows:

1. On the Infrastructure Tier, start the oidadmin tool and connect to the Oracle Directory Manager (oidadmin) tool as the orcladmin user.

2. Go to Entry Management | OracleContext | Computers | <Apps hostname> | <$ORACLE_HOME> | EmailServer | mailProcessConfig | <hostname>:um_system:gc | <hostname>:um_system:<Email Process>:<TargetID> and the parameters will display at the right panel.

3. Select All on view properties (which will show null values as well).

4. Search for the parameter orclMailAdminCollectionInterval and enter the value for the Email process selected.

5. After changing, choose Apply and repeat the process for each of the other Mail target processes.

Figure 12-16 shows the parameter being set for the Garbage Collection process (gc) to one hour (3600 seconds). Notice the tree structure on the left side.

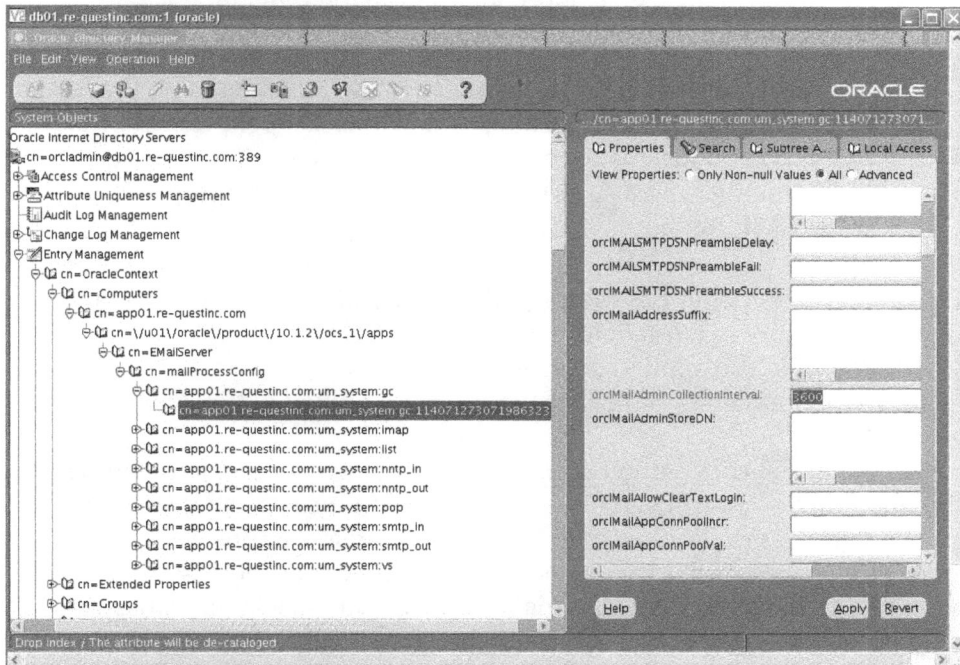

FIGURE 12-16. *Setting the orclMailAdminCollectionInterval parameter in Oracle Directory Manager*

Once statistics are being collected into the repository, it makes sense to configure the Housekeeping function to clean up and manage the statistics so that they don't get out of control in terms of the space they take inside the database. To do so, Enterprise Manager Collaboration Suite 10*g* Control Console must be used. The Housekeeper function is found on the Mail Application Service Targets page on the Applications Tier in Enterprise Manager. To navigate there,

1. Sign in to Enterprise Manager Collaboration Suite 10*g* Control Console as ias_admin and then select the Middle/Applications Tier instance from the Standalone Instances list.

2. Choose the Mail Application link from the System Components list, and then the Housekeeper from the Service Targets list.

3. Select an individual instance of the Housekeeper function from the Process Instances page.

4. Select the Statistics Cleanup option from the Operation Mode drop-down list in the Housekeeping Operations section and click Apply.

5. You get a confirmation page. Return to the Housekeeping Process Instance page and re-select the same Housekeeper process instance to which you just made the change. Then change the Age Threshold to the number of days you wish to retain statistics history for and again click Apply.

Figure 12-17 shows the values as they were modified on an example Housekeeper process instance.

Now to have the applied changes take affect, stop and restart the Housekeeper process instance for which you modified the cleanup parameters.

Now that statistics gathering has been completely configured—including cleanup functions—you can now concentrate on the reporting and graphing functionality of the *oeschart* utility. In order to create graphs, the utility requires a property file location as its single command-line parameter. The property file is a text file containing keywords and associated values that

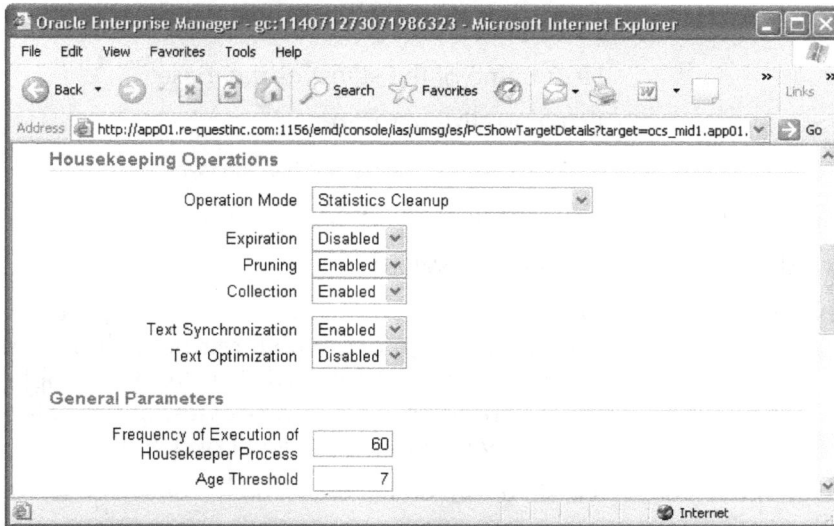

FIGURE 12-17.   *Housekeeper process instance statistics cleanup configuration*

define the information the utility needs to generate the graph. There are mandatory parameters as well as optional parameters. Table 12-1 identifies the mandatory parameters for the *oeschart* property file, while Table 12-2 identifies the optional parameters for the *oeschart* property file.

Figure 12-18 shows a sample property file for graphing one of the available IMAP metrics.

Notice that ES_MAIL is the value for the *username* parameter, which is the database user that owns the email statistics schema. This is where the associated tables are created by default with the Oracle Collaboration Suite 10*g* installation. The *graph_type* parameter tells *oeschart* what type of graph to create (current, cumulative, rate, or command_data), and the *image_dir* tells *oeschart* where to place the image file when the graph is complete. The *image_file_name* combined with the *encode_type* provide the remaining information for the filename. The other critical parameter is of course *metric_name,* which tells *oeschart* which metric you want to graph. Figure 12-19 shows the graph output to the file socketcount.png.

Parameter	Description
server	Host name of the statistics database
port	Database listener port
sid	SID or service name for the server
username	Account user
password	Account password
process_dn	Query used to gather statistics, such as *process_dn= %value_in_ini_file%*, which retrieves all processes that follow this DN pattern. This lets you graph a specific process, a set of processes, or the entire system by specifying the level of detail
metric_name	Metric to query
graph_type	Type of graph. Possible graphs are • command_data • xy_rate • xy_cummulative • xy_current
image_file_name	Choose a name for the generated file. **Note:** Either .gif or .png will be appended to this filename, depending upon which encode_type you choose
image_title	Title to display on the graph

TABLE 12-1.   *Mandatory oeschart Property File Parameters*

Message Store Administration Specifics

The last area of Email application administration I am going to cover is not only very important, but also right up a traditional Oracle guy's alley. It is the area of administering the Message Store, or the Oracle Database 10*g*

Parameter	Default
encode_type	Gif
image_dir	./
aggregate_time_period	600
max_lifetime	300
show_statistics	FALSE
debug	FALSE

TABLE 12-2. *Optional oeschart Property File Parameters*

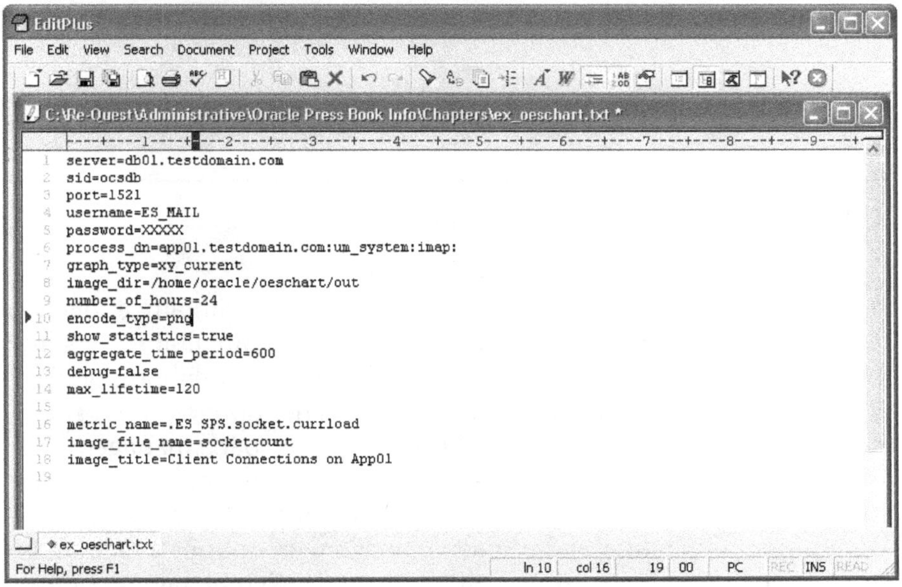

FIGURE 12-18. *Sample oeschart property files*

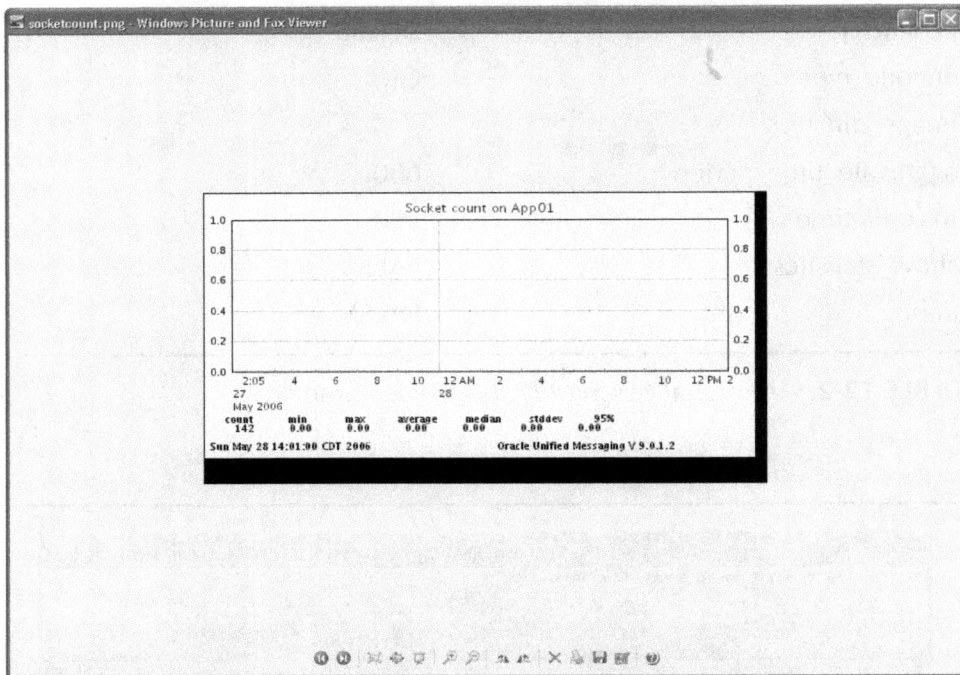

FIGURE 12-19. *Sample oeschart graph*

environment where email messages are stored. Just as with any application written on top of the Oracle core technology stack, maintaining a healthy, happy database is critical to a well-performing Oracle Collaboration Suite 10*g* environment. Two main areas are critical, in my opinion, for a stable, available, and manageable Message Store database: space management/ message archival, and deleted message retrieval if someone inadvertently deletes one or more email messages they did not mean to delete.

With proper utilization of the space management options available in Oracle Collaboration Suite 10*g*, an Administrator can maintain a controlled email environment that is properly backed up and provides consistent performance without the need to impose any unreasonable quotas on users.

(The key word in this sentence is "unreasonable." I firmly believe quotas are a necessary tool of Mail Administrators to keep users from consuming every bit of disk space in the company.) The feature that is most effective in space management is the concept of tertiary storage for the Message Store database.

Tertiary storage is defined as a separate tablespace where the associated data files are created on storage specifically configured and allocated to hold old messages. Using a separate tablespace allows administrators to use a possibly larger and less expensive storage medium, different from the active storage area for new messages. Tertiary storage can be initially planned as part of a Mail system, or it can be implemented later. By default, the ESTERSTORE tablespace is created on the same disk as all other tablespaces when initially installing Mail. Also by default, the "ESTERSTORE" tablespace datafile location is in $ORACLE_HOME/oradata/<sid> (or the data file location specified during the Oracle Collaboration Suite 10*g* installation process). Administrators can configure Mail to move messages exceeding a designated age to tertiary storage. This process frees up valuable space on the primary disk for newer messages, which are by nature more frequently accessed than the older messages, but does not prevent users from accessing messages just as they did before the messages were moved to tertiary storage. Message stores tend to grow constantly. Mail messages are continually entering the database, and although in general messages are regularly deleted, more email messages are saved than are deleted. On the average older messages are accessed less often than newer messages, so storing them on less expensive, slower disks while still keeping them accessible online for users is an acceptable way to reduce costs while not limiting user functionality. Depending on the storage mechanisms used for tertiary storage, users should really not notice that their older messages have been moved to a different physical disk location.

So, basically there are three components to implementing tertiary storage:

- Setting up the physical storage

- Creating/moving and appropriately sizing the data files associated with the ESTERSTORE tablespace to the new storage

- Creating/enabling the tertiary storage Housekeeper process

I will focus on the last two, assuming the physical storage is already available and mounted to the server where the message store is running.

In order to create the ESTERSTORE tablespace, a Database Administrator would need to log in to SQL*Plus as SYS or SYSTEM and execute the CREATE TABLESPACE command with the datafile parameter. An example to create the ESTERSTORE tablespace with an initial 2GB data file would be

```
SQL> CREATE TABLESPACE esterstore DATAFILE '<tertiary storage mount
point>/oracle/product/oradata/ocsdb/esterstore01.dbf' SIZE 2000M;
```

If the ESTERSTORE tablespace already exists, then the Database Administrator must move the datafile(s) for the tablespace to the tertiary storage mount point. To do so, follow these steps:

1. Take a full hot backup of the database (see Chapter 10 on backing up Oracle Collaboration Suite 10*g*).

2. Execute the following query in SQL*Plus to get the names of the data files (this will also provide their current locations as well):

   ```
   select file_name from dba_data_files where tablespace_name=
   'ESTERSTORE';
   ```

3. Take the ESTERSTORE tablespace offline with

   ```
   ALTER TABLESPACE esterstore OFFLINE NORMAL;
   ```

4. Physically copy the data files from the current location to the location on the tertiary storage where they will now reside.

5. Rename each data file in the database associated with the ESTERSTORE tablespace using

   ```
   ALTER TABLESPACE esterstore RENAME DATAFILE '<current mount
   point>/<datafile
   name>' TO '<tertiary storage mount point>/<datafile name>';
   ```

6. Bring the ESTERSTORE tablespace back online using

   ```
   ALTER TABLESPACE esterstore ONLINE;
   ```

Once the tablespace has been created/moved, the next step is to define the Housekeeper process that moves old email messages to tertiary storage. The steps for enabling tertiary storage on the Message Store are as follows:

1. Log in to Enterprise Manager Oracle Collaboration Suite 10*g* Control Console and display the page for the Applications Tier. Then scroll down to the System Components, and select Mail Application.

2. Click the Housekeeping Target name.

3. Create a new Oracle Email housekeeping instance by clicking Create or Create Like.

4. Select the new housekeeping process by clicking its radio button.

5. Click Default Settings to navigate to the parameter page.

6. Select Tertiary Store in the Operation Mode field.

7. Enable Tertiary Storage by selecting Enabled from the drop-down list in the Expiration field.

8. Disable Pruning, Collection, Text Synchronization, and Text Optimization by selecting Disabled from the drop-down list in the respective fields.

9. In the Frequency Of Execution Of Housekeeper Process field, enter, in minutes, how often the housekeeper should move messages to tertiary storage. In the example shown in Figure 12-20, I have set it to 1440 minutes, which equates to once a day (24*60).

10. In the Age Threshold field, enter the age, in days, of messages you want to move to tertiary storage. The default is 30 days. In the example shown in Figure 12-20, messages that are 60 days old are moved to tertiary storage.

11. Click Apply to save changes.

So, in summary, the example here shows that once a day messages that are 60 days old will be moved to Tertiary Storage.

The other main consideration for database administration related to Oracle Collaboration Suite 10*g* is setting up the Message Store database for recovery of deleted email messages. How many times have users deleted an email message only to recognize just after they pushed the big red button that they " . . . *really* didn't *mean* to delete *that email*!" With some email solutions, getting that deleted email back is impossible; with others, it's

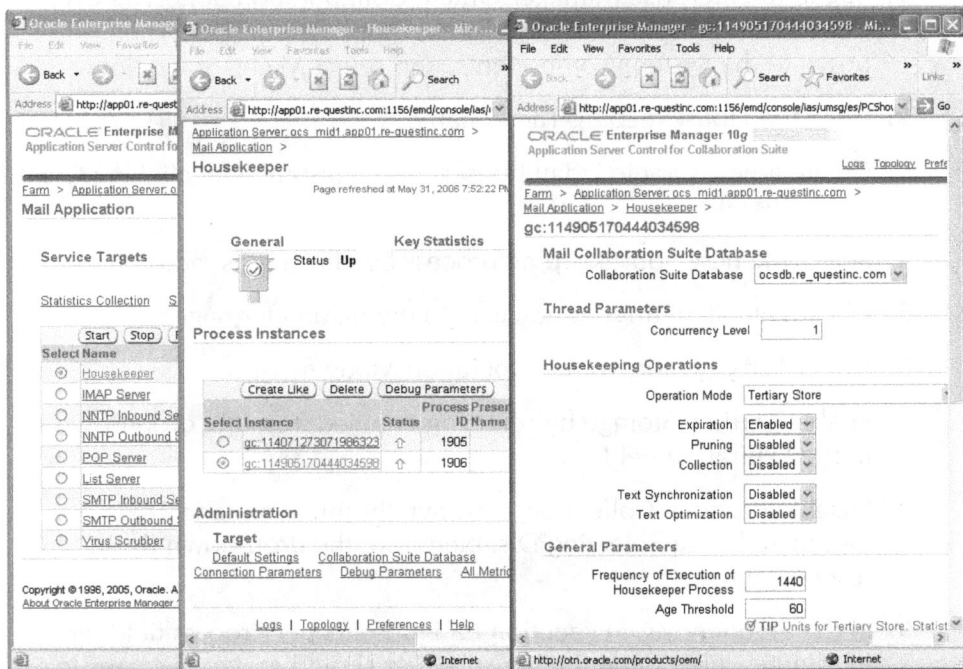

FIGURE 12-20. *Setting up tertiary storage in Enterprise Manager Control Console*

doable, but not without a lot of heartache and pain. The *oesbkp* utility gives you the capability to back up and recover mail folders, email messages, address book entries, and server-side rules for individual users. When restoring email component data with *oesbkp,* all messages are restored to a new restore folder named restore_<date> <time> to avoid overwriting existing messages in the target folders. Private address entries are restored in the user's private address book only if an identical entry does not already exist there, but server-side rules that are restored will overwrite existing server-side rules with the same name.

The *oesbkp* utility is pretty easy to use, provided one can make sense of the syntax and appropriate values for the command-line parameters. For example, the Oracle documentation refers to the user parameter as a fully qualified username when it actually is asking for the email address of the email account to be backed up or restored. Also, the password parameter must contain the password that is associated with the OID admin username–given admindn parameter, which is usually orcladmin. In terms of the admindn parameter, the value *must be* provided with the cn= preceding the username, for example cn=orcladmin.

The syntax for the entire oesbkp command, including all parameters, looks like this:

```
oesbkp task={backup | restore} user=userid@domain password=admin_password
[type={all | mail | rules | addrbook}] [admindn=OID_account_with_admin_
privileges] [ldaphost=host_name] [ldapport=port_number]
[backupdir=directory] [folder=folder_name]
```

The task, user, and password parameters are all mandatory. All the other parameters are optional, but I recommend filling all of them in whenever possible. Table 12-3 contains the entire list of possible command-line parameters for the oesbkp utility, along with a good idea of what they actually require, as well as example values for each.

Parameter Name	Valid Values	Default Value	Description
TASK	{backup | restore}	None	oesbkp can be used to either back up or restore email information.
USER	Fully qualified username (email address)	None	Fully qualified email address, including the domain, of the user being backed up or restored. For example, a valid value for user is test.user1 @domain.com, whereas user@domain and user are not valid values.
PASSWORD	Any string	None	Password for the Admin distinguished name (ADMINDN parameter).

TABLE 12-3. *oesbkp Utility Command-Line Parameters*

Parameter Name	Valid Values	Default Value	Description
TYPE	{all | mail | rules | addrbook}	all	Indicates the objects to be backed up or restored: all (folders, messages, server side rules, and address book entries); messages only; server-side rules only; or address book entries only.
ADMINDN	Any valid admin for the LDAP server	cn= orcladmin	DN that the tool uses to bind to the LDAP server. The DN should have admin privileges, such as orcladmin. The cn= is required.
LDAPHOST	Any valid host name	localhost	Name of the host where Oracle Internet Directory is installed. For example, ldap.testdomain.com.
LDAPPORT	Any integer	389	Port on which Oracle Internet Directory is listening. 389 is the default value; if using SSL, the default value is 4032.
BACKUPDIR	Any valid operating system directory	user.dir	Location where the backup file is being created or read from for a restore. An example in UNIX/Linux: /u01/oesbkp.
FOLDER	Any email folder name	None	Name of the folder to be backed up or restored. If no value is specified, then all available folders are backed up or restored. Example: Inbox.

TABLE 12-3. *oesbkp Utility Command-Line Parameters* (Continued)

The *oesbkp* command can be run right from the command line on the Applications Tier server on a one-off basis. However, I would suggest setting up a script with a cron job to run at a regularly determined interval—once a day maybe—to capture Mail data with enough frequency to have value to the end users.

The oesbkp process also writes a log file for each time it is run, and that log file's location is $ORACLE_HOME/oes/log/um_system/backup/*nnnn*/ text.log, where *nnnn* is a random, unique number auto-generated by the oesbkp utility. I would also suggest creating a unique subdirectory under the main backup directory location, say based on the date or some random, unique number, where oesbkp can write the backup files on a given day so that all backup files are not being written into the same directory each time the oesbkp process runs. Again, implementing this as part of a cron job script process is the best way to handle it in my opinion.

Figure 12-21 shows a set of oesbkp commands as a real example. I first executed an oesbkp backup command to back up my Inbox. Notice the

```
[oracle@app01 oracle]$ oesbkp task=backup user=ron.zapar@re-questinc.com password=        type=mail admindn=cn=orcladmin ldapho
st=db01.re-questinc.com ldapport=389 backupdir=/home/oracle/oesbkp folder=Inbox
Logs will be generated in /u01/oracle/product/10.1.2/ocs_1/apps/oes/log/um_system/backup/9721/text.log
[oracle@app01 oracle]$ cd /u01/oracle/product/10.1.2/ocs_1/apps/oes/log/um_system/backup/9721
[oracle@app01 9721]$ ls -1
total 4
-rw-r--r--   1 oracle   oinstall      278 Jun  3 00:15 text.log
[oracle@app01 9721]$ cat text.log
((time 06/03/2006 00:15:57.427 CDT)(compclass oracle.mail.backup)(compinst )(component backup)(module )(priority notification
 16)(execid 127.0.0.1:9721.Thread[main,5,main]:1149311755-1)(msgid succ_bkp_mail)(mtext Successfully backed up mails of user
ron.zapar@re-questinc.com))
[oracle@app01 9721]$ cd /home/oracle/oesbkp/
[oracle@app01 oesbkp]$ ls -1
total 8
-rw-r--r--   1 oracle   oinstall     2370 Jun  3 00:15 ron.zapar@re-questinc.com_0
-rw-r--r--   1 oracle   oinstall       36 Jun  3 00:15 ron.zapar@re-questinc.com_foldermap
[oracle@app01 oesbkp]$ oesbkp task=restore user=ron.zapar@re-questinc.com password=        type=mail admindn=cn=orcladmin ldaph
ost=db01.re-questinc.com ldapport=389 backupdir=/home/oracle/oesbkp folder=Inbox
Logs will be generated in /u01/oracle/product/10.1.2/ocs_1/apps/oes/log/um_system/backup/216/text.log
[oracle@app01 oesbkp]$ cd /u01/oracle/product/10.1.2/ocs_1/apps/oes/log/um_system/backup/216
[oracle@app01 216]$ ls -1
total 4
-rw-r--r--   1 oracle   oinstall      277 Jun  3 00:18 text.log
[oracle@app01 216]$ cat text.log
((time 06/03/2006 00:18:13.380 CDT)(compclass oracle.mail.backup)(compinst )(component backup)(module )(priority notification
 16)(execid 127.0.0.1:216.Thread[main,5,main]:1149311890-1)(msgid succ_rest_mail)(mtext Successfully restored mails of user r
on.zapar@re-questinc.com))
[oracle@app01 216]$
```

FIGURE 12-21. *Example oesbkp backup and restore commands and results*

output from the command and cat of the log file in the figure, as well as the listing showing the files in the backup directory. Then I deleted all the Mail in my Inbox. (I did this offline from the example, as there really was no way to demonstrate this in a screen shot.) Again, notice the output from the command and associated log file list.

Figure 12-22 shows a screen shot of my Web Mail client with the restored file listed and the emails shown on the right side of the page.

There are other methods of restoring emails, including Log Miner and Flashback Query functions, but I felt those were more mainstream Oracle Database Administrator tools; I wanted to concentrate on options specific to Oracle Collaboration Suite 10*g*.

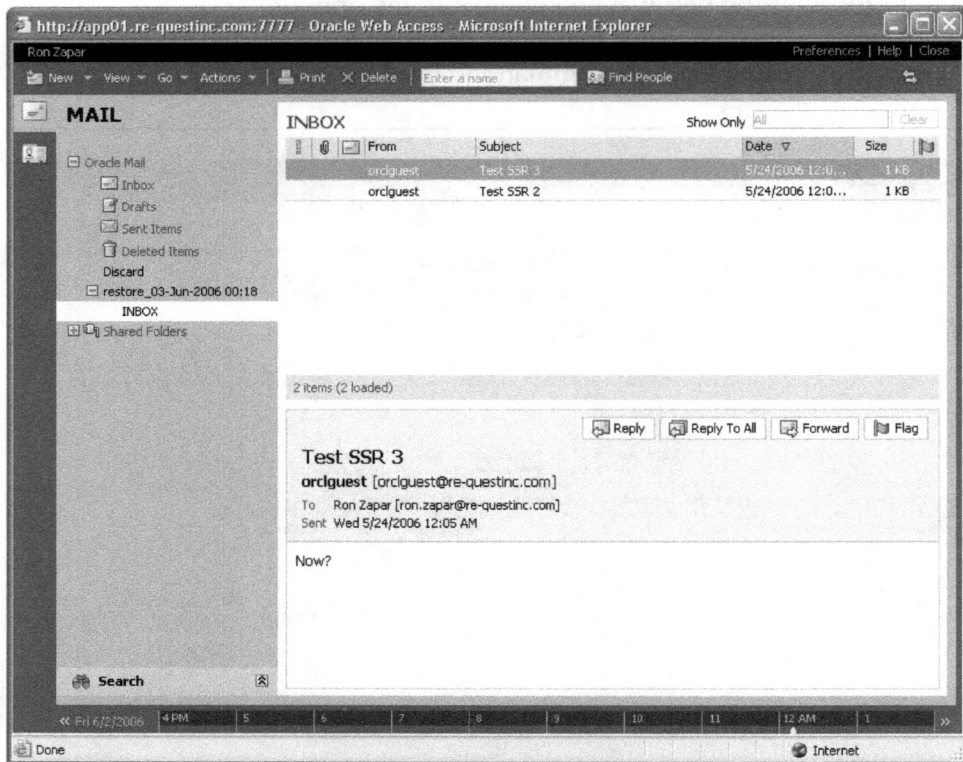

FIGURE 12-22. *Mail client after email restore*

Calendar Component Administration

I will now describe the Oracle Calendar application's architecture and cover important administrative functions for the Oracle Calendar application.

Calendar Application Architecture

The Oracle Calendar Server is defined by a collection of several processes that run on the Oracle Collaboration Suite 10g Applications Tier, each of which provides a specific function of the Calendar application (they are background processes in UNIX/Linux and multithreaded services on the Windows platform).

- The *uniengd* process is the Oracle Calendar Engine, which processes all users' requests for Calendar functionality.

- The *unilckd* process is the Oracle Calendar Lock Manager, which controls access to the Calendar data store. Remember from the earlier overview chapter that the Oracle Calendar has its own proprietary database that resides on the Oracle Collaboration Suite 10g Applications Tier, rather than storing its data in a schema in the Oracle database on the Infrastructure Tier.

- The *unisncd* process is the Oracle Calendar Synchronous Network, a process that maintains TCP/IP connections between nodes (if there are multiple Calendar nodes created) and grants connections to the Directory Access Server.

- The *unidasd* process is the Oracle Calendar Directory Access Server, which is the process that allows Calendar users and processes to access the Oracle Internet Directory on the Infrastructure Tier.

- The *unicwsd* process is Oracle Calendar Corporate-Wide Services, the process that replicates data between nodes and exchanges information between remote users and notification services external to the Calendar. In addition, the *unicwsd* process sends email notifications through an SMTP mail server, sends wireless notifications through Oracle's wireless services, processes server-side reminders, and synchronizes the calendar database with the directory server.

- The *unicsmd* process is the Oracle Calendar Server Manager, a process that provides remote management of the Calendar Server.

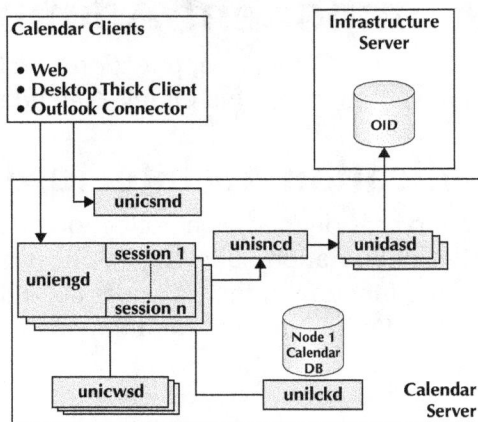

FIGURE 12-23. *Calendar architecture*

Figure 12-23 shows the Calendar architecture with each of these processes identified, as well as a high-level diagram of how they interact.

Calendar Process Management

Common management tasks for the Oracle Calendar application processes include

■ Starting/Stopping the Calendar Server

■ Checking the status of the Calendar Server

■ Viewing the current user activity

In terms of starting and stopping the Oracle Calendar processes, they have now been integrated with the Oracle Process Management and Notification utility (OPMN) in Oracle Collaboration Suite 10*g* (in previous releases of Oracle Collaboration Suite, the Calendar Server processes were only manageable from the command line using their proprietary commands). So, to start and stop the Calendar processes, I use opmnctl from the command line, or Enterprise Manager Collaboration Suite Control Console just like the email processes in the preceding section. To start the Calendar Server from the command line, use the following command:

```
[oracle@app01 oracle] opmnctl startproc ias-component=
CalendarServer
```

To stop the Calendar Server from the command line, use this:

```
[oracle@app01 oracle] opmnctl stopproc ias-component=CalendarServer
```

The unistart and unistop utilities—the utilities that were used in place of OPMN commands to manage Calendar processes in previous releases of Oracle Collaboration Suite—are still available for use in Oracle Collaboration Suite 10*g*, but I highly recommend using OPMN for normal operations. There may be times when the Calendar processes get out of synch, or when they will not start/stop with normal commands; at such times the unistart/unistop utilities can be employed to resolve issues. Eventually, however, in future releases of the product, the further integration of Calendar Server processes with the Applications Tier will make the unistart/unistop functions obsolete.

In addition to starting and stopping the entire Calendar Server (all processes), I can also start and stop specific processes by using the process-type=<Calendar Process> parameter in place of the ias-component= CalendarServer parameter. To get a complete listing of all the processes associated with a particular installation of Oracle Calendar, as well as to check their status, use the following command:

```
[oracle@app01 oracle] $ORACLE_HOME/opmn/bin/opmnctl status ias-
component=CalendarServer
```

In addition to the OPMN status, I can also do a status on the Calendar Server and its associated processes by executing the following:

```
[oracle@app01 oracle] $ORACLE_HOME/ocal/bin/unistatus -d
```

Another important Administrator function is to monitor user activity on the Calendar Server. The *uniwho* command provides the following information:

- The PID, or process ID, associated with the individual user session

- The ADDRESS (IP address) of the device where the user is signed on to Calendar

- NODEID, the Calendar node ID that the user logged in to

- XITEMID, the X.400 address of the user process

- USER, which displays the actual name of the user (Last, First)

- A connection summary, which contains the following information:

  - TOTAL is the total number of connections.

  - STANDARD is the number of standard or user connections.

  - SHARED is the total number of shared connections, which are connections from the Web client applications.

  - CONNECTIVITY identifies the number of reserved connections, as SYSOP and CWSOP.

Calendar Administration Specifics

There are administrative utilities with specific functions: *unidbbackup, unicheck, uniclean, unidsup, unilogons, unireqdump* and *unirmold, uniaccessrights, uniadmrights, unidsdiff, unidssync,* and *uniuser.* These administrative utilities provide the following functionality:

- The *unidbbackup* utility is used to back up the Oracle Calendar Server.

- The *unicheck* utility is used to verify the Oracle Calendar Server file system and also to check the settings for permissions, owner, and group information.

- The *uniclean* utility is used to remove or correct any problems found running unicheck. Transient files will be removed, and permission and ownership settings restored to the default.

- The *unidsup* utility is used to report the status of the directory server.

- The *unilogons* utility is used to display Oracle Calendar Server statistics for signing on and off.

- The *unireqdump* utility is used to view and delete requests in the Oracle Calendar Corporate-Wide Services (CWS) queue.

- The *unirmold* utility is used to remove old data from the Calendar Server database.

- The *uniaccessrights* utility is used to manage user and resource access rights.

- The *uniadmrights* utility is used to grant, modify, or remove administration rights.

- The *unidsdiff* utility is used to report differences between the Calendar Server and the directory server.

- The *unidssync* utility is used to synchronize the information in the Calendar Server with that in the directory server.

- The *uniuser* utility is used to manage user, resource, and event calendar accounts.

Another critical utility is necessary for resetting the password of a Calendar user, especially the SYSOP user. The *unioidconf* utility can be run at the command line of the operating system and prompt the Administrator for a new password for the SYSOP Oracle Calendar Administrator user. The main Administration account *cn=orcladmin* is required because the change is being made in the Oracle Internet Directory (OID) and not in a local database for the Calendar node. In Oracle Collaboration Suite 10*g*, changing the SYSOP password changes the SYSOP password on all the other nodes in the node network if they exist. The syntax is as follows:

```
$ORACLE_HOME/ocal/bin/unioidconf -setsysoppassword -D cn=orcladmin
```

It first prompts for a Bind password (the password for the cn=orcladmin account). Then it asks for the new Administrator password and then again for verification. The initial SYSOP password is set for a node during the Oracle Collaboration Suite 10*g* installation process.

Real-Time Collaboration (RTC) Administration

Oracle Real-Time Collaboration (RTC) is the real-time conferencing component of Oracle Collaboration Suite 10*g*. Oracle RTC enables users to publish their availability and presence to the RTC community of their site, send and receive instant messages between users, and participate in chat or web conferences. Oracle RTC can be configured to support both public and private conferences (meaning either type can be executed simultaneously), provide the ability to deliver online seminars, or (as is especially appealing to the technical and educational departments) enable live support/training that begins with a chat session and ends with a full Web conference, with desktop sharing between the support agent/trainer and customer/student.

Oracle RTC features can also integrate into company web sites, or multiple sites can be created that are customized specifically for company's lines of business, yet all running on the same RTC system.

Oracle RTC provides a platform for secure information exchange with built-in system scalability and high availability of all system servers. Administrative functions include the ability to monitor processes and system components in real-time capacity, quality of service, usage, system reports, and complete archiving of all conference and messaging data.

RTC Application Architecture

The architecture for the RTC application consists of three main components: Infrastructure, the Oracle Real-Time Collaboration Server, and, of course, the User Interface. Figure 12-24 provides a high-level definition of the RTC application.

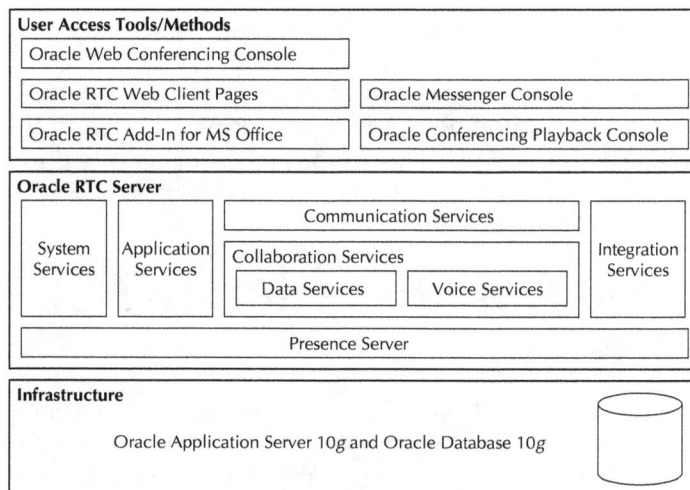

FIGURE 12-24. *Real-Time Collaboration application architecture*

I am going to discuss the architecture from the bottom up, since any good architecture begins with a solid foundation. At the foundation of the Oracle Collaboration Suite 10*g*—which includes the Real-Time Collaboration application—lives the Oracle Application Server 10*g* and Oracle Database 10*g* at the Infrastructure layer. The repository holds all the configuration information, user information, status information, etc., for all users and components of the Real-Time Collaboration application. Oracle Application Server 10*g* serves up the user interfaces and administration tools for the RTC functions.

At the next layer—the Application layer—is the Oracle RTC Server itself, which has several components that are the core of the RTC application function. Again, operating from the bottom up, the Presence Server provides information to all users about the status or presence of other users or groups in the RTC console, Instant Messaging, or Chat applications. The System Services module provides system administration and monitoring functions through properties; statistical reporting on such things as usage, performance, and availability; and process monitoring. The Application Services module provides the RTC conference scheduling and reporting functions presented through the RTC Web Client pages. The Collaborative Services component, composed of the Data Services and Voice Services functions (a later release will include Video Services as well), provides the functionality for sharing screen data for Web Conferences and text data for Chat and IM, as well as the ability to stream voice within Web Conferences and Voice Chat sessions. The Communications module handles all requests for connection—inside or outside firewalls—to/from the system to the Data and Voice Services functions. The Integration Services module provides the functionality for third-party applications, web sites, etc., to integrate with the RTC application functions.

The last layer of the RTC architecture is the User Access layer, which provides all the interfaces from the users to the RTC application and back. Inside the User Access layer are the Web Conferencing Console, Oracle Conferencing Playback Console, Messenger Console, and MS Office RTC Add-In, which are the "client" interfaces for accessing the RTC application functions. Users will also interact with the RTC application through the Web Client pages, which provide the core functionality of the RTC application for signing into RTC, scheduling and joining conferences, and managing download clients, as well as reviewing archived conference materials and recordings.

All of the layers of this architecture, along with all of their respective components and functions, work in unison to present the RTC functionality to the end user.

RTC Process Management

As with all other applications within the Oracle Collaboration Suite, the RTC application has its processes that must be running on the RTC Server (on the Applications Tier) in order to serve up the user functions and interfaces. Therefore, where there is process, there must be proper process management. This section will discuss the process management necessary for the Oracle Collaboration Suite 10*g* RTC application.

The processes running in the background of the Applications Tier server that support the RTC functions are listed in Table 12-4.

Component Type	Component Name	Description
confsvr	rtc-confsvr	Oracle Web Conferencing Server
OC4J	OC4J_imeeting	RTC OC4J Java Container
mx	rtc-mx	Multiplexer
connmgr	rtc-connmgr	RTC Client Connection Manager
imrtr	rtc-imrtr	ORACLE Presence Server, Oracle Messenger Router
rdtr	rtc-rdtr	The Redirector
voiceproxy	rtc-voiceproxy	The Voice Stream Proxy Server
rtcpm	rtcpm	RTC Process Manager
voiceconv	rtc-voiceconv	RTC Voice Conversion Server
docconv	rtc-docconv	RTC Document Conversion Server

TABLE 12-4. *RTC Application Component Processes*

The main command-line utility for managing the RTC processes is the *rtcctl* utility. Running *rtcctl* from the command line puts the Administrator in the RTC Control command-line prompt, where certain functions are valid and available. By typing **help** at the *rtcctl* prompt, you can review the valid *rtcctl* functions. Figure 12-25 shows the output from the *rtcctl* help command.

The *rtcctl* command can be used to get the status of the processes, start and stop the entire RTC Server (all processes) or individual processes, and manage other functions related to managing the RTC processes, all of which are displayed in Figure 12-25.

I want to at least run through a series of *rtcctl* commands to status, stop, and start a complete RTC instance, as well as individual components of an instance based upon different identification options. Figure 12-26 shows the individual commands and their associated output.

```
[oracle@app01 bin]$ pwd
/u01/oracle/product/10.1.2/ocs_1/apps/imeeting/bin
[oracle@app01 bin]$ ./rtcctl
rtcctl> help
Commands are:
start - Start a specified component or complete instance.
stop - Stop a specified component or complete instance.
getstate - Gets the state of a specified component or complete instance.
getPids - Returns the process identifiers for running iMeeting processes.
listComponents - List all the components.
listInstances - List all the instances.
setProperty - Get property for system/instance/component.
getProperty - Get property for system/instance/component.
getProperties - Gets all properties for system/instance/component.
getMonitorStats - Get monitor statistics for iMeeting components.
runTests - Run tests against midtier instances for service availability
modifyRole - modify role for a given user.
modifyMenu - modify menu for a given role.
addSysDialin - add a system dialin for voice conferencing.
deleteSysDialin - delete a system dialin.
getSysDialins - list all the system dialins.
updateHostName - updates the hostname, apachewebhost, apachetunnelhost, globalwebhost, ldaphost, instancename.
versions - list version information for a particular instance.
exit - Quit control shell.
quit - Quit control shell.
help - Prints this help message.
rtcctl>
```

FIGURE 12-25. *rtcctl command help option*

```
app01.re-questinc.com:1 (oracle)
oracle@app01:/u01/oracle/product/10.1.2/ocs_1/apps/imeeting/bin
File  Edit  View  Terminal  Go  Help
[oracle@app01 bin]$ ./rtcctl
rtcctl> getstate
ID      COMPONENT_NAME  TYPE        STATUS          NUM_PROCS
10007   rtc-connmgr     connmgr     UP              2
10000   rtc-confsvr     confsvr     UP              4
10006   rtc-imrtr       imrtr       ACTIVE-OK       1
10008   rtc-voiceproxy  voiceproxyUP                1
10004   rtcpm           rtcpm       UP              1
10003   rtc-rdtr        rdtr        UP              1
10002   rtc-mx          mx          UP              1
rtcctl> stop -cname rtc-imrtr
rtcctl> getstate
ID      COMPONENT_NAME  TYPE        STATUS          NUM_PROCS
10007   rtc-connmgr     connmgr     UP              2
10000   rtc-confsvr     confsvr     UP              4
10006   rtc-imrtr       imrtr       DOWN            0
10008   rtc-voiceproxy  voiceproxyUP                1
10004   rtcpm           rtcpm       UP              1
10003   rtc-rdtr        rdtr        UP              1
10002   rtc-mx          mx          UP              1
rtcctl> start -cid 10006
rtcctl> getstate
ID      COMPONENT_NAME  TYPE        STATUS          NUM_PROCS
10007   rtc-connmgr     connmgr     UP              2
10000   rtc-confsvr     confsvr     UP              4
10006   rtc-imrtr       imrtr       ACTIVE-STARTING1
10008   rtc-voiceproxy  voiceproxyUP                1
10004   rtcpm           rtcpm       UP              1
10003   rtc-rdtr        rdtr        UP              1
10002   rtc-mx          mx          UP              1
rtcctl> stop
rtcctl> getstate
ID      COMPONENT_NAME  TYPE        STATUS          NUM_PROCS
10007   rtc-connmgr     connmgr     DOWN            0
10000   rtc-confsvr     confsvr     DOWN            0
10006   rtc-imrtr       imrtr       DOWN            0
10008   rtc-voiceproxy  voiceproxyDOWN              0
10004   rtcpm           rtcpm       DOWN            0
10003   rtc-rdtr        rdtr        DOWN            0
10002   rtc-mx          mx          DOWN            0
rtcctl> start
```

FIGURE 12-26.   *rtcctl commands and output*

After starting the rtcctl Console, I execute a getstate command to retrieve the status of all the background processes. Notice in the example that everything is up. I then stop the imrtr process by using the –cname parameter to shut it down by name. I then status the RTC instance again to show the process is down. I then start the imrtr process again, this time by using the –cid parameter and listing the 10006 component ID number for the imrtr process. I status the RTC instance again to show the process is up again, and then I execute a stop command with no parameters, which stops the entire RTC instance. Executing a getstate shows the entire instance (all processes) to be down. I end the example with a start function, which then brings all the processes for the RTC instance back up as they were when I started the example.

As a final *rtcctl* command option to discuss, consider the modifyRole command. This command is used to modify the role, or level, of a particular RTC user. There are three role options for the parameter: enduser (default), businessmonitor, and businessadmin. The specific syntax for the function is rtcctl modifyRole –username <RTC User> –rolename <enduser, businessmonitor, businessadmin>. An example of modifying my username to be the Business Admin looks like this:

```
rtcctl modifyRole -username test.userz1 -rolename businessadmin
```

Before moving on, I just want to take a moment to explain the various roles within the RTC application. There are three possible roles, which are mutually exclusive, meaning a user can only be assigned one role at any given time. The list and associated definitions are as follows:

- **enduser**   You can use any of the standard RTC features, such as scheduling a conference, uploading materials, and viewing conference and instant messaging archives.

- **businessmonitor**   You can use the standard RTC features, and can also view the Monitor and Reports tabs to monitor current conferences and see reports regarding conference and messaging history, component usage, system problems, security information, and user feedback about conferences.

- **businessadmin**   You can use any of the previously listed features and can also view the Site and System tabs to create and manage RTC sites and view statistics about all instances and components of the system.

RTC Administration Specifics

The administration requirements for the RTC application are really pretty minimal. This application basically runs itself. Good monitoring and reporting functions are available to provide an Administrator with information for managing the RTC environment. It is a good idea to review the information provided periodically in order to ensure that the RTC instance/server(s) aren't consistently being overtaxed. With RTC, even if an organization starts out with a small footprint of RTC users, over time the popularity and range of uses for the RTC applications will expand, in many cases exponentially. I guarantee that productivity seekers will adopt Web Conferencing just as they adopted web searches instead of paper phone book lookups! Having said that, it is extremely important to monitor the RTC instance so usage does not get out of hand, or if it does, an Administrator knows about it early enough to either change behavior or implement another RTC instance on another server.

The Administrator user (like the one I created in the preceding section) will have access to management and monitoring tools right through that user's RTC Web Client pages. Figure 12-27 shows the tabs from a user's RTC Web Client that was granted the businessadmin role through rtcctl.

Notice the user gets the Monitor, Reports, Sites, and System tabs at the end of the tab list. Figure 12-28 shows the Reports tab on the RTC Web Client page and its many options for reporting information regarding the RTC instance. This and other information like it are extremely important to Administrators charged with keeping performance and availability of the RTC application at acceptable levels for the end user community.

For my last example regarding RTC administration, refer to Figure 12-29, which is a sample System tab on the RTC Web Client page showing the status for the various components of the RTC system.

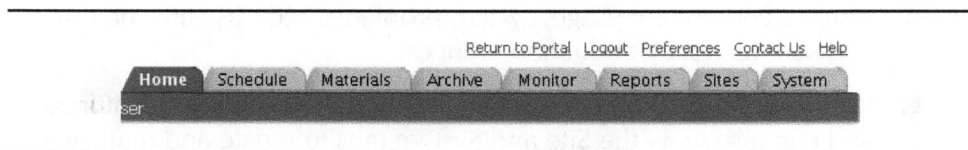

FIGURE 12-27. *Tabs that display for Business Admin role user*

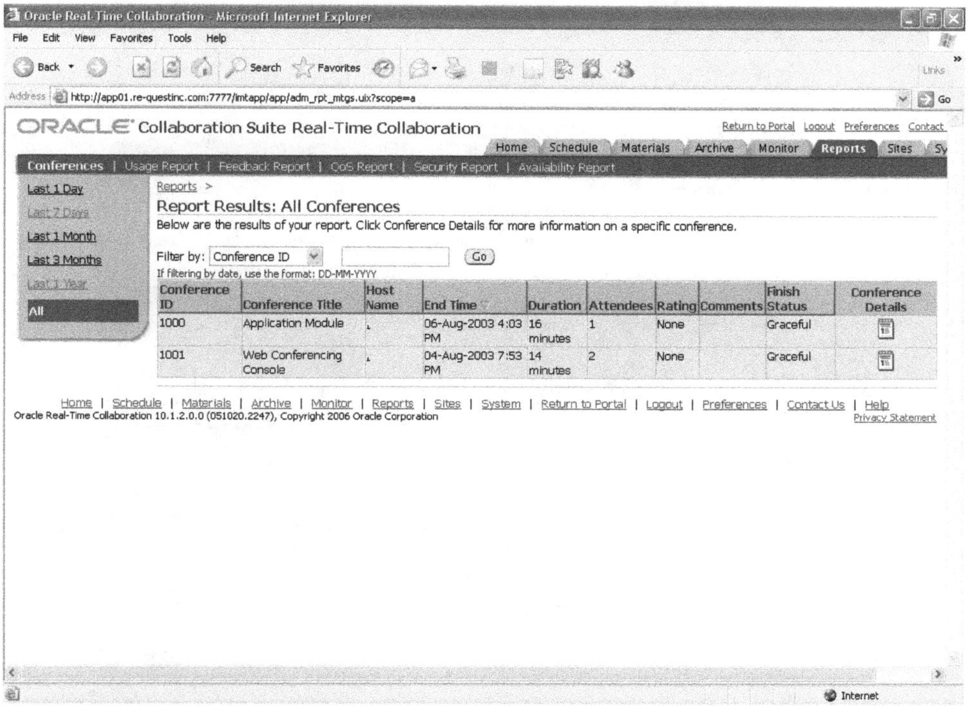

FIGURE 12-28. *Reports tab options for Business Admin*

From this page you can drill into each of the system components, whether they are a usage statistic, a system property, or site Type target. There are a plethora of possibilities on this page for reviewing and monitoring the entire RTC instance, including everything from the background processes down to individual RTC users. So my best advice is for an Administrator to spend a lot of time reviewing the information available here and understand its best fit into the way he/she manages the specific RTC environment.

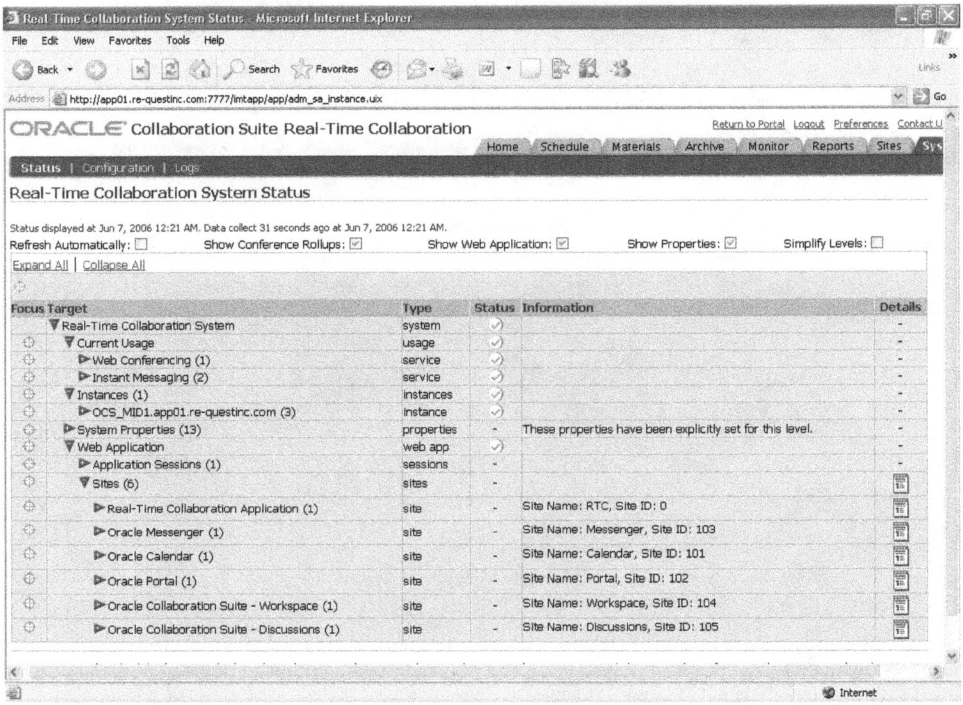

FIGURE 12-29. *RTC administration: System Status page*

Summary

Application Administration is a critical and valuable component to the overall process for managing Oracle Collaboration Suite 10*g*. While the preceding information is a good start in terms of important administrative tasks, this chapter only scratches the surface in terms of the various areas to manage and maintain in the product. Oracle has published Administrator Guides for each of the application components, as well as providing Oracle Education classes for various Administrator roles. I strongly suggest reviewing the Administrator Guides as well as keeping them close at hand to assist in the event of an issue. I also suggest reviewing the class profiles and determining if taking these classes is worthwhile for gaining additional knowledge.

PART
IV

Oracle Content
Services

CHAPTER
13

Content Services
Functional Overview

Our days are a kaleidoscope. Every instant a change
takes place in the contents. New harmonies, new contrasts,
new combinations of every sort. Nothing ever happens
twice alike. The most familiar people stand each moment
in some new relation to each other, to their work,
to surrounding objects. The most tranquil house,
with the most serene inhabitants, living upon
the utmost regularity of system, is yet
exemplifying infinite diversities.

—Henry Ward Beecher

Oracle Content Services is both new and old. It is "old" in the sense that portions of the capability have existed for years under another name (i.e., "Oracle Files,") but, also, "new" in terms of the full scope of the current functionality *and* the way that it has been integrated and deployed as part of the Oracle Collaboration Suite 10*g* product. But regardless, the current name is extremely appropriate, since Content Services is not simply another widget thrown into the mix of Oracle Collaboration Suite 10*g*. As the word "Services" implies, Oracle Content Services really is a set of services that, collectively, allows for the creation, use, and management of intelligent containers for the storage and accessibility of unstructured—document or file—data. That sounds an awful lot like any garden-variety "shared drive" on your local area network (excluding the "intelligent" aspect, of course), and yes, there are some similarities. In fact, Content Services does attempt to project the same general hierarchical folder/file paradigm to the end user through various interfaces. Beneath that simple comparison, however, is where the similarities end.

From the earliest versions of the "Oracle Files" product, the objective has been the same: store unstructured data along with associated metadata inside an Oracle database to facilitate the superior search, management, scalability, and recoverability capabilities that are inherently available to *any* data that resides within an Oracle database—in effect, using database storage to provide for traditional "file server" storage. Of course this isn't a trivial exercise, since databases are organized to store data in rows and columns of tables while file servers store data in tree-structured directories (folders within folders). Aside from that challenge, the issues of user identification, file ownership, and security quickly emerge as related requirements when seeking to replace the common file server with a database—not to mention how to bridge the gap from SQL*Net (the database's native network communication protocol) to the Windows, Unix, or Mac native formats expected by users and applications alike. All of those challenges can be overcome by using various Oracle products in concert (i.e., a database, an LDAP server, drive mapping software, etc.). Since virtually all the necessary technology stack components are already being used within the Oracle Collaboration Suite 10*g* product, the integration of "Oracle Files" capabilities under the new moniker of "Content Services" is a natural fit and not merely something "bolted on" to fill a gap in functionality.

And while it is helpful, at first, to think of the Content Services component of Oracle Collaboration Suite 10*g* as a database-based file server, one would seriously understate the true value of the product unless the full range of the Content Services' functional capabilities are understood.

Content Services Objects

In order to understand how Content Services works (and what capabilities are available), you need to become familiar with a vocabulary of terms that have specific meanings within the context of Content Services. This is no different from understanding what is meant by the term "drive" or "directory/folder" or "file" when describing the use of a traditional file server. Content Services also organizes and manages content using those terms, but it also involves new objects and concepts that might require some explanation. The most important object types/terms to understand include:

- Site/Realm
- Category
- Container
- Group
- Library
- Quota
- Folder
- Archive
- Access roles

Site/Realm

During an Identity Management installation (OID/DIP/DAS/SSO—typically as part of the default Oracle Collaboration Suite 10g/iAS installer run), a single identity management domain is specified in an LDAP format (e.g., dc=testdomain,dc=com). And while the term "domain" might seem intuitive, since we're used to referring to, say, "testdomain.com" as a domain, the term "realm" might be a new one. It is, however, simply a synonym for the term "domain." It is, in plain English, a high-level organizational grouping of users. It might refer to an entire company, a geographical or functional division, or even just an arbitrary segment of the complete user population within an organization. But in all cases, each Oracle Identity Management installation must have one or more domains/realms defined. In most cases there will be only one (the initial domain specified during installation), but it is possible to create multiple domains/subdomains/realms within a single OID/LDAP directory.

Within Content Services, an Identity Management Realm is the basis for the "Site" object. Sites are related to Realms on a strict 1:1 basis (there may only be one Site per Realm), and a Site forms the "root" of all other Content Services objects for the related Realm/Domain (i.e., Containers, Libraries, Folders, etc.). And while a given Oracle Collaboration Suite 10g/Content Services installation may host/service multiple Sites concurrently, users defined in different Realms/Sites may not share access to each other's content. Each site is a separate, stand-alone island of resources that has its own overall disk quota and set of administrators. From a functional perspective, the Site object is uninteresting. It is merely the root of all other subdivisions of content. Creating more than one Site does, however, involve defining the additional realm to the Single Sign-On server (SSO) and the qualification of usernames when accessing Content Services resources. Creating multiple Sites is not recommended unless absolutely required. If you need them, you should consult Chapter 9 ("Managing Oracle Content Services Sites") of the Oracle Content Services Administrator's Guide.

Category

Unlike Sites, which map to Realms and are very intuitive because of preexisting exposure to the concept of a domain, a Content Services "Category" is probably a very new concept. Categories are, fundamentally, the mechanism by which metadata is associated with the unstructured (document) data that is stored within Content Services. Categories contain attributes ("fields," if you like) and may be made Required or Optional. If the Category is required for a given document, then the document may not be stored unless the user supplies the necessary Category-specified metadata. This is the first example of how Content Services goes beyond the capability of a traditional file server–based shared drive. Note that, first of all, Categories to satisfy any requirement may be defined, from scratch, by a Category Administrator—Content Services does not lock you into a fixed set of static (or even "flex") fields to capture additional descriptive information about documents. Next, the metadata captured per the Category definition is stored with the document in the database and is indexed and searchable. Finally, the metadata is also available for routing, approval, and any other programmatic purpose. That goes way beyond the meager "create date, size, etc." metadata typically associated with simple file system–based documents. Categories may be associated with Containers, Libraries, or Folders and can be applied to individual Files (documents).

Container

Containers are special-purpose Folder objects that may only contain either 1) other Containers or 2) Library objects. If not created within another Container, a Container must be created as a direct child object of the Site itself. And since Library objects haven't been described yet, it wouldn't seem that Containers do much, since (aside from Libraries) they can hold only other Containers. In terms of where they fit in an object hierarchy, that's pretty much true, but Containers exist to capture configuration information/rules that are intended to apply to all objects that, in turn, are created within the Container. So, for example, user access may be specified at the Container level. (This can be done either for individual users or for a Group of users. A user Group, within the context of Content Services, is not the same as an LDAP group, but it functions in the same manner. Once defined by a Content Services user, a Group may be used in lieu of an individual username when specifying Sharing rules.) Once access is granted at the Container level, all of the "children" of the container will "inherit" the permissions. But Sharing rules are but one of several important rules that may, optionally, be defined at the Container level. Others include

- Associating Categories with Files
- Specifying Versioning rules

- Specifying Records Management rules

- Specifying Workflow rules

And while the meaning of some of those configuration types may not be clear at this point, it should be sufficient to understand that Containers allow the definition of "default" settings at a high level in the object hierarchy. If not overridden at a lower level, the values specified within a Container definition allow for consistent treatment of similar documents without the need for tedious manual specification of each possible option value. Containers may only be created/modified/deleted by users that have been granted the "Container Administrator" role.

Library

Library objects are similar, in some respects, to Container objects in the sense that they allow for the specification of the same configuration settings as may be defined at the Container level. And since a Library must be defined within a Container, it will (by default) inherit the values of any configured values of the parent Container. If the Container does not provide for a default—or if the Container allows the default to be overridden—then different configuration values may be specified at the Library level. So, for example, the Container may specify that no Workflow approval rules are necessary. But when creating a new Library within that Container, the owner might decide that documents to be stored in the new Library should, in fact, require Workflow-based approvals. So general rules specified at the Container level may be changed at the Library level—unless the rule is defined as mandatory or locked at the Container level. This might seem like an awful lot of administrative plumbing to go through before even getting to the point of creating a simple Folder, but what appears to be a time-consuming effort for the first few folders quickly becomes a huge productivity enhancer when hundreds of users are creating thousands of objects using well-thought-out (and centrally managed) rules. Again, we see a degree of configurability and fine-grained control that traditional file server–based storage could never come close to matching.

Library objects are not, however, merely "subcontainers." They also have some additional attributes:

- Associated disk space quotas

- Trash and recycle bins

- Additional Folder privileges (end users with rights to use the Library may create/rename/delete Folders within the Library at will)

Depending upon how one chooses to configure Content Services, requests for new Libraries may be submitted online by end users and the request routed, via Workflow, to approvers. As Library space usage approaches the Quota limits, Quota Administrators can be automatically notified (so as to, possibly, increase the Quota). But regardless, once the Library's Quota limit has been reached, no new content may be saved to Folders within the Library. And once again (and not to sound like a broken record), we see how Content Services handles resources better than traditional file server–based solutions in the way Quotas at the Library level allow for more timely notifications of space issues rather than waiting until an entire storage device is close to being filled.

Folder

The Folder object is created within a Library, and as a Library may inherit configuration rules from a Container, a Folder may inherit configuration rules from its parent Library (and/or override optional defaults as well). Unlike Libraries, however, Folders have no Quotas or Trash bins associated with them. Users may also create and manage Folders without formal review/approval processes (all of that has been handled at the Container and Library levels). Content Services Folder objects serve, humbly, the same simple functions as Directories/Folders anywhere else—organization and access control (determining who may share the contents of the folder). Folders, then, contain the Files (documents) themselves.

Archive

Recall that Library objects contain user-defined Folders and a system-created Trash folder (or Recycle Bin) object. When a user deletes a File or Folder within a Library, the content is moved to the Library's Trash folder instead of being physically removed from the database. While the file(s) reside within the Trash folder, the disk space they consume continues to count against the Library's Quota. The user may restore files from the Trash folder at any time without assistance/approval. Once they are deleted from the Trash folder, however, the situation changes. Once again, the content is moved rather than deleted, but this time the disk space consumed by the content is no longer counted against the Library's Quota. The second difference is that the user may no longer restore the content without the assistance of the Site's Content Administrator, since the data now resides within the Archive (a second-level Trash folder managed at the Site level). Archive data may be converted to read-only storage (as BFILEs) before being totally purged from the system after an expiration period specified by the Content Administrator. Whether space consumed by the Archive should count against the Site-level Quota is also configurable (as is the frequency with which purges of the Archive occur).

Access Roles

Not to be confused with Oracle Database roles, but functioning in a similar way, Content Services uses the concept of roles (or access roles) to segregate and distribute responsibility for the various functions and components of the product. I have made reference to some of these roles already in describing Content Services objects. For example, the "Content Administrator" is just an ordinary Oracle Collaboration Suite 10g user that has been granted an access role to permit the user to perform restricted operations. There are thirteen roles broken down between "Site Only Level" and "Site and Container Level" types.

- Site-Only level
    - Site Administrator
    - Role Administrator
    - User Administrator
    - Category Administrator
    - Records Administrator

- Site and Container levels
    - Quota Administrator
    - Configuration Administrator
    - Library Administrator
    - Library Creator
    - Container Administrator
    - Container Viewer
    - Security Administrator
    - Content Administrator

Upon installation of Content Services, the orcladmin user has global access and may grant all of these roles to other users. Each role must be granted to at least one user but, obviously, may also be granted to more than one. Refer to the Oracle Content Services Application Administrator's Guide for complete details concerning each role.

As you gain an understanding of the Content Services Object types (and their relationships to one another), much of the essence of what Content Services is and how it works necessarily emerges naturally. If you've understood what has been presented thus far, then the remaining macro descriptions of Content Services features should be fairly simple to grasp.

Content Services Features

While many of the core capabilities of Content Services have already been discussed, a number of core and optional features require a minimal level of discussion, even though detailed descriptions are probably best left to the original documentation set.

Integration with Antivirus Software

As a separately licensed and installed option, the Symantec Antivirus Scan Engine may be configured to scan files (documents) uploaded to Content Services. If installed, it need not scan all content. In fact, scanning may be specified on a case-by-case basis depending on the MIME type of the file.

If viruses are detected, the file will be placed in a quarantined state and be unavailable until such time as a new virus signature file is downloaded and a repair/cleansing operation can render the file safe for use.

Records Management

Although a separately licensed option, the Records Management product ships with and installs with Content Services (although it is installed in a disabled state). Records Management permits full records life cycle management based upon formal policies (known as "File Plans") to ensure the authenticity and reliability of records, to control their use, and also to ensure that such records are not deleted too soon or retained for too long. Note that the term "record" is used as opposed to "file" or "document," since a record could be something like an email message. In fact, as of release 10.1.2.3 of Oracle Collaboration Suite 10g, Oracle supplies a Records Management Add-in for Outlook that allows email messages to be easily transformed into Records and uploaded to Content Services. In today's regulatory compliance–aware business environment the Records Management option provides a disciplined means of limiting corporate liability.

Data Aging, Archiving, and Near-Lining

Data uploaded to and managed by Content Services is, by default, stored in Binary Large Object (or "BLOB") columns of relational tables, providing for the greatest degree of performance, manageability, and recoverability. This setting does, however, come at a higher price than for some alternatives (including slower disks or "write once read many"—WORM—optical storage devices). Content Services may, optionally, be configured to take advantage of an advanced capability of the Oracle Database known as BFILEs. BFILEs allow content to be moved outside of the database into OS files while retaining pointers within the database so that the information may be accessed (albeit more slowly and with some restrictions) as if the data still physically resided within the database. The term "data aging," then, refers to configuring Content Services to move data that has not been accessed within a specified time frame from expensive internal BLOB storage to less-costly external BFILE storage. Once configured, the process is automatic and transparent to end users. Likewise, content that has been moved to the Site Archive (content deleted by users) may be configured to move to BFILE storage after a configured period of time (i.e., data "Archiving" BFILE support). Finally, when the Records Management option is licensed, integration with third-party "near-line" storage subsystems (Network Appliance SnapLock and EMC Centera) allows for completely automated end-to-end implementation of File Plans (including movement of BLOB data to secondary BFILE storage *and* the removal/destruction of said data once the retention period/policy has been satisfied).

Automatic and Manual Versioning, Check-in/Check-out, Locking

Versioning of files allows for the preservation of copies of files as they appeared in each distinct prior form. A new version may be Manually created (i.e., upon request) or Automatically created (i.e., whenever a changed file is saved to the Content Services repository). Checking out a version-enabled file will automatically result in the file being locked against update by other users. Changes made to a checked-out file do not result in a new version until the file is checked in again. Checking in the file also automatically releases the lock. Files may also be locked and unlocked manually by a user (whether the file is version-enabled or not) and automatically by Content Services during Workflow-enabled Approval processing.

Workflow/BPEL Integration

Both Oracle Workflow and BPEL (Business Process Execution Language) provide facilities for the definition of business process automation rules. Content Services comes with predefined (or "seeded") Workflow definitions to support both parallel and serial approval of various standard operations (for example, check-in, copy, delete, move, read, or upload of files). Additionally, JDeveloper may be used to define custom BPEL-based workflow definitions. Note, however, that custom BPEL-based workflows may only be deployed and run against the default Site (an important consideration in deciding whether to create multiple Realms/Sites). BPEL support means that events occurring within Content Services can, via Web Services processing as part of a BPEL workflow, result in processing elsewhere within and/or outside of the Oracle Collaboration Suite 10*g* environment—or even outside of the enterprise. This is, once again, an example of what becomes possible once data and processing move inside of the Oracle technology stack.

Searching

Capturing both documents and metadata within the database means that all of the industrial-strength search and retrieval capabilities of Oracle's database product may be brought to bear in order to locate desired content. There are basically two types of search capabilities available for Content Services data:

- **Quick Filename Search**   A search based on a partial or complete filename

- **Advanced Search**   A search that can look for an arbitrary search term in both the metadata and the content of the document files themselves

Searches of the document content are processed, internally, using the database's "Text" option (formerly known as the "Context" and "InterMedia" options).

With the exception of a discussion of the various Protocol Servers that may be used to access Content Services storage (i.e., upload, download, edit-in-place files), virtually every feature of Oracle Collaboration Suite 10*g* Content Services has now been presented.

Protocol Servers/ Content Services Access

Now that you understand the internal architecture and features of Content Services module, our focus turns to the mechanisms that are available to move files (and metadata) into and out of the Content Services Datastore. Most of the available methods fall under the generic heading of "protocol servers," but additionally, a complete Java API also exists in order to permit programmatic access to virtually all of the functionality previously discussed (including, of course, the ability to upload/download content in a user-prescribed manner). See the Content Services Application Developer's Guide and the Content Services Web Services Java API Reference (Javadoc) for details concerning coding directly to the APIs. Most users, however, will find that one or more of the ready-made "protocol server" interfaces will meet their needs. The "out of the box" protocols are:

- HTTP

- FTP and FTPS (FTP, Secure)

- WebDAV

Each protocol (and related tools) will now be examined.

HTTP (Hypertext Transfer Protocol)

The Oracle Content Services User Interface (http:// <host:port>/content/app) is the default user interface for Content Services. This client is entirely HTML- and JavaScript-based and permits the user to perform the full range of Content Services functions. Because this interface is entirely browser-based, it may be accessed from a variety of browsers and operating system platforms.

FTP and FTPS (File Transfer Protocol)

Any FTP client (running under Unix, Windows, Mac, etc.) may be used to transfer files to/from the Content Services repository. If the FTP protocol is used, then because of the inherent insecurity of the protocol, a password is required (each user must choose their own FTP password unless Anonymous FTP is configured). If Content Services has been configured to support FTPS (not to be confused with SFTP), then passwords are not required. Note that FTPS configuration requires the use of certificates and wallets. And, whether using FTP or FTPS, documents with Categories containing required attributes cannot be uploaded via these protocols, since (under FTP) no user interface exists to allow entry of the required information.

WebDAV (Web-Based Distributed Authoring and Versioning)

The WebDAV protocol allows, under Windows, the definition of a Web Folder to access a Content Services Datastore. To configure a Web Folder, simply run the Add Network Place Wizard under My Network Places in

Windows Explorer. Enter http:// <host:port>/content/dav as the network location and supply your Single Sign-On username and password. Once the wizard completes, you'll be able to move content to and from Content Services as easily as you move data between any other Windows Explorer folders. Again, as with FTP protocols, functionality is limited to uploading and downloading files without metadata requirements that cannot be met by the UI.

Oracle Drive

A second means of accessing the Content Services repository using the WebDAV protocol is via the Oracle Drive application. Oracle Drive is a 20MB Windows client that must be downloaded from http:// <host:port>/welcome/download.jsp and installed locally. Once installed and configured, the client presents the Content Services Datastore as an additional drive letter to Windows. So, as in the case of the Web Folder approach, manipulation of remote objects directly from Windows Explorer is possible. But in addition to Windows Explorer, the Content Services Datastore will appear to be a native Windows volume to *any* program running on the Windows client. And if all of that isn't enough of a reason to download and install Oracle Drive, copies of Content Services data can also be made available while the Windows client is "offline" (i.e., while disconnected from the Content Services Datastore) and automatically resynchronized once the connection is reestablished.

Summary

This chapter opened with a description of Content Services as "a set of services that, collectively, allows for the creation, use, and management of intelligent containers for the storage and accessibility of unstructured data." Hopefully that now sounds like a concise description of the feature-rich and powerful set of capabilities that is Content Services.

CHAPTER
14

Content Services
Technical Overview

Lots of folks confuse bad management with destiny.

—Kin Hubbard

As you read in the preceding chapter, Oracle Content Services is not a single, new, monolithic product. Much of the intelligence behind the product is drawn from the technology stack upon which it is built (i.e., the Oracle Database, Oracle Text, Oracle Workflow, and Oracle Application Server). If you're an old hand at dealing with those products, then much here will seem familiar. But additionally, there are components that are designed only to implement Content Services as a product. With the exception of the Oracle Drive tool, which is a Windows application that may be installed on end users' PCs, virtually every other Content Services–specific component runs on the Applications/Middle Tiers and is managed via the Enterprise Manager Collaboration Suite Control. Understanding those components (and how to manage and monitor them) is the focus of this chapter.

Architectural Components

As was the case from the functional perspective, Content Services brings with it a number of new terms that need to be understood. In many cases the terms sound familiar but have a Content Services–specific meaning. It is, therefore, vital that you understand the terminology for each architectural component (and its function) before attempting to make any changes in the environment. The most important component types/terms to understand include

- Oracle Application Server Middle Tiers
- OC4J Containers
- Nodes
- Services, servers, and agents
- Domains

Oracle Application Server Middle Tiers

Recall that Oracle's Application Server (iAS) is one of the key architectural components of Oracle Collaboration Suite 10*g* (generally) and Content Services (in particular). In general, Oracle Application Server installations consist of components installed and running on two (or more) different computers (but it is possible—if not recommended—to make do with a single computer). One computer serves as the Infrastructure Tier, which hosts OID/SSO and the infrastructure metadata repository database. The same database may also provide storage for Oracle Collaboration Suite 10*g*, Portal, and other applications. The second (and perhaps third, fourth, . . . *n*th) server is configured as a Middle Tier and serves as the platform to deploy and run applications code (typically written in Java). Applications like Portal and Content Services make heavy use of Middle Tier servers in order to execute the code (Java-based and otherwise) that implements their functionality. Virtually *all* of our attention in this chapter will be focused on the different Content Management components that are deployed to (and run on) one or more Middle Tier computers. Please note that in each case that the physical hardware that is home to Middle Tier software installation(s) has been referenced, the term *computer* has been used. This is intentional, since in a Content Services context, terms like "node" and "server" have quite specific meanings—and they are *not* synonyms for "computer."

OC4J Containers

OC4J (Oracle Containers for Java) Containers are J2EE-compliant runtime environments for applications written in Java and deployed using standard XML-resource descriptors. OC4J Containers play a prominent role within Oracle Application Server, Portal, and Oracle Collaboration Suite 10*g* Content Services. And while the application code deployed to a given OC4J Container may be unique, remember that the containers themselves are industry-standard infrastructure components. The containers function, in some respects, like operating systems for Java applications—they're merely the context within which a program runs. But unlike an operating system, which is in control of all of the resources of a computer, an OC4J Container is configured with limits within which it must exist (primarily memory limits). Also, unlike an operating system, it is common to create multiple OC4J Containers on a given computer. And that is precisely the case with

Content Services, since a minimum of two OC4J Containers is created during installation of the product (even though one is disabled/shut down by default). The important thing to understand is that OC4J Containers are pieces of infrastructure delivered by Oracle Application Server itself, they are created and run on Middle Tier computers, and they serve as "virtual machines" for the execution of Java Application code. While Content Services deploys a good deal of its code within OC4J Containers, they, themselves, are not part of Content Services.

Nodes

Recall that within the context of any discussion of Content Services architecture, the term *node* does *not* refer to a piece of computer hardware. It is indeed unfortunate that Oracle chose to assign a unique, product-specific meaning to such a common term. But "it is what it is," and the sooner one gets used to using the term in the way that Oracle intends, the better. Okay, so what's a "node" within Content Services? The answer, in a nutshell, is: "a bundle of application code that implements Content Services functionality." Recall from the OC4J Container discussion that OC4J Containers are where J2EE application code is deployed and executed. Some Content Services nodes include such applications (HTTP nodes), while the other major type of node (the Regular node) does not require an associated OC4J Container. The two major types of node are

- **HTTP nodes** During installation of Content Services, by default, two different HTTP nodes are created: one to provide the application code for the core Content Services features and another to provide the application code for the Records Management option. Note that although the node to support Records Management is installed, it is disabled/shut down by default, since it is a separately licensed product/option. In both cases, however, HTTP-type nodes deploy code to OC4J Containers and become known, commonly, by the names of their associated OC4J Containers (by default, OC4J_Content and OC4J_RM).

- **Regular node** A single Regular node is created and deployed to the Middle Tier during installation of Content Services. Unlike HTTP nodes, however, there is no associated OC4J Container. Even though the Regular node still contains application code, it just doesn't require a J2EE Container of its own.

Different types of servers (again, not as in "computers") run on the different types of nodes. For example, the FTP and FTPS protocol servers described in Chapter 13 run from the Regular node, while the WebDAV protocol (supporting Web Folders and Oracle Drive) is implemented by code running in the HTTP OC4J_Content node. But in all cases, nodes form the first meaningful units of configurable, manageable, and monitorable code that implement Content Services.

No more than one instance of each of these types of node may be created within any given Middle Tier. If your installation includes multiple Middle Tier installations, each Middle Tier may have its own set of nodes installed. That is not to say that all servers and agents (to be discussed) may run in more than a single node—quite the contrary. In most cases a given server or agent must run on one and only one node—although the nodes they run within needn't all reside within the same Middle Tier installation on the same computer. This allows for processing to be distributed among a number of different computers in order to provide for superior scalability and manageability.

Services, Servers, and Agents

We began by drilling down from the computer to the Oracle Application Server Middle Tier software installation, into J2EE Containers, and finally into nodes, which, as we saw, are bundles of Content Services application code. We've even seen that there are different types of nodes and that they may be distributed among multiple computers. It is now time to descend once again and to examine the major components of a node, namely: services, servers, and agents.

- **Service** Upon node start-up, a *service* is started that creates and manages shared resources within the node (such as credential managers, database connection pools, and committed data cache). Servers and agents running within the same node make use of the resources provided by the service.

- **Servers** More properly called "protocol servers," *servers* listen on network ports for (and service) requests made by client applications (FTP, etc.). Refer to Chapter 13 for a more detailed discussion of protocol servers. The FTP protocol server would, for example, accept a connection request from an end user, use service-provided resources to validate the user's identity, and then also to store the user's files in the database.

- **Agents** *Agents* are fundamentally different from servers in the sense that they are not accessed from outside of the node. Instead, they more closely resemble the Oracle Database's asynchronous background processes, with each agent responsible for some specific management task. There are many different types of agents defined, and—with the exception of the Service Warmup and Statistics agent types—any given agent may run only within a single node (but that node may exist within any Middle Tier installation). Agents are similar to servers, however, in the sense that they make use of the shared resources made available by the node's service component.

All three node components are configurable using the Enterprise Manager Collaboration Suite Control. Note that both servers and agents (as defined here) are referred to generically as "servers" within Collaboration Suite Control. Each is identified correctly with a value in the Type column of the node's Service and Server administration page, where they are both managed in the same way.

Domains

A Content Services *domain* is defined, simply, as all of the nodes defined within all of the Middle Tiers for a Content Services installation. Leveraging the capabilities of the Oracle Process Manager and Notification Server (OPMN), the entire Content Services domain may be started, stopped, and/or restarted from a central location and with a single command (whether using the "opmnctl" CLI or the Collaboration Suite Control web interface).

It is absolutely vital to understand the architecture of Content Services, what each component does, and how each component is related to the others. If you've understood the material presented to this point, you'll be well equipped to grasp the remaining topics. If some of the terms are still confusing to you (i.e., if the distinction between "server," "node," and "computer" isn't crystal-clear), you should go back and review the definitions once again.

Administration Overview

Initial installation, configuration, monitoring, and tuning are the major administrative activities associated with Content Services. Thankfully, the installation and initial configuration of the product is largely automatic, and so it is easy to get up and running without lengthy preparation. Additional (optional) components—such as the Anti-Virus scanning engine or the Records Management feature—may be added at any time, if desired. Such tasks (if necessary) are one-time activities best performed after a careful review of the relevant documentation. As an overview of administration topics this chapter will focus, instead, on understanding the tools and concepts necessary for the routine, ongoing care, and feeding of Content Services, beginning with the primary administrative interface: Collaboration Suite Control.

Collaboration Suite Control

Really just the Oracle Enterprise Manager Application Server Console enhanced to allow for administration of the Content Services domain (i.e., all nodes and associated subcomponents), Collaboration Suite Control's interface and general operational principles are instantly recognizable to anyone who has used Oracle 10g Enterprise Manager tools previously. Completely web-based, the tool is portable, since it may be run from Windows, Linux/Unix, etc. And while it makes Content Services administration an easy visual task, behind the scenes, operations like node or service startup/shutdown/restart are still being carried out by the same command line–accessible utilities (OPMN, DCM, etc.), which is convenient if one prefers to skip the GUI and manage the application directly (or write scripts to, say, automatically start and stop the environment on computer startup/shutdown).

From the Collaboration Suite Control Home page, access to Content Services domain components (nodes, services, and servers) is via the "Content" System Component. Figure 14-1 shows the Collaboration Suite Control Home page with both "Content" and "OC4J_Content" shown in the list of System Components running on the Applications Tier for this sample instance.

Clicking that link displays the Content Services Home page, which contains a list of each node within the domain. Each node may be started/ stopped/restarted individually or the entire domain (all nodes on all Middle Tiers on all servers) may be started/stopped/restarted as a unit. This page also has links to Domain Properties; Performance pages; and node, service, and server configurations (all of which will be discussed). Additionally, links

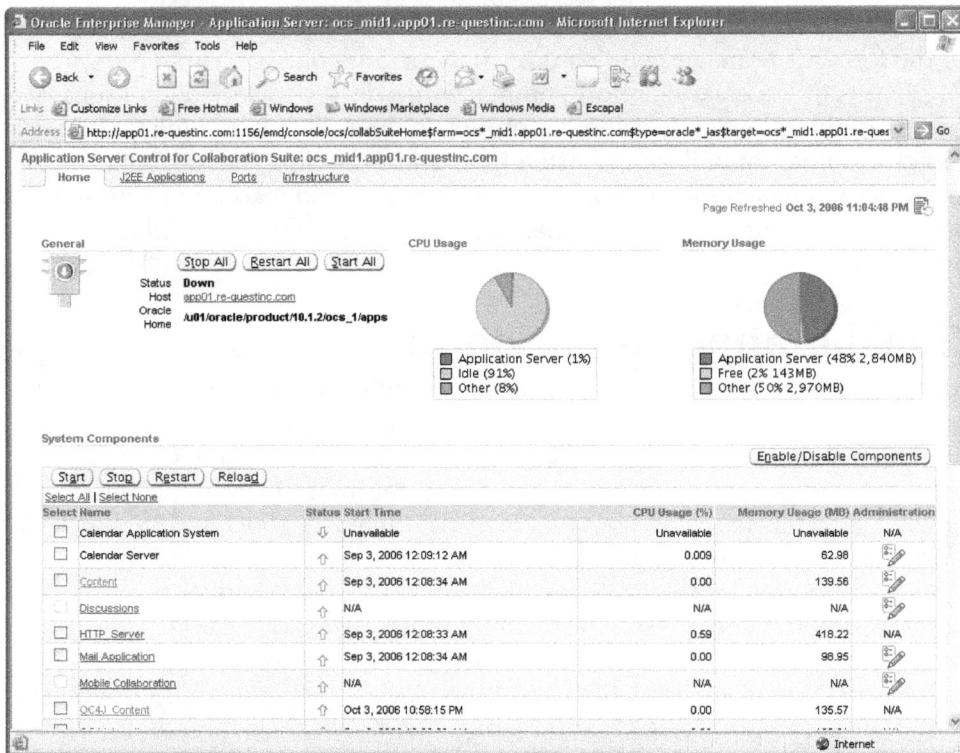

FIGURE 14-1. *Collaboration Suite Control Home page*

to allow Site, Format, Retention Hardware, Storage Management, and Custom Workflow administration are also available. Figure 14-2 shows the Content Services Home page in Collaboration Suite Control.

Note that while the OC4J Containers supporting the HTTP nodes can be administered from the Collaboration Suite Control Home Page as seen in Figure 14-1 (listed as peers of the "Content" System Component), they are also listed and available for administration on the Content Services Home page, as seen in Figure 14-2.

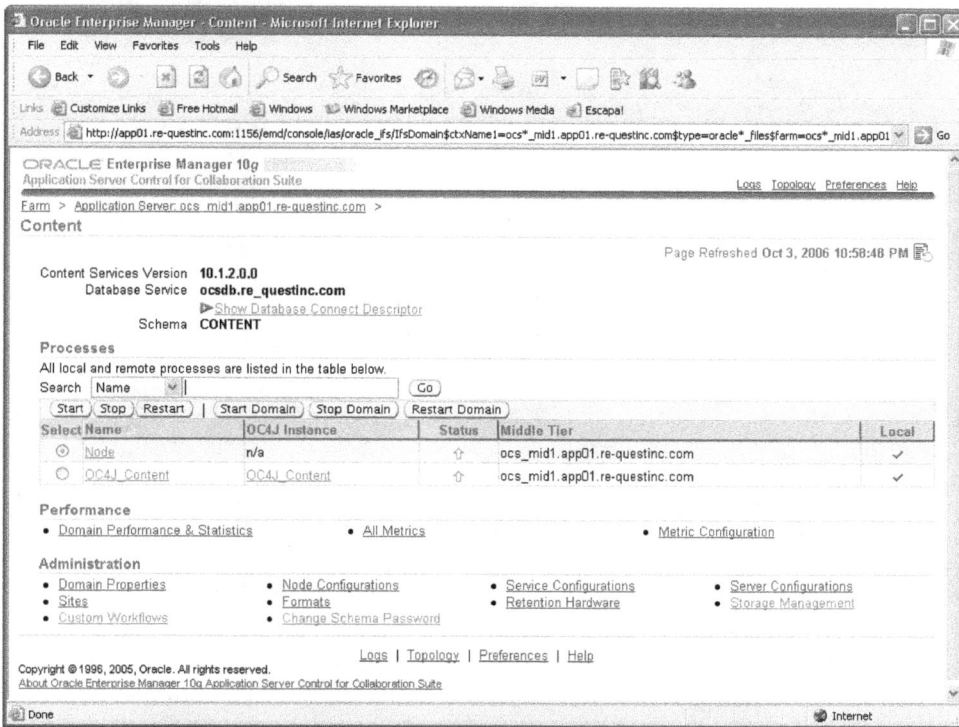

FIGURE 14-2. *Content Services Home page*

Domain Properties

This link displays a list of all configuration properties defined at (and that apply to) the domain as a whole. Think of them as functioning like database p-file parameters. Some (but not all) may be changed, but saved changes will not take effect until the domain has been restarted. Many property names are very descriptive and self-explanatory, but none should be changed without a full understanding of the impact. Some administration tasks (such as, for example, installing the Anti-Virus engine or setting-up BFILE Aging and Archiving functionality) involve setting Domain Properties. The point is that other activities will lead you to the Domain Properties

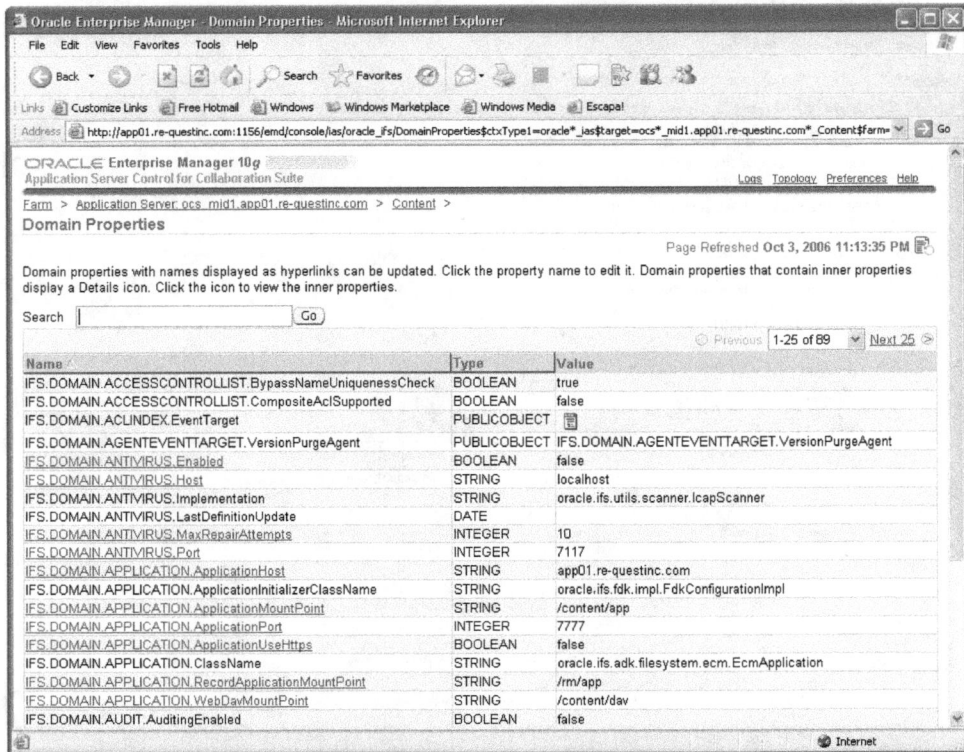

FIGURE 14-3. *Domain Properties page*

page. They are not a destination of interest in and of themselves. Figure 14-3 shows the Domain Properties page displayed in the browser.

Performance

Actually a set of three links under the heading of Performance on the Content Services Home page, the heading is very deceptive. The links are

- **Domain Performance & Statistics**   This leads to a page with subtabs for a number of high-level statistics, but there isn't actually any meaningful performance data on these pages. Figure 14-4 shows the Domain Performance & Statistics Collaboration Suite Control Console page.

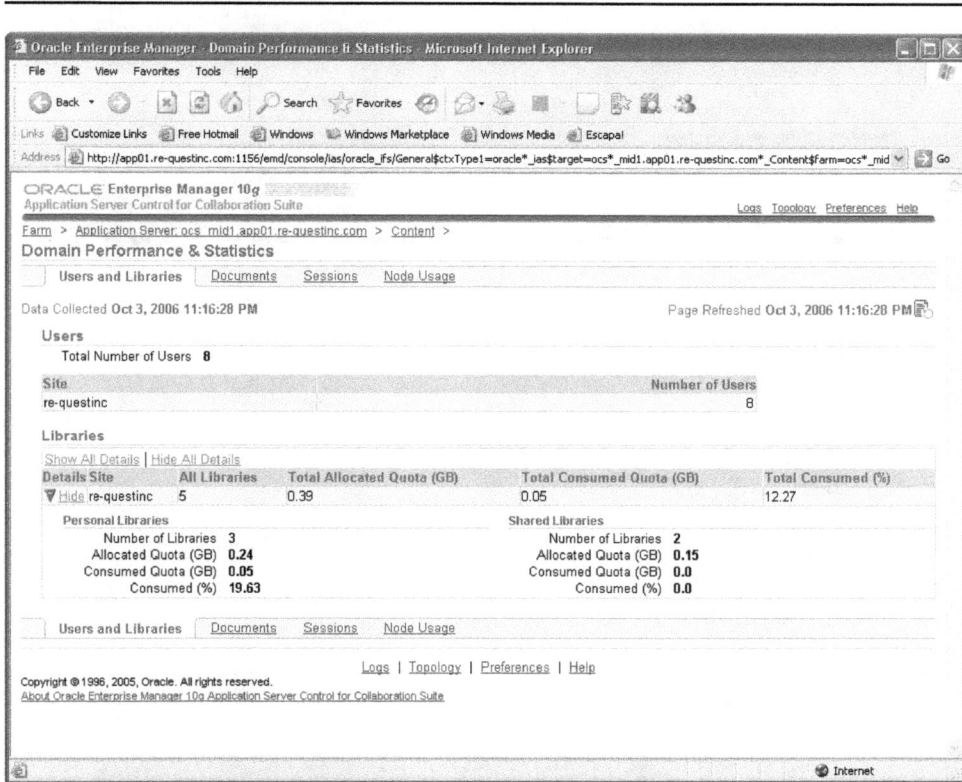

FIGURE 14-4. *Domain Performance & Statistics page for Content Services*

■ **All Metrics** This leads to a page with an expandable tree of all available statistics classified into categories such as "Processes" and "Documents By MIME Type." This is a superset of the selected statistics shown under "Domain Performance & Statistics," but again, there isn't actually much in the way of actionable performance information published here. Figure 14-5 shows the All Metrics page.

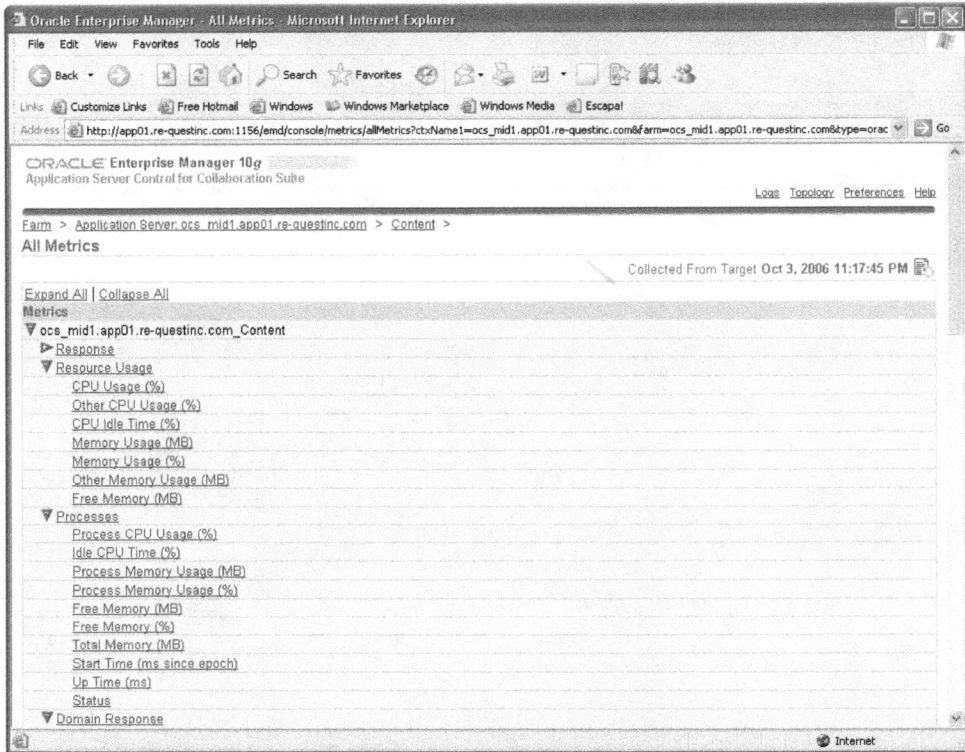

FIGURE 14-5. *All Metrics page for Content Services*

■ **Metric Configuration**   This leads to a page that identifies what
metrics are to be collected. The categories include: Repository
Metrics, Web Application Response Time, Load-Balanced Web
Application Response Time, RM Application Response Time, and
Load-Balanced RM Application Response Time. Figure 14-6 shows
the Metric Configuration page.

These links provide quick and easy access to any number of statistics,
but the most useful (for purposes of performance tuning) are actually related
to the service components of the nodes. Recall that the service component is

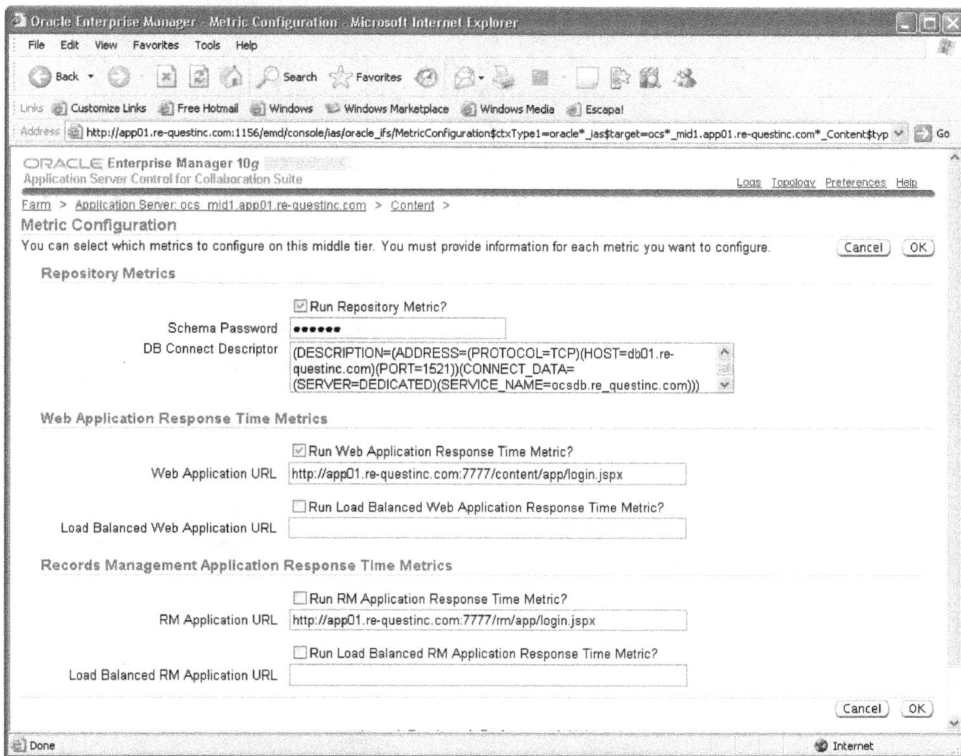

FIGURE 14-6.   *Metric Configuration for Content Services*

responsible for maintaining database connection pools and committed data caches for use by the servers and agents that run within the nodes. Hit ratios and actual vs. limit statistics are maintained for the connection pools and caches. If those statistics indicate the need for the allocation of more resources, the service may be reconfigured in real time.

Those service-level statistics (and associated configuration parameter settings) are accessed by clicking the link for the desired node from the Content Services Home page and then the link for the service (typically named IfsDefaultService). The resulting page has links for Performance

Statistics and Administration of the Connection Pools and Committed Data Cache. Changes to the configuration parameters of these components may be made in real time, but in order to survive as permanent changes (i.e., beyond a restart of the node), the service's configuration must also be changed. Figure 14-7 shows the IfsDefaultService page Connected Sessions section, while Figure 14-8 shows the Performance and Administration sections, as well as the remaining portion of the Connected Sessions section of the page.

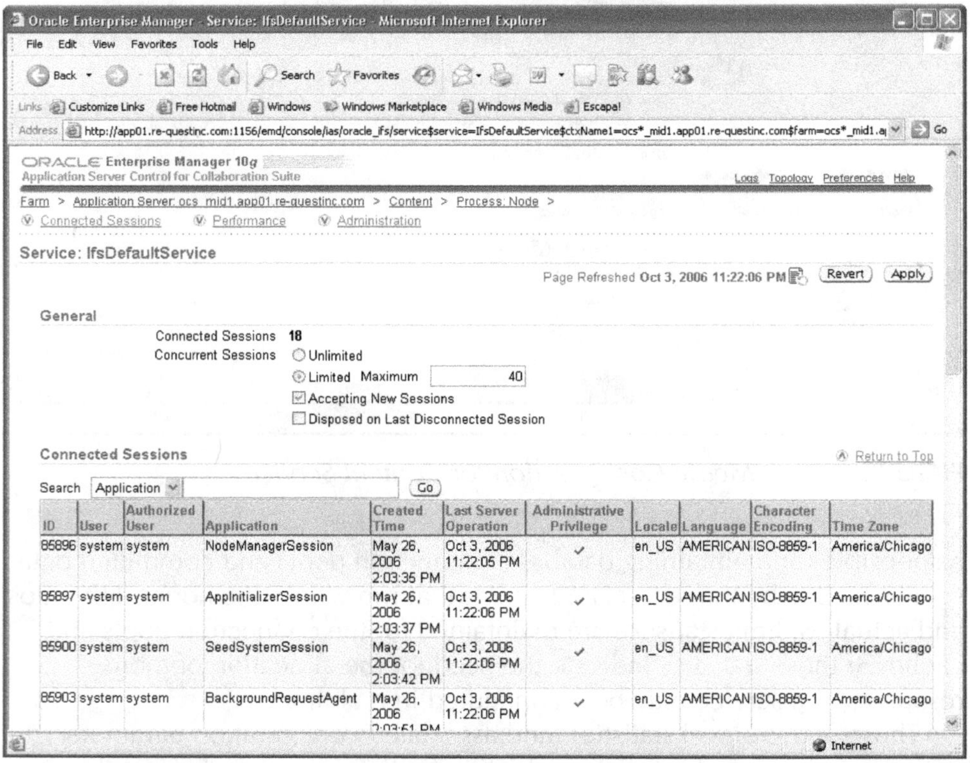

FIGURE 14-7. *IfsDefaultService page Connected Sessions section*

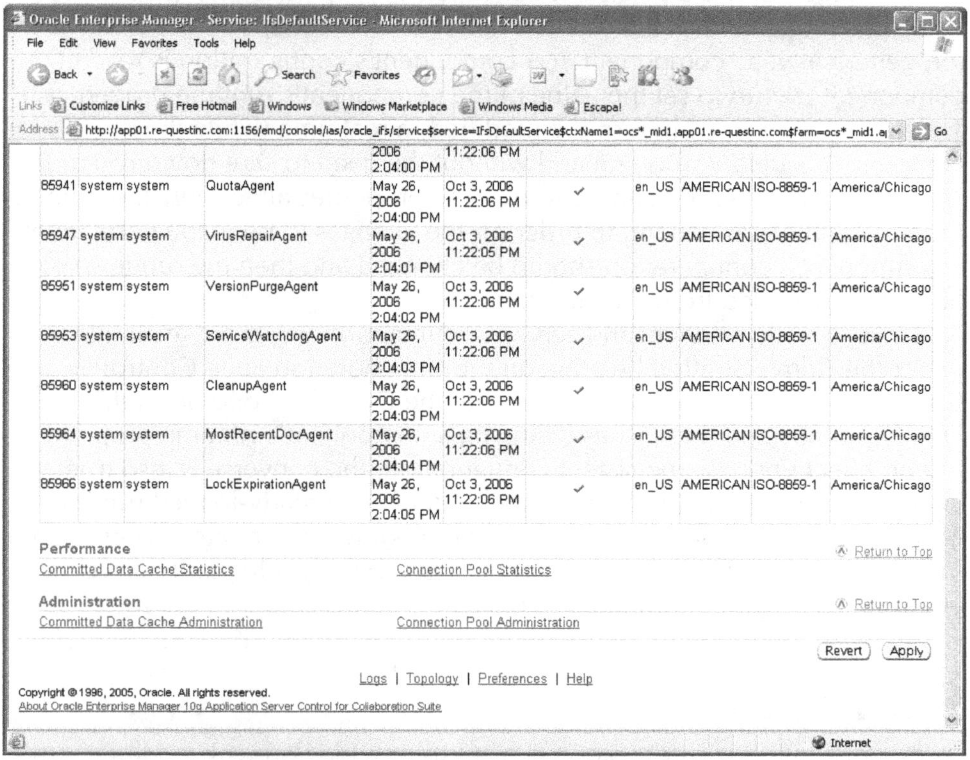

Oracle Enterprise Manager - Service: IfsDefaultService - Microsoft Internet Explorer

File   Edit   View   Favorites   Tools   Help

Back   Search   Favorites

Links   Customize Links   Free Hotmail   Windows   Windows Marketplace   Windows Media   Escapa!

Address   http://app01.re-questinc.com:1156/emd/console/ias/oracle_ifs/service$service=IfsDefaultService$ctxName1=ocs*_mid1.app01.re-questinc.com$farm=ocs*_mid1.a   Go

				2006 2:04:00 PM	11:22:06 PM					
85941	system	system	QuotaAgent	May 26, 2006 2:04:00 PM	Oct 3, 2006 11:22:06 PM	✓	en_US	AMERICAN	ISO-8859-1	America/Chicago
85947	system	system	VirusRepairAgent	May 26, 2006 2:04:01 PM	Oct 3, 2006 11:22:05 PM	✓	en_US	AMERICAN	ISO-8859-1	America/Chicago
85951	system	system	VersionPurgeAgent	May 26, 2006 2:04:02 PM	Oct 3, 2006 11:22:06 PM	✓	en_US	AMERICAN	ISO-8859-1	America/Chicago
85953	system	system	ServiceWatchdogAgent	May 26, 2006 2:04:03 PM	Oct 3, 2006 11:22:06 PM	✓	en_US	AMERICAN	ISO-8859-1	America/Chicago
85960	system	system	CleanupAgent	May 26, 2006 2:04:03 PM	Oct 3, 2006 11:22:06 PM	✓	en_US	AMERICAN	ISO-8859-1	America/Chicago
85964	system	system	MostRecentDocAgent	May 26, 2006 2:04:04 PM	Oct 3, 2006 11:22:06 PM	✓	en_US	AMERICAN	ISO-8859-1	America/Chicago
85966	system	system	LockExpirationAgent	May 26, 2006 2:04:05 PM	Oct 3, 2006 11:22:06 PM	✓	en_US	AMERICAN	ISO-8859-1	America/Chicago

Performance   ⊗ Return to Top

Committed Data Cache Statistics   Connection Pool Statistics

Administration   ⊗ Return to Top

Committed Data Cache Administration   Connection Pool Administration

Revert   Apply

Logs | Topology | Preferences | Help

Copyright © 1996, 2005, Oracle. All rights reserved.
About Oracle Enterprise Manager 10g Application Server Control for Collaboration Suite

Internet

FIGURE 14-8.   *IfsDefaultService page Performance and*
Administration sections

Node, Service, and Server Configurations

Although most of the terms with special/precise meanings in a Content
Services context were defined up front in order to facilitate later discussion,
the term "configuration" (as it applies to nodes, services, and servers) hasn't
been described until this point because the distinction between a component's
configuration and its runtime properties is a subtle one—best tackled once
the meaning of the other terms has become second nature.

A *configuration* is a persistent collection of properties (i.e., parameter/ value pairs) that control the runtime behavior of a node, service, or server (or, generically, a "component"). A component's configuration is read at component startup to set the value of the component's runtime properties. Those properties may, in turn, be modified in real time (while the component is up and running and without the need to shut down/restart the component). Any such changes to runtime properties affect *only* the running instance of the component. In order for the changes to be made permanent, a component's configuration should be changed and then the runtime properties reloaded from the configuration.

Links to node, service, and server Configuration pages are available under the Administration heading on the Collaboration Suite Control Content Services Home page (along with the Domain Properties link). Finally, understand that just as changing a component's runtime properties has no effect upon the persistent configuration, the converse is also true: changing a configuration, by itself, will not affect already-loaded runtime properties. After a configuration has been modified, the related component must be restarted (or the runtime properties explicitly reloaded) before the changes will impact running components.

Summary

As the objective of this chapter has been to provide you with a solid conceptual foundation for understanding the technical architecture of Content Services, its conclusion represents a jumping-off point and not a destination in and of itself. The material presented herein should, however, be sufficient to allow you to use the Oracle Enterprise Manager Collaboration Suite Control to visually explore and inspect the Content Services components of your installation—and to understand what you see!

APPENDIX

References

E very effort has been made to provide you with a list of all the material we used as references for this book. Any omission from this list is purely unintentional.

Publication	Date	Part Number
Oracle® Calendar Administrator's Guide 10*g* Release 1 (10.1.2)	July 2006	B25485-04
Oracle® Collaboration Suite Administrator's Guide 10*g* Release 1 (10.1.2)	June 2006	B25490-05
Oracle® Collaboration Suite Deployment Guide 10*g* Release 1 (10.1.2)	October 2005	B25492-01
Oracle® Collaboration Suite High Availability Guide 10*g* Release 1 (10.1.2)	March 2006	B25481-03
Oracle® Collaboration Suite Installation Guide 10*g* Release 1 (10.1.2) for Linux	October 2005	B25465-01
Oracle® Collaboration Suite Migration and Coexistence Guide 10*g* Release 1 (10.1.2)	December 2005	B25493-01
Oracle® Content Services Administrator's Guide 10*g* Release 1 (10.1.2)	June 2006	B25275-04
Oracle® Content Services Application Administrator's Guide 10*g* Release 1 (10.1.2)	April 2006	B25276-04
Oracle® Database Backup and Recovery Reference 10*g* Release 2 (10.2)	November 2005	B14194-03
Oracle® Mail Administrator's Guide 10*g* Release 1 (10.1.2)	April 2006	B25499-03
Oracle® Real-Time Collaboration Administrator's Guide 10*g* Release 1 (10.1.2)	May 2006	B25460-03

Index

References to figures and illustrations are in italics.

GET YOUR **FREE SUBSCRIPTION**
TO ORACLE MAGAZINE

Oracle Magazine is essential gear for today's information technology professionals. Stay informed and increase your productivity with every issue of *Oracle Magazine*. Inside each free bimonthly issue you'll get:

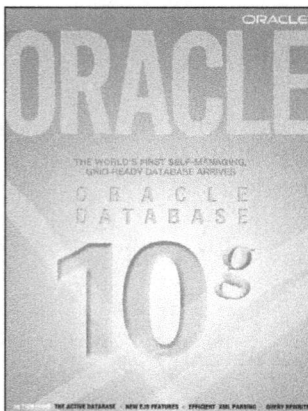

- Up-to-date information on Oracle Database, Oracle Application Server, Web development, enterprise grid computing, database technology, and business trends
- Third-party vendor news and announcements
- Technical articles on Oracle and partner products, technologies, and operating environments
- Development and administration tips
- Real-world customer stories

IF THERE ARE OTHER ORACLE USERS AT YOUR LOCATION WHO WOULD LIKE TO RECEIVE THEIR OWN SUBSCRIPTION TO ORACLE MAGAZINE, PLEASE PHOTOCOPY THIS FORM AND PASS IT ALONG.

ORACLE
M A G A Z I N E

Three easy ways to subscribe:

① Web
Visit our Web site at otn.oracle.com/oraclemagazine. You'll find a subscription form there, plus much more!

② Fax
Complete the questionnaire on the back of this card and fax the questionnaire side only to +1.847.763.9638.

③ Mail
Complete the questionnaire on the back of this card and mail it to P.O. Box 1263, Skokie, IL 60076-8263

ORACLE®

FREE SUBSCRIPTION

○ **Yes, please send me a FREE subscription to _Oracle Magazine_.** ○ **NO**

To receive a free subscription to _Oracle Magazine_, you must fill out the entire card, sign it, and date it (incomplete cards cannot be processed or acknowledged). You can also fax your application to +1.847.763.9638. **Or subscribe at our Web site at otn.oracle.com/oraclemagazine**

○ From time to time, Oracle Publishing allows our partners exclusive access to our e-mail addresses for special promotions and announcements. To be included in this program, please check this circle.

○ Oracle Publishing allows sharing of our mailing list with selected third parties. If you prefer your mailing address not to be included in this program, please check here. If at any time you would like to be removed from this mailing list, please contact Customer Service at +1.847.647.9630 or send an e-mail to oracle@halldata.com.

signature (required) | date

X

name | title

company | e-mail address

street/p.o. box

city/state/zip or postal code | telephone

country | fax

YOU MUST ANSWER ALL TEN QUESTIONS BELOW.

① WHAT IS THE PRIMARY BUSINESS ACTIVITY OF YOUR FIRM AT THIS LOCATION? (check one only)
- ☐ 01 Aerospace and Defense Manufacturing
- ☐ 02 Application Service Provider
- ☐ 03 Automotive Manufacturing
- ☐ 04 Chemicals, Oil and Gas
- ☐ 05 Communications and Media
- ☐ 06 Construction/Engineering
- ☐ 07 Consumer Sector/Consumer Packaged Goods
- ☐ 08 Education
- ☐ 09 Financial Services/Insurance
- ☐ 10 Government (civil)
- ☐ 11 Government (military)
- ☐ 12 Healthcare
- ☐ 13 High Technology Manufacturing, OEM
- ☐ 14 Integrated Software Vendor
- ☐ 15 Life Sciences (Biotech, Pharmaceuticals)
- ☐ 16 Mining
- ☐ 17 Retail/Wholesale/Distribution
- ☐ 18 Systems Integrator, VAR/VAD
- ☐ 19 Telecommunications
- ☐ 20 Travel and Transportation
- ☐ 21 Utilities (electric, gas, sanitation, water)
- ☐ 98 Other Business and Services

② WHICH OF THE FOLLOWING BEST DESCRIBES YOUR PRIMARY JOB FUNCTION? (check one only)
Corporate Management/Staff
- ☐ 01 Executive Management (President, Chair, CEO, CFO, Owner, Partner, Principal)
- ☐ 02 Finance/Administrative Management (VP/Director/ Manager/Controller, Purchasing, Administration)
- ☐ 03 Sales/Marketing Management (VP/Director/Manager)
- ☐ 04 Computer Systems/Operations Management (CIO/VP/Director/ Manager MIS, Operations)
IS/IT Staff
- ☐ 05 Systems Development/ Programming Management
- ☐ 06 Systems Development/ Programming Staff
- ☐ 07 Consulting
- ☐ 08 DBA/Systems Administrator
- ☐ 09 Education/Training
- ☐ 10 Technical Support Director/Manager
- ☐ 11 Other Technical Management/Staff
- ☐ 98 Other

③ WHAT IS YOUR CURRENT PRIMARY OPERATING PLATFORM? (select all that apply)
- ☐ 01 Digital Equipment UNIX
- ☐ 02 Digital Equipment VAX VMS
- ☐ 03 HP UNIX

- ☐ 04 IBM AIX
- ☐ 05 IBM UNIX
- ☐ 06 Java
- ☐ 07 Linux
- ☐ 08 Macintosh
- ☐ 09 MS-DOS
- ☐ 10 MVS
- ☐ 11 NetWare
- ☐ 12 Network Computing
- ☐ 13 OpenVMS
- ☐ 14 SCO UNIX
- ☐ 15 Sequent DYNIX/ptx
- ☐ 16 Sun Solaris/SunOS
- ☐ 17 SVR4
- ☐ 18 UnixWare
- ☐ 19 Windows
- ☐ 20 Windows NT
- ☐ 21 Other UNIX
- ☐ 98 Other
- 99 ☐ None of the above

④ DO YOU EVALUATE, SPECIFY, RECOMMEND, OR AUTHORIZE THE PURCHASE OF ANY OF THE FOLLOWING? (check all that apply)
- ☐ 01 Hardware
- ☐ 02 Software
- ☐ 03 Application Development Tools
- ☐ 04 Database Products
- ☐ 05 Internet or Intranet Products
- 99 ☐ None of the above

⑤ IN YOUR JOB, DO YOU USE OR PLAN TO PURCHASE ANY OF THE FOLLOWING PRODUCTS? (check all that apply)
Software
- ☐ 01 Business Graphics
- ☐ 02 CAD/CAE/CAM
- ☐ 03 CASE
- ☐ 04 Communications
- ☐ 05 Database Management
- ☐ 06 File Management
- ☐ 07 Finance
- ☐ 08 Java
- ☐ 09 Materials Resource Planning
- ☐ 10 Multimedia Authoring
- ☐ 11 Networking
- ☐ 12 Office Automation
- ☐ 13 Order Entry/Inventory Control
- ☐ 14 Programming
- ☐ 15 Project Management
- ☐ 16 Scientific and Engineering
- ☐ 17 Spreadsheets
- ☐ 18 Systems Management
- ☐ 19 Workflow

Hardware
- ☐ 20 Macintosh
- ☐ 21 Mainframe
- ☐ 22 Massively Parallel Processing
- ☐ 23 Minicomputer
- ☐ 24 PC
- ☐ 25 Network Computer
- ☐ 26 Symmetric Multiprocessing
- ☐ 27 Workstation
Peripherals
- ☐ 28 Bridges/Routers/Hubs/Gateways
- ☐ 29 CD-ROM Drives
- ☐ 30 Disk Drives/Subsystems
- ☐ 31 Modems
- ☐ 32 Tape Drives/Subsystems
- ☐ 33 Video Boards/Multimedia
Services
- ☐ 34 Application Service Provider
- ☐ 35 Consulting
- ☐ 36 Education/Training
- ☐ 37 Maintenance
- ☐ 38 Online Database Services
- ☐ 39 Support
- ☐ 40 Technology-Based Training
- ☐ 98 Other
- 99 ☐ None of the above

⑥ WHAT ORACLE PRODUCTS ARE IN USE AT YOUR SITE? (check all that apply)
Oracle E-Business Suite
- ☐ 01 Oracle Marketing
- ☐ 02 Oracle Sales
- ☐ 03 Oracle Order Fulfillment
- ☐ 04 Oracle Supply Chain Management
- ☐ 05 Oracle Procurement
- ☐ 06 Oracle Manufacturing
- ☐ 07 Oracle Maintenance Management
- ☐ 08 Oracle Service
- ☐ 09 Oracle Contracts
- ☐ 10 Oracle Projects
- ☐ 11 Oracle Financials
- ☐ 12 Oracle Human Resources
- ☐ 13 Oracle Interaction Center
- ☐ 14 Oracle Communications/Utilities (modules)
- ☐ 15 Oracle Public Sector/University (modules)
- ☐ 16 Oracle Financial Services (modules)
Server/Software
- ☐ 17 Oracle9i
- ☐ 18 Oracle9i Lite
- ☐ 19 Oracle8i
- ☐ 20 Other Oracle database
- ☐ 21 Oracle9i Application Server
- ☐ 22 Oracle9i Application Server Wireless
- ☐ 23 Oracle Small Business Suite

Tools
- ☐ 24 Oracle Developer Suite
- ☐ 25 Oracle Discoverer
- ☐ 26 Oracle JDeveloper
- ☐ 27 Oracle Migration Workbench
- ☐ 28 Oracle9i AS Portal
- ☐ 29 Oracle Warehouse Builder
Oracle Services
- ☐ 30 Oracle Outsourcing
- ☐ 31 Oracle Consulting
- ☐ 32 Oracle Education
- ☐ 33 Oracle Support
- ☐ 98 Other
- 99 ☐ None of the above

⑦ WHAT OTHER DATABASE PRODUCTS ARE IN USE AT YOUR SITE? (check all that apply)
- ☐ 01 Access
- ☐ 02 Baan
- ☐ 03 dbase
- ☐ 04 Gupta
- ☐ 05 IBM DB2
- ☐ 06 Informix
- ☐ 07 Ingres
- ☐ 08 Microsoft Access
- ☐ 09 Microsoft SQL Server
- ☐ 10 PeopleSoft
- ☐ 11 Progress
- ☐ 12 SAP
- ☐ 13 Sybase
- ☐ 14 VSAM
- ☐ 98 Other
- 99 ☐ None of the above

⑧ WHAT OTHER APPLICATION SERVER PRODUCTS ARE IN USE AT YOUR SITE? (check all that apply)
- ☐ 01 BEA
- ☐ 02 IBM
- ☐ 03 Sybase
- ☐ 04 Sun
- ☐ 05 Other

⑨ DURING THE NEXT 12 MONTHS, HOW MUCH DO YOU ANTICIPATE YOUR ORGANIZATION WILL SPEND ON COMPUTER HARDWARE, SOFTWARE, PERIPHERALS, AND SERVICES FOR YOUR LOCATION? (check only one)
- ☐ 01 Less than $10,000
- ☐ 02 $10,000 to $49,999
- ☐ 03 $50,000 to $99,999
- ☐ 04 $100,000 to $499,999
- ☐ 05 $500,000 to $999,999
- ☐ 06 $1,000,000 and over

⑩ WHAT IS YOUR COMPANY'S YEARLY SALES REVENUE? (please choose one)
- ☐ 01 $500, 000, 000 and above
- ☐ 02 $100, 000, 000 to $500, 000, 000
- ☐ 03 $50, 000, 000 to $100, 000, 000
- ☐ 04 $5, 000, 000 to $50, 000, 000
- ☐ 05 $1, 000, 000 to $5, 000, 000

100103

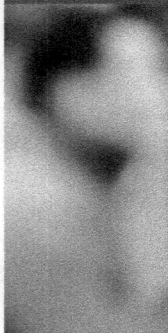

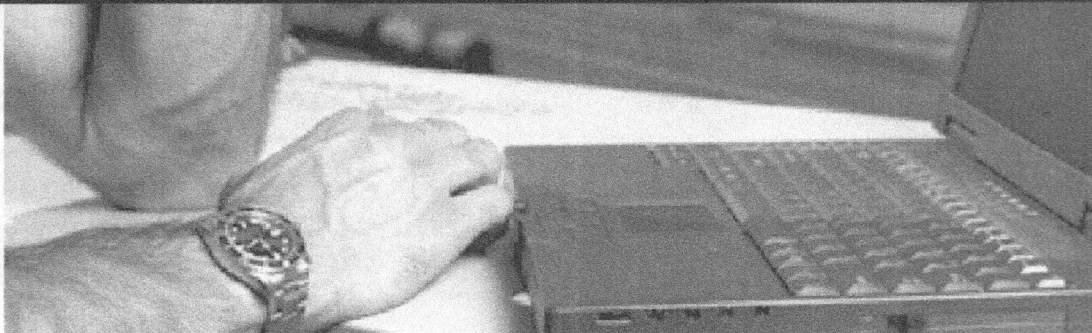

www.ingramcontent.com/pod-product-compliance
Lightning Source LLC
Chambersburg PA
CBHW080135220326
41598CB00032B/5070